NATURAL DISASTER AND NUCLEAR CRISIS IN JAPAN

The March 2011 earthquake and tsunami in Japan plunged the country into a state of crisis. As the nation struggled to recover from a record-breaking magnitude 9 earthquake and a tsunami that was as high as 38 meters in some places, news trickled out that the Fukushima nuclear power plant had experienced meltdowns in three reactors. These tragic catastrophes claimed some 20,000 lives, initially displacing some 500,000 people and overwhelming Japan's formidable disaster preparedness.

This book brings together the analysis and insights of a group of distinguished experts on Japan to examine what happened, how various institutions and actors responded, and what lessons can be drawn from Japan's disaster. The contributors, many of whom experienced the disaster first hand, assess the wide-ranging repercussions of this catastrophe and how it is influencing Japanese politics, civil society, energy policy, the economy, and urban planning.

This book is essential reading for anyone seeking an understanding of the events of March 2011 in Japan and the wider consequences for the future of the country and the rest of the world.

Jeff Kingston is Professor of History and Director of Asian Studies at Temple University, Japan. He is the author of *Japan's Quiet Transformation* (2004) and *Contemporary Japan* (2011).

THE NISSAN INSTITUTE/ROUTLEDGE JAPANESE STUDIES SERIES

Series Editors:

Roger Goodman, Nissan Professor of Modern Japanese Studies, University of Oxford, Fellow, St Antony's College

J.A.A. Stockwin, formerly Nissan Professor of Modern Japanese Studies and former Director of the Nissan Institute of Japanese Studies, University of Oxford, Emeritus Fellow, St Antony's College

Other titles in the series:

Japan and Protection
The growth of protectionist sentiment and the Japanese response
Syed Javed Maswood

The Soil, by Nagatsuka Takashi
A portrait of rural life in Meiji Japan
Translated and with an introduction by Ann Waswo

Biotechnology in Japan
Malcolm Brock

Britain's Educational Reform
A comparison with Japan
Michael Howarth

Language and the Modern State
The reform of written Japanese
Nanette Twine

Industrial Harmony in Modern Japan
The intervention of a tradition
W. Dean Kinzley

Japanese Science Fiction
A view of a changing society
Robert Matthew

The Japanese Numbers Game
The use and understanding of numbers in modern Japan
Thomas Crump

Ideology and Practice in Modern Japan
Edited by Roger Goodman and Kirsten Refsing

Technology and Industrial Development in Pre-war Japan
Mitsubishi Nagasaki Shipyard, 1884–1934
Yukiko Fukasaku

Japan's Early Parliaments, 1890–1905
Structure, issues and trends
Andrew Fraser, R.H.P. Mason and Philip Mitchell

Japan's Foreign Aid Challenge
Policy reform and aid leadership
Alan Rix

Emperor Hirohito and Shôwa Japan
A political biography
Stephen S. Large

Globalizing Japan
Ethnography of the Japanese presence in America, Asia and Europe
Edited by Harumi Befu and Sylvie Guichard-Anguis

Japan at Play
The ludic and logic of power
Edited by Joy Hendry and Massimo Raveri

The Making of Urban Japan
Cities and planning from Edo to the twenty-first century
André Sorensen

Public Policy and Economic Competition in Japan
Change and continuity in antimonopoly policy, 1973–1995
Michael L. Beeman

Men and Masculinities in Contemporary Japan
Dislocating the Salaryman Doxa
Edited by James E. Roberson and Nobue Suzuki

The Voluntary and Non-Profit Sector in Japan
The challenge of change
Edited by Stephen P. Osborne

Japan's Security Relations with China
From balancing to bandwagoning
Reinhard Drifte

Understanding Japanese Society
Third edition
Joy Hendry

Japanese Electoral Politics
Creating a new party system
Edited by Steven R. Reed

The Japanese-Soviet Neutrality Pact
A diplomatic history, 1941–1945
Boris Slavinsky translated by Geoffrey Jukes

Academic Nationalism in China and Japan
Framed by concepts of nature, culture and the universal
Margaret Sleeboom

The Race to Commercialize Biotechnology
Molecules, markets and the state in the United States and Japan
Steve W. Collins

NATURAL DISASTER AND NUCLEAR CRISIS IN JAPAN

Response and recovery after Japan's 3/11

Edited by Jeff Kingston

LONDON AND NEW YORK

First published 2012 by Routledge
2 Park Square, Milton Park, Abingdon, Oxon OX14 4RN

Simultaneously published in the USA and Canada
by Routledge
711 Third Avenue, New York, NY10017

Routledge is an imprint of the Taylor & Francis Group

Typeset in Bembo by Saxon Graphics Ltd, Derby, DE21 4SZ

British Library Cataloguing in Publication Data
A catalogue record for this book is available from the British Library

Library of Congress Cataloging in Publication Data
Natural disaster and nuclear crisis in Japan : response and recovery after Japan's 3/11 / edited by Jeff Kingston.
p. cm. -- (The Nissan Institute/Routledge Japanese studies series)
Includes bibliographical references and index.
ISBN 978-0-415-69855-9 (hbk.) -- ISBN 978-0-415-69856-6 (pbk.) -- ISBN 978-0-203-12410-9 (ebk.) 1. Tohoku Earthquake and Tsunami, Japan, 2011. 2. Nuclear power plants--Accidents--Japan--Fukushima-ken. 3. Disaster relief--Japan. I. Kingston, Jeff, 1957- II. Series: Nissan Institute/Routledge Japanese studies series.
HV6002011.T64 N37 2012
952.0512--dc23
2011038746

ISBN 978-0-415-69855-9 (hbk)
ISBN 978-0-415-69856-6 (pbk)
ISBN 978-0-203-12410-9 (ebk)

Printed and bound in Great Britain by MPG Printgroup

CONTENTS

ILLUSTRATIONS

Figures

Maps

Tables

CONTRIBUTORS

Daniel P. Aldrich is an Associate Professor of Political Science at Purdue University and for the academic year 2011–2012 an AAAS fellow at USAID who has been a Visiting Scholar at the University of Tokyo's Law Faculty in Japan, Harvard University's Program on US-Japan Relations, Sciences Po in Paris, France and the Tata Institute for Disaster Management in Mumbai, India. He is the author of the book *Site Fights* from Cornell University Press (2008, 2010) and *Building Resilience* (University of Chicago Press 2012) along with 40 articles, reviews, and book chapters.

Chris Ames is an Associate Professor in the Undergraduate School at University of Maryland University College. He holds a PhD in Anthropology from the University of Michigan and an MA in East Asian Studies from the University of Pittsburgh. His research focuses on ethnic and gender diversity in contemporary Japan.

Simon Avenell is Associate Professor in the Department of Japanese Studies, National University of Singapore. His publications include *Making Japanese Citizens: Civil Society and the Mythology of the Shimin in Postwar Japan* (University of California Press, 2010) and "From 'Fearsome Pollution' to Fukushima," *Environmental History* (forthcoming April 2012).

Kenneth Neil Cukier is the Japan business correspondent of *The Economist*, and extensively covered the March 11 disaster and aftermath. He is a frequent commentator on the Japanese economy for the BBC and America's NPR. His work has also appeared in *Foreign Affairs* and *Prospect*, among others.

Gerald L. Curtis is Burgess Professor of Political Science at Columbia University. He is the author of numerous books and articles written in both English and Japanese and is the recipient of the Chunichi Shimbun Special Achievement Award, the Masayoshi Ohira Memorial Prize, the Japan Foundation Award and the Order of the Rising Sun, Gold and Silver Star.

Andrew DeWit is Professor in Rikkyo University's School of Policy Studies. His latest work includes 'The Politics of Fixing Financial Crises' in *Keynes and Modern Economics* (2011) and (in Japanese) *The Energy and Environmental Crises: Getting Beyond the Political Treatment of the Tax State as an Economic Parasite* (2011).

Peter Duus is William E. Bonsall Professor of History Emeritus at Stanford University. He has written numerous books and articles on modern Japanese history. His most recent publication is *Rediscovering Japan: Japanese Perspectives on the American Century* (2011), an anthology of Japanese visitors to the United States.

Iida Tetsunari is Executive Director of the Institute for Sustainable Energy Policies (ISEP). He is also a member of the Ministry of Economy, Trade and Industry Advisory Committee on Energy and Natural Resources. He is author of *Northern Europe's Energy Democracy* (2011), *The Japanese Green New Deal* (2009), and numerous other publications.

Kaneko Masaru is Professor of Public Finance in the Faculty of Economics at Keio University in Japan. His specialty areas include public finance and institutional economics. Perhaps the most notable among his extensive publications include (in Japanese) *Long-Term Stagnation* (2002), and *The Political Economy of the Safety Net* (1999).

Kawato Yuko is a postdoctoral researcher at the France-Japan Foundation of the École des Hautes Études en Sciences Sociales in Paris. She obtained her PhD in political science from the University of Washington. She is preparing a book manuscript on US military bases and protests in Asia, with a grant from the East-West Center. She has also co-authored some book chapters on Japan's civil society.

Jeff Kingston is Director of Asian Studies and Professor of History at Temple University Japan. Author of *Contemporary Japan: History, Politics and Social Change Since the 1980s* (Wiley-Blackwell, 2011) and *Japan's Quiet Transformation* (Routledge, 2004). Editor of *Tsunami: Japan's Post-Fukushima Future* (ebook by *Foreign Policy*, June 2011).

Love Kindstrand is a graduate student at Sophia University. Recent publications include "The Politicization of Precarity: Anti-nuke protests in Japan since the Great Tohoku Earthquake," in Hot Spots (*Cultural Anthropology*, 2011) and

"Rethinking Neoliberal Urbanism" in *Glistering Streets, Displaced Populations: the Theme park-ification of Urban Commons* conference proceedings.

Yuiko Koguchi-Ames is an Associate Professor in the Department of Social Welfare at Takasaki University of Health and Welfare. She holds a PhD in Family Relations from the University of Guelph and an MA in Education from Michigan State University. Her research focuses on socialization and multicultural education in Japan.

John F. Morris, Professor, Department of Intercultural Studies, Miyagi Gakuin Women's University. Author of *Kinsei Bushi no "Kō" to "Shi" Sendai Hanshi Tamamushi Jūzō no Kyaria to Zasetsu* (Seibundō, Osaka, 2009) and *150 Koku no Ryōshu Sendai Hanshi Tamamushi Jūzō no Ryōchi Shihai* (Ozaki Hachiman Gū, Sendai, 2010).

Ōtani Junko, Graduate School of Human Sciences at Osaka University, obtained her MPH/MS in international health and population science from Harvard University and her PhD in social policy from the London School of Economics. She has worked for the World Bank and the World Health Organization, based mainly in China. Her areas of specialization include area studies, and research methodology.

Nishimura Keiko is a Master's student in Japanese Studies at Sophia University in Tokyo, where she researches female fandom and participatory media culture. She is especially interested in how new technologies intervene in social activities. Her most recent publication is "On exhaustion, self-censorship, and affective community" (*Cultural Anthropology*, 2011).

Robert Pekkanen is Associate Professor at the University of Washington. He has published articles in the *American Political Science Review*, the *British Journal of Political Science*, and *Comparative Political Studies*, among others. His *Japan's Dual Civil Society* won an award from the Japan NPO Research Association and the Masayoshi Ohira award. His most recent book, co-authored with Ellis Krauss, is *The Rise and Fall of Japan's LDP: Political Party Organizations as Historical Institutions* (Cornell, 2010).

Paul J. Scalise is JSPS Postdoctoral Fellow at the Institute of Social Science, University of Tokyo. A former Tokyo-based financial analyst and contributing associate to several consulting firms since 1998, he is the author of numerous publications on Japan's energy sector, including the chapter on Japan's national energy policy in Cutler Cleveland's *Encyclopedia of Energy* (2004).

David H. Slater is an associate professor of Cultural Anthropology and Japanese Studies at Sophia University. Related publications include *Social Class in*

Contemporary Japan (co-edited with Ishida Hiroshi) and an edited collection of short essays in *Cultural Anthropology* entitled "Hot Spots: 3.11 Politics in Disaster Japan."

Leslie M. Tkach-Kawasaki is an Associate Professor at the University of Tsukuba. Her research interests include Internet use by Japanese political actors, Internet Studies methodologies, and comparative website analysis. Dr. Tkach-Kawasaki's research papers have appeared in journals such as *Party Politics* and *Social Science Computer Review*.

Tōgo Kazuhiko (PhD 2009, Leiden University) is Professor and Director of the Institute for World Affairs, Kyoto Sangyo University. He served in the Japanese Foreign Ministry, retired as Ambassador to the Netherlands and, since then, taught at various universities, including Leiden, Princeton and Seoul National. His publications include *Japan's Foreign Policy 1945–2009* and *The Inside Story of the Negotiations on the Northern Territories*.

Riccardo Tossani With a 30-year career in master planning in Japan, Italy and the USA, Tossani founded the Tokyo-based practice of Riccardo Tossani Architecture in 1997, addressing multi-cultural community development and sustainability. Harvard GSD's top 1988 graduate in architecture and urban design, he has studied at MIT and the University of Adelaide, Australia.

Tsujinaka Yutaka (PhD, Kyoto University, Japan) is a vice president and a professor of politics, University of Tsukuba. He is the author of *Pressure Groups in Japan* (1986), *Interest Groups* (1988), *Politics in Japan* (2001), *Comparing Policy Networks* (1996), *Local Governance in Japan* (2010) and *Political Functions of Social Organizations in Contemporary Japan* (2010).

SERIES EDITORS' PREFACE

Japan's triple disaster of March 11, 2011 (now known widely as '3/11') is reminiscent of the myth of Achilles. According to a late version of the story, the mother of Achilles, seeking to make him invulnerable, dipped the child Achilles into the River Styx, holding him by his heel. But this failed to save him when, as an adult warrior, he was wounded in his unprotected heel.

Japan is home to some 20 per cent of the earthquakes that occur on the planet, so that government authorities had come to enforce extremely stringent building regulations designed to minimise damage and casualties from shaking of their unstable land. Officials were well aware that the Great Kantō earthquake that destroyed much of Tokyo and Yokohama in 1923 cost over 100,000 lives. If the even stronger quake (an extraordinary 9 on the Richter scale) that occurred on 3/11 had hit an inland area, no doubt the government would have derived satisfaction from the success of its policies, since only a few hundred people died as a result of the quake alone. But a major fracture of a tectonic plate some 150 km off the north-eastern coast of Japan's main island of Honshū caused a tsunami that reached a maximum height of 38 m at places along the coast, overwhelming local communities and raising the death toll to more than 20,000. The lesson of a similar occurrence in the 1890s had apparently not been learned. Moreover, it caused the cooling system to fail at the Fukushima No. 1 nuclear reactors, bringing about meltdown and radiation leakage. The Japanese Achilles was unprotected, not in one heel, but in two.

The present multi-authored volume seeks to assess the extent and nature of the disaster, the multiple crises that it caused, the performance of central and local governments and their agencies, the private sector and civil society – not forgetting US forces stationed in Japan – in working for recovery from the disaster. Much of the writing in this book has great immediacy, given that several of the authors work and live in Japan, and their accounts are closely engaged with the events.

This imparts to their sharply analytical approaches an unusually compelling character.

The timing of 3/11 is particularly important and is reflected in much of the analysis. In government and politics the disaster occurred at a time when the political system was being criticised for inadequate leadership and sclerotic procedures – this despite the fact that a rare change of government had taken place in 2009. As a case study of political disaster-response, it showed that the system was hard put to rise above petty politics and unite behind a clear strategy of recovery. Kan Naoto, Prime Minister for the first six months after the disaster, had good intentions but was frustrated at every turn by rivals within his own party, a recalcitrant opposition party determined to get rid of him, and hostile mass media.

Several authors throw a critical light on the so-called 'nuclear village,' and its cosy relations with past governments, leading to complacency about the security of nuclear reactors in an earthquake-prone zone. The Fukushima crisis has turned public opinion strongly against nuclear energy, but the future implications are far from clear. As we write this preface, 42 of Japan's 54 nuclear power plants are currently either off-line for regular maintenance or shut down for stress-testing. It is far from clear as to what will happen with them next. Should Japan phase out nuclear energy as a key part of its energy mix and go for renewable sources, or simply reinforce safety regulations? This book examines both possibilities.

Another area covered extensively here is that of volunteering and the development of civil society. Impressive efforts were made by an army of external volunteers in the stricken communities, as well as by local authorities and local people themselves. The implications of this for the potential decentralisation of politics are crucial, as several authors point out. But the magnitude of the problem still remaining is shown by the numbers still living in temporary accommodation, the difficulty of reviving ravaged communities on low-lying coastal land, many of whose surviving inhabitants are elderly, in a region of Japan that is outside the economic mainstream. One substantial area is rendered uninhabitable for the long term by the radiation leakages.

The present volume is a timely and indispensable guide to understanding Japan's triple disaster and its aftermath, as well as the prospects for the future.

Arthur Stockwin
Roger Goodman

A NOTE TO THE READER

All Japanese names that feature in this volume are given with the family name first, corresponding with actual usage in the Japanese context.

Macrons are used throughout to mark long vowels in Japanese, with the exception of well-known places (such as Tokyo, Osaka, Kobe, and Kyoto) and certain cases where the individual in question prefers a different way to romanize his or her name.

For political parties we have used their common English names and acronyms: Democratic Party of Japan (DPJ) and Liberal Democratic Party (LDP).

For the utility operating the Fukushima Daiichi nuclear power complex where the nuclear crisis took place, we use the English name Tokyo Electric Power Company (TEPCO). For the various government ministries we use their common English names, e.g. Ministry of Economy, Trade, and Industry (METI).

We designate the massive seismic event on March 11 as the Tōhoku Earthquake.

Fukushima can be used in a descriptive sense, like Chernobyl, to reference the nuclear crisis even though it refers to a specific prefecture where the nuclear meltdowns took place.

Monetary values are given in yen (¥) when discussing financial issues in Japan, since conversions into pounds or dollars are rendered almost meaningless by highly volatile exchange rates. For the purposes of comparison, however, in mid-October 2011 US$1 = ¥77 and £1 = ¥122.

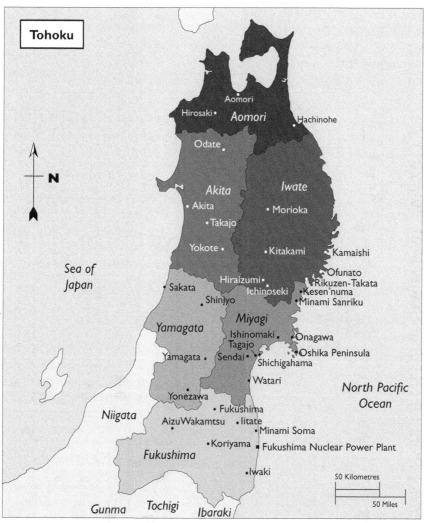

Map of the Tōhoku region.

Nuclear Power Plant Operational Status Map, July 2011

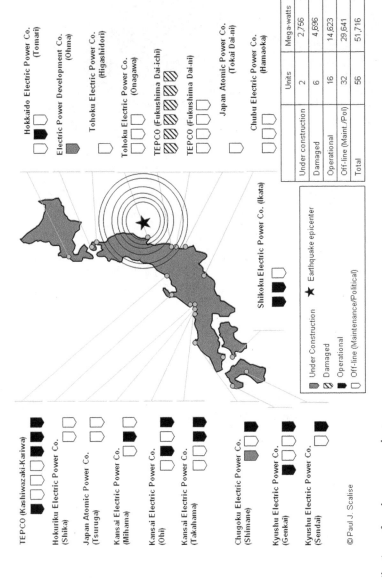

	Units	Mega-watts
Under construction	2	2,756
Damaged	6	4,696
Operational	16	14,623
Off-line (Maint./Pol)	32	29,641
Total	56	51,716

© Paul J. Scalise

Map of distribution of nuclear power plants.

INTRODUCTION

Jeff Kingston

The 3/11 complex catastrophe that devastated Japan's northeastern coastline and caused a nuclear accident was triggered by a magnitude 9.0 undersea earthquake off the northeast coast of Japan, a region known as Tōhoku, that occurred at 2:46 PM on March 11 2011, lasting nearly six minutes. It is the most powerful quake recorded in Japan and one of the four most powerful in the world since 1900 when record keeping began. It generated forces five hundred times stronger than the 2010 magnitude 7 earthquake that devastated Haiti. The Tōhoku quake launched a massive tsunami that battered and inundated coastal villages along 500 km of coastline and in some areas wreaked destruction as far as 5 km inland. The island of Honshū was shifted 2.4 m east by the earthquake and there has subsequently been significant land subsidence in coastal areas, approximately 0.6 m, along 400 km of coastline, making them prone to flooding.

The official casualty toll as of August 2011 is 15,760 deaths, 5,927 injured and 4,282 people missing. Some 580,000 people were displaced initially and some 120,000 buildings were destroyed and a further 220,000 houses and buildings were damaged, leaving twisted piles of waterlogged rubble and debris where communities used to exist. Infrastructure suffered extensive damage, closing many ports along the coast, the major regional airport at Sendai, railroad lines and roads, complicating relief and recovery efforts. Initially 4.4 million households lost electricity and 1.5 million lost water services.

In addition, the earthquake and tsunami compromised reactor-cooling systems causing meltdowns and subsequent hydrogen explosions at three of the reactors at the Fukushima Daiichi nuclear plant, spreading radioactive contamination and leading the government to eventually evacuate 80,000 residents living within 20 km of the plant. The economic and public safety fallout from radioactive contamination is gathering as the Japan brand has been tarnished, food safety compromised, farming communities ruined and parents have become increasingly vocal about inadequate measures to safeguard children. The overall cost of the disaster is estimated between $210–300 billion, dwarfing the $125 billion damage caused by Hurricane Katrina, making it the most expensive natural disaster on record. The 6.8 magnitude earthquake in Kobe in 1995 killed 6,434 people and caused an estimated $130 billion in damage.

3/11 is the biggest crisis that Japan has faced since World War II ended in 1945. Looking at how Japanese people and their government have responded to this cataclysm helps us better understand disaster emergency planning, rescue and relief operations and yields broader insights about Japan. One major reason for trying to distill the lessons of 3/11 as they are still unfolding is to give policymakers everywhere an early opportunity to study how the country best prepared in the world for such eventualities has coped with the cascading disasters of earthquake, tsunami and nuclear meltdown. Obviously no country anywhere could possibly be prepared adequately for such a nexus of devastation, but seeing how Japan has struggled to manage this compound disaster carries widespread implications for every other country, because nowhere else is as experienced or prepared to deal with such disasters. It behooves policymakers around the world to draw lessons from 3/11, as the greater intensity and frequency of natural disasters over the past two decades heightens the need to improve planning for disaster mitigation and management, emergency rescue and relief, and reconstruction and recovery. Crisis and disaster management officials must respond quickly to mega-catastrophic events and it is important to understand how they react to the pressures of such a situation, and the mistakes they inevitably make, in order to be better prepared. 3/11 is also a poignant reminder for the global community about vulnerabilities and risk, and the imperative of reducing them through de-concentration and hedging strategies along the lines suggested by Charles Perrow in *The Next Catastrophe* (2007).

Japan has gotten lots of things right when it comes to disaster resilience. It is one of the world's most seismically active areas and experiences about 20 percent of the world's earthquakes of magnitude 6 or greater. Strict building codes meant that the seismic damage was relatively limited given the level of ground motion. Evacuation drills paid off as people in tsunami-vulnerable communities knew to move quickly and where to go, minimizing the loss of life. Strong community ties and social cohesion has been a significant asset as people in destroyed towns and villages struggle to cope. Civil society organizations have grown much stronger after the Kobe quake in 1995 and played a critical role in organizing volunteers and translating good intentions into effective responses. Social media sites like Twitter, Mixi and Facebook and Google's People Finder have been effectively used to disseminate timely information, mobilize and deploy volunteers, assess needs and distribute supplies, and help people find relatives and friends, making a huge difference in rescue and relief efforts. Understanding how social media enabled mobilization of networks of people, providing a means of social and political activism, is another valuable lesson our contributors explore. For example, citizens skeptical about reporting on radioactive contamination have been collecting their own data and using social media to expose discrepancies and challenge mainstream sources. Social media also played a crucial role in mobilizing an estimated 30,000– 60,000 anti-nuclear energy demonstrators in Meiji Park in central Tokyo on September 19, 2011, the largest demonstration in the nation's capital since the 1960s.

The Fukushima nuclear crisis has had an enormous impact and carries implications for nuclear and renewable energy policies that are hotly debated. Only 12 of Japan's 54 reactors are operating as of September 2011 as idled plants are not restarted, others go offline for regular maintenance and the utilities administer stress tests. Aside from the catastrophic failure of cooling systems that caused the meltdown, apparently due to design flaws in the backup power system, the disaster response of Tokyo Electric Power Company (TEPCO) has been fumbling and further undermined public confidence in nuclear energy. Progress towards achieving a cold shutdown of the stricken reactors has been slow and raised questions about the wisdom of operating nuclear reactors in such a seismically active nation. In addition, the International Atomic Energy Agency has admonished the utility for not providing accurate information in a timely manner. Inadequate information disclosure has harmed TEPCO's credibility while radioactive contamination has triggered alarm bells throughout the nation and the world. TEPCO's miscues have also tarnished the reputation of nuclear energy for safety and reliability, sparking increased support for renewable energy alternatives and electricity conservation measures. The crisis has also drawn attention to institutional problems, notably the nuclear watchdog agency being part of the ministry responsible for promoting nuclear energy. Given the potential conflict of interest, the nuclear watchdog agency will be reconstituted and shifted to the Environment Ministry in an effort to reassure the public that regulations will be enforced robustly and public safety not compromised in favor of industry interests.

Preliminary assessment

This volume covers the consequences of, and responses to, the natural disasters and nuclear crisis in post-3/11 Japan throughout the summer of 2011. As such this is a preliminary assessment and very much a contemporary document that we hope will prove valuable to future historians and students of disaster and energy policy, as they sift through the numerous articles and assessments that will accumulate over the ensuing years. We assume there will be more definitive reports in the future about the triple catastrophe that struck Japan on 3/11, and hopefully they will draw on the initial impressions, observations and analysis that we provide here, along with a sense of the evolving national mood and policy fray that has shaped contemporary discourse about the disasters.

It is already possible to discern what has happened, what lessons can be drawn and what some of the long-term implications may be. There have been decisive developments, and non-developments, that enable us to give an early and timely account of this traumatic period and what it portends. In these chapters one can get a sense of what it has been like to experience Japan in crisis, a revealing moment and fraught climate that will fade as time passes.

This project took shape in early April when I first visited the disaster zone. The scenes and smells of devastation from those days linger vividly in my memory, contrasting with memories from 1982 when I first visited this hauntingly beautiful coastline on my honeymoon. Gazing out over endless piles of waterlogged debris and the tsunami flattened landscape where communities once existed, it was hard to imagine that anyone survived this cataclysm. Charming hamlets of oyster farms and fishing villages had literally vanished and what remained looked like a war zone.

While I acknowledge that there is much to be said for analytical detachment and judicious assessment honed over time, this volume speaks to the strengths of first-hand accounts and immediacy. Our contributors rose to the task of pulling together information quickly and using their expertise to ask the right questions and provide thoughtful answers. I wish to thank this group of dedicated professionals for taking on this arduous task with a shared sense of urgency and personal commitment, while meeting ambitious deadlines.

The contributors have been urged to write in an accessible style and to share their insights, bypassing typical scholarly conventions involving methodological or theoretical issues. They have also been urged to keep citations and notes to a minimum and not dwell on disciplinary specific discourse. The results, I think, are gratifying for the non-specialist and an inspiration for other experts who seek to more broadly disseminate their findings.

Lessons

This wide-ranging examination of post-3/11 Japan conveys some crucial insights about how Japan is responding to its darkest moments since 1945. Peter Duus reminds us that what we are observing today is similar to post-disaster historical patterns in Japan, with overlapping phases of blaming, coping, hoping, learning, and forgetting. He notes that the incredible acts of generosity and mutual assistance we have witnessed in 2011 are also an established pattern. It is less encouraging to learn that the opportunities of substantial transformation created by disaster have been squandered in the past and according to many of our contributors will probably be frittered away again. It is perhaps a harsh and hasty assessment, but few of our contributors hold out hope that something new and better will be built in Tōhoku and early signs suggest reconstruction will be based far too much on past patterns rather than bold innovations. I think we all hope to be proven wrong on this score and would like to share Tossani's and Tōgo's tempered optimism about realizing a more redeeming vision.

This volume sheds light on a variety of fundamental issues and consequences arising from 3/11:

Natural disaster

1   Disaster preparedness in Japan undoubtedly saved numerous lives as well-drilled people knew where to evacuate, acted quickly, and had emergency supplies on hand.
2   Strict seismic codes meant that the magnitude 9 earthquake inflicted relatively little damage, but did cause significant land subsidence in coastal areas that renders such areas more vulnerable to flooding.
3   The tsunami caused most of the damage to buildings and transport networks, and deaths of people by drowning. Massive seawalls in many cases did not provide sufficient protection and many were broached. Complacency induced by such protection and the "cry wolf" syndrome may have added to the death toll.
4   The cascading disaster poses special problems that raise questions about emergency disaster planning. The interaction between the initial tsunami warnings understating the threat, and the quake-induced blackout compromising tsunami alarm systems, prevented many people from getting crucial updates about the scale of the tsunami, slowing evacuation. This problem was compounded by the relatively high proportion of less mobile elderly people in affected coastal communities who were unlikely to access social media and unable to move quickly. In addition, vulnerable transport networks, government offices, and evacuation centers that were in some cases overwhelmed by the tsunami, complicated rescue and relief efforts. About two-thirds of the recovered bodies were aged 65 or over, indicating that aging societies face special needs in preparing for disasters.

Society

1   Social cohesion has played a significant role in helping communities cope with the devastating consequences of 3/11.
2   Social capital in Tōhoku is less than in Kobe and coupled with a relatively aged population raises questions about the capacity for the region to bounce back.
3   The evident perseverance of the Tōhoku people should not obscure the fears, frustrations, and hopelessness that pervade, nor become an excuse for not providing desperately needed assistance. There are widespread apprehensions, and few reassuring answers, about relocation of communities and livelihood restoration.
4   Volunteering is more organized in Tōhoku 2011, and arguably more effective, than in Kobe 1995 as NPOs/NGOs (nonprofit/nongovernmental organizations) have developed significantly since then. Civil society organizations have played a critically important role in filling in gaps where government capacity has been lacking and contributed significantly to mitigating the consequences and helping people and communities rebound.

5　Google's People Finder proved instrumental in reuniting people, while social network services like Twitter were crucial for a nimble response, assessing needs, collecting and distributing supplies, mobilizing volunteers and donations, and gathering and disseminating up to date news about the situation.

Nuclear disaster

1　The first Fukushima meltdown occurred within five hours of the tsunami and the other two within 80 hours, but this information was not made public by TEPCO until the end of May. The age of the reactors, all 1970s' vintage, played a role in the world's worst nuclear accident since Chernobyl. The earthquake caused critical structural damage with implications for seismic safety at other nuclear plants while the tsunami knocked out backup electricity generators, crippling cooling systems that lead to the meltdown and subsequent hydrogen explosions.

2　TEPCO and government oversight authorities compromised safety by underestimating and downplaying tsunami risk despite credible warnings, while human error exacerbated the nuclear crisis and efforts to manage it.

3　The poor management of the nuclear crisis by TEPCO and the government has undermined the credibility of both organizations and casts a cloud over the future of nuclear energy in Japan, as 77 percent of Japanese surveyed in July favor gradually phasing it out in line with Prime Minister Kan's July 13 announcement.

4　Public concerns about the long-term health effects of radioactive contamination have increased considerably since 3/11, sparking anger towards the government's handling of the crisis and fueling support for renewable energy alternatives. Bans on food shipments from contaminated areas due to anxieties about food safety are ruining farmers' livelihoods and raise concerns about their ability to resume their livelihoods.

5　Anti-nuclear activism is constrained in hosting communities because they are chosen precisely because they are poor and dependent on nuclear-related subsidies, but this calculus may be changing as revelations emerge about the government and utilities falsifying support for nuclear power and, more importantly, as the media draws attention to evacuees in Fukushima who have received little assistance and face uncertainties about being able to return to their homes anytime soon, if ever.

6　Renewable energy enjoys considerable public support and growing political and corporate support as Japan reconsiders its national energy strategy and the risks of nuclear power. Some important steps have been taken to promote renewable energy projects, but there is a long way to go as renewables currently provide only about 1 percent of Japan's electricity needs.

Leadership

1   Japan's political elite has consistently underwhelmed the public throughout this crisis, wasting too much time and energy on petty politics and failing to act effectively or with sufficient urgency, leaving the public disenchanted with Tokyo and forcing the people of Tōhoku to rely on their own initiative.

2   There needs to be clearly organized disaster management decision-making structures and rigorous training, as in MBA programs and the military, in making decisions under stress and in situations of uncertainty that help officials rise to the occasion.

3   Local political leaders, community and neighborhood associations, cooperatives, NPOs and NGOs, and the private sector have been key actors in recovery, making up for central government inertia with timely, appropriate and generous interventions.

Politics and realities of disaster

Post-3/11 Japan reveals a society that is coping relatively well with adversity, trying to maintain hope against steep odds and giving full vent to the need to assign blame. Finger pointing over the emergency response to the earthquake and tsunami, and the handling of the nuclear crisis in Fukushima, remains in full gear and there are few signs that this will abate anytime soon. Clearly, as noted by several of the contributors, Prime Minister Kan Naoto was a lightning rod for widespread frustration and dissatisfaction. His ineffectual leadership skills and inability to formulate coherent policies and means to achieve them earned him widespread obloquy. Kan did not act effectively to mitigate the consequences of 3/11 and, as Curtis argues, failed to articulate a vision that would give the people of Tōhoku hope for the future. Curtis and Kingston agree that the public is disgusted with the political elite, including both the LDP and DPJ, and believe that ousting Kan holds little promise of improvement. His successor Prime Minister Noda Yoshihiko inherits the same problems of a divided diet, a divided party, a stagnant economy, high yen, and staggering public debt. Prime Minister Noda moved quickly to nurture party unity and reach out to the opposition, but with mixed success. Reconstruction, economic recovery, and managing the nuclear crisis remain key challenges. Time will tell if Noda will have any more success than his predecessor. Curtis and Kingston also agree that in comparison to leaders elsewhere in the world faced with far less daunting disasters, Kan did not perform as badly as the media insists. Kingston further argues that Kan has been the target of an orchestrated campaign of vilification by what Japanese refer to as the nuclear village (pro-nuclear energy advocates in the utilities, bureaucracy, LDP, media, and academia) because he advocates policies on nuclear and renewable energy that harm its interests, a perspective shared by DeWit, *et al.*, and Tōgo.

The failures of the central government to come to grips with the scale of the disaster and need for urgent action explains why few people in Japan believe that the potential for change will be realized. The absence of this buoying promise hangs like a storm cloud over Tōhoku's future and serves as a barometer for the nation's future as well. Much as people understand the sort of policies needed to generate transformation and would like to re-imagine Japan, the central government has been methodical and careful, eschewing the bold initiatives and reformist zeal that could translate concepts and visions into progressive reforms. As a result, hopes and dreams are in scarce supply.

Cukier asserts that the government's precarious financial circumstances will shape reconstruction efforts as will depopulation of the region. Younger residents are seeking better futures elsewhere, leaving behind smaller and less resilient communities that will be disproportionately elderly. The problems in Fukushima are compounded by radioactive contamination and nuclear anxieties that have forced large-scale evacuations. Indeed, the nuclear disaster assures that the implications of 3/11 will be far greater and persistent than previous disasters because of greater uncertainties about how to resolve the attendant problems and the global ramifications.

Disaster is a humbling experience. Despite all that we can learn from the past and all the advances in technology, the cascading Tōhoku catastrophe demonstrates that there is no way to prepare for every contingency. The major lesson policymakers can draw is that nations can act to improve disaster preparedness through a variety of measures ranging from improving evacuation drills, public education about managing risks, creating more resilient and vulnerable communications and transport systems, promoting diffusion of social network services, enforcing stricter building codes and land use zoning, while developing backup systems, emergency rescue, relief and public health services, and hedging strategies that avoid placing too many eggs in one basket. Another key lesson is the need to guard against complacency.

As Curtis argues, the Tōhoku story is one of resilience, community solidarity, and self-help. It is also the story of humanitarian assistance by private sector firms of unprecedented scope, offset by divided politics and the stifling hand of excessive government regulations and a segmented bureaucratic system. He laments that,

> Japanese politics today is dominated by men consumed by petty politics and power struggles and who are out of touch with the views of the public. There is not a political leader on the scene with the skill to connect with the public and exercise the power of persuasion that is so essential to effective political leadership.

A younger, and more cosmopolitan generation of politicians is advancing into positions of influence, however, and learning some important post-3/11 lessons about politics, policymaking and crisis management.

Civil society

Civil society makes for a much more uplifting story than politics. Morris points out problems he experienced firsthand with some NPOs, but Avenell, Slater, *et al.*, and Kawato, *et al.*, make a compelling case for the enormous contributions of volunteers, community groups, and civil society organizations to the Tōhoku relief and recovery efforts. Clearly, social media played a key role in maximizing such initiatives. Our contributors argue that volunteering has gained social legitimacy since Kobe 1995 and has become more organized and sustainable because of NPO efforts and also due to declining faith in government.

Avenell points out that Prime Minister Kan Naoto quickly established a governmental support structure for Tōhoku volunteering, a key development that demonstrates how far state-civil society relations have evolved since Kobe 1995 when local officials did not know what to do with volunteers. Overall, in the first four months after the Tōhoku Earthquake there were 499,300 registered volunteers, while 1,305,000 people volunteered in the first four months after the Kobe Earthquake. The numbers, however, do not tell the story of how much more difficult it has been to mount such efforts in relatively inaccessible Tōhoku, nor our contributors' expectations that Tōhoku volunteering will be sustained at significant levels for a longer duration.

Energy

Our contributors disagree about energy, certainly one of the more important debates facing Japan post-Fukushima. Scalise is skeptical that renewables can replace nuclear energy and makes a case that the imperatives of electricity demand and the need to contain costs and emissions make a renewable revolution unlikely. DeWit, *et al.* concede that the nuclear village holds important advantages in defending the energy status quo, but see signs that the solidarity of the village is unraveling and argue that renewables can be cost efficient. Furthermore, they argue that the true costs of nuclear energy have been systematically understated and assert that the global experience in renewables indicates that costs decrease as capacity expands. In their view, the benefits of nuclear power are highly concentrated while the costs are spread widely, while Scalise argues that nuclear energy is reliable, clean, and a boon to the economy, meaning widespread benefits. Noting increasing interest of Japanese business in developing and exploiting opportunities in renewables, DeWit, *et al.* conclude, "A green energy policy at the core of a smart post-3/11 reconstruction, could create robust and sustainable demand in Japan's domestic economy, opening up lucrative opportunities and generating both electricity and jobs."

Aldrich and Kawato, *et al.* draw attention to the constraints on anti-nuclear activism, pointing out how utility companies carefully select impoverished, remote communities where civil society and social capital is weak to host nuclear plants because they can be co-opted through generous subsidies. Aldrich stresses that these host communities are likely to remain quiescent because of budget and job concerns. Kingston acknowledges the subsidy addiction, but also notes that in some of these communities there are growing distrust, anxieties, and opposition stemming from the plight of Fukushima evacuees, and recent scandals involving utilities and central government stage-managing town hall meetings to fabricate local support for nuclear energy. An October, 2011 poll conducted by NHK found 80 percent of host community mayors opposed restarting idled nuclear reactors once stress tests are completed, reflecting widespread skepticism about how rigorous and reliable these safety checks really are.

There is general agreement that the Fukushima accident has reinvigorated anti-nuclear activism in Japan, but less consensus on whether this will be decisive in reshaping national energy policy. DeWit, *et al.* and Kingston believe there is momentum evident in a massive shift in public opinion polls against nuclear energy and in favor of renewable energy, which is increasingly echoed in the media and civil society, and by politicians and business leaders. They believe that a gradual shift towards renewable energy and away from nuclear energy is possible, but also recognize the power of the nuclear village to defend its turf.

Aldrich is more skeptical, writing, "In Japan, while there have been some moderate demonstrations against nuclear power in the post-3/11 days, there are few signs of broad-based, sustained anger or opposition to nuclear power." He adds,

in the arena of nuclear power, Japanese leaders and civil servants envision public opinion as malleable; in this approach, the people's perspective should be changed to match the perspective of the administration rather than elevated as a guidestar which should be followed.

As the energy battle heats up, it is important to bear in mind that the nuclear village is influential and wields a wide array of policy instruments designed to sway public opinion in line with national ambitions. While Scalise downplays the political influence of the utilities, Kingston and DeWit, *et al.* note the high level of political contributions by power company executives, constituting 72 percent of all individual donations to the LDP in 2009. In addition, it remains to be seen if the anti-nuclear movement can withstand the stress tests of prolonged conservation measures, possible blackouts, rising electricity bills, CO_2 emissions, and job losses associated with business flight.

Rebuilding and the Reconstruction Design Council

Our contributors are mostly critical of the Reconstruction Design Council (RDC) appointed by Prime Minister Kan to provide a vision and guidelines to achieve that. Curtis is skeptical about "reform by committee." Tossani shares Curtis' criticism about the suitability of the committee members for the task, calling into question their relevant professional expertise. Cukier doubts that the lofty principles of the interim report issued at the end of June can be translated into concrete results while Tōgo, despite some disappointments, finds more inspiration in the proposals than other contributors. Tossani agrees with the RDC that it is important for communities to take the initiative, and notes that a "one-size-fits-all" policy is inappropriate. He also raises important questions about local capacity and vision, while stressing the need for overall coordination of rebuilding efforts.

In thinking about reconstruction it is important not to forget that what makes for rational policy may not be appealing. Consolidating ravaged communities into safer, planned new towns rather than just rebuilding them might be sensible, but holds little appeal in a region marked by strong local loyalties and deep attachments. In addition, Ōtani reminds us that the post-disaster needs of the elderly in Japan's rapidly aging society must be integrated into rebuilding projects.

Prospects

In assessing prospects for Tōhoku's recovery Aldrich reminds us that the affected areas in the Tōhoku region have lower levels of social capital than elsewhere and residents in this region spend less time on informal socializing, have more single-member households, and are older than residents in Hyōgo prefecture where the Kobe Earthquake occurred. He suggests that, "these lower social capital metrics have accompanied slower, less-focused recoveries. Along with more shallow reservoirs of social capital, the Tōhoku areas have fewer financial resources as well compared to other parts of Japan." Given these handicaps, the absence of effective national political leadership or timely government action, there are good reasons to be pessimistic that Tōhoku will become an inspiring model for recovery.

On the other hand, the resourcefulness and initiative of local political and community leaders, massive corporate social responsibility programs undertaken by Japanese companies, and the flowering of civil society, are bolstering the gritty determination of local residents who are determined to rebound against the odds. And the odds are very steep indeed. Perhaps that is why the nation collectively and openly rejoiced in the victory of the underdog Japanese women's soccer team over Team USA to win the FIFA World Cup in July 2011. The nation thrilled to see the effective teamwork and gutsy, high-octane performance of the Japanese players offset the physical and athletic advantages of the US team. Gracious in victory, the Japanese women embodied qualities that made people feel collectively proud, basking in the glow of victory earned in a style that conforms with cultural traits many believe are the wellspring of national strength. The women's spirited, come-from-behind triumph inspired the nation, a rare bit of feel-good news in a nation that has been coping with an unending flow of bad news and is still in mourning and shock. Many hoped that the improbable championship might augur well for Tōhoku, drawing on the intangibles of humanity and collective determination that surprise and inspire in equal measure.

PART I

Disaster

Reports from Tōhoku

I

TŌHOKU DIARY

Reportage on the Tōhoku disaster

Gerald L. Curtis

There are towns along the Pacific coast in Tōhoku, the region northeast of Tokyo, with names like Ōfunato and Rikuzen Takata in Iwate prefecture, and Minami Sanriku, Kesennuma, and Watari in Miyagi prefecture that until March 11 of this year meant little more to most Japanese than the names of towns along the Maine coast mean to most Americans. Many people knew little more about these towns than that they were places where Japanese got a lot of their fish, and that they have a harsh winter climate and hardworking people of few words.

The 9.0 magnitude earthquake and the tsunami that struck Tōhoku on that day in March changed all that. Now the names of these towns, towns that I visited over several days at the beginning of May, and others on the northeast coast, evoke images of miles upon miles of devastation where houses, ports, fishing boats, merchant shops and small factories, rice fields and hot houses for vegetables and strawberries have disappeared, turning the landscape into an endless vista of debris punctuated by the occasional presence of a boat or car perched on the roof of some concrete structure that did not collapse under the incredible force of the tsunami.

Earthquake damage to the train station at Sendai, Miyagi prefecture's capital, had been repaired by the time I got there on May 4, a few days after bullet train service resumed along the entire Tokyo-Aomori route. Neither at the train station nor anywhere else in the city center was there evidence that Sendai had been violently shaken by the strongest earthquake in its history.

In Tokyo high-rise buildings swayed, and did so for so many minutes that it made some people feel as though they were seasick, but none collapsed. Falling objects killed or injured several people but overall damage was minimal. In the north the earthquake knocked out electricity, gas, and water lines, but power was restored relatively quickly in areas that were beyond the reach of the tsunami, and deaths and injuries were few.

I stayed one night at an old inn in Ichinoseki in Iwate prefecture, one of the inland cities hard hit by the earthquake. There were cracks in the walls of the inn but there was electricity and gas and running water. The owner told me that her elderly mother, who was standing at the entrance looking confused and anxious, became so frightened by the intensity of the earthquake that she completely lost her hearing. The owner said that she was putting off fixing the cracks and repairing other damage that the earthquake had caused because she assumed that at some point there will be a much more powerful aftershock than any they had experienced so far. The only question was when it would come. If the inn survived that quake, she would make repairs then. Lying on my futon on the second floor, I fell asleep hoping that we would not find out the answer about the inn's survival that night. We didn't. If there had not been the tsunami, the lead story about March 11 would have been about the remarkably successful earthquake disaster prevention measures Japan has adopted.

After arriving in Sendai and checking into the hotel, I headed out to the Sendai airport. Driving toward the ocean from the city center, everything looked normal for the first ten kilometers or so. Then the scenery suddenly turned bizarre: a smashed car sitting in the middle of a rice field, wood, metal and other debris scattered here and there. The closer I got to the ocean the more destruction I saw: a two-story building for example whose walls were still intact but without any windows left on either the first or second floor. The tsunami had blown them out, washing away most of the things that had been inside and drowning people who were living there. I could see large characters painted at the top of what had been the building's entrance. They indicated that this had been a community old age home.

There was an incredible number of cars tossed about helter-skelter throughout the area along the coast, many so crushed and mangled that it looked as though they had been involved in head-on collisions. One car was perpendicular with the front half of its hood buried in the ground, looking as though someone had tried to plant it. Others were upside down and one looked as though it was trying to climb a tree. The Self Defense Forces have been collecting and sorting the debris and piling it up – wood here, scrap metal there – for eventual disposal. Every so often along the side of a road there would be a stack of ruined automobiles piled on top of each other and taking up the equivalent of half a New York city block. Since automobiles are virtually the sole mode of transportation for people who live in this coastal part of Sendai, it is not unusual for a household to have several cars for family members to commute to work. Never have I seen so many ruined automobiles.

It is going to take imagination, money, bold planning, and strong political leadership to rebuild this area. The rice fields have been inundated with salt water and the land in many places has sunk 70–80 centimeters. Restoring this land to agricultural use will be difficult and expensive. The port will be restored and airport repairs will be completed, but in the absence of some development scheme that at the present time seems to be nowhere in sight, the population of this corner of

Sendai and even more so in the affected towns along the coast undoubtedly will decline, leaving behind mostly elderly people who cannot or do not want to leave the only place they have ever known, even if there is nothing there.

The tsunami rolled across the Sendai airport, washing mud and debris onto the runways and doing extensive damage to the terminal building. With the bullet train system down, the airport not functioning, boats unable to enter the Sendai port, and roadways cracked and covered with debris, it was a monumental task to get relief supplies and rescue workers into the region.

In the days immediately following the earthquake, the US military in Japan launched "Operation Tomodachi" (*tomodachi* meaning friend), ferrying supplies by helicopter from the aircraft carrier *Ronald Reagan*, which had changed course to go to Japanese waters to assist the humanitarian effort. A team of Air Force special forces flew from Okinawa to a Japanese Self Defense Force (SDF) airbase near Sendai and then travelled to the airport in Humvees they had brought in with them. Within a few hours the team had enough of one of the runways cleared for C-130s to land with emergency supplies. When I got to the airport a month and a half later, the runways were open for limited domestic civilian traffic, but the passenger terminal building had been so badly damaged that there was only one small area being used for ticketing and passenger check in.

The Japanese press and television, unlike the US media, gave prominent coverage to the activities of the American troops. The favorable publicity no doubt reinforced Japanese public support for alliance with the United States, which was strong to begin with. Whether that will change anything about issues that the US military cares about is another matter. Operation Tomodachi is not going to make it any easier to solve the problem of what to do with the Marine Corp's Futenma air station in Okinawa. Building a new base at Henoko off Okinawa's northeast coast does not appear to be a viable option. Staying put at Futenma is an option, but hardly a desirable one. This base sits smack in the middle of Ginowan city where the eardrum-breaking noise of fighter jets and other planes taking off and landing and the ever-present danger of a major accident are what led the US and Japanese governments to decide more than a decade ago to close it down.

In the aftermath of the earthquake, three influential US Senators – Democrats Carl Levin and Jim Webb and Republican John McCain – publicly called on President Obama to abandon the Henoko option, saying that it was unrealistic to expect Japan to provide the funding needed to build the base at Henoko when it faced a huge reconstruction bill in Tōhoku. They proposed closing the Futenma base and moving the Marines that are stationed there to the Kadena air force base, the largest US military base in Okinawa.

Even if the US air force were to agree to joint use with the Marines and the Obama Administration were to abandon its commitment to the Henoko relocation, the Japanese government would still face the formidable task of convincing the Okinawa government to go along. Okinawans want less of a US military presence on their island, where most US bases in Japan are located. As for Japanese living on Japan's main islands, appreciation of the US military effort in Tōhoku is heartfelt but it has not changed their Not In My Backyard attitude toward the disposition of US military bases in their country.

US military personnel, in addition to their work in opening the airport and ferrying in supplies, worked with the SDF in the offshore search for victims. They also cleared the debris at one of the many damaged train stations. I met with a US army major stationed in Sendai who serves as liaison between US Forces Japan, which now have returned to their bases elsewhere in Japan, and the Self Defense Forces' Northeast Army. Major Brooke took me to the Nobiru train station to show me the work the US military did in cleaning up debris from the platform and the adjacent tracks. Visiting this site as well as seeing the damage done to railway tracks, stations, bridges, and trains throughout the disaster area left me dubious that this effort was of much more than symbolic value. The debris at Nobiru station was gone, but the tracks were bent and half buried in sand and mud, a train that had been at the station looked beyond repair, and you could not see the tracks for more than a few hundred yards beyond the station platform in either direction because of all the detritus that has yet to be cleared away.

It is doubtful that restoring the Nobiru station and the railroad bridges and tunnels along the battered coast makes much sense. Many of the people whose homes were swallowed up by the tsunami are going to relocate to higher ground away from the current rail lines. The destruction offers an opportunity to build a new railway system that could take advantage of the latest technology and be designed more rationally than the one that now is in ruins. But to do that would require quick and decisive action by the government, an unlikely prospect.

American participation in efforts to help people in Tōhoku has not been limited to the military. There are American and other foreign volunteers working with Japanese and international NGOs throughout the disaster zone. One of these is an international disaster relief organization called All Hands that is active in Ōfunato city in Iwate prefecture. What the American volunteers working with All Hands are doing is a reminder that the US-Japan relationship is far more than a military alliance. The great majority of Americans working in Tōhoku with All Hands and with other NGOs are people who are living in Japan. A typical case is that of a businessman who has been in Kanazawa for more than 15 years who took time off from work to volunteer with All Hands, saying that after all Japan has done for him he could not stay away and do nothing.

Another American there turned out to be my student from 20 years ago. (Teach long enough and former students show up in all sorts of unexpected places.) Having gone from Columbia to a successful career as an investment banker, he became prosperous and was enjoying retired life in Tokyo until the earthquake struck. Able to set his schedule as he likes, he decided to do volunteer work with All Hands. This subsequently became his new calling. He heads the All Hands operation in Tōhoku, and when he is not shoveling mud and debris along with other volunteers he gives financial advice to local government leaders and businessmen and fishermen trying to get their businesses up and running again.

An American woman who runs a consulting company in Boston was there working with the volunteers as a translator. Born in Tokyo and having lived there through high school, she said that for her Japan is home. She felt that she had to come to do something to help.

When I caught up with the All Hands volunteers, they were working on a house that had been badly damaged by the tsunami but was repairable. Mrs. Chiba, the owner of the house, was watching them work when I got there. She was staying in an evacuation center with her husband, who is confined to a wheelchair, and her son. She said that a couple of nights earlier she had slept soundly through the night for the first time in the nearly two months that she has been at the evacuation center. "I went to bed thinking that in the morning those nice volunteers would be back at my house," she said. "I felt so relieved."

There are countless uplifting stories about the foreign volunteers and the reception they have found, but there also have been problems with government bureaucrats telling volunteer organizations that their help wasn't needed or that there were no accommodations for them. It would be a mistake simply to chalk this up to xenophobia or to conclude that it is typical of the government's response. Rather, these frazzled functionaries seem incapable of doing anything for which there is no precedent, to think "outside the box," and they find dealing with NGOs, Japanese or foreign, to be more trouble than it is worth.

All Hands got lucky in Ōfunato. The mayor, who had worked for the Shimizu Corporation before deciding to run for mayor of his hometown, had spent time at the architecture school at Harvard. He met with the representative of All Hands, discussed the situation with him in English, and not only welcomed the volunteers to his city but found a place for them to live. Although there have been glitches, on the whole the Japanese government and local communities have welcomed foreign volunteers and have been grateful for their help.

There has been an outpouring of sympathy for Tōhoku's victims from across Japan. Innumerable ad hoc groups have emerged to collect donations of money and of clothing and other needed items. Many Japanese have been volunteering. Estimates of the number of volunteers who have gone to Tōhoku during the first three months range from half to three-quarters of a million people. The number is impressive especially when you consider how much time it takes to reach the devastated areas from Tokyo and the lack of adequate accommodations.

It is difficult to take unscheduled vacation time in the typical Japanese company, especially on short notice, but many companies are making special arrangements to make it easier for their employees to take time off to do volunteer work. The Mitsubishi Corporation, for example, has established an employee volunteer program whereby employees go to Tōhoku in groups of ten for three nights and four days. They receive their regular salaries during this time. This program is scheduled to run for one year initially.

Relief activities in Tōhoku, whether removing debris, providing psychological counseling, or rebuilding damaged facilities, are hampered by the lack of a sufficient infrastructure and of people with the management skills needed to coordinate these kinds of activities. Finding housing for volunteers, for example, and putting them in touch with reliable organizations requires having people on the ground tasked with these responsibilities. Tōhoku's recovery is a long-term challenge that will require continued assistance of various kinds. Along with all the other problems they face, prefectural authorities and the national government need to build an infrastructure to facilitate and coordinate the help that so many individuals and organizations would like to offer.

I met many people and heard many terribly sad and terrifying stories. I spent a couple of hours with Mayor Sato of Minami Sanriku town. He was in the town office with more than 30 town officials when the earthquake struck. They all ran up to the roof, anticipating that a tsunami would come. What they could not know was that this tsunami would be so powerful – it was measured at one location at 39 meters and it wrought its destruction as far as six miles inland – that it would be higher than the town hall. Sato and a few others were thrown by the wave toward one end of the roof where he was able to grab onto a steel pole. He managed to hold on as the tsunami washed over him. Most of the others were pushed to the other side where there was only a flimsy metal fence. The fence broke under the force of the water and they were swept away to their death. Only ten people working in the town office including the mayor survived.

Photographs and television footage do not do justice to the incredible scale of the devastation that struck Minami Sanriku town. There is almost nothing left of the homes and businesses that were there. The fish market, the seafood processing plants and canneries along the wharves, and almost all the boats that had anchored in its harbors were badly damaged or destroyed. (According to the Miyagi prefectural government, about 90 percent of the 13,400 fishing boats in the prefecture were damaged or destroyed. Most of the boats that survived were those that fishermen sailed out into the open ocean as soon as the earthquake struck to ride out the tsunami.)

When I visited evacuation centers in Minami Sanriku and other towns the first thing that struck me, and that is immediately apparent to anyone who has seen television footage of the evacuation centers, is how orderly they are. This is Japan after all and people are incredibly – that is incredibly to someone who is not Japanese – neat and polite. Of course shoes are taken off before entering the room, there are special slippers to wear at the bathrooms, which are immaculate, there is no one playing loud music that might disturb someone else and people keep their voices down so as not to bother their neighbors. Their neighbors in this case are people living on the other side of a cardboard partition. Whatever meager belongings they have are arranged neatly along the outer perimeter of the small space that these people have had to live in for the past months, ever since their homes and possessions and in all too many cases their loved ones perished.

At the end of June there were still just under 90,000 people living in evacuation centers. The government has promised that by August it will complete the building of temporary housing where people can stay for up to two years while they make arrangements for their permanent relocation. But moving homeless and elderly people – an estimated 30 percent or more of the population in the tsunami affected areas is over 65 years old – into temporary housing is not a simple matter.

The government has been building housing blocks on public land outside the tsunami zone, mostly on the soccer fields and baseball diamonds of local elementary and middle schools and on land adjacent to community and town-run cultural centers. But there is not enough of this kind of land available for the more than 72,000 temporary housing units the government plans to construct in Iwate, Miyagi and Fukushima prefectures. In many of the towns along the coast, higher elevation land is too steep to build on or it is privately owned. The government has to negotiate lease arrangements with private landowners and it also has to level some mountainous land, processes that take both time and money.

The effort to build temporary housing as quickly as possible and move people out of the evacuation centers has created problems of its own. The government has adopted a lottery system to determine who should be eligible to move into these housing units as they become available. While that may seem fair, it has created considerable anxiety among people who have lived their entire lives in the hamlets that are the basic units of rural Japanese society.

One elderly lady drove the point home to me. She does not want to leave the evacuation center, she said, if it means moving to temporary housing somewhere where she is separated from her friends in the village where she has lived all her life. She would prefer to stay there until all the people in her village could be resettled together. She is afraid of the loneliness and worries about becoming entirely dependent on her son to drive to wherever she might be relocated to take her to her doctor. She was not alone in this view: I heard the same lament from others as well.

A misguided desire to be equitable has collided with the norm of community solidarity that remains so pervasive in isolated, poor areas in rural Japan. (In terms of per capita GDP, Miyagi ranks number 32 of Japan's 47 prefectures and Iwate number 39.) Even more, government policy seems oblivious to the special problems faced by the elderly. I was told of a landowner in Ōfunato who donated hilltop land he owns to be used for temporary housing but in doing so insisted that the agreement with the city stipulate that all the residents of the local hamlet would be offered the opportunity to move there before housing would be made available for occupancy by others. Resettling these displaced people in a manner that not only gives them a roof over their heads but that sustains community ties and mitigates the isolation of elderly people living on their own requires a much more fine-tuned approach than the one-size-fits-all policy approach favored by government bureaucrats.

Even in the urban setting of Kobe, there were many cases of "death in isolation" (*kodokushi*) of elderly people living alone in temporary housing after the 1995 Hanshin Awaji Earthquake. Not only did they die alone, in many cases their bodies were not discovered for several days or weeks after their death. Elderly people in the evacuation centers in Tōhoku have good reason to be frightened at the prospect of living separated from friends and relatives. Most of the victims of the earthquake and tsunami have nothing left except each other. The government's resettlement program threatens to take even that away from many of them as well.

Many observers have noted the bravery, stoicism, and resilience of the Tōhoku people. They have a dignity about them, an instinctive readiness to band together to help each other, a courage and an inner strength that has impressed the entire world but that perhaps has impressed no one more than the Japanese themselves. People who thought that cherished core traditional Japanese values had weakened or disappeared stared at their television screens transfixed as they watched people forming long lines to wait patiently for water and for a single rice ball for dinner, and as tens of thousands of people who had crammed into evacuation centers got themselves organized, chose leaders, and formed groups to perform the various tasks needed to make their refuge as civilized and comfortable a place to live as possible. The pictures and stories coming out of Tōhoku were heartbreaking and at the same time inspiring. They have given the Japanese a renewed sense of pride. That could be a source of energy if only Japan had leaders who had a sense about how to mobilize and channel it.

It is important not to exaggerate and idealize the stoic, patient, resilient Tōhoku victim. You do not have to spend much time talking with people in the evacuation centers before you are overwhelmed by how frightened they are and how hopeless they feel. They are bitterly disappointed in their government's inadequate response to their predicament, and they are desperate about their future. These are brave people who have nothing and have no idea what the future holds.

One woman told me that her only worldly possession is the cell phone she had with her when she fled the tsunami. But she smiles and says that she will be okay. Another lady, perhaps in her mid-60s and with the sweetest, softest smile told me that she shares her small space in the evacuation center with three other people. I assumed that one of them was her husband and asked her what his occupation is. "Oh, my husband," she said very gently, "he got swept away by the tsunami and died." As she spoke she strained to keep her smile on her lips but there were tears in her eyes and every muscle in her face seemed pulled taut.

I visited an evacuation center in Watari, a town about 30 kilometers south of Sendai that is famed for its strawberries, accompanied by a local town assemblyman whom I had met through a mutual friend. It was the middle of the afternoon and there were perhaps 100 people sitting around chatting quietly or napping, or just staring out into space. The assemblymen went over to three men who were sitting together, introduced me and asked one of them to talk to me and tell me what he thought the government should be doing to deal with their situation. The man said that he did not have anything to say and turned away. I would have given up but the assemblyman persisted. Being friends from the same village, he asked the man to do him a personal favor and just answer a question or two.

I sat down on the floor next to him and tried to engage him and his companions in casual conversation. For the first few minutes all I got were short and guarded replies and a kind of when-are-you-going-to-get-out-of-here look from the three of them. But in this and other interviews I had in Tōhoku, people spent the first few minutes trying to figure out who is this Japanese-speaking American and deciding whether they wanted to talk to me.

It did not take long before their guard came down. Usually it was sparked by some innocent question, as happened when I asked the lady what her husband's occupation was. In this case I asked the man sitting next to me what he did for a living before the tsunami hit. He said that he was a strawberry farmer. When I then asked him whether he planned to go back to strawberry farming, the floodgates opened up. "How can I," he said,

> I am 70 years old, my house is gone, the strawberry hothouses have all been destroyed, the land is full of salt water and has sunk 75 centimeters, I still have a loan on equipment I bought that is ruined. I have no income and no way to take out another loan on top of the one I already have.

The other two men were sitting across the table from us. One of them had been sitting there stone-faced but suddenly he too became animated and chimed in to tell me that to buy a new thresher costs more than 8 million yen, or roughly $85,000. He does not have that kind of money and at his age he is not going to get a loan. So he sits there with little more to do than contemplate the dead-end predicament he finds himself in.

The third man told me that he was 43 years old and was also a strawberry farmer. His facial expressions and body language left me with the disquieting feeling that he was perhaps the most stressed and depressed person of all I had met. I tried to be encouraging and said that he was still young and physically fit and what did he think about moving to Sendai or somewhere else where there were job opportunities and getting a new start. His answer was that he has lived his whole life in the village where he was born, that he never wanted to move away and does not want to now, that growing strawberries is all he knows how to do and is the only thing that he loves to do, and that he has no idea what is going to become of him now that everything is gone.

There is no place for him to turn for well-informed advice. He can get a temporary job cleaning up debris or fill out an application at one of the "Hello Work" employment centers. He might have the opportunity to talk with a psychiatrist or one of the other mental health specialists who have been going to Tōhoku from around the country to offer their services. But since they stay for only a few days at most and are not familiar with local conditions, it is questionable how helpful their psychological counseling is. More than a psychiatrist, what this strawberry farmer and others like him need are government policies that give them some reason to have hope about their future.

There was a lively old lady at the Watari evacuation center who started out our conversation by saying with a chuckle that she got divorced when she was 37, raised her children by herself, made a living all these years growing strawberries, and that she would survive this tsunami disaster too. But after several minutes the bravado disappeared as she told me in a very heavy Tōhoku dialect known as *zuzuben* that she has no hope. "You have no hope?" I repeated, partly to make sure that I did not misunderstand what she had just said in her Tōhoku accent. "None," she said, "no hope or anything." She added that she is 80 years old and strong and was planning to work until she is 100. But she was afraid that just sitting here in the evacuation center day after day with nothing to do except worry about the future was going to kill her. When I asked her what was most important to give her hope, this countrywoman's answer echoed what the other elderly lady said to me about moving to temporary housing. "There are so many things, but what is most important is that all of us [from her village] can live together and bring our farmland back to life."

I had planned to be at this evacuation center for no more than an hour but ended up staying for almost three. These brave people are neither as stoic nor as resilient as others who do not share their plight might like to believe. They try their best to be positive but cannot hide their stress and the grief that lines their faces. Nor are they as reticent and reserved as many people seem to think they are. Give them an opportunity to talk with a sympathetic listener, Japanese or foreigner, and they give eloquent expression to their fears. Their homes are destroyed, the land has sunk 70 centimeters or more so they cannot rebuild where they once lived even if they wanted to, and many of them do not want to rebuild where a tsunami might hit again. They have no jobs, their fishing boats, farm equipment and everything else is gone and in many cases they have loans on no longer existing homes and on factories and machinery that are beyond repair and little or no insurance to cover their loss. This is the daunting reality that political leaders in Tokyo need to contend with. They have fallen far too short in doing so.

There are local political leaders who have innovative ideas about how to rebuild their communities. The mayor of Minami Sanriku, the man who barely missed being swept off the roof of the town hall, would like to turn this disaster into an opportunity to reshape the fishing industry that is the heart of the economy of this town. Minami Sanriku has 23 ports, which means that there is a port in just about every inlet with just a few fishermen in many of them who eke out a meager income. Mayor Sato would like to consolidate them into two or three ports equipped with modern equipment and have the fishermen band together in a corporate structure that could buy and lease a modern fleet of boats and equipment.

The owner of a fish packing plant in Ōfunato showed me the battered remains of a machine for smoking fish that he purchased the previous fall for a million dollars and other now useless machinery. He said that it would cost somewhere between $5–10 million to recover from his loss. He is determined to get his business up and running again and hire back the employees whom he had to let go. He is investing what money he has and getting bank loans wherever he can but getting back into business without government assistance seems like an almost insurmountable hurdle. He and other local businessmen have been urging adoption of a program by which the government would purchase the equipment that is needed and lease it to people like him who want to restart their businesses.

The media and the political opposition were unrelenting in their criticism of Prime Minister Kan. Less than 20 percent of the public supported the prime minister. More than 70 percent disapprove of the way he was dealing with what Japanese call the Great Eastern Japan Earthquake Disaster and wanted to see him resign before the end of August. But the public entertained no illusions that the political situation would improve with Kan's resignation. No political leader had been able to capture the public's imagination. Support for the DPJ, LDP and other parties was in a kind of free fall.

By any comparative measure, the Kan government's response to the triple catastrophe of the earthquake, tsunami, and nuclear meltdown was not as awful as his critics made it out to be. (The response to the crisis at the nuclear power plant at Fukushima Daiichi is another story.) It was far better than the way the Bush Administration dealt with the aftermath of Hurricane Katrina and compares favorably to how other governments have responded to disaster situations.

But the Japanese rightfully credit the people in Tōhoku and not the government for being law abiding and orderly and for doing so much to take care of themselves and each other. They have not received the assistance from the government that they should have gotten. There are stories of elderly people who managed to survive the tsunami only to die in evacuation centers from hypothermia because of delays in getting blankets and dry clothing to them.

The owner of the fish packing plant in Ōfunato went right to the core of the problem with the way the Kan Administration has dealt with the situation in Tōhoku when he said,

> I know that coming up with detailed policies takes time. I understand that. But what we need to hear from the prime minister are words that would give us some comfort and hope about the future. Words are important. I am investing my own money to try to recover my business but I am doing so not knowing whether to believe that the government will come through with policies that will support the reconstruction of this area or not.

Prime Minister Kan did not succeed in convincing the public that he had a vision for Tōhoku reconstruction and for Japan's future, and that there were things that he cared deeply about that he wanted to accomplish as prime minister and on which he was ready to stake his government's survival.

The mood in Tōhoku would be much less despondent if Prime Minister Kan had said something like "I know that the land on which you have lived is not safe to build on again and that your farms have been ruined by sea water. I cannot tell you at this moment exactly how we will do it but we will make it possible for you and your neighbors to relocate to higher ground, to stay together as a community, and provide assistance so that you can get the boats, machinery and other equipment that you need to get back to work. Don't give up hope. We will make Tōhoku prosperous." He should have appointed a Reconstruction Minister immediately and tasked him with producing a basic reconstruction plan and to present it to him within weeks. Instead he created a reconstruction commission chaired by a political historian and president of the National Defense College and appointed several other academics to the Commission who also have little in the way of relevant expertise. The Commission's final report is not due until near the end of 2011.

Reliance on this Reconstruction Design Council will delay decisions. The report that finally emerges is certain to be a consensus document, and not offer the hard-hitting, bold, and precedent-breaking approach that is needed. Commissions and other consensus building approaches may have a role to play in normal times, but the situation in Tōhoku is a state of emergency even if Japan does not have a law on the books that enables the government to define it as such. Neither Prime Minister Kan nor the leaders of the political opposition convey enough of the sense of urgency that the situation demands. It is of course important to resettle people from evacuation centers to temporary housing and to clean up the debris as quickly as possible. But there is just as urgent a need to adopt policies to create jobs and to give people hope about their future.

In a conversation I had with Prime Minister Kan on April 24, I expressed skepticism about the usefulness of the Tōhoku Reconstruction Design Council and asked him whether he really thought that it had an important role to play. His answer could not have been more discouraging. "Definitely," he said, "the Reconstruction Design Council will amass diverse public views and come up with a concept [for Tōhoku's reconstruction]."

This is akin to President Obama saying that the United States needs to restructure its health care system so he is appointing a committee comprised of people with diverse opinions to come up with a concept for health care reform. It was tough enough for Obama to get his health reform program through the Congress knowing what he wanted to do. It was impossible for Prime Minister Kan to come up with a meaningful reconstruction plan by waiting until a committee told him what to think about everything from nuclear energy policy to city planning to tax policy and just about anything and everything else that might be relevant to recovering from 3/11.

It is the responsibility of the prime minister himself to come up with a basic concept for rebuilding Tōhoku and to then seek expertise from within and outside the government to translate that concept into a concrete plan of action. What made Kan's failure to provide leadership all the more troubling was that there was no other political leader in sight with the vision and political will to take the bold action that was required.

The opportunity to create a new Tōhoku development model exists. The key is to designate Tōhoku as a special economic zone (SEZ) and transfer power and money to the prefecture and local governments. Domestic and foreign businesses would be offered tax holidays and other incentives to invest in the Tōhoku SEZ and prefectural governments would have the authority to decide whether to apply or suspend ministerial rules and regulations and whether to impose restrictions of their own, for example on rebuilding in the tsunami danger zone. The people who best understand what is needed are those who are there on the ground, not politicians and their advisers in Tokyo who fly in for a few meetings with local officials and fly right back to Tokyo again. The Reconstruction Council's proposal in its interim report to create special economic zones, in the plural, offers far less than meets the eye. Specific to particular industries and towns, it has the fingerprints of central government ministry bureaucrats all over it.

If action is not taken quickly the opportunity will be lost. Life will get back to normal for people who live outside the Tōhoku region and, as it does, enthusiasm for radical change will decline. Supply chain problems are temporary. Special budgetary allocations for Tōhoku recovery will have a stimulatory impact on the economy. Recovery from catastrophe is likely to be quick; six to eight months after the earthquake, the nation's growth rate is likely to be just about where it would have been had the disaster never occurred.

In Tōhoku itself some people who lost their homes and businesses to the tsunami will decide nonetheless to try to resume life as they knew it before March 11 and rebuild on the land where their houses and businesses once stood. Once that happens the chance to move entire communities to new housing on higher ground, to spread a network of solar energy panels across land close to the shore, to have fisherman band together in a new corporate structure and to effect other radical reforms favored by thoughtful leaders at the local level will have been lost.

The exodus of young people from the region will accelerate but there will be enough people left to catch and package the fish that is the mainstay of this relatively impoverished region. Tōhoku could sink back into obscurity and the rest of the country would hardly notice. An opportunity lost perhaps, but not the end of the world.

The three Tōhoku prefectures of Fukushima, Miyagi, and Iwate account for about 4 percent of Japan's GDP and the areas directly affected by the tsunami for less than half of that. The truth is that if nothing much is done to give Tōhoku a new start, Japan will not suffer appreciably as a consequence. That of course is a good reason to make a bold and radical policy shift. The downside risk is small, and if it were to succeed a Tōhoku development model would become a beacon for Japan's future.

Politicians in Tokyo use words like crisis and emergency situation to describe the impact of the March 11 earthquake but it is not possible to square their rhetoric with their behavior. If they had believed that they were dealing with a crisis they would have shifted their focus from trying in every which way to cause the Kan government to fall to looking for ways to forge policy cooperation across party lines. At least the opposition parties would be trying to persuade the public that they have a better program than what Prime Minister Kan was offering to respond to the crisis in Tōhoku and to come to grips with the larger issues of fiscal and social security reform. But the LDP as well as Kan's opponents in his own Democratic Party could not seem to be able to turn their attention away from trying to figure out how to bring down the government long enough to say anything constructive.

Prime Minister Kan seemed to have little idea about how to structure a coherent policy-making process – and he got no help from bureaucrats who wanted to see him fail. He seemed incapable of delegating responsibility and the crisis spawned by the catastrophe of March 11 deprived him of the luxury of time to figure out how to develop a sensible decision-making system.

Japanese politics today is dominated by men consumed by petty politics and power struggles and who are out of touch with the views of the public. There is not a political leader on the scene with the skill to connect with the public and exercise the power of persuasion that is so essential to effective political leadership. It is not surprising that public opinion polls show widespread public disgust with both the DPJ and the LDP.

There was no short-term remedy for Japan's political woes. Japan, like the United States, had divided government. With their control of a majority of seats in the upper house, the opposition parties found the temptation to block the DPJ from passing legislation all but irresistible. The only way for the government to force the opposition to cooperate was to rally public opinion strongly to its side. That is how Prime Minister Koizumi was able to overcome intense opposition to his program from within his own party. But unfortunately for Japan, Kan was no Koizumi.

Forming a grand coalition is not the answer to Japan's political predicament either. In Germany or in Britain parties are able to enter into coalition without forsaking their separate identities and core bases of support. But in Japan where social cleavages – class, region, religion, ethnicity, and so on – that help structure the party system elsewhere are weak, a grand coalition would signify the effective end of the existence of a major opposition party and the virtual collapse of competitive party politics. That would not produce more enlightened policies; it would only threaten Japan's political democracy.

A grand coalition that is not based on a policy accord would move the power struggle out of public view into the backrooms of the coalition government. For the LDP the attraction of a grand coalition is the opportunity to get its hands on power once again. For the DPJ it is the hope that the LDP would in reality become hostage to the DPJ government.

There is considerable resistance to forging a coalition in both the LDP and the DPJ. Many in the LDP believe that the best course of action for their party is to hammer home the argument that the DPJ is incompetent and press for an early election. Many in the DPJ as well oppose forming a coalition because of the fear that they would become hostage to the LDP's policies rather than the other way around. So a grand coalition is not likely to materialize and if it were it would not be a palliative for a deeply troubled political system.

The Japanese public faces the dismal political reality that there is not likely to be a strong and effective government anytime soon and that the opportunity that the Tōhoku tragedy presents to open a new and dynamic era probably will be lost. My experience in Tōhoku left me inspired by the people I met, saddened beyond words by what I saw and what I heard, and dismayed by the failure of Japan's political leaders to grasp the opportunity that the Tōhoku tragedy presents for bold and innovative policies to rebuild Tōhoku and revitalize Japan.

I do not want to conclude this essay on an entirely pessimistic note, however. There are new developments at the local level that contrast sharply with the political gridlock in Tokyo and that are in part at least a response to the political vacuum that exists there. There has been a rise of dynamic local political leaders, an unprecedented level of business involvement in civic affairs and significant private sector initiatives to restore the Tōhoku economy, and a blossoming of volunteerism and the strengthening of non-governmental organizations. Japanese citizens have not rioted or engaged in large-scale protest demonstrations but neither have they been indifferent to the political disarray in Tokyo. For now their activism is taking place at the local level but Tokyo will not be able for long to ignore these growing pressures from below.

I returned to the disaster zone four times over two months since making the trip in early May that formed the basis for this essay. During these visits I met with seven mayors, the governor of Miyagi prefecture and other politicians. These local leaders wrestle with what is a crisis situation day in and day out. They do not enjoy the luxury to engage in the kind of political squabbling and gamesmanship that consume the energies of so many politicians in Tokyo, and they can barely contain their frustration at having to spend valuable time meeting with Diet men whose visits to their towns and cities produce no tangible results.

Japan has a parliamentary system at the national level but a system of direct election of government leaders in the localities. Governors and mayors are elected directly for four-year terms. They have local assemblies to contend with but they are not beholden to their legislatures for their very existence as is the prime minister. There is great variety among them of course in terms of personality and political skill but in Tōhoku and around the country there are increasing numbers of governors and mayors who are not hesitant to express their views and criticize the central government. They have their own ideas about how to rebuild their communities, administrative experience as their government's chief executive, and a realistic appreciation of what is doable.

Since they are there working on the ground, they understand what the issues are in a way that bureaucrats and politicians in Tokyo do not. Although needs vary from community to community, the central government adheres to its traditional one-size-fits-all administrative approach. Moreover, bureaucratic ministries are as segmented as ever. With the organization of the prime minister's office under the DPJ still very much a work in progress there is little coordination among ministries that are involved in the reconstruction effort. Observing the situation in Tōhoku has given me a new appreciation of the advantages of federalism, and of the disadvantages of Japan's overly centralized governmental system.

There is a tug of war going on between local leaders and the political leadership in Tokyo. Every mayor I met had the same grievance – that the government's response is too slow and too encumbered by bureaucratic red tape. Leaders of the DPJ have their own complaint – that these local politicians are quick to say that things should be left to them to handle and then turn around and blame the central government for not doing everything for them.

The Minister for Reconstruction, Matsumoto Ryū, was forced to resign just a few days after being appointed for lashing out precisely in this manner at the governor of Miyagi. This was followed a few weeks later by a similar outburst on television by the chairman of the DPJ's Diet Management Committee Azumi Jun. The DPJ came into power two years ago trumpeting the importance of greater local autonomy but that has been pretty much swept aside by its irritation with local leaders, something that members of the LDP, whose ties to the local political establishment are far deeper than the DPJ's, rarely if ever express publicly.

There is a serious coordination problem between local governments and Tokyo that is the result of the halfway decentralization reforms that Japan adopted over the past decade and a half. The goal of the comprehensive decentralization reform bills that the Diet adopted in 1999 was to give localities more autonomy vis-à-vis the central government. In the Japanese terminology this meant a shift from a system of agency-delegated functions (*kikan i'nin jimu*), essentially a system in which the central government told local officials what to do, to something that is referred to as "a cooperation among equals system" (*taitō kyōryoku*). But the latter term is pure hyperbole. The reality is that the reforms weakened central government authority over local governments without giving those governments the resources and power to act on their own, thus making coordination among national, prefectural, and local governments more complicated and cumbersome. Local governments are now expected to do more for themselves but they have not been given expanded authority to increase revenue. Japan still has so-called "30 percent autonomy," with local governments dependent on central government disbursements for nearly two-thirds of their income.

The solution to this problem is to adopt far-reaching decentralization reforms. So far, however, the DPJ has not matched its rhetorical support for greater local autonomy with concrete proposals, and Diet members in the LDP exude little enthusiasm for reforms that would reduce their ability to use subsidies to get the support of local interest groups for their election campaigns.

The fact remains that many local political leaders are pushing back against the center, looking for ways to maximize their ability to act autonomously, and to respond to growing public demands for policies that the national government is either too slow or opposed to adopting. The most interesting and popular politicians in Japan today are not Diet members but governors and mayors. It is a new and encouraging development in Japanese politics.

It is the private sector that responded quickly and decisively to the disaster in Tōhoku. Within days of the earthquake and tsunami Japanese automobile manufacturers sent upwards of 2,000 engineers to Tōhoku to assist companies that they depended on for parts to get them back in operation. Electronics companies responded with similar speed to get companies that had been knocked off line back in business. The severe disruption of supply chains in Tōhoku has lasted for a much shorter time than many observers anticipated. They are expected to be completely resolved before the end of 2011.

Humanitarian assistance by companies large and small has been of unprecedented scope, and continues months after March 11. Several firms have set up funds in the one hundred million dollar range and many other companies have made large contributions as well. Having no faith in the ability of the bureaucracy to distribute their funds quickly and efficiently, businessmen have been channeling their funds through various non-profit organizations or have taken their contribution directly the mayor of the town or city they decided to help. Individuals as well as companies have provided both money and supplies.

When I travelled to Tōhoku at the end of July I visited with the owner of the fish packaging plant whom I met in May and who at the time, as described in this essay, was despondent about his ability to recover without government assistance. A little more than two months later the situation could hardly be more different. He was all smiles. He had secured bank loans to repair salvageable equipment and make necessary repairs and was proud to tell me that he would begin operating again at the beginning of August. What was most telling was that he did it without any government assistance. The Ministry of Economy, Trade, and Industry (METI) has a program to provide financial support to local businessmen. He had filed the necessary paperwork to receive assistance but, as he told me, if he waited for the government to act he would be out of business.

Entrepreneurship, risk taking, individual initiative, and community cohesiveness are what are bringing hope to people in Tōhoku. There are other examples like this one of local companies getting back on their feet and of some large companies making new investments in the region. But these actions will be the exception to the rule in the absence of government policies to foster investment in the tsunami zone that would create jobs and keep young people from fleeing the area. This is not so much a matter of money as it is of creating an incentive structure that would attract private investment to the region. That is what local political, business, and community leaders are asking for. What is impressive about the situation in Tōhoku four months after disaster struck is how much local communities are fending for themselves and how much support they are getting from the private sector and from volunteer groups around the country.

As of July 20, according to official government figures, 570,000 volunteers had been to Tōhoku. The total number is probably over a million. What is especially impressive is that the flow of volunteers remains high months after disaster struck. There were 130,000 volunteers in the month of June and 75,000 in the first half of July.

Non-governmental organizations that had been accustomed to operating on a shoestring and managing a small number of volunteers suddenly have found themselves inundated with cash and people. They are struggling to recruit managerial talent and strengthen their organizational infrastructure and to better coordinate among themselves and with local governments. These are the inevitable growing pains of a newly vibrant civil society.

The Tōhoku story is one of resilience, community solidarity, and self-help. It is also the story of weak and divided politics and of the difficulty of fostering innovation and quick response in the face of excessive government regulations and a segmented bureaucratic system. And herein lies the story of the promise and the perils of post–3/11.

2

RECOVERY IN TŌHOKU

J.F. Morris

Welcome to the city of Tagajō, home to myself and my wife Machiko for some 20 years, and where our children grew up. Tagajō has a population 61,693 people, as of 30 April 2011. It is 20 minutes by local train east of Sendai, placing the city on the coast halfway by train between Sendai and the famous tourist site of Matsushima. To most foreign tourists, it is probably just another anonymous train stop slowing down their progress to their destination at Matsushima or elsewhere.

The 'city' is an untidy amalgamation of sleepy rural villages, an industrial complex dating back to the city's role as a munitions manufacturing base for the Japanese Imperial Navy up until 1945, and very recent urban development as a bed town for the neighbouring urban sprawl of Sendai. A small river, the Suna'oshi River, acts as a natural barrier between the inland parts of the city on low hill land, and the flood-prone eastern part opening out to the sea at Sendai Port. I live in a high-rise housing complex on the western banks, the safe side, of the Suna'oshi River.

At 14:46 on Friday 11 March 2011, an earthquake of magnitude 9.0 hit north-eastern Japan. The initial shock lasted for six minutes, and in Tagajō, its intensity was around 5 on the Japanese scale. Some 30 minutes or so later, the tsunami hit. The tsunami was seven metres high at Sendai Port, and decreased in size to two to four metres as it moved inland, until it was stopped by the banks of the Suna'oshi River. By the time the tsunami reached the river, it was more like a flood than a towering wave, but it wreaked havoc nonetheless. The tsunami affected approximately 33.7 percent of the city's area, leaving 5,356 houses wrecked or damaged, and 150,000 cubic metres of debris to be disposed of. The cost of disposing of the debris alone is equivalent to the annual budget of the city. Many public facilities have been damaged or destroyed, including the sewerage treatment plants.

This is a record of how I and my wife, Kamiyama Machiko[1] experienced the compound disaster of earthquake, tsunami, and nuclear disaster. This disaster directly affected a belt stretching about 500 kilometres down the north-eastern side of the main island of Honshū. How this disaster affected any given area depends on whether the area is on the coast or inland, the shape of the coastline, and afterwards, the distance and direction of prevailing winds from the nuclear reactors in Fukushima. If I lived anywhere else in the affected area, my story would be very different. Even within the eastern part of the city of Tagajō, moving just 50 metres in any direction would directly affect the impact of the initial disaster, and in the case of the tsunami, the distance between life and death was often much less. For those of us who live within this 500 km belt, there can be no single coherent story of the disaster; just a multitude of stories all of equal validity, but incoherent and often mutually contradictory. I cannot claim that my story has any special validity because it is a story directly from the scene. On the other hand, I do hope that it may provide a sense of what it was like living through one part of the disaster, and some perspectives that you may not find in media reporting.

Disaster strikes: the first day

When the earthquake hit, I was in a public building owned by Tagajō City, on the higher ground to the west of the river. Seconds before the shock, the internal announcement system came on with a recorded message that a quake would hit in a few seconds. We had had four large earthquakes within the last eight years, including a rather large quake just two days before.[2] It was already 33 years since the devastating Miyagi Offshore Earthquake of 1978, and we all knew that another big earthquake was overdue. On the other hand, there was no way of knowing just how big the imminent quake was going to be; the computer-controlled alarm system did not distinguish between big quakes and little quakes, and I did not bother to react to the warning. Japan's early warning system for earthquakes and tsunami is a wonder of modern technology, but even the most sophisticated warning system can only provide information. Ultimately the success or otherwise of the system depends on how the recipients of such information react, which is a problem beyond the realm of high science and technology. In my case, an over-familiarity with earthquakes and tsunami warnings did not matter, but elsewhere complacency cost many people their lives.

The city official responsible for disaster procedures within the building made sure we all evacuated outside. I grabbed my coat, and resignedly walked down the three flights of stairs and out into the sleet in the car park outside the building. People from other buildings were mulling around. Those who could view TV on their cellular phones were trying to catch news reports, but at this stage there was nothing that we did not know from our direct experience: there had been a huge earthquake and our lifelines would be out for a few days. At this stage, nobody was talking about an imminent tsunami.

After collecting my personal belongings I headed for home, a 15 minutes' walk away. I felt exhausted, and the cold was draining what energy I had left. My first urge was to head over the river to the local patisserie and purchase some of their delicacies before they closed down. I knew that it would take some time, I expected a week at the worst, before I would be able to purchase anything as good again, but the baggage I was carrying weighed heavily, and I trudged straight home, not knowing that this might have made the difference between life and death.

Once home, I ran up the stairs to my apartment on the fifth level, dropped off my baggage and went to the disaster assembly area in the tiny park within our complex, according the disaster drill that we did once a year. The key elected officers of the local neighbourhood association (*chōnai-kai*, hereafter abbreviated to NA) happened to be home at the time of the disaster, and already had put the disaster drill into effect: report that you are safe to the person responsible for your building, and then mull around in the sleet again, waiting for word that it is safe to enter the buildings. However, this time, something went wrong. Suddenly, someone called out that a tsunami was coming. Most of those who had bothered to take the disaster drill seriously and were in the park headed for the high land west over the train lines.

At this stage I did not know how anyone knew that the tsunami was coming. I later discovered that the city's disaster announcement system had been silenced by the impact of the earthquake. In an interview, Mr Nishi, the head of our NA said that he heard a car from the local fire brigade broadcasting the imminent impact of the tsunami over its loudspeaker system. I spent the remaining hours until just before sunset out in the snow on the road between the farmhouses on the high land in Shibiki. As Mr Nishi later pointed out, I would have been equally safe and much less cold if I had taken refuge in my apartment, but those who fled to high ground probably felt more comfortable with firm ground under our feet. The local families took in the elderly amongst us and kept them warm.

Just before sunset, the NA officials came over the train tracks and announced that it was safe to return to our apartments. On returning to my building, we discovered a group of some 20 to 30 people, shivering in the cold, who had fled from over the river. Several households had unexpected guests that night, and this was our first inkling of what had happened on the other side of the river. Electricity, water and gas (heating and cooking) were all dead. Darkness was already setting in. I discovered part of the store of emergency goods that Machiko had accumulated, and got out a small battery-operated lantern, a 24-hour candle, and a radio. There was little sense that we could make of the news. It turned out that I had some guests too. We slept in our clothes, with the candle glowing for reassurance, and shivered all night despite the layers of dry bedding we had. The aftershocks were endless, and were to continue so often and for so long that no one even bothered to count or notice any but the most severe for several weeks afterwards.

A shell of isolation/withdrawal

The next morning, my first concern was to establish communications with my family. My wife, Machiko was at Yamagata University, where she teaches clinical psychology, a two-hour commute by public transport through the mountains west of Sendai. Our daughter works as a nurse in a major hospital in Sendai and lives by herself nearby the hospital. Our two sons study overseas.

Machiko arrived back unannounced from Yamagata on the afternoon of the day after the disaster. Colleagues at Yamagata University who live in the Sendai region had commandeered a university van, stocked up on bottled water and emergency rations and gasoline, and drove over the mountains back home. One of them living in the suburbs in the hills of western Sendai said that the land under his house had subsided.

Machiko was relieved and amazed to find that the inside of our apartment was intact. The total immediate damage was two broken teacups. The location of our apartment on the fifth level of a 15-storey building meant that our apartment had experienced much less shock than those with better views higher up. Moreover, we had left nothing to chance, and we had earthquake-proofed our furniture as far as possible. Machiko dug out the supplies of emergency food, the little butane gas cooker, and the remaining radios and lanterns I had failed to find. Our weekly delivery of vegetables and groceries had arrived on 11 March, just before the earthquake. With the refrigerator dead, Machiko started pickling all the vegetables she could, and I was saved from the dire fate of having to survive on my own cooking. For the next few days, we dined in style as we set about consuming the perishables before they went rotten. We had the radio on full-time as we were hungry for news, in particular about when public utilities, transport and gasoline supplies would be restored, but the radio just kept up a litany of disaster. At this stage, nobody could assess the full extent of the disaster: it did not stop, but just kept on unfolding, with the nuclear disaster in Fukushima increasingly spreading its own ghostly pall over everything else.

For the first few days, we rarely ventured outside our house. Machiko consciously stayed inside, busying herself with restoring our apartment as close as possible to 'normal'. I made two trips over the river on foot, and discovered that the highway just about 200 metres away looked like a war zone from the Middle East. Battered cars were piled up three high, shattered debris lined the road, shops looked as if they had been bombed, and a layer of dry, stinking mud covered everything, curling up in little white clouds of dust behind the vehicles which were tentatively moving up and down the road. Here and there, families stopped their cars for mum and the children to dash out into the mounds of debris to scavenge for usable essentials. Not everyone had adequate stores for an emergency like this. When I got home from these excursions, I was visibly shaken. Machiko, the psychologist, gave me a knowing look and quietly went on with her work of cleaning up the house. With only the radio as our contact to the outside world, almost everyone else across the planet knew more about what was happening to us than we ourselves.

Probably from the third day, I started visiting the community centre, a small building that usually functions as a meeting hall for our neighbourhood association. The NA had set up a gasoline-powered electrical generator, from which they ran a large television screen, and electrical outlets where we could recharge the batteries for our cellular phones. News, such as it was, from the city office was posted up on the notice board, and from 13 March they started up a communal soup and rice kitchen for residents. For the next few days, I occupied myself by participating in the crew organised to collect unused timber from the farmhouses on the high land in neighbouring Shibiki, and in a bucket brigade to collect water from the river to use in flushing the toilet in the community centre. Machiko was still busy at home, and making a point of not going outside. I was over-active, and she was introverted.

Breaking out: saved by children

In the noisy confusion in the communal space in the community centre, I noticed a young mother, sitting for hours in the same place, trying to keep two infant boys from crying. The boys had badly running noses, and were already showing signs of an unbalanced diet. I tried negotiating with the executives of the NA to set up a separate space for little children but was not able to present them with an acceptable plan for how to do this. I told Machiko of my troubles that night, and the next morning, she met the NA and gave them an outline for a child-friendly space that would not disrupt the other activities within the limited space of the community centre, and therefore be acceptable to all parties concerned. Thus the first child-friendly space in Tagajō City was born. Over the next few days, the mother and her boys looked increasingly healthy and socially adapted.

This little event galvanised Machiko. That afternoon, she walked to the nearest major relief centre, looked around, and in no short time came back to collect the cuddly stuffed toys that remained as mementos of our children's infancy, and marched back to the relief centre. Sometime later the same day, I used some of the remaining gasoline in our car to deliver a more substantial collection of toys and books. On her first visit, the first thing to enter Machiko's sight had been a little boy nursing a PET bottle as his 'dolly' in the sleet and snow under a tree outside the relief centre building; there was no place for a tiny little boy to play and regain his equilibrium inside. That night, Machiko started talking about the children she had met inside the relief centre: children who had seen people being washed away, who had spent the night taking refuge on a pedestrian bridge over the highway and had to watch the destruction unfold beneath them, children who had lost playmates and spoke about it with no signs of emotion, children who had lost their homes, and children with parents unsure about how to survive the next day.

The next day, Machiko found a student volunteer at the relief centre, who himself had no home to return to, and who wanted to do something to help the children. They negotiated with the city official responsible for the running of the relief centre, found a windy corner at the end of a corridor where nobody had taken up residence, and 'Kids' Land,' a child-friendly space was born.

Machiko set the space up on firm principles based on play therapy. The space was operated in two sessions a day, for clearly set hours. Children needed their parents' permission to participate. Rumbustious play was prohibited, as were electrical toys and devices, and toys that might elicit aggressive or anti-social behaviour. Reading books, drawing pictures, or playing with toys that would occupy the children's hands and minds were encouraged. After each session, the children themselves had to tidy up and put everything back in its proper place. It was to be a quiet, secure place where children could occupy themselves and re-establish a daily routine. Very soon after the space was opened, its efficacy became apparent. Children were now disentangled from their parents/mothers who could move unhampered, to stand in lines at the city office to apply for documents, search for a safe place to live or start the task of cleaning the stinking mud out of the ground floor level of their house, go to work or look for a job. The stress levels of the parents/mothers went down, and the children were able to be quietly active by day and started to sleep at night. Later on, when the children discovered that the elderly people in the relief centre used to play with the same toys when they themselves were children, they started to venture into the old people's area to challenge them to tests of skill, thus bringing laughter, smiles and a daily routine into the lives of the elderly as well. Adults could now attend to the business of restoring their lives, and the children had their own routine to restore balance to their lives. Problematic behaviour amongst children started to drop off markedly. Moreover, Machiko now had a routine other than cleaning the apartment: the children had saved us.

Adapting: disaster in the twenty-first century

It took much longer than anyone had anticipated to restore essential utilities after the earthquake. Even three months after the disaster, areas hit worst by the tsunami did not have electricity, running water nor gas. Where I live, electricity came on five days later, running water on 23 March, and gas on 4 April. The local NA closed down the soup and rice kitchen and other community-run relief activities on 25 March.

Machiko had had an uneasy premonition after the nasty quake two days before the main one, and had topped up our stores of emergency food and water, and while we occasionally had guests for dinner, we ourselves never had recourse to the communal kitchen. We dug out the two kerosene heaters that we had not used for 20 years but had saved up for this kind of emergency, discovered that we still had a few days' supply of kerosene in a plastic jerrycan, and that the smaller of the two heaters still actually worked. This saved us from the worst ravages of the biting unseasonal chill that was to continue for some weeks. Machiko had previously added a special emergency toilet kit to our supplies to treat 'solid waste,' but the odour, along with that of urine, was to pervade our apartment until running water returned.

When the electricity came back on, after the lights, the first appliance that we turned on was the stereo set. Television was an unending horror show: we needed relief, and music was food to the soul. You know things are pretty bad when your wife lets you play your bassoon in the living room: you know they are really grim when she starts singing along when you stumble out of tune through a collection of popular songs. Normalcy means that you are reassigned to the back room.

After the electricity came back on, the local Farmers' Co-operative Store opened up. At this stage, nothing was coming in from the outside, but we were able to purchase fresh vegetables grown locally. If anyone wants to argue that Japan is being irrational in fighting to maintain its inefficient agricultural sector, they should try surviving here after a major natural disaster. Despite the benefits of having access to fresh vegetables, most of what else we were eating came out of a vacuum-tight plastic pack or a can. My nails started to crack. We washed our toothbrushes thoroughly after use, but did this in a cup of water, not running water, and we both developed viral infections in our throats. Our state of hygiene and nutrition was superb compared to conditions in the relief centres, particularly the bigger ones, but despite our best efforts, our bodies reminded us that things were different from usual.

Having electricity but not running water and gas made for many anomalies, the single largest of which was having the Internet. We were unable to flush the toilet, but we could communicate with the whole globe. Machiko and I vented our frustration at being immobilised by the gasoline shortages by periodically writing reports on what we were experiencing and perceiving around us. Our sons overseas told us that the world had given up on Tōhoku, if not all Japan, as destroyed beyond all saving, and we wanted to tell them otherwise. People across Japan and over the globe were reading what we wrote as 'true reports' from 'the front', even though we were very privileged 'victims', with dry feet and clothes, a home, electricity, fresh vegetables to eat, and people outside the disaster zone were actually seeing more of the overall disaster relayed on their television screens than we ourselves could see in our narrow, restricted little world. Whether our reports were true or reliable, they went through networks and across the globe, and then we discovered that 'the world' would in no short time reach back out to us, and we would be kept busy.

This narrative brings us somewhere into the second week, maybe, after the first impact. Life moved on, centring on important things like finding a bath or washing the clothes, getting to catch up with our daughter after she survived the first week of initially being on duty non-stop for four days and living on a ration of one rice ball per day and lots of adrenalin as a nurse in a major base hospital, having long conversations with our sons overseas to reassure them, and talking to my family in Australia. For us, normalcy was very slowly creeping back into place. This recovery was very rudely interrupted by the major magnitude 7 earthquake that hit around 11:30 PM on 7 April. This cut off our lifelines again for another two days. It was a shock to wake up the following morning to discover that I had forgotten how to prepare breakfast without electricity, gas, nor running water. My subconscious was working hard to create 'normalcy' around me, and was fast throwing out memories and information that interfered with this project.

There is much more that I could write about the progression towards normalcy, such as it is even today, but I shall change my narrative to a series of themes.

Victims and voices

For many people, it is probably important to identify who are the victims of the present disaster, and who speaks for the victims. For example, if you are trying to assess what goods are needed at a relief centre, it is important to be able to determine whether the senior gentleman you are most likely to first speak to really knows the needs of the people he purports (or you assume him) to represent. The needs of a feeding mother for herself and her baby may not be apparent to him, nor the needs of very young children, nor teenagers, nor schoolchildren who want to study, whereas the needs of middle-aged men and women will rank high on his agenda. This does not mean that his agenda will necessarily be invalid, but it might be very inadequate. For an experienced aid worker, or an informed journalist, this much seems to be taken as a given.

However, watching/reading news in a rather haphazard way, I cannot help but wonder about the depiction of victims, and how our voices are represented.

The total personal damage that Machiko and I suffered in the two earthquakes, both of them extremely serious ones, was four broken teacups. However, even having a secure roof and walls around you and your loved ones safe, or living far away from the areas hit by the tsunami, does not mean that you have not been affected.

For one thing, the degree and extent of damage by the tsunami has diverted attention away from the seriousness of quake damage done inland, particularly by the second earthquake on 7 April. In terms of magnitude it was smaller than the first earthquake, but in terms of intensity it paralleled it. In rural inland areas far away from the tsunami, the damage of the two earthquakes in 2011 came on top of the earlier four over the past eight years, resulting in further damage to old homes and shops. Many aged people and owners of low-profit businesses will not be able to manage yet another loan to repair things, and the already decaying centres of local towns and cities throughout the eastern side of the Tōhoku region are facing further accelerated decay.

On the other hand, it is a moot question as to how much the economic demand created by the rebuilding after the disaster will create economic growth and revival in this region: the lion's share will most likely go to companies and employees elsewhere. Most of the goods and services that will be consumed in the rebuilding of the region are produced outside of here. The jobs produced locally by the sudden increased demand in the building industry require special skills, leaving low-paid retail and sales jobs for the rest. It is too early to tell how widely and deeply it will grow, but the threat of recession is spreading like a cancer throughout the whole region.

For example, in the pyramid of job security within the local economy, my own job as a faculty member of a leading local women's university may appear secure beyond doubt, but we were already facing a serious drop in student enrolments due to the double effects of the post-Lehman Brothers' depression, and the increasingly sharp drop in the university age population before the disaster. Now, we have to pay the cost of repairing the damage done to university buildings and property, re-buy a large proportion of the computers and other equipment on campus, and provide free tuition and educational loans to students whose families, homes, or livelihoods have been affected by the disaster, even as our revenue base itself is increasingly being eroded, disaster or not. Even though we will get national funding to pay for half of this, the other half of these emergency expenditures will have to come out of a seriously depleted income. For universities outside the region, they can do the noble task of caring for and educating affected students with relative impunity as it will only affect a very small percentage of their student intake. For universities throughout Iwate, Miyagi and Fukushima prefectures whose primary student intake includes the areas worst affected by the disaster, this cost will bear heavily, and will continue to reverberate for many years to come. Even if we survive 2011, nobody knows what lies ahead, other than that it will not be easy, and nothing can be taken for granted anymore.

Another aspect to be considered in evaluating the after-effects of this disaster is that even if you yourself are not directly affected, there is a unique sense of post-disaster community or commonality that pervades the region. At a personal level, I can look with detachment at photographs of Sendai after it was devastated by bombing in 1945, but I cannot look at photographs of this current disaster without paying a large psychological and emotional cost. I live on the fringe of the tsunami disaster, but still I feel that it has affected me in ways that I cannot well explain. This sense of community and belonging is very strong, shared, and not just something imagined. I have my ethnic background, white Australian, etched indelibly into my face, yet in the 'honeymoon' period immediately after the disaster, people did not ask me where I came from or express amazement that I could converse in their language with them. If I was here, I was one of the community, 'local'.

I may feel a strong bond with areas hit by the tsunami, but I cannot guarantee that these feelings are reciprocal. After the electricity came on in our apartment block, all but the most essential of the safety lights in the corridors had to have their bulbs removed so that people over the river who would have to wait much longer to have their electricity restored would not feel abandoned and neglected. For our part, some nights earlier, Machiko and I had looked out and seen the lights come on throughout Sendai, and we had felt neglected and abandoned, and overwhelmingly jealous. This example is relatively innocuous, but in cases involving the loss of family, home and employment, this sense of being victimised more, or less, than one's neighbour can create very complicated and intense emotions.

People trying to survive in a relief centre may feel bonds of commonality with others in the same situation, but when it comes to questions of how to escape from the relief centre, where and how one should live, whether you should rebuild close to the sea or on inconveniently located high ground, whether there is any future for your children in this depressed and shattered region, then there is no simple, single answer, neither for a family nor for a community of any size or description.

Commentators and politicians in Tokyo scrambling for debating points do not appear to be cognisant of the difficulty of achieving consensus on anything when the cost of taking the road to reconstruction involves reconciling so many conflicting interests, and not rebuilding things as they were, but rebuilding things to deal with a sunken shoreline, an exacerbation of an existing problem of accelerating depopulation and economic depression, new standards of safety requirements, and a sudden naked revelation of deep and biting regional inequalities to a national population brought up in the belief that they were 'all the same'. Now they are very rudely not the same, nor its concomitant meaning of 'equal', both within the confines of any given hamlet/village/town/city, and also in terms of this region vis-à-vis the rest of Japan. The twin problems of unbalanced economic development and acute depopulation predate the disaster; the sudden riveted attention of the rest of the nation on this area only highlights the dreadful price that we have had to pay to be noticed at all.

The image of the Tōhoku region as 'victim' follows conventional discourse about this region from the early twentieth century. Tōhoku is conceived of as a poor, backward region with uncouth customs and speech, whose major role in the national scheme of things was to provide a flow of young workers for the factories around Tokyo. The region only drew attention if hit by a major famine or disaster. It existed to be spoken to and about, analysed, reformed, exploited, but never to be allowed to speak in its own right. People from this region who travel outside it have to hide outward signs of their identity, most typically speech, or else they face the risk of derisive laughter. Badgering a singer from this region about his supposed accent on popular TV and laughing at his discomfort may just seem to be typical of the bad taste and lack of sensitivity of the genre. However, things do not stop in the realm of crass vaudeville.

In historical dramas produced by NHK, the national television station, characters from Tokyo and anywhere west speak in a watered-down version of the modern form of the dialect of whatever region they are supposed to come from. In the rare case where a protagonist comes from our region, the actor mouths lines written in the Tokyo dialect: speech from this region is not allowed into the nation's living rooms unless it has been suitably sanitised. The famous Japanese psychologist Doi Takeo made an eloquent plea for the need to express patients' descriptions of their problems in their own words, in his case, using 'Japanese', and hence the Japanese term *amae* has entered the international vocabulary of psychiatry/psychology. At learned conferences within Japan, scholars and practitioners from Tokyo and western Japan move seamlessly between academic speech and local dialect as they shift between the words of their clients and their own analysis. However, when Machiko once quoted directly the speech of her clients from the fishing ports of central Miyagi prefecture at one such conference, suddenly a shocked silence filled the room. A basic social taboo had been violated, and the transgression was not acceptable.

After the disaster, the media has suddenly been filled with the speech of people from this region. In the *Asahi* newspaper, reporters writing interviews with elderly locals now often try to transcribe their pronunciation. Sometimes an adventuresome reporter may try to add the local grammar to give the interview added credibility, but the reporter transcribes not what was spoken, but what the reporter heard through a filter of Tokyo preconceptions of what local speech should be. Authenticity is only permitted within the limits of what we are supposed to be, not what we are. When the nation gets tired of the heart-rending stories dominating the media at present, and their attention moves elsewhere, will even a distorted version of our speech be accepted in public discourse, or will we have to withdraw into the corner we have been allocated since 1868 and only speak when spoken to, in a carefully enunciated Tokyo accent? On evidence so far, I fear that the latter will be the case.

The child-friendly space that Machiko helped set up in the relief centre in Tagajō became one of the sites of pilgrimage for media crews scouring the region for news in the first few weeks after the disaster. One television crew filmed the children's space, then did an interview with Machiko, the professor from Yamagata University, with her explaining as a professional why the space was necessary, and why it was set up the way it was. The footage was edited in Tokyo and broadcast some days later. Machiko was given a few innocuous words, but the important part explaining the significance of the space was given to an academic from the Tokyo region sitting in an academic office looking, well, academic, but really only restating what Machiko had clearly explained in her interview. An unwashed lady looking cold and exhausted in a very thick coat, with tousled hair and a sore throat standing in a nondescript corridor apparently was not an acceptable image. We are allowed to tell heart-rending stories, look pathetic and helpless, or even occasionally heroically brave, but we are not allowed to provide informed professional analysis of what we are doing or why: we are victims, and therefore cannot help ourselves. 'We' need 'you' to do this for 'us'.

This problem in imagining and defining 'victims' manifests itself in another way. Popular images and even official definitions of 'victims' primarily conceive of them as people in relief centres and later, in temporary housing. This convenient definition is far removed from the reality. For example, many families whose homes were still standing after being flooded by the tsunami chose to move out of over-crowded relief centres and live on the second storey of their muddied homes. Once they were out of the relief centre, they were out of the purview of both the media and the official definition of people in need of immediate support. This very narrow perception/definition of 'victims' meant that the more you exerted yourself to achieve self-dependence, the less support you received, which is a very counter-productive message to send.

Having our voices stolen and modified is of itself humiliating, but perhaps the deepest problem is that the scale of this disaster is so great, both in terms of the area affected and in terms of the depth of its consequences, that it is impossible to conceive of the victims of this disaster as a single unity in any but the most superficial terms. However, governments needing to classify people for administrative purposes, and media needing to edit their messages to fit the limitations of time and space, must simplify complicated realities in order to be able to deal with them, and too often this results in dangerous stereotyping and oversimplification.

The pall

The pall cast by the nuclear reactors in Fukushima reaches far beyond the area immediately affected. However, there was another pall that covered the area, and that is the psychological shadow cast by the media-orchestrated mood of 'self-restraint'.

For many days after the disaster, large television screens in public places, including relief centres, broadcast scenes from the disaster areas almost non-stop. Within private homes, adults were riveted to the disaster reporting, thereby exposing young children and juveniles to an endless barrage of shocking images. Advertisements disappeared from the commercial stations, replaced by publicly sponsored advertisements exhorting us to be more morally correct by exercising restraint, adding to the overall dreariness. In Miyagi this continued for more than a month, if not longer. In areas far removed from the tsunami, not only were school buildings put off limits until they could be confirmed structurally safe, the school grounds were closed as well, depriving children who wanted relief from the endless horror on TV of a healthy place to burn off energy and emotions. Within tsunami-affected regions, all usable schools had become relief centres, and here children's options for playing were even more restricted.

Within the city of Sendai, young women felt that they could no longer put on make-up and dress up as it would be inappropriate. Customers disappeared from stores selling anything that was not socially 'appropriate'. The owners of a kimono shop that Machiko frequents, more often to chat than to actually buy anything, were divided within the family as to how they could, or should, weather the total loss of customers. They had their employees and bills to pay, but absolutely no revenue. Their banker had his economically rational, but bloody ideas about what they should do, and the employees were looking tense. On the forty-ninth day after the disaster, the shop held a small charity concert for their customers in the store, and the freeze was broken. No employees have been laid off, and the store will probably be able to continue. Machiko has a new kimono on order that she did not intend to buy. For my part, our stereo has new speakers that I cannot really afford. If the pall of 'self-restraint' had continued just a little longer, an uncounted number of small businesses supporting many families would have been forced to either lay off their employees and/or go into bankruptcy, leaving the whole area with economically and socially 'appropriate' enterprises, but no cultural life at all.

In all, this dreadful pall of 'self-restraint' felt most like what it reportedly was in Japan during the Pacific War. Intense but unspoken social pressure pervaded the region, evinced seemingly innocuously in the form of public exhortations for petty moral correctness, standing up for expectant mothers in trains, helping old people up steep stairways, saying 'hello' to other people. This, coupled with the blanket on children playing in their usual public spaces outside, the indiscriminate destruction of the tsunami, and the suddenly ubiquitous presence of military vehicles and personnel in uniform everywhere, all added to the unnerving sense of living in a war zone.

This 'self-restraint' project was morale-draining and economically counter-productive. While it is understandable that there was a need for a certain amount of public consideration for victims of the disaster, the 'self-restraint' project appears to have been grossly excessive in its execution, to the point of having threatened the emotional, psychological and economic recovery of the area.

Being saved: volunteers and NGOs

The reports that Machiko and I issued to the world in general over the Internet, and the television reporting on the child-friendly space in the Tagajō relief centre, to our surprise, meant that 'the world' discovered us. People wishing to volunteer and contribute to the area started contacting us, and we were kept busy trying to comply with an increasing volume of requests that we were really in no position to respond to.

One anecdote concerning the role of volunteers I have heard involves the matriarch in one of the Buddhist temples over the river. She herself is Buddhist, but after she dies, she wants to be reincarnated as a Christian. The temple operates two kindergartens, both in the area flooded by the tsunami. I happened to visit the worst-hit kindergarten, some days after the disaster, and thought that it would take several months to restore it. It reopened on 27 April. A Christian church-related group had come in with earth-moving equipment, and in very short time, had restored the kindergarten to a usable condition. This Christian miracle had convinced the lady that next time, she wants to be reincarnated as a Christian.

This is a success story, but our own personal experience with volunteers has been ambivalent. Large scale NGOs with professional staff experienced with international standards and guidelines for providing aid in emergencies have provided invaluable expertise and support for overworked local governments struggling to find ways to deal with a disaster exceeding all expectations. On the other hand, uninformed volunteers purportedly working in the best interests of the victims of the disaster, but in ignorance of such standards and guidelines, can do more harm than good. Machiko has withdrawn from the Kids' Land that she helped set up. In more than one case we have witnessed cases of aid and support that ran counter to the purpose of achieving the social and economic independence of its recipients. Aid which does not respect the human rights of its recipients, and which does not respect nor restore their self-dignity, in the long run, will do more harm than good.

For our part, an email from an acquaintance in Yamagata resulted in us entering into a working relationship with Plan Japan, the local branch of Plan International, an NGO with a record of providing care for children in conflict and disaster areas for over 70 years. On the surface, it looks as if it was the Internet which brought us all together, but in reality, the Internet was nothing more than the medium that achieved this, and it was really old-fashioned interpersonal networks and plain good luck which got this relationship started.

This chance meeting happened at a crucial time when Machiko had started to enter into a working relationship with the Tagajō School Board to provide psychosocial support for school teachers within the city. Dr Unni Krishnan of Plan provided Machiko with invaluable advice on the theory and practice of psychosocial care after a disaster as she sought to grasp these matters new to her and develop a practical model for supporting children through providing support for school teachers. For our part, we provided Plan with an introduction into local government in Tagajō, which gave them a base from which to start their activities in the area. Four months after the disaster, Machiko is currently participating in Care Miyagi, a coalition of psychologists who are providing workshops for school teachers throughout Miyagi prefecture, as a way to effectively help as many children as possible adapt to their changed circumstances. By providing support for school teachers, one of the primary care-giver groups for children, Care Miyagi hopes to enable school teachers to discover their own latent potential, and the potential of children being with other children to enable them to overcome the shock and disorientation of their recent experiences. Plan Japan is providing financial and logistical support for Care Miyagi, and the two organisations are now engaged in a mutually productive relationship in conducting what may turn out to be one of the largest experiments in providing psychosocial care after this disaster, and provide a model for other places, in Japan and elsewhere.

It should therefore be very important to assess whether this experiment in psychosocial care by Care Miyagi really is effective, and if so, to what extent. The model for this project dates back to a workshop that was set up by the Tagajō School Board, and run by Machiko with the participation of Dr Krishnan on 11 April, exactly one month after the disaster. Data taken after this initial workshop could provide the answer to this crucial question, but this data may never be used. If for example, one headmaster sees this kind of data collecting and analysis as a self-serving exercise for opportunistic academics to further their own career at the expense of infringing on the privacy of ordinary people, then the local school board cannot release this kind of data for analysis. Furthermore, the Ministry of Education and Science has released a directive to universities throughout Japan effectively calling on scholars to exercise 'restraint' in conducting research which runs the danger of putting a burden on local governments asked to provide data, or violating the privacy and wishes of victims. Several leading academic associations have issued similar directives. A 'celebrity' disaster area, such as the city of Kesennuma in northern Miyagi, has been smothered with dignitaries, worthies, celebrities and everyone else wanting to get in on the act as well, to the point where local officials and school teachers have trouble getting on with their proper jobs. Data which could provide important answers to questions about what really was effective in helping the recovery from this disaster is going to waste or not being collected, partly due to bureaucratic intransigence and ineptitude, but also due to overkill caused by people following their own program of self-promotion. In the ensuing confusion and mutual acrimony, the baby gets thrown out with the bath water. In the absence of quantitative data, the reports from school teachers to Care Miyagi suggest that the rate of school refusal amongst children in affected areas might now be lower than before the disaster.[3]

Without the efforts of the multitude of NGOs working throughout the area, the recovery in this area and the personal toll on individuals would probably have been much higher. However, there may also be problems as well.

The first is a matter of perceptions. NGOs need to promote their activities in order to generate the flow of donations on which they depend for their revenue. Looking at the reports generated by NGOs, one might be forgiven for thinking that they were the only effective organs operating in the area. However, the most important work in the recovery process is being carried out by local government, both by the local governments within the area, and other local government bodies outside the area which are providing support for the governments of disaster-affected areas. This inflow of support staff from all over Japan is what has made the improbable task of getting damaged water and gas pipes serviceable again in an unbelievably short time, given the huge scale of the task. It filled out the ranks of overworked health professionals, insurance evaluators and many other professions and support services as well. Local government is often singled out as 'the villain' for slowing down the process of recovery, or of diverting scarce resources to suit interests other than that of the people directly affected. There may be no shortage of such examples, but witnessing at first hand the incredible hours and devotion to duty that many local government officials have displayed throughout this disaster, I would argue that local government and the people who work within it are the unsung heroes of this disaster. NGOs are doing a remarkable job, but one should keep in mind that NGOs are filling in the gaps between what local government cannot achieve, and what it is achieving despite the odds.

In the same vein, NGOs are outsiders here, and cannot achieve very much without the participation in some way of local people. The information provided in NGO reports, particularly my limited experience of what made it into English versions of NGOs' activities here, and foreign media reporting, seemed to give the impression that the NGOs were here to save us, and everyone local was a passive victim, devoid of any subjectivity, waiting to be saved. However, within my limited field of vision, NGOs that are achieving things are doing it because they have succeeded in establishing a productive relationship with a local community, organisation or network. This is not just a matter of fighting for credit or recognition, although for survivors of a disaster, re-establishing self-respect is an integral and indispensable part of the recovery process. The more important issue is that if recovery does not come from the victims themselves, if it does not engage them on centre stage, then it will not be a true recovery, but a pillaging of the region by other people who will reap the economic and other benefits of restoration work within the region. This is a very political problem at heart, and goes to the roots of how representative government at all levels really is of the people governments purport to represent. However, in such a sensitive area, it is important that public discourse on recovery does not head off in a direction that disenfranchises the people who most need to be given the leading voice in deciding their own future.

If one can accept the proposition that the work done by NGOs is by its very nature supplementary to that of local government and public utility service companies, then another problem comes into focus. People are prepared to donate money readily to NGOs, but they appear to be much less ready to donate to local government. If people consider donating to local government wasteful, then they should also bear in mind that NGOs of necessity have their own overheads as well. It is estimated that it will take up to five years to dispose of the debris created by the tsunami. Until this task is completed, we will all have to continue breathing the dust from it, looking at it as it scars our parks and skylines, have temporary housing occupying public spaces and taking away children's playing space, and in myriad of ways be constantly reminded of the devastation wreaked by the tsunami. It may take some two years to rebuild sewerage plants throughout Miyagi prefecture, and until this is done, those who live in low-lying areas will have to live with sewerage drain leakages, the smell of which permeates sweaty hot summer nights. Rebuilding sewerage treatment plants may not be as glamorous nor as exciting as the work done by NGOs, but it does contribute to maintaining essential life services on a long-term basis within disaster-affected areas. Houses subjected to flooding at high tide by the coastline subsiding will have to depend on local government to make their homes safe to live in. The image of 'victims' in relief centres is powerful and attracts public attention across the globe, but the reality of the extent of the damage is far greater, and much of it requires remedies, specialised skills and resources beyond the reach of NGOs.

One other problem concerning images of 'victims', is that donors are prepared to provide money for 'worthy' causes, the most poignant of which are the children left orphaned by the tsunami, but also children in general easily attract the attention of donors and NGOs. This is understandable, but beyond a certain point, it becomes counter-productive. The number of children orphaned by this disaster as of July 2011 is counted at 218. People understandably weep for the plight of these children, but in the long run, if other parents who have survived the disaster are deprived of hope and the chance of gaining employment to rebuild their lives, then the number of children who are orphaned or deprived of a parent by suicides, drunken driving or death by stress-related causes will in time come to exceed the number of children orphaned in the initial impact. The majority of children still have a parent/parents, and perhaps the single most important factor in making life secure for these children is to make life secure for their parents. Otherwise, domestic violence, child abuse, substance abuse, broken families and deaths due to unnatural causes will take their toll over the following years, and then reverberate as the children who experienced this during their own upbringing start to raise their own families. Helping parents should be an indispensable element of any effort to help children, yet people who will donate for children baulk at helping their care-givers.

A similar problem that is becoming evident is that the way that relief payments are allotted does little to rebuild the regional economy. A family which has lost its home qualifies for relief payments, for free housing for a limited time in temporary housing, or for cash payments to defray the cost of rented accommodation. On the other hand, a family which has not lost its house but which has lost the means of making its livelihood must take out a loan to restart the family business. If the family already has a large loan to repay, taking out another may prove to be a burden beyond their resources. Again, here the problem is that cash payments are being made in accordance with a very narrow definition of 'need', whereas a broader definition is needed that takes into account the need to restore the local economy as a whole in order to guarantee the livelihoods of individual families within local society. If you have a stable source of income you can acquire somewhere to live, and will be committed to continue to stay in the locality, but if you have a house but no way of making a livelihood, sooner or later you will have to move out of the region to find a livelihood elsewhere, assuming of course that you live that long.

Words of parting

This disaster has elicited an enormous out-pouring of goodwill, aid and volunteerism, both within Japan and also reaching out across the globe, which is playing an important part in rebuilding this region. However, despite the huge progress which has been made both internationally, and within Japan after the 1995 Kobe Earthquake, in coordinating efforts to eliminate waste and unnecessary duplication in aid, and in making sure that relief work meets the needs of the recipients rather than conforming to the donor's own personal agenda, there are still a lot of problems left to be ironed out. The Internet and computer technology have played an important role in the coordinating and making relief work more efficient, but ultimately, it is personal networks and simple good luck that seem to prove to be the crucial factors in deciding the difference between success and failure. Any attempt to contribute to rebuilding after the disaster must be connected to people in the region, and truly be in their best interests if it is to succeed. It is this area where potent media images of 'victims' are working to distort or give a very one-sided view of who are the victims of this disaster, or what constitutes being a 'victim'.

This essay has no conclusion nor end, as there will be no end to the after-effects of this disaster, at least not in my lifetime. Even after towns have been rebuilt and landscapes restored, the social and economic effects of this disaster will still be playing themselves out through succeeding generations. If you want to help, please visit this region when it becomes safe, to revel in its richness. We do not need sympathy or pity. We need jobs, our self-respect and hope.

Notes

1 Machiko's version of our experiences have been published as Kamiyama Machiko 'Hisai Shita Wagamachi kara Mananda "Tachiagari no Chikara" Tagajō Zaijū Rinshō Shinrishi no Ikkagetsu', *Gendai to Hoiku*, Vol. 80, July 2011, pp. 6–23.

2 These were an earthquake of magnitude 7.1 in 2003, of magnitude 7.2 in 2005, of magnitude 7.2 in 2008, and of magnitude 7.3 on 9 March, just two days before the major earthquake of 11 March, 2011, followed by a tremor of intensity of around 4 on 10 March. A tsunami alert was sometimes issued after these earthquakes, but the tsunami for the quake of 2008 was only 10 to 80 centimetres in height.

3 On the debit side, a paediatrician in Tagajō says that the degree of intensity of symptoms exhibited by children with problems predating the disaster appears to be increasing markedly.

PART II

Volunteerism, civil society and media

3

FROM KOBE TO TŌHOKU

The potential and the peril of a volunteer infrastructure[1]

Simon Avenell

Tōhoku 2011: Kobe 1995 redux?

On the morning of January 17, 1995, the Kobe region of Japan experienced what was *then* the country's most destructive earthquake in the postwar era.[2] Close to 6500 died, infrastructure was crippled, and hundreds and thousands of buildings were destroyed or damaged. Magnifying the earthquake was the woeful national government response that arguably made Kobe as much a man-made disaster as a natural one. Officials quarreled over jurisdictional matters and enforced regulations that ultimately cost lives and severely dented the legitimacy of Japan's bureaucracy. The flipside of this administrative debacle was a historically unprecedented outpouring of volunteering which by December 1995 boasted some 1.3 million participants, including many young people who travelled hundreds of miles to help. Undoubtedly one of the milestones of civil society in postwar Japan, 1995 was soon christened 'Year One of the Volunteer Age' (*Borantia Gannen*) and heralded as a 'volunteer revolution' (*borantia kakumei*).

Some 16 years later Japan now faces recovery after the triple blow of a mega earthquake, a tsunami, and a nuclear meltdown. As one pundit bluntly put it, "this is no Kobe 1995 redux" (Winter 2011) and the reconstruction will most certainly require a larger, more comprehensive, and longer-term effort than after the 1995 temblor. Although there have been numerous natural disasters in the intervening period, the current disaster is undoubtedly the greatest test of Japan's voluntary sector since the 1995 crisis. How the voluntary response plays out in Tōhoku will have ramifications not only for those receiving assistance but also for civil society in Japan more generally.

In this chapter I analyze the volunteer response in the first few months after the Great East Japan Earthquake. How have individual volunteers, civic groups, and related business, government, and quasi-government organizations acted and interacted in the current crisis? What does this response tell us about the evolution of volunteering in Japan from Kobe to Tōhoku? Though still an unfolding saga, a number of developments in the months after the quake suggest that the voluntary sector in Japan has reached a new level of professionalism, organization, social legitimacy, and institutionalization. The spread of the Internet and diffusion of electronic social networking has empowered volunteers and coordinating organizations in ways unimaginable 16 years ago (Suga, *et al.* 2008, Ch. 5). Almost immediately after the March 11 quake and tsunami national, local, and quasi-governmental institutions moved to facilitate and organize disaster relief volunteering in concert with civic groups. Disaster Volunteer Centers (DVCs) set up primarily by local social welfare council offices (*shakai fukushi kyōgikai, shakyō*) and disaster relief NGOs were providing services within days (if not hours). Ordinary Japanese also dug deep into their pockets, making substantial donations not only for victims but, importantly, for disaster relief NGOs, NPOs, and voluntary groups.

Though sweeping characterizations are difficult at this point, the major differences with the voluntary response after Kobe appear to be, first, the level of integration and collaboration among civic groups, the business sector, and state/quasi-state agencies; second, the larger and more readily accessible funding for volunteer relief work; third, the level of professionalization of NGOs and other volunteer groups; and, fourth, the greater institutional (both state and non-state) mediation of individual volunteers. After Kobe, voluntary groups scrambled to form ad hoc networks with other social, political, and economic groups. Individual volunteers travelled to affected areas on their own accord and, in some cases, even initiated their own relief efforts. In Tōhoku, however, the volunteer response appears to be a far more structured and systematized affair, with some even questioning excessive 'regulation', 'restriction' and 'control'.[3] True or not, Tōhoku is unfolding as a pivotal moment of an advanced volunteer infrastructure which synthesizes government, business, and civic energies. The all-embracing nature of this infrastructure presents both opportunities and hazards for the future of volunteering in Japan.

Below, I examine Tōhoku volunteering from five perspectives. For historical insight I first survey the voluntary response after the 1995 Kobe Earthquake and beyond. How did volunteering unfold after that event and what were the take-away lessons for later activism? I then turn to volunteering in Tōhoku, examining the response by the national government, quasi-governmental groups, businesses and business groups, and civic groups and networks. In the conclusion I consider the implications of Tōhoku for volunteering in Japan. While a valuable national asset in times of crisis, the volunteer infrastructure also runs the risk of constraining or inhibiting volunteering in the country. In the context of neoliberal retrenchment in the public sector, it also raises questions about the boundary between state and societal responsibilities.

Kobe 1995 and its legacies

Civil society and volunteering did not suddenly materialize in Japan after the Kobe Earthquake; they had been developing steadily throughout the postwar era in areas such as elder care, support for the disabled, and overseas relief operations (Avenell 2009, 2010; Hasegawa, *et al.* 2007; Mega 1999; Nakamura 1999; Imada 2003: 40). Such earlier activism and networking provided a solid foundation for the impressive voluntary response in 1995. Nevertheless, Kobe remains a watershed for civil society and volunteering in contemporary Japan and the successes, failures, and learning from it are clearly evident in the current Tōhoku crisis. Unfolding as it did against the backdrop of Japan's largest postwar natural disaster (at that time), Kobe volunteering became visible on a national scale as never before. The event transformed the image of volunteering from obscure activity by an exclusive group of altruists to something ordinary people could easily participate in (Tanaka 2005: 161). The media contributed by relaying stories about the thousands of ordinary individuals – mostly youths – who flocked to the region to help. Underneath this spontaneous outpouring of goodwill was an even more significant development involving volunteer groups and networks which, for perhaps the first time ever, took the lead in coordinating and implementing the post-disaster voluntary response. Many of these groups predated the quake, but in the turmoil after January 17, they were pushed to new levels of professionalization and organization. Important too, many of the activists and groups involved at the time are playing key roles in the Tōhoku response.

Perceived and actual government failure after Kobe also helped raise the profile and social legitimacy of volunteering. Added to the haphazard response of the Murayama Administration, people were shocked by bureaucratic foot-dragging, infighting, and red tape. Ministry of Health and Welfare Officials, for instance, argued that foreigners with expired visas were ineligible for medical attention and that medical services provided to citizens prior to the establishment of official emergency medical centers were not covered under national health insurance. Tokyo bureaucrats also made unreasonable demands on already over-burdened local officials, ordering them to prepare vehicles for site investigations, to organize guides, and to prepare conference rooms (CODE 2004: 178). In the long run central government officials and politicians learned hard lessons from this administrative fiasco as too did local officials in Kobe who forged substantive ties with voluntary groups that would become templates for later government-civil society cooperation.

From January 17, 1995 through to January 20, 1996 some 1,377,300 volunteers were involved in relief and reconstruction efforts – the bulk of whom assisted during the first three months (see Figure 2.1) (Fujii 2002:18). In terms of composition, 34 percent were in their twenties, 16 percent in their thirties, and 19 percent in their forties. Thirty-three percent were university or college students, 23 percent company employees, and the remainder housewives, 'freeters,' and the self-employed. Around 52 percent had no prior volunteering experience (Fujii

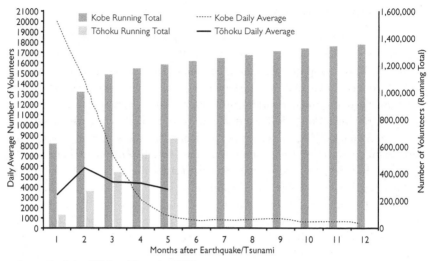

Source: Zenshakyō (2011) and Hyōgo-ken (2006)

FIGURE 3.1 Volunteering in Kobe and Tōhoku (source: Zenshakyō 2011 and Hyōgo-ken 2006)

2002: 18; Nishiyama 2007: 77). Different from the comprehensive management and systematization of volunteering in Tōhoku, most of these individual volunteers went to Kobe uninvited, joining groups only after their arrival. The rudimentary volunteer infrastructure at the time was simply ill-prepared to administer so many people – one of the most important lessons civic leaders took away from the experience.

Though neat categorization is difficult, it is possible to identify at least five types of groups/networks involved in the voluntary response. After Kobe they became the nongovernmental backbone of Japan's disaster volunteering infrastructure.

1. Professionally qualified voluntary groups
2. Local residents' groups
3. Volunteer groups for those with special needs
4. Pre-existing volunteer associations and organizations
5. Volunteer coordination networks

First, professionally qualified volunteer NGOs such as the Association of Medical Doctors of Asia (AMDA), Médecins Sans Frontières (MSF), the Japan Overseas Christian Medical Cooperative Service (JOCS), and the Japan Red Cross were among the first on the ground, providing specialist medical and other emergency services (CODE 2004: 169). Though small in terms of total numbers of volunteers, these groups embodied the kind of professional, 'self-sufficient' (*jiko kanketsu*) model of disaster volunteering pursued and, to a great extent, realized in the years after Kobe.[4] At the other end of the spectrum, locals from unaffected areas spontaneously formed groups of so-called 'patrolling volunteers' (*junkai borantia*) who provided door-to-door services. The Ōmura Group comprising organic farmers and volunteers from a local preschool, for example, established emergency kitchens and meal distribution services in Kobe (CODE 2004: 167).

Volunteer groups also mobilized for those with special needs such as foreigners, the elderly, and the disabled. The Foreigner's Earthquake Information Center (*Gaikokujin Jishin Jōhō Sentā*) began providing telephone consultations in numerous languages soon after the temblor, while the Foreigner Relief Network (*Gaikokujin Kyūen Netto*) fought health officials over medical services for visa overstayers, set up a 'subrogation fund' (*katagawari kikin*) to pay foreigners' medical bills, and demanded that the families of foreign individuals killed in the disaster receive governmental condolence monies similar to Japanese citizens.[5] The Disaster Area Center for the Disabled (*Hisaichi Shōgaisha Sentā*) established by some forty groups in February 1995 provided similar service and advocacy for the physically and mentally disabled. Along with immediate relief services, the group provided special prefabricated shelters for individuals whose needs could not be accommodated in official shelters, and even coordinated volunteering by the disabled themselves.[6] Finally, Kobe witnessed the emergence of specialist IT/computer volunteer groups and networks. Soon after the quake the Inter-V-net User Conference (*Intā V Netto Yūzā Kyōgikai*) began using Internet bulletin boards to provide disaster updates and information about volunteering and material needs. In 1995, of course, Internet diffusion rates were still relatively low, but these rudimentary computer-based volunteer networks sowed the seeds for an amazing technological transformation in all aspects of volunteering thereafter. The intensive utilization of the Internet for volunteer coordination and information transmission we have witnessed after Tōhoku really began in 1995 with such efforts.

Preexisting voluntary associations and NGOs active overseas also played a high-profile role after Kobe, with many drawing on nationwide membership and years of experience both within Japan and abroad. Space prohibits any thorough treatment of these groups that included well-established volunteer associations such as the Osaka Voluntary Action Center (OVAC, *Ōsaka Borantia Kyōkai*), the Japan Youth Volunteer Association (JYVA, *Nihon Seinen Hōshi Kyōkai*), and various chapters of the YMCA and YWCA. Religious groups also chipped in with volunteers from Tenrikyō and the Shanti Volunteer Association (SVA, *Shanti Kokusai Borantia Kai*) of the Sōtō sect of Zen Buddhism.

One interesting group worth highlighting is Peace Boat, a staunchly antiestablishment group started by activist and later socialist politician Tsujimoto Kiyomi and her colleagues in the 1980s. Prior to the Kobe quake Peace Boat activists focused primarily on forging reconciliation and understanding among Japanese and youth around Asia and beyond, and the group was roundly detested by national bureaucrats and conservative politicians for promoting abroad what they saw as an anti-Japanese agenda. Around a week after the disaster, however, 88 Peace Boat activists brought a printing machine into Kobe City and began distributing a newsletter, *Daily Needs* (*Derī Nīzu*), for people in shelters who lacked access to up-to-date information. Towards the end of January the group expanded its activities, distributing supplies to the needy and providing a range of volunteer services. After an appeal by group leaders for assistance on Asahi Television, the Peace Boat office was overwhelmed by some 850 inquiries from would-be volunteers (*Asahi Sonorama* 1995: 219–220; CODE 2004: 168).[7]

Significantly, all of the groups I mention here are involved in the Tōhoku relief effort. Kobe proved to be a turning point for many of them: groups such as Peace Boat which had a strong antiestablishment image (or no image at all) among both elites and ordinary Japanese generated unprecedented levels of popular goodwill and social legitimacy. After a number of political ups and downs, Peace Boat's leader Tsujimoto Kiyomi now finds herself on the 'other side' as the Japanese government's volunteer czar for Tōhoku. Tsujimoto always manages to generate controversy, but after her Peace Boat activities in Kobe few challenge her qualifications in the voluntary sector. From another perspective, the fact that the Japanese government has appointed a chief volunteer coordinator and that this person is Tsujimoto also speaks volumes about changing official attitudes to volunteering after Kobe.[8]

The numerous volunteer coordination networks established after Kobe also helped lay the foundation for later disaster volunteer management in the country and some are leading the Tōhoku response. The four most high-profile networks were the Disaster Area NGO Collaboration Center (DANCC, *Hisaichi NGO Kyōdō Sentā*), the Nippon Volunteer Network Active in Disaster (NVNAD, *Nippon Saigai Kyūen Borantia Nettowāku*), the Citizens' Association to Assist People in the Hanshin-Awaji Earthquake Disaster Area (CAA, *Hanshin-Awaji Daishinsai Hisaichi no Hitobito o Ōen suru Shimin no Kai*), and Rescue Stockyard (RSY, *Resukyū Sutokkuyādo*).[9]

DANCC was established by eight NGOs including the Kobe NGO Association and chapters of the YMCA and YWCA two days after the quake (January 19). All groups in the network had extensive experience in volunteering, many of them in developing countries such as Bangladesh. DANCC primarily played a liaison role, matching volunteers with individuals, regions, and groups in need of help. The absolute necessity of such intermediate volunteer coordinating institutions in post-disaster situations, it must be noted, was one of the major lessons to come out of Kobe. Assisted by local youth bike gangs (*bōsōzoku*), immediately after the quake DANCC set up a tent in a Hyōgo ward park and began providing services for the elderly and disabled (CODE 2004: 58–59). As with Peace Boat's Tsujimoto, DANCC's leaders came from a strongly antiestablishment background having been involved in support groups for Minamata disease sufferers and resident Koreans. The group maintained a rather detached approach to officialdom: cooperate if needed and oppose vehemently when required (Tanaka 2005: 162). Over time the group's operations evolved into volunteer coordination and, some months after the quake, leaders created two subcommittees – one to assist foreigners and the other to deal with issues in temporary housing communities. The latter housing subcommittee, the Temporary Housing Support NGO Liaison Committee

(*Kasetsu Shien NGO Renrakukai*), became an important model for longer-term community-reconstruction volunteering as opposed to the more high-profile yet shorter-term disaster relief work.[10]

Presenting a rather different model to DANCC was NVNAD, set up about a week after the quake in the Kobe city hall. Originally called the Nishinomiya Volunteer Network, the group comprised representatives from the city bureaucracy, quasi-governmental institutions (such as *shakyō*), and civic groups who worked together to coordinate the many volunteers pouring into the city as well as to distribute supplies. This collaborative model of state-civil society volunteer coordination – called the Nishinomiya Method (*Nishinomiya Hōshiki*) – proved highly successful and in April 1999 NVNAD became Hyōgo prefecture's first incorporated nonprofit organization (Tanaka 2005: 162). Thereafter the network participated in various post-disaster initiatives such as disaster preparedness programs and training volunteer coordinators.[11] Although some criticized the Nishinomiya Method as 'bureaucratic subcontracting,' the collaborative model it established in Kobe took root and forms the backbone of volunteering in Tōhoku.

Rescue Stockyard, another volunteer coordination group, was set up by activists from Nagoya in July 1995 based on their experiences in Kobe.[12] Dissatisfied with the poor coordination and management of volunteers, in the months and years thereafter RSY activists focused on ways to link the goodwill of volunteers to concrete and useful activities. As the group's name suggests, RSY hopes to build a 'stock' of knowledge and materials to facilitate rapid post-disaster volunteer response. To this end, its local disaster preparedness activities in Nagoya have included volunteer coordinator training, disaster workshops, and drafting of community preparedness plans (Tanaka 2005: 180). RSY played a particularly important role in the rescue and relief operations after torrential rains in the Tōkai area in September 2001. Implementing the collaborative Nishinomiya Method, RSY managed volunteer centers and deployed volunteers in close partnership with NPOs/NGOs, local officials, and representatives from *shakyō*. Tapping into the 'stock' of experience from Kobe, RSY also coordinated the volunteer response in Tōkai via fax with DANCC activists in Kobe City (Tanaka 2005: 162; CODE 2004: 162). RSY activists are playing a leading role in the Tōhoku volunteer effort.

As the above groups and networks demonstrate, the response after Kobe was a quantum leap for volunteering. But just as important were the shortcomings and the lessons learned by officials and volunteer leaders. Kobe exposed the abysmal financial situation of volunteer groups. Although the Red Cross and other organizations offered some financial support, there was no systematic process for fund raising and dispersal to voluntary groups. The inhospitable regulatory environment was partly to blame but so too were popular attitudes toward donations: before Kobe ordinary citizens did not fully appreciate the function of voluntary groups and many preferred to give their contributions to disaster victims. Kobe changed such attitudes dramatically to the extent that, in the current crisis people are generously donating funds specifically for voluntary groups (as opposed to victims) and see such action as a form of volunteering – albeit passive.

Despite regulatory impediments and lack of funding, however, Kobe also proved that effective networks of volunteers could be built both within affected areas and with groups and individuals from the outside and even abroad. Related to this, Kobe also stimulated volunteer leaders and officials at all levels to reconsider their mutual relations. While some groups maintained a tense if cordial stance with officials, many others wholeheartedly embraced engagement and collaboration – the dominant model we see today.

Finally, the issue of volunteer coordination became particularly important after Kobe. The reality of 1995 was that both officials and civic groups were poorly prepared to deal with the thousands of volunteers. The Nishinomiya Method, while successful, was somewhat of an anomaly, and the general level of coordination among government institutions and volunteer groups was minimal. Because of this poor coordination, many so-called 'unsolicited volunteers' (*oshikake no borantia*) were simply turned away by city officials. In search of something to do, on their own initiative some went to evacuation shelters or wandered the streets until they found somebody to help. Needless to say, goodwill did not always result in good deeds and complaints about 'nuisance volunteers' (*meiwaku borantia*) began to spread. Some even criticized idle volunteers for taking meals at emergency kitchens and buying up valuable supplies at convenience stores (Kotani 1999: 9). The most cynical of observers even suggested that some volunteers came primarily out of curiosity to enjoy 'disaster area tours' (ibid.).

Despite it being mid-winter, many were certainly ill prepared with no sleeping bag, tent, rations, or place to sleep. These 'refugee volunteers' (*nanmin borantia*), as they were sardonically labeled, brought the necessity of coordination into sharp relief (Suga, *et al.* 2008: 112). Individual acts of spontaneous altruism made for good news copy, but volunteer experts in government and civil society became convinced that, for disaster volunteering to be effective, it had to be channeled through a mature and highly integrated voluntary infrastructure based on volunteer centers, registrations, training, and experienced coordinators. As I have argued elsewhere, this was hardly a novel realization: although often seen as the beginning of a new volunteer age, in many ways Kobe helped solidify developing ideas about the need to facilitate and manage the spontaneity of volunteering in the country (Avenell 2010: 81).

As the table shows, in the years from Kobe to Tōhoku Japan has experienced around 15 natural and manmade disasters involving 9000 or more volunteers. In 1997, for instance, some 274,000 volunteers helped in the clean-up effort after the Russian tanker, the *Nakhodka*, spilled crude oil onto the Japan Sea coast. Volunteer specialists in government and civil society responded quickly with groups such as RSY establishing disaster volunteer centers and coordinating operations with shakyō and local officials (Kotani 1999: 16). Local residents also showed new appreciation for volunteers, with inns and pensions offering lodgings and meals, and physicians providing first-aid services. Airline companies also offered free flights into the area for volunteers (as they are doing in Tōhoku) (Kotani 1999: 14). By the time of the Niigata-Chūetsu Earthquake in 2004 an advanced volunteer

TABLE 3.1 Disaster volunteering from Kobe to Tōhoku

Year	Event	Number of Volunteers
1995	Hanshin Awaji Earthquake	1,377,300
1997	Nahotoka Oil Spill Japan Sea	274,600
2000	Hokkaido Usuzan Eruption	9,300
☐	Tōkai Torrential Rain	19,600
2001	Kōchi Prefecture Torrential Rain	11,500
2004	Niigata Prefecture Torrential Rain	45,200
☐	Fukui Prefecture Torrential Rain	60,200
☐	Niigata-Chūetsu Earthquake	95,000
☐	Typhoons Meari (No.21) and Ma-on (No.22)	11,900
☐	Typhoon Tokage (No.23)	44,500
2005	Typhoon Nabi (No.14)	12,200
2006	Nagano Prefecture Torrential Rain	21,000
2007	Nōtō Peninsula Earthquake	15,300
2009	Chūgoku and Northern Kyūshū Torrential Rain	9,700
☐	Typhoon Etau (No.9)	22,700

Source: Naikakufu 2010.

infrastructure involving government, quasi-government, business, and nongovernmental groups was more or less in place – though still untested in a major disaster. Nongovernmental groups, in particular, were playing a significant role in volunteer training and coordination, liaison with officials, fund raising, and direct action at disaster areas. At the same time, the National Social Welfare Council (*Zenkoku Shakai Fukushi Kyōgikai*, *Zenshakyō*) and its many regional shakyō volunteer centers had fast become the nerve center for disaster volunteer response and coordination throughout the country. National bureaucracies were also far more receptive to volunteers and the government could boast a robust portfolio of policies for volunteer facilitation. The bitter experience of Kobe combined with subsequent institutional improvements and modifications meant that the Japanese voluntary sector could not have been more prepared for its greatest challenge after March 11, 2011.

3/11: the official government response

How then are these earlier developments playing out in the current crisis? For some preliminary indications, I analyze government, quasi-government, business, and civic group initiatives for volunteering in Tōhoku. Consider first the government response that has focused on active liaison with volunteer leaders, information sharing, and regulatory support measures. Strikingly different to the central government's ignorance about volunteering after Kobe, Prime Minister Kan Naoto was quick to establish a substantive governmental support structure for Tōhoku volunteering. One day after the disaster Kan appointed Tsujimoto Kiyomi as prime ministerial aide in charge of disaster volunteering and civic activist, Yuasa Makoto, as director of the Cabinet Secretariat's Volunteer Coordination Office (*Naikaku Kanbō Shinsai Borantia Renrakushitsu*, VCO). Officially launched by Tsujimoto and Yuasa at a press conference on March 16, the VCO comprises three non-governmental appointees and seven bureaucrats. Apart from direct liaison with volunteer representatives, the VCO is communicating directly with the public through its disaster relief information portal 'Tasukeai Japan', launched on March 22 to provide information on volunteering and donating in Japanese and English.[13]

It is worth highlighting the appointment of Tsujimoto and Yuasa as the official government representatives for volunteering in Tōhoku. Tsujimoto's strongly leftist, anticonservative background, coupled with her activities after Kobe give her great credibility among nongovernmental groups. Yuasa brings an elite and activist pedigree, having graduated from the Tokyo University law faculty as well as being a tireless advocate for the homeless and working poor and for issues of poverty more generally.[14] Yuasa leads two influential NPOs in these areas and was an advisor to Kan prior to the quake. For many years he has advocated the need for social inclusion for women, the disabled, the poor, and foreigners and, in keeping with this agenda, at the VCO press conference on March 16 highlighted 'inclusion' as one of the long-term goals post-Tōhoku (Tsujimoto and Yuasa 2011). Like Kobe, the reintegration – or 'social inclusion' – of people in disaster areas will be a major issue in the coming years and both Yuasa and Tsujimoto are eminently qualified to lead this project.

The national government also rapidly implemented a series of regulatory and administrative measures to facilitate volunteering. After a request to officials by civic leaders, volunteer groups were able to obtain special road passes usually reserved for emergency service vehicles (Tsujimoto and Yuasa 2011). Certification procedures for new nonprofits (NPOs) were streamlined, reporting requirements for existing groups eased, and procedures for relocation, amalgamation, and dissolution simplified. The government also allocated emergency funds for NPOs assisting the disabled and the elderly in affected areas and reduced duties and taxes for the purchase of vehicles. With respect to donations, officials expedited implementation of new regulations raising the upper limit of personal income tax deductions for individual contributions to charities and voluntary groups. NPOs were also given greater freedom in the use of donations and the so-called public support test (PST) required for qualification as a designated NPO was significantly eased.[15] Finally, on March 15, the Ministry of Finance (MOF) recognized the Disaster Volunteer-NPO Activities Support Fund (see below) of the Red Feather Community Chest Movement as a designated donation (*shitei kifukin*) which means enhanced tax exemptions for individual donations, no ceiling amount for contributions, and greater flexibility in usage of funds.[16]

Almost all of the ministries and agencies have some disaster volunteer initiative for Tōhoku. The Tourism Agency, for instance, is helping coordinate and promote 'volunteer bus tours', the Ministry of Foreign Affairs (MOFA) is working with Japanese NGOs to help coordinate assistance from overseas groups, and many other ministries are encouraging employees to take special 'volunteer leave.'[17] In sum, government measures for volunteering have been swift and substantive and profoundly shaped by the humiliating legacy of Kobe where bureaucrats floundered and volunteers flourished.[18] Societal focus on the problematic government response to the Fukushima nuclear crisis, while understandable, has overshadowed these proactive and effective governmental initiatives in support of Tōhoku volunteering. After Kobe, volunteers made officials look incompetent but post-Tōhoku officials are actively encouraging volunteerism and, together with civic leaders, helping administer the country's extensive volunteer infrastructure.

The role of quasi-governmental institutions

Two quasi-governmental organizations – *Zenshakyō* and the Red Feather Community Chest Movement (RFCC, *Akai Hane Kyōdō Bokinkai*) – are also central players in the Tōhoku volunteer infrastructure, providing key coordination, funding, and liaison services.[19] With its nationwide network of volunteer centers (VCs) in local *shakyō* offices, over the past two decades *Zenshakyō* has fast become the backbone of independent volunteering in Japan.[20] As I have explained elsewhere (Avenell 2009), from the late 1980s onwards *Zenshakyō* began to establish many new VCs in prefectural and municipal *shakyō* offices, enhanced its training for volunteer coordinators, and intensified its registrations of individual volunteers and groups.[21] The results of this campaign were impressive: in 1989 only 39 percent of localities had *shakyō* VCs but by 2005 the percentage had risen to 96 percent (Zenshakyō 2008: 26; Suga, *et al.* 2008: 138). Volunteer registrations also rose sharply from approximately 1.6 million people nationwide in 1980 to 7.4 million in 2005 (Zenshakyō 2007: 3).[22] Over the same period *Zenshakyō* articulated an expansive agenda for VCs that went beyond the traditional emphasis on welfare. Especially after the first seven-year volunteer plan of 1993 and Kobe in 1995, VCs began to provide more logistical support for volunteer groups, and became more active as nodes connecting government institutions, medical and health services, NPOs/NGOs, and individual volunteers – what was called 'constructive collaboration' (*kensetsutekina kyōdō*) between each sector (Zenshakyō 2008: 7).

As part of *Zenshakyō*'s policy of 'needs catching' (*nīzu kyacchi*) in the voluntary sector, after Kobe the organization paid far more attention to disaster volunteering (Zenshakyō 2008: 18). As Figure 3.2. shows, in the early 2000s *Zenshakyō* envisioned a multilevel, multi-organizational disaster response system based on VCs as central coordination points but involving all levels of government, volunteer groups, and other relevant sectors (such as the media). Prefectural and municipal VCs have also contributed, preparing detailed manuals for the establishment and management of disaster volunteer centers.[23] The year 2004 proved to be a

Level 1: Local Disaster Networks

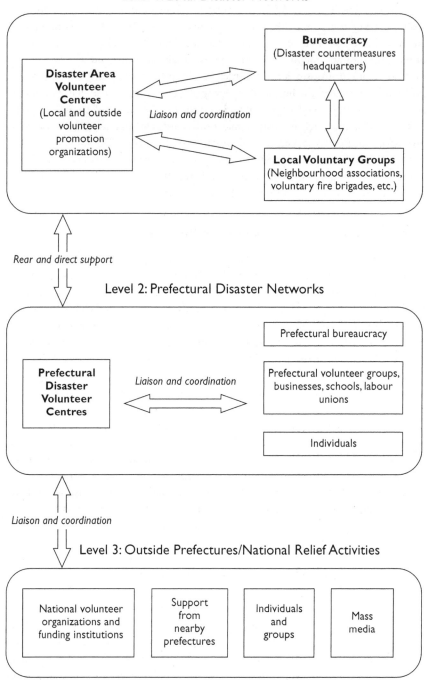

FIGURE 3.2 The Zenshakyō Vision: Japan's Disaster Prevention and Volunteer Support Network (source: *Zenshakyō* 2001).

particularly important moment in the development of *Zenshakyō*'s volunteer infrastructure with earthquakes and flood damage in Niigata and Fukuoka prefectures. Some 87 VCs were established in regional *shakyō* throughout that year. In keeping with *Zenshakyō*'s multilevel disaster response plan, these VCs actively brought in outside experts from nongovernmental groups and borrowed *shakyō* staff from other regional blocks. VCs also began to make extensive use of the Internet and other information technologies to circulate disaster volunteering information (Suga, *et al.* 2008: 142–143).

Post-Tōhoku, *Zenshakyō* has adopted a similar system. *Shakyō* disaster VCs were operational in Chiba and Ibaragi prefectures on March 12 and soon after in the hardest hit prefectures: Fukushima (March 17), Miyagi (March 18), and Iwate (March 19). As areas return to relative normalcy some of these disaster VCs have ceased operations, but VCs in badly affected areas of Fukushima and Iwate continue to operate and may do so for some time. *Zenshakyō* had staff surveying volunteer needs in affected areas by March 13, and the *Zenshakyō* homepage issued some 42 disaster volunteer reports through until late July and continues to update VC data almost daily.

As Figure 3.1 reveals, compared to Kobe, the total number of volunteers (as registered by *shakyō* VCs in Iwate, Miyagi, and Fukushima) in the first four months post-disaster has been considerably lower.[24] There were practical reasons for this early on. Disaster VCs and volunteer coordinators capable of handling large numbers of individual volunteers were not in place until around a week after the quake (though NGOs were on site). Different from Kobe, where volunteers could catch trains almost to the city center, road conditions made access somewhat difficult and short supplies of gasoline and other necessities hindered access. The danger of aftershocks and other disaster area hazards also inhibited large inflows of individual volunteers. Interestingly however, whereas the average daily number of volunteers per month for Kobe dropped sharply in the first four months post-disaster, in Tōhoku daily averages began to exceed those for Kobe after the third month and may be leveling off (although it is still rather early to be sure).

As I discuss more in the conclusion, some have pointed to the role of *Zenshakyō*, volunteer organizations, and the media in actively discouraging volunteers until around the end of Golden Week in May. *Zenshakyō* through its disaster volunteer web portal and local *shakyō* VC homepages have been a first point of contact for many would-be volunteers and, in this way, are directly influencing many individuals' decisions about if, when, and how to volunteer.[25] Figure 3.3, which shows daily volunteer numbers from *shakyō* VCs in Iwate Miyagi, and Fukushima, also hints at institutional factors behind the different volunteer patterns in Kobe and Tōhoku. After the sharp spike during the Golden Week holiday, the graph shows a fairly regular weekly cycle in Tōhoku. My argument here is that Tōhoku differs from Kobe in terms of the advanced institutional mediation of volunteering through *shakyō* VCs and nongovernmental organizations. I believe such mediation is having a systematizing impact on volunteering. Organized or 'packaged' volunteer buses and volunteer tours, registrations, homepage updates, training, and 'pre-briefings', for example, not only make volunteering more accessible but also facilitate its management by organizations like *Zenshakyō*. The regular number of around 5000–7000 weekend volunteers at *shakyō* VCs suggests a level of institutional influence in Tōhoku largely absent in Kobe – hence the sharp decrease in volunteers in the first months after the Kobe Earthquake versus the cyclical weekly trend after Tōhoku.

The Red Feather Community Chest Movement is the other key quasi-governmental organization facilitating volunteering in Tōhoku. Like *Zenshakyō*, RFCC is formally autonomous but, as a social welfare corporation, is subject to significant bureaucratic oversight and control. RFCC is playing a dual role in the Tōhoku volunteer infrastructure: one financial, the other logistical. One of the key concerns for Japanese civic organizations from the late 1980s onwards was the dearth of funding for operations – a problem only underscored by the financial difficulties of post-Kobe volunteer groups. In response, in 1998 the RFCC established the Disaster Volunteer Activities Support Fund aimed at raising one billion yen over ten years to support post-disaster volunteering (Kotani 1999: 18). Along with the NPO Law passed the same year, the fund was one of the most substantive institutional outcomes after Kobe, building on widespread public recognition of the voluntary sector. Four days after the disaster in Tōhoku (March 15), the RFCC established the Disaster Volunteer-NPO Activities Support Fund as a second-generation version of the earlier fund. Visitors to the RFCC's homepage are now given a choice between donating to disaster victims or to voluntary groups. NPOs, NGOs, and voluntary groups active in post-disaster activities can apply directly to RFCC for funding of up to three million yen.[26]

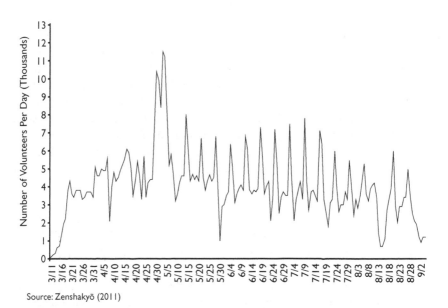

Source: Zenshakyō (2011)

FIGURE 3.3 Number of daily volunteers in Iwate, Miyagi, and Fukushima (source: Zenshakyō 2011).

The RFCC has also played a logistical role post-Tōhoku as organizer of the Joint Committee for Coordinating and Supporting Disaster Relief Activities (CSDR).[27] Perhaps more than any other organization involved in Tōhoku volunteering, this committee exemplifies the extensively networked and interlinked character of Japan's contemporary volunteer infrastructure. Set up by the RFCC after the 2004 Niigata-Chūetsu Earthquake, the project brings together representatives from *Zenshakyō*, RFCC, business (e.g. the Keidanren's '1% Club,' JAL), and the voluntary sector, and its primary aims are to fund and train volunteer coordinators, and to help organize finances, resources, and people in times of disaster. The committee's first substantial operation was after the Nōtō Peninsula Earthquake of 2007 when it created a special mechanism for 1% Club member organizations to make tax-free donations for the dispatch of volunteer coordinators, transportation of supplies, and various reconstruction projects.[28] Building on this experience, after the Tōhoku disaster the committee had representatives on the ground by March 18 and it has been instrumental in providing a steady stream of experienced volunteer coordinators to *shakyō* disaster VCs. The committee is also tapping into corporate resources through the 1% Club whose member corporations have provided various 'new year school packs' and 'ladies packs' for distribution by volunteers at shelters.

The contribution of corporations and business organizations

The direct and indirect contributions of the corporate sector post-Tōhoku also warrant mention. At a meeting between civic groups and government officials on May 12, a representative from the NGO Peace Boat called on corporations to make 2011 'Year One of the CSR Age' (*CSR Gannen*, Corporate Social Responsibility) – just as volunteers made 1995 'Year One of the Volunteer Age.' Such pleas have not gone unanswered. The 1% Club and its member corporations have actively provided supplies and personnel to the CSDR. As a member of the 1% Club, Japan Airlines also offered free domestic flights for affiliated volunteer groups. The mobile communications company, Softbank, donated 300 free mobile phones (and mobile plans) to the Nippon Foundation and the NGO, Japan Platform. Online search engines such as Yahoo Japan, goo, Nifty, and MSN have all established portals with disaster volunteering information.[29]

In terms of funding, in early May the Mitsubishi Corporation established a ¥2 billion grant for NPOs and voluntary groups, which will provide up to ¥2.5 million to two hundred voluntary groups over the coming four years.[30] Mirroring the national bureaucracies many companies – including Wacoal, SMBC Nikko Securities, Mitsui, and Mitsubishi Corporation – have announced special 'volunteer leave' programs for employees (Mainichi Shimbun 2011; NHK Nyūsu 2011b). And, in one of the most creative innovations post-Tōhoku, tour companies and agencies such as JTB Kantō and Kinki Nihon Tourist are running 'volunteer bus tours' to affected areas in collaboration with volunteer groups. Though schedules vary, participants usually spend one or two days involved in volunteer work after which they visit nearby shopping areas, hot springs, and/or tourist spots. Purists might be troubled by this unabashed commodification of volunteering, but the reality is that it brings both helping hands and money to regional economies devastated by the tsunami.[31] From the perspective of volunteering, it is also emblematic of the new synergies from increased corporate-voluntary sector interaction over the past two decades. Recall Kobe where uninvited volunteers were roundly criticized for making 'disaster area tours.' In Tōhoku organized volunteer tours combining altruism and enjoyment seem almost commonsensical.

Civic groups and networks

The other important story of Tōhoku volunteering is the high public profile, greater social legitimacy, and enlarged role of nongovernmental organizations and voluntary groups. Again, it is impossible to fully capture the scope of this involvement here but, in broad strokes, three kinds of activism have been conspicuous in the months after Tōhoku: relief efforts for affected areas both on- and off-site, network building within and beyond the voluntary sector, and provision of funding for voluntary initiatives. Needless to say, all of these initiatives build on the experience and lessons of Kobe.

Non-governmental groups – many with extensive experience in troubled areas across the globe such as JEN, SVA, and Peace Winds Japan – were among the first to reach Tōhoku after the disaster. Peace Boat, for example, which cut its disaster-relief teeth in Kobe, began operations in cooperation with the Japan Youth Chamber in the devastated Ishinomaki region of Miyagi almost immediately.[32] Like many other NGOs active in Tōhoku, Peace Boat has been organizing volunteers and volunteer buses independently of the *Zenshakyō* VC network and holding its own briefings for volunteers in major cities.[33] From its headquarters in Tokyo Peace Boat has also conducted street donation campaigns, and organized emergency supplies. Rescue Stockyard, another Kobe veteran, has conducted similar relief efforts in Shichigahama City, transporting volunteers by minibus all the way from Nagoya City. Rescue Stockyard is also spearheading network-building initiatives among relief groups. Continuing the Nishinomiya Method of cross-sectoral collaboration, the Tokyo Voluntary Action Center (TVAC) has been coordinating volunteer bus tours in cooperation with the Tokyo municipal government and private tour companies. Emblematic of the professionalization of volunteering nowadays, like Peace Boat, TVAC asks volunteers to attend explanatory sessions and pre-departure briefings (*gaidansu*) (NHK Borantia Netto 2011). Consumer cooperatives (*seikyō*) throughout Japan are tapping into their nationwide distribution networks and organizational cultures of volunteerism to support relief efforts. Apart from collecting donations and delivering supplies, many *seikyō* are encouraging members to buy products from affected areas to help rebuild local business and agriculture.[34] In an effort to stimulate local employment the Tōhoku Disaster Relief NGO Center has begun a 'cash for work' program in which residents of Ishinomaki and Kesennuma made jobless by the tsunami are employed on an hourly basis to engage in debris clean-up efforts.[35] Such 'remunerated' or 'paid' volunteerism (*yūshō borantia*) has been an ongoing point of controversy in the voluntary sector but, with Tōhoku, the argument in favor now seems irrefutable (Mega 1999: 44–45; Nakayama 2007: 118–119, 130–131).

I also note the role of 'embedded' or traditional community-based volunteering in affected areas through neighborhood and village associations and volunteer fire brigades (although many such organizations were devastated by the tsunami).[36] There are, moreover, myriad individual voluntary efforts by locals and citizens nationwide that will never be captured in the macro data. One enterprising volunteer, for example, set up an ingenious system for people to purchase and send necessary items through amazon.co.jp to people in affected areas who have specific needs. The diversity and depth of individual and nongovernmental group involvement in Tōhoku is indeed striking and provides irrefutable evidence of the substantial material strength of many civic and voluntary groups in contemporary Japan – not to mention the ingenuity of volunteer leaders.

As I explained above, Kobe witnessed the creation of many rudimentary civic networks for volunteer coordination and liaison – a trend which continues in an ever-more intensified form post-Tōhoku. Among the most important networks is the Japan Civil Network for Disaster Relief in East Japan (JCN), established in Tokyo by leading voluntary and nongovernmental groups on March 16 and comprising some 581 member organizations (as at July 4, 2011) (JCN 2011b). Divided into eight specialist teams (volunteer financing, local networking, systems and administrative issues, volunteer guideline setting, information dissemination, youth volunteering, international liaison, and media relations), JCN is led by three prominent civic groups which are themselves networks of volunteer groups and civil society advocates: Rescue Stockyard (RSY), the Japan NPO Center, and the 'Spread the Circle of Volunteers' Liaison Committee (SCV).[37] Launched on March 22, the JCN homepage provides extensive data on volunteer activities in the Tōhoku region (including an impressive interactive map), as well as information for both volunteer groups and would-be volunteers. JCN has also organized and chaired the frequent liaison conferences between government officials and relief volunteer groups held in Tokyo and affected prefectures, providing volunteer leaders with an unprecedented conduit to Japan's policymaking elite.[38] Beyond JCN, other networks such as the National Network for Earthquake Disasters (NNED) (established after Kobe) and Japan Platform, a consortium of some 30 major NGOs (including Peace Winds Japan, JEN, and SVA) are also uniting the civic sector as never before.[39]

Finally, in striking contrast to Kobe, some voluntary and nongovernmental groups are helping to fund volunteer efforts in Tōhoku. Such initiatives are not completely new, of course: nongovernmental foundations such as the Nippon and Toyota Foundations have a long record of funding civic groups – the latter, of course, with substantial corporate backing. In the specific area of disaster relief, the Niigata NPO Association created the Niigata Flood-Damage Relief Volunteer Activities Fund after torrential rain in 2004, which raised an impressive ¥9.3 million from around 400 donors in three months (Suga, *et al.* 2008: 133). Post-Tōhoku, however, the scale of such nongovernmental funding has reached new heights. Most notably, Japan Platform has made available a ¥1 billion fund to support groups involved in post-quake relief and reconstruction efforts. The scale of the disaster in Tōhoku partly explains Japan Platform's ability to amass such funds, but I believe this is also a result of the greater public appreciation for the services volunteers provide, as well as an increased willingness among Japanese people to entrust nongovernmental groups with their donations.[40]

Conclusion

After the triple disaster in Tōhoku we have witnessed the operation of a highly organized, professionalized, networked, and financed volunteer infrastructure, involving extensive cooperation and collaboration among state authorities, quasi-government organizations, NGOs and NPOs, corporations and business organizations, and voluntary groups. This volunteer infrastructure did not come about spontaneously or by chance: in the decade or so before Kobe and even more so thereafter, volunteer advocates in all of these sectors worked together to institutionalize new forms of volunteering beyond traditional, community-embedded activities, and in keeping with the challenges faced by both government officials and ordinary citizens in contemporary Japan. From the mid-1990s, regulatory reform, media and corporate attention, the emergence of new social issues and values, and a cadre of committed volunteer leaders and advocates helped transform the 'volunteer revolution' of Kobe into the robust volunteer infrastructure we see at work in Tōhoku today.

At a time of crisis like Tōhoku, this volunteer infrastructure has become a potent national asset. Instead of volunteers impulsively rushing to help and sometimes hinder (as in Kobe), now institutions – governmental and nongovernmental – are better matching individual goodwill with actual needs. Resources are also arguably being more sensibly and maximally utilized. Up until after the May Golden Week holidays, both media and voluntary organizations loudly and clearly announced that 'unsolicited volunteers' (*oshikake no borantia*) should control their altruistic impulses and only act through volunteer coordinating agencies and groups. The message was clear: there would be no 'nuisance volunteers' in Tōhoku. Based on media reports so far, this has largely been the case (Kyōdō Tsūshin 2011).[41] Institutionally, Japan's volunteer infrastructure creates a mutually beneficial atmosphere in which volunteer leaders who accept the system can collaborate easily with government and business representatives.

Of course, there have been critical voices that question a volunteer infrastructure that endeavors to systematize the spontaneity and empathy produced between volunteer and beneficiary. Writing in *Newsweek Japan* on April 5, Murosaki Yoshiteru (2011) of Kansai Gakuin argued that 'nuisance' volunteers doing their own thing are needed – so long as they are 'one hundred times more useful' than 'troublesome.' Murosaki worried that the registration, training, and briefings required nowadays might be discouraging some from committing their time. Imase Masashi, Kobe veteran and director of the NGO, Civic Action Clearing House, similarly wonders why the volunteer effort must be so 'coordinated' and why volunteers must be 'trained.' Talk of 'nuisance volunteers', he argues, will only hamper (*yokusei*) individual spontaneity, as too will the reliance on money and business-like NPOs.[42]

As Atsumi Tomohide (2008: 89) has noted, after Kobe the trend in volunteering has been to shun spontaneity in favor of systematization, efficiency, speed, and coordination. In the years after the 1995 disaster, he asserts, voluntary activities were 'mutually coordinated' and 'stuck into networks,' and volunteer centers established so 'relief efforts could proceed in the most efficient way' in moments of crisis. Atsumi (2008: 101) is not questioning the motives, sincerity, and basic goodwill of individual volunteers, but rather, points out the risks and limitations of narrowly defining the 'disaster volunteer' within a rigid schema (*zu*) based on an inflexible cluster of preconceived ideas. The danger with schemas is that they may constrain the otherwise limitless potentialities of human altruism.

Conclusive interpretations about the historical significance of the Tōhoku disaster for volunteering are difficult so soon after, but the event has undoubtedly brought a number of key issues into sharp relief. While the country's volunteer infrastructure has made for an efficient and orderly response in Tōhoku, from a broader historical perspective of state-society relations in Japan, the close collaboration between state and civic groups, the mobilization of civic activists into government posts, and the management of volunteers through the VC infrastructure deserve close scrutiny. Such processes, while efficient, also risk stifling involvement by narrowly defining the boundaries of volunteering or, to use Atsumi's terminology, schematizing it. The risk is not so much a return to the dark past of total social mobilization but, rather, the containment of potential. After all, having volunteers participate through predetermined channels of participation, by default, excludes or makes invisible other types of involvement and other meanings of volunteering. Individuals uncomfortable with donning the predetermined attire of the *borantia* may avoid involvement altogether. Or, if they do become involved as critical and contentious actors, they will not be considered volunteers since they contribute nothing 'constructive' and only 'criticize.' The *borantia* as manifest in contemporary Japan contributes and does not criticize – a fact patently obvious in Tōhoku. Conversely, nor are *borantia* or the volunteer infrastructure subject to much critical scrutiny. For instance, who decides the scope of volunteering and what agendas inform such decisions? Could the seamless web of collaboration obscure more fundamental questions about the roles and responsibilities of the state on the one hand, and the autonomy and critical capacity of civil society on the other?

We need to keep in mind that the origins of Japan's volunteer infrastructure precede Kobe and derive from state concerns about meeting the country's growing welfare challenges. The spread of VCs and increase in volunteer registrations formed part of an overarching policy to channel voluntary energies into the provision of services, mostly for the elderly. One effect of this strategy has arguably been to shift perceptions about the locus of responsibility from the state to society. After Tōhoku, for example, the media rightly sang the praises of volunteers operating emergency kitchens in evacuation centers but only a few wondered why the government did not hire professional caterers and restaurant owners (many left unemployed after the disaster) to do the job. To do so, of course, might be construed as criticism of the volunteers who gave selflessly of their time and energy. But this is to miss the point. From a public finance perspective, supporting and managing volunteerism through a volunteer infrastructure is more economical and politically expedient than using state resources for service provision. It also serves the dual purpose of fashioning or patterning volunteering in terms of state priorities and reinforcing official preferences for a compliant civil society centered on service provision.[43]

Indeed, asking questions about the operation of Japan's volunteer infrastructure after Tōhoku is not a criticism of individual goodwill but, rather, an opportunity to scrutinize the potential pitfalls of an ever-more systematized sphere of activity in the country. Who *is* and *is not* a volunteer and who decides? How are state- and quasi-state institutions, policies, and systems shaping and perhaps constraining volunteerism and associational life in Japan? Could the extensive collaboration and coordination between government officials and civic groups we have witnessed after Tōhoku intensify such trends? The answers are, as yet, unclear.

Notes

1   I thank Robert Pekkanen and Jeff Kingston for valuable feedback on earlier drafts of this chapter.
2   The official name of the disaster is the Great Hanshin-Awaji Earthquake which takes into account the full area affected by the event.
3   See the conclusion for more discussion.
4   The term 'self-sufficient volunteer' (*jiko kanketsu borantia*) was a mantra of government officials and volunteer leaders in the first months after Tōhoku. Volunteer centers and associations provided detailed inventories of necessities for would-be volunteers. For example, Zenshakyō advises the following preparations: food, water, transportation, sleeping bag, dustproof mask, rubber gloves, and rubber boots. See: www.saigaivc.com (accessed June 9, 2011).
5   For discussion of these initiatives for foreigners see CODE (2004: 80–84). Other groups for foreigners included: The Center for Multicultural Information and Assistance (*Tabunka Kyōsei Sentā*, see: www.tabunka.jp). The NGO Network for Foreigners' Assistance KOBE (NGO *Gaikokujin Kyūen Netto*, see: www12.ocn.ne.jp/~gqnet). Kobe Foreigners' Friendship Center (*Kōbe Teijū Gaikokujin Shien Sentā*, see: www. social-b.net/kfc). FMYY (*FM WaiWai*, see: www.tcc117.org/fmyy/index.php). The Association of Foreign Schools in Hyogo prefecture (*Hyōgo-ken Gaikokujin Gakkō Kyōgikai*, see: www.hyogo-ip.or.jp), all accessed July 3, 2011. Most of these groups have established volunteer initiatives for Tōhoku.

6   A similar group, the Disabled Relief Headquarters (*Shōgaisha Kyūen Honbu*) established in Osaka, engaged in fundraising and sent caregivers to Kobe. In 1999 this group incorporated as a nonprofit organization, the Lifespace Support Center Hyōgo (*Seikatsu no Ba Sapōto Sentā Hyōgo*), operating a small workshop, day services, and a group home for the disabled (CODE 2004: 71–72).

7   Also see Peace Boat's home page: www.peaceboat.org (accessed July 3, 2011).

8   Admittedly, Tsujimoto had an ally in Prime Minister Kan Naoto, but I suspect that a similar pro-volunteer policy would have been pursued even under a conservative administration.

9   See DANCC: www.pure.ne.jp/~ngo; NVNAD: www.nvnad.or.jp; CAA (space does not permit discussion of this group here but readers are directed to an electronic book of the group's activities held by Kobe University: www.lib.kobe-u.ac.jp/directory/eqb/book/7-113/index.html); and RSY: www.rsy-nagoya.com/rsy.

10 This group officially became DANCC in April 1996.

11 For example the Indonesia earthquake (1996); the Japan Sea Oil Spill (1997); Tōhoku-Kanto torrential rains (1998); Taiwan and Turkey earthquakes (1999); Usuzan Eruption (2000); the Iran earthquake (2007).

12 The group was originally called the Volunteer Network Association to Learn from Earthquake Disasters (*Shinsai kara Manabu Borantia Netto no Kai*) (Tanaka 2005: 179).

13 Online, available at: www.tasukeaijapan.jp. See below for more discussion about these liaison meetings.

14 Yuasa is actively involved in the following groups: The Anti-Poverty Network (*Han-Hinkon Nettowāku*, see: www.k5.dion.ne.jp/~hinky, accessed July 3, 2011) and the Independent Life Support Center MOYAI (*Jiritsu Seikatsu Sapōto Sentā Moyai*, see: www.moyai.net, accessed July 3, 2011). See also Yuasa (2008) for his ideas on poverty in contemporary Japan.

15 Qualification as a designated NPO previously required 30 percent of total income from donations. Now NPOs pass the test if they receive ¥3000 or greater per donor from one hundred or more donors. Many of these reforms were already under discussion before the earthquake which served to hasten their implementation. These government initiatives are outlined in JCN (2011a).

16 For example monies from this fund can now be used by NPOs for hiring staff. The ceiling or upper limit of the fund was previously ¥1.5 billion (Cs 2011).

17 On Tourism Agency support for bus tours see: www.rescuenow.net/2011/06/post-1593.html (accessed July 2, 2011); www.mlit.go.jp/kankocho/news02_000096.html (accessed July 3, 2011); and www.tasukeaijapan.jp/?page_id=3813 (accessed July 3, 2011).

18 After Kobe the government acted quickly amending both the *Basic Plan for Disaster Prevention* (*Bōsai Kihon Keikaku*, amended July 1995) and the *Disaster Countermeasures Basic Law* (*Saigai Taisaku Kihonhō*, amended December 1995) to make it a responsibility of the government to create an infrastructure for the facilitation of disaster volunteering (Suga, *et al.* 2008: 101). The *Basic Plan* is available at www.bousai.go.jp/keikaku/kihon.html (accessed July 3, 2011). Prime Minister Kan Naoto and his predecessor Hatoyama Yukio were also strong proponents of a so-called 'New Public Commons' (*Atarashii Kōkyō*) based on civic self-help through active volunteering nurtured and facilitated by government (specifically, the Cabinet Office). A number of leading civic activists involved in the Tōhoku volunteer response have also been members of the promotional

committee for this government initiative (for example, Matsubara Akira from the NPO 'Cs' is also a central figure in the JCN movement). For more on the New Public Commons (including its response to the Tōhoku disaster) see: www5.cao.go.jp/npc/suishin.html.

19 Legally, at least, these organizations are nongovernmental but, as Imada notes, 'since [*shakyō*] are established under the older Social Welfare Service Law, they are regulated and controlled by central and local governments and have only limited independence' (Imada 2003: 48).

20 *Zenshakyō*'s volunteer web portal is: www3.shakyo.or.jp/cdvc/volunteer/index.html.

21 These efforts were further strengthened by a series of long-term plans: the First seven-year plan of 1993 (Zenshakyō 1993); the Second five-year plan of 2001 (Zenshakyō 2001); and the Third five-year plan of 2008 (Zenshakyō 2008).

22 This did not, of course, necessarily mean the total number of volunteers was growing: rather, that more volunteers were being registered.

23 For an example of one such manual from Sendai City, see: www.ssvc.ne.jp/?p=417 (accessed July 3, 2011).

24 However we need to keep in mind that many people are also volunteering through nongovernmental volunteer organizations and traditional groups like neighborhood associations and voluntary fire brigades and, at this stage, we do not have any definitive numbers for such groups.

25 *Zenshakyō*'s disaster volunteer web portal is accessible at: www.saigaivc.com, and contains links to local *shakyō* disaster VCs in affected areas.

26 For details, see: www.akaihane.or.jp/topics/detail/id/61 and www.akaihane.or.jp/er/p6.html.

27 In Japanese: *Saigai Borantia Katsudō Shien Purojekuto Kaigi*.

28 For information on the 1% Club, see: www.keidanren.or.jp/japanese/profile/1p-club.

29 See: http://shinsai.yahoo.co.jp; http://busshi.311.goo.ne.jp; www.nifty.com/navi/cs/volunteer/list/1.htm; and http://eastjapaneq.jp.msn.com/volunteer (all accessed July 5, 2011).

30 See: www.mitsubishicorp.com/jp/ja/fukkou/110506.html (accessed June 16, 2011).

31 On volunteer tours see: www.mlit.go.jp/kankocho/news02_000096.html; www.kenpokukanko.co.jp/volunteerliner.html#volunteerliner-miyako; and www.tvac.or.jp/di/20960.html (all accessed June 16, 2011).

32 Peace Boat activists outlined their activities at the government-NGO liaison conferences on 7 and 19 April 2011. For streamed video of the conferences see JCN (2011b) (specifically: www.jpn-civil.net/news/2011/04).

33 For a list of some of the nongovernmental groups independently mobilizing volunteers, see: www.tvac.or.jp/di/20960.html (accessed June 19, 2011).

34 The Seikatsu Club is one such example. See its homepage at: www.seikatsuclub.coop (accessed July 7, 2011).

35 This group is affiliated with the International Volunteer Center of Yamagata. See the center's homepage, available www.ivyivy.org (accessed July 7, 2011). The 'cash for work' program was also explored on the television documentary series *Gaia no Yoake* (*The Dawn of Gaia*), June 21, 2011.

36 See Kawato, Pekkanen, and Tsujinaka in Chapter 4 of this volume for more on such groups. For discussion of 'embedded' volunteering see Haddad (2007).

37 The SCV ('*Hirogare Borantia no Rin' Renraku Kaigi*) is a classic example of the deep state-corporate-voluntary sector ties which have developed in Japan over the past two decades. Headquartered in *Zenshakyō*, SCV brings together volunteer groups, NPOs/NGOs, local governments, and businesses for the purpose of nurturing volunteering in the country. See SVC's homepage at: http://blog.hirogare.jp (accessed July 7, 2011).

38 At the time of writing there have been eight meetings: Tokyo: April 7 and 19, May 12, June 6 and 22; Miyagi: May 25; Fukushima June 29. Video streams for most of these meetings are accessible via the JCN homepage (JCN 2011b).

39 Nevertheless, some newly established networks such as the Nationwide Project to Support NPOs involved in Reconstruction after the East Japan Earthquake (*Higashi Nihon Daishinsai Fukkō NPO Shien – Zenkoku Nettowāku*) do not seem to be functioning in any substantive way (*NHK Nyūsu* 2011c).

40 On the Japan Platform Fund see: www.japanplatform.org/top.html (accessed July 7, 2011).

41 See also *47 News* (2011); *NHK Nyūsu* (2011a); *Japan Times* (2011); *Asahi Shimbun* (2011); and Takeuchi (2011).

42 Imase was a member of the important Kobe group the Citizens Association to Support People in Areas Affected by the Great Hanshi Awaji Earthquake (*Hanshin-Awaji Daishinsai Hisaichi no Hitobito o Ōen suru Shimin no Kai*). The University of Kobe library contains a digitized book documenting the group's activities after that quake (see: www. lib.kobe-u.ac.jp/directory/eqb/book/7-113/index.html, accessed June 22, 2011).

43 On state molding of civil society, see Pekkanen (2006).

References

47 News (2011) 'Borantia Kakusho de Ukeire Seigen Tōhoku 3ken "Kyōkyū Kajō",' April 26, online, available at: www.47news.jp/CN/201104/CN2011042601000148.html (accessed April 26, 2011).

Asahi Shimbun (2011) 'Borantia, Renkyū de Shūchū Miyagi de Ukeire Chūshi,' April 30, online, available at: www.asahi.com/national/update/0429/TKY201104290413.html (accessed April 30, 2011).

Asahi Sonorama (ed.) (1995) *Borantia Gannen – Hanshin Daishinsai 12nin no Shuki*, Tokyo: Asahi Sonorama.

Atsumi, T. (2008) 'Borantia ni tsuite Mōichido Kangaeru,' in M. Suga, Y. Yamashita, and T. Atsumi (eds.) *Saigai Borantia Nyūmon (Shirīzu: Saigai to Shakai – 5)*, Tokyo: Kōbundō.

Avenell, S. (2009) 'Facilitating Spontaneity: The State and Independent Volunteering in Contemporary Japan,' *Social Science Japan Journal*, 13(1): 69–93.

Avenell, S. (2010) 'Civil Society and the New Civic Movements in Contemporary Japan: Convergence, Collaboration, and Transformation,' *Journal of Japanese Studies*, 35(2): 247–283.

CODE Kaigai Saigai Kyūen Shimin Sentā (ed.) (2004) *Kobehatsu Saigai Shien: Sasaeai wa Kokyō o Koete*, Kobe: Kobe Shimbun Sōgō Shuppan Sentā.

Cs (Shīzu – Shimin Katsudō o sasaeru Seido o Tsukuru Kai) (2011) *NPO Shien Bokin, Shitei Kifukin ni*, March 16, online, available at: www.npoweb.jp/modules/news1/print. php?storyid=3426 (accessed April 30, 2011).

Fujii, A. (2002) 'Shakaigakusha wa Donoyōni Borantia o Katattekitanoka,' *Borantia Katsudō Kenkyū*, 11: 13–28.

Haddad, M.A. (2007) *Politics and Volunteering in Japan: A Global Perspective*, Cambridge/New York: Cambridge University Press.

Hasegawa K., Shinohara C., and Broadbent, J.P. (2007) 'The Effects of "Social Expectation" on the Development of Civil Society in Japan,' *Journal of Civil Society*, 3(2): 179–203.

Hyōgo-ken Kenmin Seikatsubu Seikatsu Bunkakyoku Seikatsu Sōzōka (2006) *Hanshin Awaji Daishinsai Ippan Borantia Katsudōshasū Suikei*, online, available at: http://web.pref.hyogo.lg.jp/wd33/wd33_000000144.html (accessed August 27, 2011).

Imada, M. (2003) 'The Voluntary Response to the Hanshin Awaji Earthquake: A Trigger for the Development of the Voluntary and Non-Profit Sector in Japan,' in S.P. Osborne (ed.) *The Voluntary and Non-Profit Sector in Japan: The Challenge of Change*, London/New York: Routledge Curzon.

Japan Times (2011) 'Too Many Volunteers to Put Up,' April 27, online, available at: http://search.japantimes.co.jp/print/nn20110427a6.html (accessed April 27, 2011).

JCN (2011a) *Haifu Shiryō: Daiikkai Shinsai Borantia-NPO tō to Kakushōchō to no Teirei Renraku Kaigi*, Tokyo, April 7, online, available at: www.jpn-civil.net/news/2011/04/post_9.html (accessed April 11, 2011).

JCN (2011b) *Higashi Nihon Daishinsai Shien Zenkoku Nettwāku*, online, available at: www.jpn-civil.net (accessed 7 July 2011).

Kotani, N. (1999) *Shimin Katsudō Jidai no Borantia*, Tokyo: Chūō Hōki Shuppan.

Kyōdō Tsūshin (2011) 'Borantia Kakusho de Ukeire Seigen Tōhoku 3ken "Kyōkyū Kajō",' April 26, online, available at: www.47news.jp/CN/201104/CN2011042601000148.html (accessed 15 November, 2011).

Mainichi Shimbun (2011) 'Mainichi Fōramu Kigyō Fairu: Sumitomo Ringyō nado,' May 11, online, available at: http://mainichi.jp/select/seiji/forum/kigyo/archive/news/2011/20110509org00m010057000c.html (accessed May 11, 2011).

Mega, F. (1999) 'Borantia Katsudō: Kore made to Kore kara,' in Y. Nakamura and Nihon NPO Sentā (eds.) *Nihon no NPO 2000*, Tokyo: Nihon Hyōronsha.

Murosaki, Y. (2011) 'Borantia wa Oshikakete ii – The Goodwill Dilemma,' *Newsweek Nihonban*, April 4, online, available at: www.newsweekjapan.jp/stories/world/2011/04/post-2035.php (accessed July 7, 2011).

Naikakufu – Bōsai Tantō (2010) *Chiiki no 'Juenryoku' o Takameru tameni*, Tokyo: Naikakufu, online, available at: www.bousai-vol.jp/juenryoku (accessed July 8, 2011).

Nakamura, Y. (1999) 'Shimin Katsudō' no Tōjō to Tenkai,' in Y. Nakamura and Nihon NPO Sentā (eds.) *Nihon no NPO 2000*, Tokyo: Nihon Hyōronsha.

Nakayama, A. (2007) *Borantia Shakai no Tanjō: Giman o kanjiru Karakuri*, Tsu: Mie Daigaku Shuppankai.

NHK Borantia Netto (2011) 'Ima, Watashitachi ga Dekiru Koto,' April 13, online, available at: www.nhk.or.jp/nhkvnet/spots/column-03.html (accessed May 10, 2011, now taken down, copies with the author).

NHK Nyūsu (2011a) 'Hisaichi Renkyū de Borantia ni,' April 9, online, available at: http://www3.nhk.or.jp/news/html/20110429/k10015632971000.html (accessed April 29, 2011, now taken down, copies with the author).

NHK Nyūsu (2011b) 'Borantia Kyūka Dōnyū Hirogaru,' May 10, online, available at: http://www3.nhk.or.jp/news/html/20110507/k10015743081000.html (accessed May 10, 2011, now taken down, copies with the author).

NHK Nyūsu (2011c) 'Hisaichi NPO Shien de Zenkoku Soshiki Setsuritsu,' April 24, online, available at: http://www3.nhk.or.jp/news/html/20110424/k10015519881000.html (accessed April 29, 2011).

Nishiyama, S. (2007) *Kaiteiban Borantia Katsudō no Riron*, Tokyo: Tōshindō.

Pekkanen, R. (2006) *Japan's Dual Civil Society: Members Without Advocates*, Stanford, CA: Stanford University Press.

Suga M., Yamashita Y., and Atsumi T. (2008) *Saigai Borantia Nyūmon (Shiñzu: Saigai to Shakai – 5)*, Tokyo: Kōbundō.

Takeuchi, A. (2011) *Interview on NHK Volunteer Net*, March 25, online, available at: www.nhk.or.jp/nhkvnet/spots/column-02.html (accessed November 15, 2011).

Tanaka, T. (2005) 'Bōsai Borantia ni taisuru Shien,' in Fukkō 10nen Iinkai (ed.) *Fukkō 10nen Sōkatsu Kenshō – Teigen Dētabēsu*, online, available at: http://web.pref.hyogo.lg.jp/wd33/wd33_000000126.html#h01 (accessed April 20, 2011).

Tsujimoto, K. and Yuasa, M. (2011) *Establishment of the Cabinet Secretariat's Volunteer Coordination Office*, press conference, Tokyo, March 22.

Winter, R. (2011) 'This is No Kobe 1995 Redux,' *The Wall Street Examiner*, online, available at: www.wallstreetexaminer.com/blogs/winter/?p=3746 (accessed July 1, 2011).

Yuasa, M. (2008) *Han-Hinkon: 'Suberidai Shakai' karano Dasshutsu*, Tokyo: Iwanami Shoten.

Zenshakyō (Zenkoku Shakai Fukushi Kyōgikai – Zenkoku Borantia Shimin Katsudō Shinkō Sentā) (1993) *Borantia Katsudō Suishin 7kanen Puran Kōsō*, online, available at: www3.shakyo.or.jp/cdvc/volunteer/center/7yearsplan.html (accessed July 3, 2011).

Zenshakyō (Zenkoku Shakai Fukushi Kyōgikai – Zenkoku Borantia Shimin Katsudō Shinkō Sentā) (2001) *Dai 2ji Borantia Shimin Katsudō Suishin 5kanen Puran*, online, available at: www3.shakyo.or.jp/cdvc/data/files/DD_48261056172620.pdf (accessed July 3, 2011).

Zenshakyō (Zenkoku Shakai Fukushi Kyōgikai – Zenkoku Borantia Shimin Katsudō Shinkō Sentā) (2007) *Borantia Katsudō Nenpō 2005nen (Gaiyō)*, online, available at: www3.shakyo.or.jp/cdvc/shiryo/joho1_v.html (accessed July 3, 2011).

Zenshakyō (Zenkoku Shakai Fukushi Kyōgikai – Zenkoku Borantia Shimin Katsudō Shinkō Sentā) (2008) *Shakai Fukushi Kyōgikai ni okeru Dai 3ji Borantia Shimin Katsudō Suishin 5kanen Puran*, online, available at: www3.shakyo.or.jp/cdvc/data/files/DD_8631440162620.pdf.

Zenshakyō (2011) *Hisaichi Shien Saigai Borantia Jōhō*, online, available at: www.saigaivc.com (accessed July 12, 2011).

4

CIVIL SOCIETY AND THE TRIPLE DISASTERS

Revealed strengths and weaknesses

Kawato Yūko, Robert Pekkanen, and Tsujinaka Yutaka[1]

The triple disasters—9.0 earthquake centered in Tōhoku, the massive accompanying tsunami, and the Fukushima nuclear accident—that rocked Japan on March 11, 2011 tested the country as nothing has since the end of World War II. Both the strengths and the weaknesses of Japan's civil society were on display during the crisis. The vitality of Japan's local civil society groups greatly mitigated the painful effects of the triple disasters, and there can be no doubt that many owe their lives to these groups, directly or indirectly. At the same time, the inability over many years of civil society groups to act as effective monitors or checks on state action also arguably contributed to the magnitude of the nuclear catastrophe, by failing to spur improvements in safety practices.

We understand civil society to be the organized non-state, non-market sector that exists above the family and individual. This includes nonprofit organizations (NPOs) as well as community groups like neighborhood associations and volunteer firefighter groups. On one hand, activities of community groups before the disaster improved preparedness and created social capital that facilitated the response to the disaster. NPOs outside of the affected area had developed expertise through past disasters and rushed to provide relief. On the other hand, a weak advocacy role of civil society in Japan may have been a contributing factor in the nuclear disaster by providing an ineffectual check on an errant nuclear industry. The state and electric power companies closely collaborated to implement an expansive nuclear energy policy while marginalizing civil society in their decision-making. The state and power companies also offer significant compensation to local communities that accept nuclear plants, making local advocacy and protest mobilization difficult. The configuration of Japan's civil society and its relationship to the policy-making process hampered effective contestation of nuclear policy.

This chapter first describes the general characteristics of Japan's civil society to explain why civil society organizations could not act as effective watchdogs to help prevent the nuclear accident. Second, we will discuss how community organizations provided a strong foundation for immediate response to the earthquake and tsunami. We will also highlight the activities of NPOs from outside Tōhoku. This chapter concludes with a discussion about how the general characteristics of NPOs are likely to shape their participation in the recovery efforts, and how NPO response to the disaster will (or will not) change policy and policy-making process in the future.

Japan's civil society

In comparative perspective, most civil society organizations in Japan are small, local organizations.[2] They have four defining characteristics. First, they have small membership. According to the Cabinet Office's survey of 2,345 NPOs in 2010, 67 percent of the NPOs had less than 20 members, and only 11 percent had more than 100 members. Second, most NPOs have a small number of professional staff. In the aforementioned survey, 50 percent of the NPOs said they had less than 20 staff. Third, most organizations have small budgets. The survey showed that in the previous year 54 percent of the NPOs had income of less than ¥10 million (about $123,000), while only 13 percent had income of more than ¥50 million ($616,000). Finally, most organizations have a small area of operation. Thirty-nine percent of the NPOs responded that they engage in activities within one city, town, or village, and 40 percent said they work in multiple communities within one prefecture. Only 7 percent engaged in nationwide activities (Cabinet Office 2011: 3–7). Many small local groups, and a few large professional advocacy groups, make up Japan's civil society.

There are four main reasons for this. First, beginning with the Civil Code of 1896, the state has encouraged the growth of organizations that serve the "public interest," instead of advocacy organizations that challenge the state and its policies (Pekkanen 2006). The Special Nonprofit Organization Law of 1998 liberalized the conditions under which NPOs could form and operate, but this law did not lead to a fundamental change in the type of organizations that compose Japan's civil society or the state–civil society relationship (Kawato and Pekkanen 2008). Legal status is easier for many groups to acquire, but government red tape continues to handcuff groups. Onerous reporting requirements and the limitations on charging for overheads hamper the growth of nonprofit organizations in the country. The reporting requirements vary by organization, but it might be surprising for the American reader to know just how time-consuming they are. For example, even an organization that employs a very small number of staff might have to devote six months of one staff person's time to completing just the annual reporting duties. This burden is compounded by the fact that many Japanese government contracts do not permit the charging of overheads by the organization, paying only for actual project work.

Second, most NPOs remain local and small because they have few opportunities to participate in policy-making at the national level, except for some organizations that work closely with the state (Tsujinaka 2002; Tsujinaka and Pekkanen 2007). According to Pharr (1990), the limited access reduces civil society organizations' incentive to increase staff and other organizational resources for advocacy. Furthermore, a relatively greater access to local governments has reinforced NPOs' tendency to work locally.

Third, many organizations remain small and local because they are short of funds. A series of reforms in the last decade has enabled individuals and corporations to obtain tax privileges for donating to NPOs with special certification from the National Tax Agency, including a major revision in June 2011. However, the number of certified NPOs is still vanishingly small at 223 out of over 42,000 (0.5 percent) and donations remain only a minor portion of organizational revenue on average. In addition, the state prioritizes funding to organizations that it considers important, like social welfare corporations and cannot fund all organizations that wish to receive funding. Private foundations have not been an important source of funding for NPOs. Corporate foundations that tend to be politically and socially conservative are not enthusiastic about funding advocacy organizations either (Reimann 2010: Ch. 2). With limited funding, NPOs face challenges in expanding membership, paid staff, budget for activities, and area of operation. Organizations with a small membership generally have less policy influence than those with a large membership. Organizations with small resources are also less likely to develop expertise and policy influence because they are less likely to hire paid staff that can devote time to develop expertise and influence policy.

Fourth, Japan's relatively rigid labor market makes working for a nonprofit less attractive. In many countries, a young person could work for a few years after graduation in a low-paying nonprofit job, build skills and then switch to the corporate sector. Such a course is more difficult in Japan. This means that a new graduate choosing to work for a nonprofit must contemplate working her/his entire career for a low-paying, financially insecure group. The instability of nonprofit funding works against the groups even more, as many groups have extremely volatile income streams. In a given year, for example, a group employing on average ten people might have to let five go, only to hire seven the next year, then reduce staff the following year. Mitsubishi and other corporations' decision to allow their employees to volunteer in Tōhoku without taking vacation time is a marked step forward, but it does nothing to address the workings of the labor market, which are a more serious impediment to the development of civil society organizations in the long run.

Civil society and nuclear energy policy: a subdued watchdog

The weak advocacy role of civil society organizations in Japan may have been a contributing factor in the nuclear disaster. This is of course not to say that civil society groups pushed policies that caused or exacerbated the disaster. Rather it is that they were ineffective in monitoring or checking government policies or industry excesses. In contrast, civil society groups as well as scholars now are active in creating a shadow-monitoring grid of radiation levels. So, in addition to the official figures on radiation levels, citizens can also see an independent set of measurements collected by civil society groups, scholars, and other citizens. The existence of this "shadow" measure perfectly illustrates the ability of civil society to monitor the state and provide an independent source of information (the existence of which no doubt helps to maintain the integrity of the official information source, too).

Before March 11, 2011, however, civil society groups were not as successful in preventing problems in nuclear policy or the nuclear industry. Instead, the state and electric power companies collaborated to implement an expansive nuclear energy policy to support Japan's economic development and greater independence from foreign sources of energy. A nationwide citizens' movement against nuclear energy emerged to contest this policy and question the safety standards at nuclear plants. Key umbrella organizations include Japan Congress against A- and H-Bombs (Gensuikin) and the National Network against Nuclear Energy. However, they are not professional advocacy organizations with strong influence on policy-making. These organizations' main functions are to educate the public about the dangers of nuclear plants and to facilitate information sharing among member organizations. Of course, when push came to shove, these organizations were more strongly opposed to nuclear weapons than to nuclear power. The sometimes byzantine and lurid internal struggles of these groups might also have undermined their public credibility. Moreover, despite a limited number of victims of nuclear accidents both in Japan and abroad, these groups were never effective in tapping into the "victim" and "pollution" frames that resonated so powerfully for other groups contesting the political intersection of the environment and business (see Avenell forthcoming). Nonetheless, the point stands that state and electric power companies were able to develop the nuclear energy policy in this civil society context, without having to deal with strong advocacy against their plans during policy-making and implementation processes.

The state and electric power companies tried to preserve their freedom of action. When they searched for sites to construct nuclear plants, they purposefully chose communities in which civil society was weak (Aldrich 2008). They offered large compensation packages to local communities that accepted nuclear plants, making local protest mobilization difficult. Electric power companies also benefited from weak state oversight. In 2006, a government panel with many experts with ties to electric companies drafted some guidelines and permitted the companies to check their own adherence to the standards. Although an agency for nuclear safety exists, the aftermath of the nuclear disaster has made clear that the agency played a passive role and that the state did not exercise effective control over the nuclear operators.

Few local protests to nuclear plants occurred because the economic benefits that the state and electric power companies conferred on host communities made protests difficult to organize. Since the late 1970s, small groups of local residents with support from lawyers and scientists filed 14 major lawsuits against the state or power companies. Many of these lawsuits sought to shut down nuclear plants. Plaintiffs pointed to new seismic research that revealed previously unknown fault lines under or near nuclear plants, and argued that the plants' quake-resistance standards were inadequate to withstand a major earthquake. Nuclear operators often contested the research that plaintiffs used, and sometimes responded by denying the existence of a fault line even when they knew it existed. Power companies often underestimated the dangers of continued operations in order to avoid costly safety upgrades.

Courts sided with the state and nuclear operators most of the time. Plaintiffs have not won in any of the 14 lawsuits. Two lower courts ruled in favor of plaintiffs, but higher courts overturned those rulings. Although plaintiffs relied on credible research from seismologists and other experts, it seems judges perceived that the state and nuclear operators were more reliable sources of information. According to a former chief judge at a district court who ruled for the plaintiffs, it is difficult for plaintiffs to prove that a nuclear plant is dangerous. He also said:

> I think it can't be denied that a psychology favoring the safer path comes into play. Judges are less likely to invite criticism by siding and erring with the government than by sympathizing and erring with a small group of experts.
>
> (Ōnishi and Fackler 2011)

Plaintiffs might have been able to overcome this type of bias more easily and win favorable rulings more often if there were credible advocacy organizations with expertise on nuclear energy and operations. We certainly are not claiming that civil society in any way caused the accident, but believe that stronger civil society oversight could have led to stricter standards and more rigorous monitoring of nuclear plants, which might in turn have prevented or diminished the scale of the accident in Fukushima.

The nuclear accident has reinvigorated anti-nuclear activism in Japan. On June 11, 2011, a network of civil society groups called for a nationwide demonstration. According to the organizers, 79,000 people participated in demonstrations and other activities across the nation between June 10 and June 12. The organizers did not publicize their group names, saying that they were calling for a broad mobilization solely based on their demands, which are: (1) Stop nuclear reactors that are operating, do not reactivate reactors that are currently not running, and do not create new reactors; (2) Do not relax the level of exposure to radiation officially considered as dangerous; and (3) Shift from nuclear energy to natural energy. This type of mobilization without a publicized central committee is rare in Japan, but might have encouraged participation by various grass-roots organizations and individuals. Organizations in places that host nuclear reactors, such as Hokkaido and Kyūshū, have also become active since the disaster. They have sent demands to electric power companies and prefectural governors to stop the reactors that are currently running, to cancel plans for new construction of reactors, and to switch to natural energy. One neighborhood association in Satsumasendai City in

Kagoshima prefecture asked the city mayor to tell the Kyūshū Electric Power Company to "freeze" the plan to construct a new reactor and test all the existing reactors. It is not clear how these expressions of opposition and concern will influence Japan's nuclear energy policy. However, anti-nuclear activities by various civil society organizations continue amidst media reports about the difficulty of dealing with the nuclear accident in Fukushima, scandals involving nuclear operators, and the central government's errant leadership.

Community organizations: disaster preparedness and response

The earthquake and tsunami also revealed the strength of Japan's civil society. Local civil society groups saved lives in three ways: (1) through preparation and disaster drills before the earthquake; (2) during and immediately after the disasters through direct action; and (3) by contributing to social capital and cohesion in local communities, indirectly strengthening community response. Neighborhood associations and volunteer firefighter groups are two important examples of these local groups.

Neighborhood associations

Neighborhood associations (NHAs) are the most common form of civil society organization in Japan. There are about 300,000 NHAs and nearly all Japanese belong to one. Local governments encourage NHAs to engage in activities that improve disaster preparedness and response. Local governments explain on their websites that residents may have to help each other to provide initial response to disasters, especially when a large disaster severs roads leading to the communities or when it overwhelms professional rescue teams. Tasks that local residents may have to carry out include communicating with each other, checking on neighbors' safety and rescuing them if necessary, putting out fires, helping each other to evacuate to designated areas, and distributing food and other relief materials.

Many NHAs circulate information about preparedness and organize training to enable quick and efficient response to disasters. Tsujinaka, *et al.* (2009) show that nearly half of all neighborhood associations (of the 18,000 or so in their national survey) engage in disaster preparedness drills. NHAs can also create maps indicating potential sources of hazard in their neighborhood and where people who require special assistance live, including the elderly, disabled people, pregnant women, small children, and foreigners who do not understand Japanese. Local governments also offer funds to NHAs to purchase materials such as ladders and stretchers that might be useful in case of disaster.

For example, Sendai City has encouraged NHAs to organize disaster prevention and response groups (*jishu bōsai soshiki*) since the earthquake off the coast of Miyagi in 1978. According to the city's website, 95 percent of the NHAs in the city had organized such groups by January 2010. One NHA in Kesennuma City had prepared a list of elderly who would need special assistance in case of disaster, and this list (and local residents' memory of who were on this list) helped organize visits to these people by doctors, nurses, and care managers after the disaster. This suggests that NHAs' efforts to improve preparedness had some positive impact, although there is at this early stage no official report yet about the extent to which NHAs' efforts facilitated local response to the disaster.

In addition to improving preparedness, NHAs provide various social services and socializing opportunities to local residents. NHAs typically organize cleaning, maintain roads, organize local festivals, support elderly groups, organize garbage collection, participate in celebrations and funerals, organize sports and cultural events, support school education, and maintain buildings where residents meet (Tsujinaka, et al. 2009). These activities encourage local residents to work together and consequently generate social capital (network, trust, reciprocity). This social foundation became crucial in responding to the Tōhoku Earthquake. The high level of social capital is likely to have maintained general order, although some thefts from evacuated homes, ATMs and gas stations took place. The absence of riots, looting and other disorderly conduct in affected areas impressed the world and were a source of pride for Japanese.

Residents continued to value NHAs as an essential mechanism to facilitate coordinated action and to maintain social networks. In fact, NHAs remained important even among evacuees whose neighborhoods were washed away by the tsunami. Residents in some NHAs evacuated to other towns or prefectures together as a unit in order to maintain their social network and facilitate communication during recovery efforts. NHA-like self-governing groups also emerged in evacuation centers to organize and carry out various tasks. In a center in Fukushima, for example, evacuees organized themselves by dividing into two groups, selecting leaders and conducting a needs assessment. These groups assumed responsibility for various tasks at the evacuation center, and their members worked together to clean, prepare food, and organize garbage disposal, just like in NHAs.

NHAs outside of the devastated areas also played an important role after people from Tōhoku evacuated there. For example, after 11 families (44 people) from Fukushima prefecture evacuated to a public facility in Tokyo's Katsushika ward, the NHA provided food and other materials to the evacuees. This NHA called neighboring NHAs and volunteer associations to help as well. NHAs remain an important coordination mechanism for supporting the victims outside of Tōhoku, together with other types of NPOs.

Another function of NHAs is building consensus among residents and communicating their needs to local governments. NHAs continued to serve as a bridge between residents and local governments after the disaster. For example, in Urayasu City in Chiba prefecture, where liquefaction due to the earthquake damaged roads and homes, NHA members met to discuss their situation and how to respond. They decided to submit a list of requests to local government, including stabilizing the ground (*jiban*) and restoring infrastructure.

Finally, the disaster has prompted NHAs outside of Tōhoku to encourage non-members to join them, as a way to improve local disaster preparedness. The 1923

Kantō Earthquake similarly prompted the state to encourage NHAs to form around the country. The current effort is more pronounced in Tokyo and other large cities, where the NHA membership rate is lower than in rural areas due to greater mobility and individualism. Media attention to NHAs and how strong social capital facilitated coordination of local responses in Tōhoku has prompted local governments and NHAs in metropolitan areas all over Japan to rejuvenate community-based associations by inviting non-members to join and raising public awareness of the benefits of NHAs. Some local governments have distributed brochures about NHAs, with extra focus on residents in apartment complexes where interaction between neighbors can be limited. It appears that some residents, especially older people living alone in apartments, are responding positively. Sumida ward in Tokyo will also start funding a project to help young people develop expertise on NHA management. The project aims to nurture future NHA leaders, as current leaders are growing older. The extent to which these efforts will be successful remains to be seen, but it is highly likely that NHAs will remain important for improving local emergency preparedness and disaster response.

Volunteer firefighters

According to the Fire Services Act (*Shōbō soshiki hō*), cities, towns, and villages can create volunteer firefighting groups. Volunteer firefighters learn and maintain their skills in disaster response, and engage in public education to prevent fire and improve disaster preparedness. Once disaster occurs, they respond by putting out fires, rescuing people, and guiding people to safety. According to the Fire and Disaster Management Agency, in April 2010 there were 2,275 groups (divided into 22,926 subgroups) with 883,698 volunteer firefighters in Japan. Their role is especially important in isolated and sparsely populated communities. In Iwate prefecture, for example, there were 23,420 volunteer firefighters as of April 2010, about 12 times more than full-time firefighters in the prefecture. Volunteer firefighting groups greatly contribute to disaster preparedness and response all over the country.

Volunteer firefighters responded immediately to the tsunami in March. In the town of Ōtsuchi, Iwate prefecture, volunteer firefighters rushed to close the gates of a tidal embankment. The 1 km-long embankment along the ocean has eight gates every 100 meters or so, which allow people to pass through it. Volunteer firefighters were responsible for closing them in case of tsunami and, after closing the gates, they helped local residents escape to higher ground. Media reports show that they served their community selflessly. One of them sacrificed his life by staying at the firefighters' post to warn other residents about the tsunami by ringing a bell, because the emergency siren did not work without electricity. In Rikuzen-Takata City, 26 volunteer firefighters went missing or died as they helped local residents escape the tsunami.

Those that survived continued to volunteer. In Ōtsuchi, they fought the fire that broke out in many parts of the town in the aftermath of the tsunami. In this and other towns struck by the tsunami, volunteer firefighters helped look for missing people and identified the dead. They also cleared the debris, collected photo albums and other materials that they found, and helped local residents carry their belongings out of their homes. They also looked for tanks and drum cans that might contain chemicals and combustible materials such as gasoline while at night they patrolled neighborhoods. They did all of this even when many of them had also been victimized by the tsunami. In one firefighter group in Iwate's Miyako City, 22 of 25 volunteer firefighters lost their houses in the tsunami. According to a media report from mid-April, they left their families in evacuation centers and relatives' homes in order to stay together and serve the community in the aftermath of the tsunami.

Volunteer firefighting groups were an indispensable part of disaster response. Their operation is possible only with the members' strong commitment to their communities (Haddad 2007). As such, they reflect the strength of Japan's civil society. However, the number of volunteer firefighters in Japan has steadily declined over several decades, although the number of female volunteer firefighters has increased steadily. The Fire and Disaster Management Agency has engaged in PR campaigns to increase the number of volunteer firefighters. Would the recent media reports about volunteer firefighters' heroic work in their communities encourage others to join? Or, in an increasingly individualistic society, would the reports emphasizing the selfless service and sacrifice of volunteers in dangerous conditions discourage others to join? The Agency's statistics from this year and the next will be an important indicator of whether people's participation in community organizations has increased since the disaster.

NPOs outside of Tōhoku

NPOs generally have clear and focused objectives, and are able to work with great flexibility often in cooperation with each other. These characteristics allowed them to play important roles in response to the disaster. In addition, local governments and NPOs in Japan traditionally have a close working relationship through contract projects (*itaku jigyō*). Collaborative work generates a shared expectation that state and civil society actors can work together, and this becomes an asset when responding to disasters that require coordinated action between those actors. NPOs with their swift and focused actions have complemented the efforts of governmental organizations that attend to a broader set of issues and require time for decision-making and implementation. NPOs have also guided local governmental action by proposing specific measures to alleviate local residents' hardship.

One example of coordinated action between local governments and NPOs is the Volunteer Center. Following the Kobe Earthquake of 1995, a large number of volunteers rushed to the affected areas. However, it soon became clear that lack of coordination mechanisms among the volunteers, between NPOs, and between NPOs and local governments complicated their efforts. The Volunteer Center, often maintained by local social welfare councils, emerged as a coordination mechanism in 1997 after heavy oil leaked out of a Russian tanker near the Oki Islands in Shimane prefecture. Since then, local governments and NPOs have cooperated through Volunteer Centers by sharing information about local needs and coordinating volunteer efforts, although there are some NPOs that eschew the Volunteer Centers and work independently. Volunteer Centers further spread after the Chūetsu Offshore Earthquake of 2007 and the 2008 earthquake in Tōhoku.

NPOs developed their expertise and coordination mechanisms as they responded to past disasters. Some Japanese NPOs that work overseas have also developed their expertise through their response to disasters abroad, such as in the Indian Ocean tsunami in 2004 and the earthquake in Haiti in 2010. Their experience became useful after the recent earthquake. Within days after the earthquake and tsunami, NPOs sent staff to gather information and offer immediate help such as medical attention and food. NPOs identified local needs to plan further action and looked for places with lifelines to set up their bases of operation. Some NPOs played a crucial role in identifying houses and other places away from main evacuation centers where local residents stayed, oftentimes without official assistance or relief materials. NPOs made lists of these places, communicated them to local governments and other organizations, and distributed relief materials.

Simultaneously, NPOs cautioned the Japanese public against rushing to the affected areas as volunteers or sending relief materials individually. There were several reasons for this. First, Volunteer Centers were difficult to set up where local governments lost their bases of operation in the tsunami. In Kesennuma City, for example, the tsunami damaged the social welfare council's building, limiting its capacity to coordinate volunteer efforts by destroying computers, fax machines, and documents. Second, immediately after the disaster it was difficult to secure volunteers' safety due to aftershocks, unstable debris, and in some places due to concerns related to the nuclear accident in Fukushima. Local communities could not provide places to sleep for the volunteers either. Furthermore, accessing the affected areas was difficult. Roads were cut off and there was an acute shortage of gasoline. These problems led to shortages of food and water in the affected areas, leaving them without enough supplies to support volunteers who arrived without their own provisions. For these reasons, NPOs discouraged the public from entering the affected areas as volunteers unless they could bring their own food, water and gasoline, and secure a place to stay. NPOs encouraged the public to donate money for the relief effort until local communities would be ready to accept volunteers. With this communication through the media and the Internet, NPOs coordinated public participation in the relief efforts. Towards the end of March, Volunteer Centers in devastated areas became ready to accept volunteers, and NPOs dispatched their first groups of volunteers.

Some NPOs prepare volunteers before they go to Tōhoku. They organize explanatory meetings to tell prospective volunteers what to expect in Tōhoku and how they should behave as volunteers (e.g. prioritizing local needs rather than the tasks they are interested in performing). NPOs also advise them about clothing and protective gear, and encourage them to purchase insurance for volunteer activities in case they become injured or damage someone's property. Some NPOs also organize "volunteer buses" which transport the volunteers, necessary provisions for the volunteers, and relief materials for the affected areas. These NPO-organized volunteers that come in groups are easier for local communities to accept, as administrative work is less than for the same number of individuals arriving separately. Volunteers have performed various tasks in Tōhoku, including cooking and serving food to local residents, distributing relief materials, caring for the elderly, teaching and playing with children, clearing mud and debris, and cleaning houses and public facilities. In March, 54,700 volunteers worked in Iwate, Miyagi and Fukushima combined. In April there were 148,200 volunteers, 168,800 in May, and 127,600 in June.[3] Due to the nature of the disaster and the aforementioned difficulties, the number of volunteers in Tōhoku has been much lower than following the Kobe Earthquake. In the first four months after the Tōhoku Earthquake 499,300 people volunteered in the three prefectures, while 1,305,000 people volunteered in the first four months after Kobe Earthquake.[4]

NPOs also created a national network to coordinate their relief efforts (*Higashinihon Daishinsai Shien Zenkoku Nettowāku*), and 141 organizations participated in the network's inaugural meeting in Tokyo on March 30. These NPOs, providing different services, share information about local needs through a mailing list in order to respond to them quickly and efficiently. In addition, organizations like the Nippon Foundation and the Central Community Chest of Japan (*Chūō Kyōdō Bokin Kai*) have created a new mechanism that channels donations to some of the NPOs. Those high profile organizations accept donations from the public not only for the victims of the disaster, but also for the NPOs working in the affected areas. Such low profile NPOs would otherwise have a difficult time gathering donations. This funding mechanism aims to support NPOs' long-term efforts, which are necessary given the large scale of the disaster. As of April 1, 2011, people donated about ¥759 million through various channels for NPO activities, in addition to ¥18 billion for distribution among the victims.

Various types of NPOs responded to the disaster in ways that corresponded with their expertise and mission, and to help similar groups in Tōhoku. For example, the Japanese Consumers' Cooperative Union has agreements with 46 prefectures and 310 local governments to help provide relief materials in case of natural disasters. These agreements allowed the Co-op to deliver relief swiftly in response to the disaster in Tōhoku. By April 1, 2011, the Co-op dispatched about 10,170,000 water and food deliveries in 852 trucks, involving 2,777 staff. The staff delivered relief supplies and helped clean the damaged Co-op shops, enabling local Co-ops to recover more quickly. Agricultural cooperatives (*nōkyō*) have responded to the disaster as well. The Central Union of Agricultural Cooperatives collected information from agricultural co-ops in different prefectures about damages caused by the nuclear accident, and has represented them in negotiations over compensation from the Tokyo Electric Power Company and the government. The agricultural co-ops seek compensation for reduced sales due to bans on selling nuclear-contaminated products and rumors of contamination, as well as for restrictions preventing many farmers from planting crops. Co-op affiliated banks are also providing interest-free loans to farmers who incurred damages from the disaster.

Fishing cooperatives in some of the devastated areas have also emerged as a coordinating mechanism among fishermen. In one co-op in Iwate prefecture, for example, members with undamaged and repairable ships agreed to transfer the ships' ownership to the co-op. Five hundred and eighty co-op members operating in four zones now share about 50 ships, and divide the profits equally within each zone. Meanwhile, the co-op plans to purchase new ships with governmental subsidies and no-interest loans repaid with deductions from members' earnings. The co-op will have ownership of the new ships and members will operate them jointly until the co-op has enough ships to distribute to all members. This scheme allows members who lost ships in the disaster to continue working and obtain new ships without taking out individual loans. Other fishing co-ops are also engaging in similar efforts, facilitating recovery through mutual assistance.

NPOs are engaged in a great variety of important activities that are not being performed by local governments. An NPO opened a telephone hotline for women to report cases of domestic violence, anticipating that there might be an upsurge in the wake of the disaster. Another NPO started a telephone counseling hotline in cooperation with psychiatrists, priests and lawyers, for people who lost loved ones in the disaster. Yet another telephone hotline is for children under the age of 18. Other NPOs are financially supporting children who lost their parents during the disaster. An NPO composed of car enthusiasts has provided cars and drivers for free to doctors volunteering in Tōhoku, so that they can conserve energy and focus on their medical activities. There are also NPOs who support people who have evacuated outside of Tōhoku. One of them has established a system in which a registered evacuee could receive support in finding jobs, receiving social welfare services and education, even when they move to different places. Other NPOs support foreigners by providing free interpreters, or help farmers by testing the levels of radioactive materials in their crops, livestock and soil. In sum, the disaster highlighted the strengths and breadth of Japan's civil society in responding to the needs of those affected by the disasters and supplementing relief and recovery work by government offices.

The small size of Japan's NPOs did create some difficulties in interacting with their (typically larger) international counterparts in relief operations. One non-Japanese executive of an American group with strong ties to Japanese nonprofits, noting that Mercy Corps reported raising US$1 billion for relief efforts, explained it this way in a personal communication with the authors (July 23, 2011):

> The small size and weakness of Japanese NPOs conflict with the large, professional, and rather wealthy international NGOs. Numerous international NGOs arrived with funding that was on a different scale than local NGO funding. This disparity in resources created a situation where the INGO wanted the Japanese NGOs to run the international NGO's program, and the [Japanese] NGOs could hardly resist being told what to do because of the funding. Some

Japanese NGOs feared they would be dominated/controlled, and also feared that the international NGO may be in Japan only a short time. As a result, some chose not to partner.

Comparing the response of Japan's civil society groups to the triple disasters to the response to the Kobe Earthquake shows the development and strengthening of Japan's NPOs. Although the Kobe Earthquake mobilized many individual volunteers, this time around organized NPOs were much more prepared and effective in transforming this goodwill into concrete actions addressing urgent tasks.

Conclusion

Overall, the disasters highlighted the great strengths and serious limitations of Japan's civil society. Community organizations like the NHAs and volunteer firefighting groups played important roles in disaster preparedness and response. High levels of social capital facilitated evacuation and local coordination after the disaster. Weakness in the advocacy sector, however, may have been a contributing factor in the nuclear disaster. How anti-nuclear activism evolves and the amount of influence it will have on Japan's nuclear energy policy will be an important topic of research.

How are the general characteristics of NPOs likely to shape their participation in the recovery efforts in Tōhoku? What are some of the challenges and opportunities that they face? First, given their small membership, NPOs will continue to rely on volunteers and donors from outside of their organizations. These non-members, through activities organized by NPOs, might wish to become members. If membership increases, the proportion of NPO income that comes from members' fees and donations might increase. Even if membership does not increase, reports in the media that highlight the dedicated work of NPOs in Tōhoku are likely to increase the legitimacy of NPOs and the sector as a whole.

Most NPOs have a small budget, and there is a challenge in gathering donations especially for those NPOs without name recognition among the public. Limited financial resources undermine the potential of NPOs' long-term efforts in Tōhoku. This lack of funds also complicates their effort to support Tōhoku residents' independence and leadership in recovery efforts by creating paid jobs. One key NPO task for the near future will be to encourage people from across Japan to donate money to their efforts (*shienkin*) by establishing mechanisms that facilitate giving. The decision by high profile foundations and organizations to accept donations on behalf of NPOs is helpful. NPOs with similar objectives across Japan (e.g. organizations for women, children, sports, environment, culture etc.) can help by establishing national networks (or rely on existing networks) to open websites to collect donations for specific NPO activities in Tōhoku. Channeling funds to NPOs that work in Tōhoku through such networks makes sense given the fact that most NPOs will not go to Tōhoku, but continue to work within their local communities across Japan. This effort will nurture expanded NPO linkages and might facilitate collective response to future disasters in other regions.

3/11 has underscored the need to create a more efficient donation system online that facilitates distribution of required materials in necessary amounts to specific receivers (individuals or neighborhoods), similar to wedding gift registries in the United States. There are already some non-NPO examples that have emerged in response to the recent disaster, such as the *Funbarō Higashi Nihon Shien* Project ("Let's Hang On!" Project to Support East Japan) and *Rakuten Tasukeai* (Rakuten Mutual Assistance). Such a mechanism will help mobilize citizens' resources more efficiently at minimal cost to NPOs, eliminate unnecessary materials that pile up in storage places, and free up NPO staff for other important tasks by delegating delivery of relief materials to donors and private companies. Tapping into the resources and expertise of private companies will also be important for resource-poor NPOs. Public campaigns encouraging companies to support NPOs as a part of their corporate social responsibility projects is necessary as CSR remains limited in Japan. Urging firms to retain existing jobs and create more employment in Tōhoku in order to restore livelihoods is as important to regional recovery as accepting volunteers and money from those companies.

Next, will the disaster and civil society's response change policy related to NPOs? It is possible that the state will help facilitate NPO efforts through legislative action, given that the state must continue to rely on NPOs and volunteers for recovery in Tōhoku. In fact, the state has already made some progress by improving the tax treatment of donations to NPOs in June 2011. A law in 2001 allowed individuals and corporations to obtain tax privileges for donating to NPOs with special certification from the National Tax Agency. These certified NPOs are a subcategory of organizations with legal status, to which individuals or corporations could make a contribution that is deductible from their income tax. Despite the law and its subsequent revisions, the number of certified organizations remains limited. According to the National Tax Agency, only 223 organizations have the special certification as of July 1, 2011. The eighth revision to the law that came into force on June 30, 2011 aims to increase the number of certified organizations by relaxing the requirements for certification. The reform also expanded tax privileges for donors by allowing them to choose between deduction from their income tax or from their total taxable amount. In addition, the law substantially relaxed the standards by which NPOs would qualify to receive tax-deductible contributions. The Ministry of Finance had strongly opposed such a move for years, despite arguments from advocates that such a bold stroke was needed to empower Japan's civil society. Passing by a unanimous vote in the Diet, these regulatory changes are arguably some of the most significant revisions to the civil society-operating environment since the 1998 NPO Law went into effect. Other types of state support for NPOs that would be helpful include measures to aid recovery and activities of NPOs from Tōhoku, so that local NPOs can assume more leadership. The state could also channel subsidies and other funding to NPOs, although this may be difficult given the massive cost of the overall recovery effort and in dealing with the nuclear accident.

Finally, will the disaster and civil society's response change the extent of their participation in policy-making? NPOs might increase their policy influence on the Tōhoku recovery and on ways to facilitate NPO activities. However, the state and the nuclear industry will probably seek to continue to limit access to policy-making by civil society organizations critical of nuclear energy. Nevertheless, the role of NPOs in policy-making could be strengthened by a sustained citizens' movement on renewable energy initiatives, given that three-quarters of Japanese now support phasing out nuclear energy and are now skeptical about government and industry assurances about the safety of nuclear power. Government fiscal retrenchment could also facilitate greater policy influence, or activity by civil society more generally, as the government seeks to cuts costs by outsourcing various functions and services. It may be too early to say, but we suspect that the triple disasters will open the door to increasing growth and influence for civil society organizations.

Notes

1   We would like to thank Yoshiaki Kubo for research assistance. We thank Simon Avenell for his comments on an earlier version of this chapter.
2   This is particularly true of NPOs. Under a broader definition of "civil society," Japan's civil society is also distinguished by the relative size and strength of business groups and, to a lesser extent, labor unions, compared to other civic elements (see Tsujinaka 2002). Our argument in this chapter holds whether one prefers a broader, more inclusive definition of civil society, or a narrow, more restrictive definition.
3   See the website of the National Social Welfare Council (*Zenkoku Shakai Fukushi Kyōgikai*) for the data: www.saigaivc.com.
4   These numbers are based on tallying monthly numbers of volunteers, and may include those that volunteered multiple times. For the number of volunteers in Kobe, see the newsletter of the Disaster Reduction and Human Renovation Institution (*Hito to Bōsai Mirai Sentā*), available at: www.dri.ne.jp/shiryo/pdf/news/021.pdf.

Bibliography

Aldrich, D.P. (2008) *Site Fights: Divisive Facilities and Civil Society in Japan and the West*, Ithaca, NY: Cornell University Press.
Avenell, S. (forthcoming) "Confronting Fearful Pollution: The Birth of Environmental Activism in Contemporary Japan," *Environmental History*.
Cabinet Office of Japan (2011) *Heisei 22nendo tokutei hieiri katsudō hōjin no jittai oyobi nintei tokutei hieiri katsudō hōjin seido no riyō jyōkyō ni kansuru chōsa*, online, available at: https://www.npo-homepage.go.jp/data/report29.html (accessed 15 June 2011).
Haddad, M.A. (2007) *Politics and Volunteering in Japan: A Global Perspective*, Cambridge: Cambridge University Press.
Kawato, Y. and Pekkanen, R. (2008) "Civil Society and Democracy: Reforming Nonprofit Organization Law," in S. Martin and G. Steel (eds.), *Democratic Reform in Japan: Assessing the Impact*, Boulder, CO: Lynne Rienner Publishers.
Kawato, Y., Pekkanen, R., and Yamamoto H. (2011) "State and Civil Society in Japan," in A. Gaunder (ed.), *The Routledge Handbook of Japanese Politics*, London: Routledge.

Ōnishi, N. and Fackler, M. (2011) "Japanese Officials Ignored or Concealed Dangers," *New York Times*, May 16.

Pekkanen, R. (2006) *Japan's Dual Civil Society: Members without Advocates*, Stanford, CA: Stanford University Press.

Pharr, S.J. (1990) *Losing Face: Status Politics in Japan*, Berkeley, CA: University of California Press.

Reimann, K.D. (2010) *The Rise of Japanese NGOs: Activism from Above*, London: Routledge.

Tsujinaka, Y. (2002) *Gendai Nihon No Shimin shakai: Rieki Dantai*, Tokyo: Bokutakusha.

Tsujinaka, Y. and Pekkanen, R. (2007) "Civil Society and Interest Groups in Contemporary Japan," *Pacific Affairs*, 80(3): 419–437.

Tsujinaka, Y., Pekkanen, R., and Yamamoto, H. (2009) *Jichikai Ni Okeru Rōkaru Gabanansu: Jichikai Zenkokuchōsa No Bunseki*, Tokyo: Bokutakusha.

5

SOCIAL MEDIA IN DISASTER JAPAN

David H. Slater, Nishimura Keiko and Love Kindstrand

Introduction

Almost everything thing we know now, and especially what we knew of the quake and tsunami in the hours and even days after the events, was significantly shaped by social media. In fact, the generation of information and images occurred at such a fast pace, that social media not only represented, but also directly mediated our experience of the quake more than any other natural disaster to date. If Vietnam was the first war fully experienced through television, 3/11 was the first natural disaster fully experienced through social media. This is the result of a number of factors, some a function of the way that technology use has developed in Japan, especially the fact of mobility of hand-held media, others due to the particular ways that the networks of people reacted in the time of crisis.

During the first crucial moments, individuals, texting and tweeting information, and uploading videos, gathered huge amounts of first-hand information, from the size and epicenter of the quake to the minutes until the oncoming waters were to arrive; the identification of dangerous and safe places, routes and contacts; those lost and those alive, and those looking for them. As events unfolded over the next days, the social media focus shifted to what we have called consolidator sites (blogs, Facebook and Mixi) where much of this dispersed information was brought together in ways that made it useful: the matching of available supplies and need; the location of open communication and travel networks to transport these supplies; the rise of various "people finders" and, then, the first reports of radiation leakage. In the next phase, we see dynamically generated "mashups" of web technologies becoming the central site for the generation of support through donations and the recruitment of volunteers as the relief efforts began. Finally, it was social media that allowed national and international anti-nuclear networks to mobilize some of the largest protests we have seen in Tokyo in decades. It is important to remember that social media has not displaced mass media, but it was images and information generated from individual users that were often the primary content on network print and TV media, and contributed alternative flows of non-official information to be disseminated. Many of these events, and our still evolving reaction to them, will probably change the way Japan, and the rest of the world, deals with natural and man-made disasters in the future.

This chapter lays out some of the ways that social media has affected our understanding of and participation in the 3/11 disaster. But we also keep in mind the converse: how the disasters have affected social media and, more generally, the mobilization of networks of people in new ways. Because social media rests on the initiative of the many (rather than the few, as in mass media), from solo texters and causal tweeters to alpha-bloggers and web engineers, part of our story is their new and different types of involvement in something we might call a digital civil sphere. While these linkages did not always get concrete aid and relief to the people who needed it most (and this failure is part of the story as well), it did create links between the people of Tōhoku and the rest of Japan (and sometimes the rest of the world), and new sorts of agentive connections among individuals, especially the young, through social networks that developed from very different goals and designs than disaster relief. Especially in the case of radiation, these same networks have become politicized as effective forms of civil engagement.

Working definition of social media

While "social media" is a contested term within a range of disciplines, we use it here to identify an inclusive category of social patterns of use of information technologies that are generally widely accessible, networked and usually web-based, often user generated and user designed. In terms of production, unlike traditional mass media, which is usually considered one-to-many (such as print, radio or TV) because it begins from a single centralized source and is unified in organization and managed in content, social media is usually many-to-many, generated through multiple paths and reproduced on multiple platforms (e.g. a collection of Twitter feeds reposted on a blog). Content is usually generated from multiple sources by a collective process that costs very little or nothing, usually decentralized in less hierarchical networks, characterized by multiple points of production, and transmitted at speeds that are often experienced as instantaneous, or a replica of "real time." The information circulated is "scalable," meaning that the content can be modified and edited, commented upon and reposted elsewhere; it is transparent, as participants are cognizant of each other's interactions and may critique, share or augment it; and it is mostly persistent, since it remains accessible for future reference. So, for example, a blog with continually updated information about the changing needs for shelter in a town would be an example of social media, both in terms of the information technology and the social practices. Finally, individual users of social media are usually both producers and consumers of the content, a dynamic captured in the term "pro-sumers," in ways that create interactional links, often producing strings of content and users, and even shared communities around this shared information.

If we define "social media" against the one-way transmission of information that characterized "mass media," then it has a long history, even in disaster situations, even in Japan. At the time of the Kobe Earthquake, only about 10 percent of the population had cell phone subscriptions, but we can easily see the importance of social media there. Even though the mass media infrastructure was far more intact than anything we saw in post-quake Tōhoku, a primary claim against the local and national authorities was about the insufficiency of relevant and accurate information circulated in ways that facilitated relief. In response, various methods of information circulation emerged, from ad hoc printing of fliers, sometimes called *mini-komi*, or 'micro-communication," to guerilla radio stations, such as FM YY, to other sorts of fact-to-face gathering, sometimes called *kuchi-komi* or "communication by mouth," that were specifically designed to contribute, share and consolidate information that was not available from the mass media. All of these would be examples of social media, albeit not in digital form. The coming together of citizens, often outside of the structures of local governments, produced networks of people that generated a wide range of civic organizations and memorialization sites to collect personal experiences (often hand-written and now housed in mini local libraries). Many nonprofit organizations (NPOs) point to the citizens' mobilization of information and aid after Kobe as a key moment in Japan's development of civil society, and the start of the NPO movement. Even today, we see this characteristic of much social media: its tactical rise as a way to compensate for, or move in alternative directions to, official statements and the mainstream media.

In Japan, both the technology and patterns of use of social media are distinctive in ways that had an enormous effect on the post-disaster response. Japan has a high penetration rate of Internet and Internet-ready mobile devices, mostly cell phones. According to a government white paper, the number of Internet users reached 94.62 million as of the end of 2010, with an Internet penetration rate of 78.2 percent (Ministry of Internal Affairs and Communications 2011). Moreover, the ratio of mobile network devices is quite high: computer connection is at about 87.2 percent, while the numbers of users who connect by mobile phones is 96.3 percent (although this figure shifts when we examine the distribution through age and geography) (Ministry of Internal Affairs and Communications 2010). This fact became important because it meant that a significant percentage of the population had, and were predisposed to use, technology in a broad range of times and places during the disaster and aftermath. The patterns of use of these information technologies are also distinctive. The primary use of mobile phones in Japan is text messaging, a format that can be re-transmitted to a website or blog, and is thus more likely to be far more widely circulated. And in fact, most users move among different types of social media, texting, posting, blogging almost every day.

Phase 1: first responses

In the minutes and hours just after the earthquake, many local cell phone transmitters malfunctioned: the network as a whole did not collapse, but the lines for calls were so clogged that only a small fraction of attempts got through. But the web packet connection on the same mobile phone when it connected to the Internet was often operative, allowing texting to continue at a relatively uninterrupted rate. Unable to reach their relatives or friends by telephone, cell phone users easily turned to social media. According to a study on post-quake Twitter usage, the number of posts (tweets) on the day of the quake increased to 1.8 times the average, reaching 330 million tweets in total (NEC Biglobe 2011). Similarly, in other SNS sites such as Mixi, users' posts increased up to three times the usual (eight times more during the hour after the quake) (IT Media 2011). The content also shifted in predictable ways. Usually 57 percent of the tweets are about entertainment, but on March 11, 72 percent of the tweets were quake-related (80 percent if transportation information is included) (NEC Biglobe 2011).

When the first major quake hit, a high volume of tweets from regular users focused on the immediate situation: "It's shaking" (*yureteru*)," and "It's an earthquake" (*Jishin da*). The National Research Institute for Earth Science and Disaster Prevention and Japan Meteorological Agency also began tweeting early alerts that were widely recirculated automatically by "bots" (i.e. automated posting robots). At 2:47 PM, an official NHK Twitter account posted: "There is an emergency earthquake alert. Miyagi, Iwate, Fukushima, Akita, Yamagata. Very big quake. Please be careful!!!! Please be careful!!!!!!" Provided with official information, individual users started to redistribute the alerts, and report real-time visual reports of their own disaster experience. In images that are now familiar to almost everyone who has followed the disaster, many individual users captured and posted the approach of the tsunami minutes before it struck. As the trains stopped in Tokyo, and millions were forced to consider other ways of reaching their homes, some of the first reports on Twitter concerned the availability of overnight shelters. A video of the explosion in a Chiba oil refinery was similarly reposted, triggering reports that "black rain will fall onto Tokyo."

Within days of the Japanese earthquake and tsunami, 64 percent of blog links, 32 percent of Twitter news links and the top 20 YouTube videos carried news and information about the crisis in Japan. Subsequently, patterns emerged where different sorts of social media generated different sorts of information flows. While micro-blogs and bulletin boards served to circulate information among those users who would not know each other, social networking platforms were used to confirm friends' and relatives' safety (Nikkei Business Publishing 2011). A survey shows that the perceptions of different social media platforms generated different ways to circulate different sorts of information. The popular perception was that Twitter was useful because it allowed for faster information gathering than did mass media. About one-third of those surveyed considered this necessary to compensate for the lack of reliable information provided by the mass media and/or the government. The format of social media reposts was especially useful because they were able to both circulate information and link to the source of this information (Tomioka 2011).

Nevertheless, this did not happen in the stricken areas. The prefectures that the disaster hit most severely also had the lowest mobile phone penetration rate. Tokyo is the highest in the mobile phone subscription rate, 133.9 percent (many individuals have more than one phone account), highest mobile Internet penetration rate, 63.3 percent, and second highest Internet penetration rate, 71.9 percent. In addition, the percentage of elderly in the Tōhoku region is larger than in other areas, and the penetration rate of mobile phones among those over 70 years old is 31.5 percent (Ministry of Internal Affairs and Communications 2011). Thus, geography and demographics limited the participation of those people who were most badly affected.

Cross-platform dissemination

While social media expands both the production and consumption of information, increases the types of content and the number of networks through which it moves, it still functions largely within the broad media environment dominated by newspapers, radio and especially, broadcast TV. And in fact, in times of crisis, more people usually turn to broadcast TV for what they deem "reliable" or "legitimate" information, that is, for "the news." Japan during the days after March 11 was no different. However, especially in a crisis situation in areas remote from the information hubs, network TV increasingly relied on social media for their own content, and in particular, user-generated footage and even reports about the events in the immediate aftermath.

In those first few hours, until the network stations had their own content, they repeatedly relied on amateur, user-generated information. In particular, there was a shot from the top of tower or building, showing the tsunami approaching the coast and sweeping onshore. Once the narrative potential of this scene was exhausted, it was often used as a background scene – unexplained or even uncommented on, just run on an endless loop. When another clip was submitted, it would also move through that same cycle. A very narrow range of images were played repeatedly as the announcers would pass on a wide variety of information – scientific measurements, damage reports, international reactions, etc. until the TV stations themselves were able to send reporters there. But this took quite a while and even once they had their own images, they often relied upon user-generated materials, both because of their vividness, but also because they were user-generated, a label which shed connotations of "amateur" and thus unreliable. Precisely because "ordinary" people were generating material while actually experiencing the events themselves, this material commanded a certain visceral veracity. By the second week, we see a shift in focus as each TV station was able to complement their own reports with other user-generated footage by canvassing the affected areas, much of it more horrific than what was shown during the first week. Two news announcers, both wearing earthquake helmets in the studio as they read the news, commented that it was remarkable that so many people thought to document this moment of sudden panic, and how lucky we are to have this authentic material. Upon reflection, it is probably less remarkable, given the shift to personal media that is so much part of the contemporary Japanese media-scape.

Of course, we also see interpenetration of platforms go the other way: social media circulating links to mainstream media reports, or taking whole stories and reposting them. On Twitter, especially, an arbitrary character limit imposed on every message makes it impossible to include longer stories or even quotes, and thus encourages linking of content from other sources and platforms. This is the creation of a media circuit from social media to mass media and back again, illustrating how users become the medium of information because information can only be passed through the conscious actions of individual users, forcing them also to play an editorial function in the selection of what constitutes important communication to whom it gets passed. One example familiar to many abroad during those first few weeks was the streaming of mainstream news programs through Ustream or Nico Nico Dōga. NHK allowed Nico Nico Dōga to rebroadcast NHK reports so as to reach a wider audience, but individual users also consistently redistributed mass media content, including TV broadcasts, using the same platforms. Nico Nico Dōga rebroadcasts also enable any viewer to submit persistent, anonymous commentary scrolling from right to left across most of the video screen, like subtitles. These on-screen commentaries thus run simultaneously to the NHK broadcast, and can be anything from "Those poor people" to "Tepco is lying ... again," but are a component part of any viewer's reading of the NHK news. (This makes for a significantly different degree of collective media experience than a YouTube comment in a separate comment box that is quickly pushed off the top screen as new comments are posted.) This sort of "mashup" of content flows through different information technologies and distribution platforms in ways that blur the lines between social and mainstream media, repositions individual users beyond the passive consumer position into selecting content from mainstream media for retransmissions and even editorializing about what counts as "the news."

Phase 2: the consolidation and use of information

The characteristics of social media – its diverse sources of information production, its wide range of flows, extensive distribution and differentiation of forms, enables it to play a particularly important role in early notifications about earthquakes and tsunami, in some ways surpassing that mainstream media. And yet, these very characteristics are also those that limit the utility of the information generated by social media in getting a full picture of the scope and dimensions of a disaster and, subsequently, in the coordination of relief efforts until these flows of information are brought together, consolidated, ordered and then made available to those who need them. In effect, the very diversity that was so important at the start of the disaster proves to be a liability as time goes on. In the days after 3/11, to a greater extent than in previous disasters and crisis situations (Haiti, Katrina, Egypt etc.), we see a second phase emerge where there were various efforts to bring the diverse sources of information generated from social media together in accessible, even searchable forms. Not surprisingly, these efforts were largely from within the technology platforms and the social networks that were active in the creation of information.

The most common example of aggregation sites are ones based on social networking sites (Facebook, Mixi etc.). Often, these were focused on a particular theme: radiation, foreign press, housing, etc. These are mostly clearing houses for information – repostings of newspaper stories or links to TV rebroadcasts, but also a place to post more personal accounts of earthquake and tsunami experiences. Many groups or pages were formed as action-oriented sites related to relief efforts around particular issues (such as saving pets or focusing on children) or geographically based ("Help Miyagi") or by a particular group of donors ("Shibuya High School Relief Page"). These provide information leading to the exchange of needs and relief, ranging from the very small scale ("I have some clothes to donate – can anyone who is going up north take them?" or "We need interpreters who can speak Chinese to help local workers") to the larger ("Second Harvest Japan is bringing five trucks to Ishinomaki and we need help unloading them."). Because they are embedded in the same social networks that individuals use for their personal sites, again, the lines are often blurred between these different functions. Sometimes, this leads to a greater integration of the relief efforts into people's online and offline presence.

Consolidation was much aided by an important feature of Twitter. Tweets can be tagged in such a way as to link them to others of a similar theme through a function called "hashtags," a label that users put on their own tweets to associate information with certain keywords. One early hashtag was "#j_j_helpme" – where the # marks the string as a hashtag, the first "j" is for Japan and the second one for *jishin*, "earthquake" in Japanese – a label that captures a representative mashup of language and symbolic codes that characterize much social media, especially in Japan. This hashtag spread among users and enabled them to mark messages of distress or disaster information, and to allow others involved in the relief effort to identify these needs. *Ushahidi* means "testimony" in Swahili and was developed as a crisis mapping platform in the aftermath of the post-election riots in Kenya in 2008 and was subsequently used in Haiti. It brings together simple texts ("A school in Sōma is running out food." Or, "There is a new shelter opening up; contact X for a place." Included were many of the above mentioned Tweets: "#j_j_helpme." These texts were coordinated with reports on the conditions of roads and other relevant logistical information within the platform of a visual map of the disaster area. This allowed everyone to directly and quickly identify areas of real need. It also allowed NPOs delivering food, blankets or other aid to check supply chains and to allow them to coordinate with other relief providers.

Probably the single most used consolidator site was Google's People Finder. While there were other, more local efforts, Google has the distinct advantage of offering a substantial preexisting database structure and the ability to allocate additional manpower to manage it (which they did). In a characteristically simple Google interface, there was one button to upload the name of any displaced person found and another to enter information for the person you are searching for. So for example, after an unsuccessful search someone could enter into the database: "I am looking for Shimada Keiko from Ishinomaki." They might then find this message: "I am Keiko Shimada and am ok in Kesennuma. Here are the names of the others with me here."). Google efforts offered database-level structuring and searching capabilities, and Google's ubiquity, in multiple languages, meant that they were making information available and useful to millions of people in real time, far beyond the scope of any government efforts, either local or national.

In addition to these large-scale, commercially based efforts, there were also many smaller and more local efforts, based on the same sort of platforms, that were generated by, and worked through, communities. One case in Tōhoku called "311help," worked through a local school that was relatively less affected by the natural disasters. The students would enter local shelters, document the needs of evacuees by going person to person, and then enter this information into their own database. This information would be posted where people would be able to ascertain the needs and match them with items that they either had in their house or could purchase new. Once someone committed to providing an item, they would mark it (so as to avoid duplication) and then send or drop it off to a local distribution site. This site was adopted by different groups, such as parent-teacher association groups at Tokyo schools, allowing them to organize their own relief efforts in a way that they knew would be effective. This example points to the social part of social media – the ways that information technology was used by users on both ends (those in need and those who provided relief) to address the disaster effort through collective efforts in ways that actually contributed to community building in this time of distress.

Ironically, the efficacy of social media in the relief effort was, if not made possible, at least facilitated by the *lack* of existing local governmental or technological infrastructure in the disaster-affected areas. Especially in the early days and weeks, individual citizens' groups and NPOs were able to establish reliable flows of information that led directly to highly effective, decentralized distribution of needed goods and services. Once the local governmental offices resumed functioning and official relief efforts were ramped up, they became gatekeepers for distribution, sometimes with mixed results due to disorganization and the unprecedented scale of the problems confronting officials who were overstretched and in some cases unprepared for the relief efforts.

As of July 1, many households have still not accessed regular governmental relief channels, and there are some instances where NPO relief organizations gathered information about needs and the goods to meet those needs, but were not being allowed to deliver them. Some NPOs were stymied, their information flows rendered useless, their supplies wasted. Others continued to deliver goods and services directly to locals in the area, outside of any governmental channels, using the information they had already been collecting. While in one sense, this is a viable work-around enabled by information collected by social media, on the other hand, it has also led to conflicts over jurisdiction and at times, an uneven distribution of aid.

Rallying support

The consolidation of information into key sites also proved important in the spread of images and information that was central to raising donations and the recruitment of volunteers. Social media has long been acknowledged as one key in raising funds for relief. Often cited examples are the Red Cross using commercial slots during the Superbowl that allowed viewers to text in their donation during half-time. In Japan, the use of social media by the business community is not as developed yet, although some of the information technologies do exist. The Japanese Red Cross, as of April 28, 2011, raised ¥166 billion (approximately US$ 2 billion), but much of this is generated from the purchase of very expensive TV slots. In ways that are now taken for granted, the first step to donating is almost always to stop on a homepage that gives fuller information, links to the related projects and easy ways to donate and, significantly, lots of visual illustration of need. In talking with one strategist for a large relief organization, she noted that "The visual aspect of the web enables it to communicate urgency and vividness – people want to have some idea of where their money is going. We cannot do that with mailings or billboards without being grotesque." While a simple (or static) website would not fully fall under our definition of many-to-many, even there, on a new generation of websites, more interactive features characteristic of social media are appearing. The same strategist noted that, "the ability of the user to actively pick and choose desired information from our site – to click on this or that according to their interest; as if they are doing research themselves. This also gets people involved." And gets them to donate. This is exactly the agentive interaction that is the key characteristic of social media.

Due to their low cost and user-to-user facility, social media also allows for more complex efforts by a wider range of players. While social media increases the total amounts of monies that are gathered, especially by the larger relief agencies, it has also generated a huge influx of smaller organizations – often with nothing more than a Twitter account or a simple website – to appeal for help and to gather volunteers on an event-basis (a fund-raising party, a weekend relief group, etc.). Often their sites are employing mashups (cross-platform sites): so on a single page, there is static content that provides information, does not change and is not interactional. But then, there are also links to Facebook or Mixi pages where more elaborate dialogues can occur, Twitter feeds to give up to the minute information to active members and news feeds linking to national and international media, in addition to regular email and PayPal donation buttons. Digital content can always be reposted here at these sites, and thus, the promotion of causes, fundraising or recruitment of volunteers can be infinitely redistributed, going "virtual" "ustreamed" or "tweetcasted," transcribed and commented upon in "realtime" and put back up on the website. The flows of information become wide and deep, far more complex than what mass media could offer.

Negative effects

The same characteristics of social media that made it such a hugely effective set of technologies, networks and practices for the generation, distribution and consolidation of information also cause effects counterproductive to the dissemination of accurate information about relief efforts. Another problematic feature is the sheer volume of information being circulated at high speeds. When each individual becomes a node in the network through which some part of this information passes, in times of crisis, the normally manageable flow of information quickly threatens to lead to overload. A number of different responses were observed. One reaction was a limiting of one's activity within the realm of social media, rather than acting on this information in ways that bring the individual out of the digital realm. While acknowledging that the distribution of information is, in some sense, meaningful activity in and of itself, it was often used as a replacement for other sorts of more concrete forms of contribution (of money, volunteering time, etc.). Reposting images of others shoveling mud in Ishinomaki from Tokyo is not the same as shoveling the mud yourself. Post-3/11 patterns are partly consistent with broader critiques of digital participation in politics not necessarily leading to off-line activism.

Other effects of social media are more psychological. With literally thousands of pieces of information flowing through a single user each day, the effects can be quite disorienting. Panic, emotional shutdown and erratic behavior are all well-known responses to this sort of information overload. The effect of media on the users in fact became a popular topic on blogs and tweets. They commented on the excitement of the shared experience of the earthquake, and how it spread throughout social media networks, often referred to as a *shinsai hai* (disaster high). An amplified feeling of excitement and exhaustion with the onslaught of information overload could trigger trauma or PTSD, according to psychiatrist Kayama Rika. Social media evangelists, such as Sasaki Toshinao suggested to his Twitter followers to turn off TV and not to use the Internet in order to stay calm. But this is hard to do in a mediated context where individual users are expected to read, select, repost, comment – respond to in some way – the information that comes from their peers and friends as a way to maintain their place within that network. The pressure brings them more into the center of a chaotic flux, compounding the disorienting effects of a crisis situation. The diversity of channels and interpersonal aspect of social media lead to more posts to raise awareness, with admonitions to "stay calm" and encouragement to "live regular life if you can." That is, through social media, people are acknowledging the need to have some sort of life that is *not* about the disaster. Calls to social media users to withdraw from the media, or to monitor, limit and even censor their own online participation were widely circulated in social media sites.

But it not only the volume of media flow that is a problem. Social media enables multiple channels of information that are often conflicting, hysterical and incorrect. The unregulated nature of social media leads to false information spreading much faster and wider than with print media, especially among the increasing number of those who use it as their primary source of information. This is true of any crisis in ways that lead to mistakes or poor judgment, but when a medium is structured around the expectation of instantaneous diffusion, this danger seems compounded (Acar and Muraki 2011). While the general consensus among users is that they are critical evaluators of the validity of different types of information, in the process of reposting, often this information is de- and re-contextualized in ways that obscure its source, a necessary piece of information in how it is evaluated and interpreted. When incomplete or inaccurate reports of available shelter locations were recirculated, evidently without confirmation, complaints from users were immediately posted. These complaints did generate a sort of internal critique, and even disciplined moments of critical reflection on the characteristics of the communication tools and their use, prompting many to look for ways to find more responsible ways of utilizing the technology. Nevertheless, misinformation disseminated over social media was clearly a problem.

One question is: what do we do with the indeterminacy of information? In a move with larger implications, the Ministry of Public Management, Home Affairs, Posts and Telecommunications issued takedown requests to a number of Internet service providers and media companies, with the briefest explanation that the information could not be confirmed and might lead to misunderstanding. (On April 1, an amendment to the penal code was proposed in the Diet that would allow for much increased control over Internet content. It was passed on June 17.) Within various social media groups, this move was seen immediately as a clear case of unjustified censorship of certain information that was critical of the state's effort to deal with the situation and control the information dissemination about these efforts. At this point, the issue of misinformation becomes political, in a wider sense. The definition and control of information as accurate and/or suitable for public consumption was one of the first cases that was recognized as part of the emerging politicization of crisis, a struggle that often played out through social media.

Phase 3: politicization of/by social media

At what point does the engagement in alternative forms of communication become a political act itself? Social media as a collaborative process of controlled information carries with it a political potential that mass media does not. But more than that, it is integrated into a set of social networks that by their very nature integrate into alternative public spheres; alternatives politicized in a variety of ways and by a wide range of social actors in post-3/11 Japan. In times of crisis, there is often a depoliticizing effect, a move towards retrenchment, to pull together in "sacrifice for the nation," sometimes at the behest of the state. As seen above, one way that this is executed today is through the attempt to limit social media. We saw this in ways that were not state-sponsored and in fact supported by social media – the rapid proliferation of "Pray for Japan" or *Ganbare Nippon* ("Stay strong Japan") slogans, adopted as "badges" of allegiance attached to personal profile images on social networks. But an equally important current ran in the opposite direction: the coalescence of a movement critical of the state, embedded in a diffuse mobilization of information, resources and people with the goal of autonomous earthquake and tsunami relief.

Sometimes these efforts are the result of small groups of individuals and communities to look out for their own welfare when they think the state is not taking sufficient measures to support and protect them. One example that can be directly attributed to the distrust of official information is the collection of radiation readings through "crowdsourcing." (Crowdsourcing is the collection and consolidation of information through many diffuse sources, a "crowd," rather than a single agent.) In response to bureaucratic reluctance to publicize radiation monitoring results, members of a Tokyo hacker collective built Internet-connected Geiger counters and drove along the outer perimeters of the evacuation zone, plotting their findings to a free map service (and even put clips of their trip on YouTube). Local citizens' groups followed suit and procured Geiger counters to take their own measurements to be posted on shared sites. The combined efforts of these and similar initiatives revealed that radiation had spread in uneven patterns, and beyond the circular 20 km evacuation zone. Here, grass-roots initiatives via social media quickly reached mainstream public discourse, for example when Diet members from the Japan Communist Party (JCP) confronted Prime Minister Kan with independently gathered radiation readings.

Other times, social media initiatives are more obviously an act of critique and protest. Perhaps the most high profile actor, at least in the early stages of the politicization of crisis, was Sakurai Katsunobu, Mayor of Minamisōma City, a city located close to Fukushima's nuclear plants. Thirteen days after the disaster, he appeared in a YouTube video that went viral with more than 400,000 views in the first month, making a direct appeal for aid to his city, which he claimed had not received sufficient relief from the Japanese government to even feed his citizens. The decision to make a direct appeal for aid and post it on the Internet is a remarkable step for any mayor, in Japan or out. But Sakurai went out of his way to point out the inadequacy of information from TEPCO and the government: "it's worse outside the 20 km zone", stated Sakurai in one interview, effectively declaring the government's evacuation strategy ineffectual. While Sakurai's decision to broadcast via YouTube is significant, his critique also explicitly targeted traditional media outlets, whose reporters "[simply] gather information over the phone. If they do not step in this area and get the direct information, they could not know or tell what is really the situation with these people". Sakurai's hunched, overall-clad figure, dourly staring into the camera (not at all the image of the tech-savvy blogger) became a symbol of the ineptitude of national government relief measures and a supine, co-opted media. Not without irony, Sakurai was quickly named one of the 100 most influential people in the world by *Time* magazine, certainly one of the highest profile instruments of mass media.

Once the struggle over information and its control is taken out of the context of community protection (as in the two above examples), which provide some degree of "cover," efforts become more explicitly political. While we have discussed many examples of everyday engagement through social media, there are also some high-profile social leaders who politicized this information, who due to the linkages and quick flow of information, sometimes exerted more influence than mass media spokespersons in shaping perceptions and framing stories. Alpha-bloggers with millions of followers, such as Softbank CEO Son Masayoshi, gave an explicit critique of the government response. Perhaps even more important were a handful of emboldened journalists challenging the information monopoly of exclusionary and co-opted "journalist clubs," sometimes called *kisha* clubs (cf. Freeman 2000), as well as mainstream media's default policy to quote verbatim from corporate press releases (including TEPCO's). From the very early phases, social media was completely integrated into the workflow of journalists like Iwakami Yasumi, who was not only in constant conversation with online readers, but insisted on broadcasting press conferences on Ustream, not standard practice in Japan. Such efforts were instrumental in challenging and exposing secretive mass media practices and sharing the results with large online readerships.

Accounts of foreign experts and relief workers challenging official narratives were collaboratively translated and distributed online and often found their way back into mainstream media. On March 22, France's nuclear safety institute IRSN started to release online bulletins in Japanese. There is some evidence that the social media activities of these rogue journalists/translators emboldened and empowered other reporters to pose more challenging questions to TEPCO and NISA officials, but the overwhelming majority of the mainstream media remained passive, reflecting longstanding patterns of deference and reticence about controversial issues, especially when powerful institutions are involved.

Of course, the revealing of relevant data through social media sources, some of which was directly related to safety information, was a public service. Much of the initial leakage of stories on radiation dangers appeared on social media, or it was social media sites that brought together a range of revealing data, some of which was then picked up by the mainstream mass media. But these efforts were also significant for stoking citizens' growing skepticism of both the state and official media outlets, seen to be either unwilling to share relevant information or incompetent in gathering and analyzing it.

Emerging alternative publics through protest

Initially, social media in Japan, as in other countries, grew and evolved largely as sites of communication and expression that went outside of more established institutions (family, school and work). After 3/11, the fast mobilization of these new networks for very different uses – the generation and distribution of information about the disaster – contributed to the recovery and relief efforts in important ways. The articulation and mobilization of anti-nuclear sentiment that lead directly to the organization of protest thus is a next step in the shift in social media usage patterns in post-3/11 Japan. Had these networks not already been made wider and denser through these earlier stages, it is difficult to imagine them subsequently serving as productive platforms for the politics of protest at is now the case.

Prior to the quake and tsunami, the anti-nuclear movement in Japan was relatively peripheral, but as the deeply engrained notion of nuclear power as "safe" unraveled, the diffuse fear of and opposition to nuclear energy increased exponentially. The urgency felt around the nuclear situation in particular provoked spontaneous mobilization in new and constantly changing network configurations. The thousands marching against nuclear power in Tokyo on April 10, June 7 and July 11 should therefore be seen not only as a result of mobilization through already existing networks, but also driven by a myriad of micro-interactions of the sort described above. Despite garnering little attention from the domestic mass media, the demonstrations were successfully promoted almost exclusively through social media, both in Japan and internationally. For the organizers – a small group in Western Tokyo known as *Shirōto no Ran* ("The Amateur's Riot") – Twitter accounts, event-specific hashtags and mashups were instrumental in disseminating information and gathering large-scale support for these events.

While, certainly, the activist left had already integrated information technology into their own efforts (their use during the Hokkaido G8 in 2008 was certainly significant), this was likely the first time in Japan that platforms for expressing dissent and organizing protest developed so fully within the domain of social media. Social media enabled collaboration between a wide range of different groups, giving them effective tools to disseminate their agenda and mobilize support. The ability to "cross-post" by tagging and retagging information allowed groups with little previous connection to work together in ways that did not require intensive and often problematic institutional and face-to-face contact. While it is, of course, too early to tell, it does seem that in a country where alliances across factions (political parties, labor unions and relief NPOs) is often problematic, especially among groups with similar ideologies, the use of social media as a platform to link these in common cause, at least around a particular event, might become a more significant feature of alternative politics and the creation of new civil societies, online and offline.

Conclusion

The diffuse and mobile information technology of social media provided immediate and vivid images of the worst disaster in the postwar period to the rest of Japan and the world. The consolidation of this information has been used in important ways by the relief effort to identify need and match it to available resources, as well as generate new resources through donations and volunteer efforts. It has been a relevant source of information flows that are often outside of those dominated by the state and mass media. Participation in this post-3/11 social media has engaged a generation of young people who were often represented as disaffected and politically apathetic in a political process that is at once at the heart of a national recovery effort, as well as part of the critically engaged participatory politics that few would have considered before. Through the networks that have been developed amid this crisis, alternative political movements are gaining ground in ways that have allowed the specific issue of radiation to be a rallying cry for a larger and more developed social and political critique. Events are still unfolding, but already we have to ask questions about sustainability. As Twitter feeds revert back to mostly tweets about entertainment, homepages devoted to relief are less frequently checked, and donations and volunteer rates decline, will activists be able to keep these issues in the public mind? Will social media, so vital in the early stages of this crisis response, still play a socially effective and politically productive role in post-3/11 Japan? It is tempting to speculate that there is no turning back, that the 3/11 social media revolution has aroused and awakened so many to the possibilities, but in this many-to-many world, it all depends on the flow of information, the management of these networks, and people's ability and willingness to reach out through these online networks to affect social change.

Acknowledgements

The authors would like to thank the members of the Social Media in Disaster Japan group for their very useful insights, in particular Mizukoshi Shin, Jonathan Lewis and Joo-Young Jung.

References

Acar, A. and Muraki Y. (2011) "Twitter for Crisis Communication: Lessons Learnt from Japan's Tsunami Disaster," *International Journal of Web Based Communities* (in press).

Freeman, L.A. (2000) *Closing the Shop: Information Cartels and Japan's Mass Media*, Princeton, NJ: Princeton University Press.

IT Media (2011) *Mixi Increase in both Sales and Profit during March 2011*, online, available at: http://bizmakoto.jp/makoto/articles/1105/10/news098.html (viewed 11 July, 2011).

Ministry of Internal Affairs and Communications (2010) *White Paper of Information and Communications in Japan*, online, available at: www.soumu.go.jp/johotsusintokei/whitepaper/ja/h22/pdf/index.html (viewed July 11, 2011).

Ministry of Internal Affairs and Communications (2011) *Result of Survey on Trend of Communication Uses*, online, available at: www.soumu.go.jp/main_content/000114508.pdf (viewed July 7, 2011).

NEC Biglobe (2011) *On Usage of Twitter during Great East Japan Earthquake: From Entertainment Tool to Collaborative Media*, online, available at: http://tr.twipple.jp/info/bunseki/20110427.html (viewed July 11, 2011).

Nikkei Business Publishing (2011) *Thanks to Twitter we Didn't Panic in the Smoke": Disaster and SNS through 550 Messages*, online, available at: http://trendy.nikkeibp.co.jp/article/pickup/20110427/1035385/?ST=life&P=4 (viewed July 11, 2011).

Tomioka, A. (2011) *Differentiating the Use between SNS and Twitter: On the Usage of Social Media among Companies after the Disaster*, IID Inc., online, available at: www.rbbtoday.com/article/2011/04/28/76606.html (viewed July 11, 2011).

6

MARCH 11, 2011 ONLINE

Comparing Japanese newspaper websites and international news websites

Leslie M. Tkach-Kawasaki

Introduction

Within minutes of the Tōhoku Earthquake that occurred at 14:46 on March 11, 2011, news spread around the world, aided by international news agencies and the Internet. Within an hour, the initial disaster was compounded by an ensuing tsunami with horrifying images and videos of great masses of water swiftly overtaking buildings, homes, and businesses located along Japan's northeastern coast. While many people in the Kantō area of Japan were still experiencing aftershocks, within 24 hours reports spread of damage to the Fukushima Daiichi nuclear power facilities located on the coast of Fukushima prefecture. The result was that in the weeks that followed, the powerful shock of the combined disasters of the earthquake, tsunami, and nuclear situation metamorphosed into "Fukushima." Yet this simple one-word description belied the ongoing aftermath of the "triple disasters" that would continue to dominate news reporting in Japan and the rest of the world in the following weeks and months as the death toll from the quake mounted to more than 20,000 people.

In the immediate aftermath, many people in Japan and elsewhere turned to televised news reports, radio broadcasts, and the Internet for up-to-date information. Within and beyond Japan, the Internet in particular played a critical role in information provision and communications. The use of social media functions such as Twitter and Facebook allowed people in Japan to exchange information on the safety of family members and friends, as well as provide updates on transportation services (a critical point as many transportation services were either cancelled or delayed in the first 72 hours following the earthquake). In the days that followed, video footage of shaking buildings and the tsunami were immortalized on YouTube, and overseas audiences turned to websites such as CNN to obtain up-to-date information on the unfolding events in Japan. According to the Pew

Research Center for the People and the Press, close to 60 percent of the American public indicated that they were closely following the events in Japan during the period between March 24 and 27, 2011 (Pew Research Center for the People and the Press 2011).

The dizzying amount of information, images, and video that were available through domestic and international news agencies continued in the weeks immediately following these disastrous events in Japan. In addition to domestic television and radio broadcasting, newspapers and their accompanying websites played major roles in reporting on the "triple disasters" and disseminating information and images concerning the aftermath of the earthquake and tsunami, as well as the unfolding situation at the Fukushima nuclear power plant. Domestic news reports focused on the loss of life, scarce resources, growing numbers of evacuees fleeing to temporary lodgings in public buildings, and desperate battles to cool Fukushima's nuclear reactors. Overseas, along with reports praising the "calmness" and "dignity" of the Japanese people, the battles to contain the nuclear situation invited comparisons to Chernobyl and Three-Mile Island.

This apparent dichotomy in the range of information available both domestically in Japan and overseas through news websites gave rise to questions as to whether there were actual differences between international and Japanese news coverage of the earthquake, tsunami, and the nuclear plant accident on the Internet, particularly through established Internet news channels. Were domestic news sources in Japan focusing too much on the disasters' initial events at the expense of providing information on the nuclear situation to the public? Were overseas news agencies being alarmist in their concentration on the nuclear accident?

These initial queries provided the rationale for an exploratory research project focusing on a content analysis of the comparative differences among Japanese newspaper websites and overseas news agency websites. The guiding research questions for this project are:

1. How prevalent was online coverage of the "triple disaster" compared to regular news coverage among Japanese newspaper websites and international news organization websites?
2. What visual means and participatory media channels were used on the websites to chronicle the disasters and contribute to the websites, respectively?
3. What types of general and detailed information were available on these websites with regard to the earthquake, tsunami, nuclear disaster, lifeline information, and aid or relief?

To answer these questions, a content analysis project was initiated to delve more deeply into the chronological and content patterns of news coverage concerning the "triple disaster" in Japanese domestic newspaper websites (the *Asahi*, *Mainichi*, and *Yomiuri* newspapers) and international news websites (*CNN International* and *CNN US*). Using the author's personal collection of the top pages of the *Asahi*, the *Yomiuri*, *CNN International*, and *CNN US*, as well as the website content archived through the Archive-It Project for the *Mainichi* newspaper's online edition,[1] three days in March 2011 (March 17, 24, and 31) were selected for the content analysis. News story headline items and links found on the top pages of these websites were coded and compared in terms of their overall coverage of the disasters vis-à-vis other news items, as well as special sections within those websites directly pertaining to the earthquake, tsunami, nuclear disaster, lifeline information, and aid or relief.

Following a brief review of the literature concerning comparisons of online news coverage concerning major events, as well as website content analysis, an overview of the websites and the method employed in this research project outlines the project in more detail. The results section demonstrates that there were differences in the overall news coverage of the disaster, as well as variations in the emphasis of certain detailed aspects of the disaster. The overall differences and variations are then situated within the broader context of the unfolding news coverage particularly concerning the Fukushima nuclear power plant in the discussion and conclusion section of this chapter.

Relevant literature

Previous studies in website content analysis of online news provide the theoretical background for this research project. With regard to different audience interpretations of the event or events portrayed in online news websites, comparison studies of online news websites (Abdul-Mageed and Herring 2008) suggest that the content and coverage of online news websites may construct different understandings of the events portrayed. In addition, Schwalbe (2006) notes that the framing of events, particularly over a period of time, tends to influence the narrative concerning those events and shape collective memories. Dimitrova and Neznanski's study of the framing of the 2003 Iraq war (2006) finds distinct differences between American and international online newspapers in terms of displays of photographs and interactive elements. Wu (2007) suggests that economic proximity and relations between countries may affect how events are portrayed in the media in general. In reference in particular to the social functions of the Internet during times of national disasters, Barak (2010) explores the possibilities of social functions including the diffusion of reliable relevant information, shared information, the maintenance of personal communication, and the location of missing people.

Owing to perhaps language barriers and difficulties in obtaining access to archived websites (or performing content analysis research on "live" websites), no prior research was found that focused directly on the differences among Japanese newspaper websites and international news websites. In addition, owing to the magnitude of the impact of the March 11 events on the Japanese nation, as well as the growing importance of online news in terms of the rapid dissemination of information concerning events and up-to-date information, this exploratory research project aims at analyzing the nature of online news reporting in Japan during this critical time in Japan's modern history.

Method

The content analysis project that was devised in order to respond to the overall query as to whether there were differences in the coverage of the disaster among Japanese newspaper websites and international websites focused on the Japanese-language top pages of the *Asahi* (asahi.com), the *Mainichi* (mainichi.jp), and the *Yomiuri* (www.yomiuri.co.jp) newspapers. The two international websites selected were CNN's International website (edition.cnn.com) and CNN's US website (us. cnn.com). The top pages of the five websites were archived daily for a two-week period commencing March 17, and the March 17, March 24, and March 31 versions of all websites were selected for content analysis coding, for a total of 15 websites. Upon undertaking the content analysis coding for this project, a more complete version was used for the content analysis coding of the Mainichi's website available through the Japan Earthquake public collection on the Archive-it website (see Note 1).

In undertaking the content analysis coding of the websites, three main categories of features and links on the top pages of the websites were identified. The first main category was comprised of top-page news items (links to news stories within the website), the graphics (photographs, videos, and illustrations or diagrams), and the availability of special sections (*tokushū*) related to the disasters. The second identified category was the use of Twitter, Facebook, and other participatory features available on the websites. The third category broadly focused on news-item links to subcategories relating to the earthquake/tsunami, the nuclear plant situation, lifeline-related information, and relief efforts. These subcategories were further broken down into topics including loss of life/missing persons, damage, human interest, radiation, scientific/technical information, the economy and business, politics, evacuation and safety, scheduled power outages (*teiden*), donations, and volunteer activities. In performing the content analysis coding, advertising and standard navigation links within the websites (not specific to information regarding the disasters) were excluded from the analysis.

Results

Overviews of the websites

Before discussing the results of the website content analysis in more detail, a brief description of the general approaches of the websites towards news concerning the disasters in Japan provides an insight into the construction of the websites and the news contained within. While the content of the newspaper websites and the international news websites was refreshed and changed constantly, the overall construction of the websites was remarkably similar throughout March 2011.

All three of the websites of the major Japanese national daily newspapers that were used for this project provided extensive coverage of the disasters that occurred on March 11, 2011 by providing special sections related to various aspects of the disasters, photographs on the top page and photograph collections, and videos. In terms of overall layout, each website had a three-column layout with links to stories concerning the disasters appearing in each column.

In the *Asahi* newspaper's online website, the right-hand column included photographs and videos (as well as collections of these), rankings for popular news items, and news items in related sites; the middle column contained the major news stories of the day with special sections concerning scheduled power outages, updated information on the nuclear plant situation, the earthquake and tsunami, and lifeline information. Throughout the course of this project, disaster-related stories consistently dominated the five-item list of rankings. The middle section also included links to photographs and videos. The right-hand column contained links related to these special sections, a link to a page with information about searching for survivors and/or missing persons, a display of "tweets" received through Twitter, and further links to photo galleries. The *Mainichi*'s website followed a similar format, but also included tabs in the middle section referring to general news topics, disaster safety information, updates on the nuclear plant situation, disaster relief and aid, as well as editorials and columns. The left-hand column of the *Yomiuri*'s website featured photographs, an updated table of the human toll of the disasters, and video links with the middle section also containing the main news stories of the day as well as special sections including lifeline information, medical information, and donations/volunteer information. The right-hand column contained notable news items of the week, and in the top-ten news story ranking on the *Yomiuri*'s website, disaster-related news stories occupied ten, six, and seven spots on March 17, 24, and 31, respectively.

Information concerning the earthquake/tsunami disaster and the nuclear situation also dominated the CNN websites, particularly on March 17 and 24. On these two days, both websites had special sections in their right-hand columns on the "Disaster in Japan" or the "Crisis in Japan." On the March 17 version of the *CNN International* website, this section provided in-depth information concerning various aspects of the disaster, including links to CNN's Live blog, a live link to Japanese television broadcasts, travel information, maps, a photograph collection, before-and-after photographs of the geographical area of the disaster, and a timeline. This section also included a link ("How to help") to a lengthy article focusing on how to contribute to aid and relief activities from overseas. Links to photographs and video reports concerning the situation in Japan also figured prominently in the middle section of the website as well as among the "Editor's Choice" listing on these websites on these two days.

Participatory media and other means for viewers to interact with or utilize the websites were also prevalent among the five websites reviewed. All websites had Twitter feeds, with the *Asahi* and the *Yomiuri* websites posting portions on the top pages of their websites and the *Mainichi* including a link to its "RT page" containing Twitter-related information. The Japanese websites also had RSS news feeds for viewers to subscribe to updated news reports, and three websites (*Asahi*, *CNN International*, and *CNN US*) also had Facebook pages. Viewers of the websites could also participate directly with the website in creating content by submitting comments, opinions, or stories. Reader blogs were available on the *Asahi* and the *Yomiuri* websites, with the latter having a *hatsugen komachi* (literally translated as "remarks from the street") featuring a mediated blog space for reader opinions concerning the disaster, among other topics. The two CNN websites also allowed for comments (through the "iReport" or citizen journalism section available on both websites), recommendations, and retweets of individual news stories. The *Asahi* and the *Mainichi* websites also had links to search functions for viewers to search for missing, deceased, or evacuated persons; the former utilizing its own search function and lists provided by regional police departments, and the latter with a link to Google's "People Finder" function.

Disaster-related coverage

To address the question regarding the prominence of disaster-related coverage on the websites, Table 6.1 shows the total number of all links to articles and the total number of links to disaster-related articles on the top pages of the five websites for the three dates in March 2011.

TABLE 6.1 Total links to general news and disasters headlines on website top pages

Website	Total news-item links on top page (N)			Disaster-related news-item links on top page (N) (%)		
	March 17	March 24	March 31	March 17	March 24	March 31
Asahi	91	92	91	73 (80.2)	73 (79.3)	64 (70.3)
Mainichi	104	105	104	65 (62.5)	56 (53.3)	48 (46.2)
Yomiuri	95	104	103	86 (90.5)	61 (58.7)	66 (64.1)
CNN Int'l	99	99	102	25 (25.3)	16 (16.2)	9 (8.8)
CNN US	130	134	135	17 (13.1)	20 (14.9)	7 (5.2)

Except for the *Mainichi* on March 31, more than 50 percent of the news reports on the reviewed websites for each of the selected three days covered disaster-related news and events or provided information concerning the disaster. While it could be expected that overall coverage of the disaster would decrease over time as a percentage of total news stories, the *Yomiuri*'s coverage fluctuated over the three days. The figures for disaster-related coverage on both CNN websites demonstrate that there was a great deal of international attention paid to the disaster as well. Disaster-related news was prominently featured particularly on the *CNN International* website, and even three weeks after the disaster, still accounted for more than 10 percent of the news stories posted on the website.

As visual effects such as photographs, videos, and figures are also an important feature on news websites, Table 6.2 shows the number of photographs, videos, and graphics relating to disaster coverage on the top pages of the websites for the three days.

TABLE 6.2 Disaster-related photographs, videos, and graphics on website top pages (as a percentage of total graphics on top pages)

Website	Date		
	No. of disaster-related graphics (% of total graphics)		
	March 17	March 24	March 31
Asahi	8 (40)	22 (100)	16 (72.7)
Mainichi	17 (45.9)	19 (48.7)	17 (45.9)
Yomiuri	6 (60)	15 (100)	15 (100)
CNN Int'l	9 (100)	5 (26.3)	0 (0)
CNN US	7 (63.6)	10 (76.9)	0 (0)

Photograph collections of earthquake and tsunami damage featured prominently on the Japanese newspaper websites, particularly on March 24 and 31. In fact, among the three newspaper websites, on these two days, the *Asahi* website had at least five collections of photographs pertaining to the disaster overall. In addition to photographs and videos, the *Mainichi* website included graphics of the scheduled power outages throughout the three days, and the *Yomiuri* website also had a small graphic showing the current power consumption estimated by the Tokyo Electric Power Company (TEPCO). On the contrary, the visual displays on CNN's international and US websites peaked on March 17 and steadily declined until there were no photographs or other visuals means concerning the disaster on its websites at the end of March.

Differences in the focus of news stories on the earthquake/tsunami, the nuclear situation, lifeline-related information, as well as aid and relief started to appear towards the end of the first week immediately following the initial disasters. The data concerning the number of news stories concerning each of the four categories displayed chronologically for each day reviewed for this project. Table 6.3 highlights these differences.

The focus of overseas news agencies on the nuclear situation towards the end of the first full week after the disaster could also be interpreted as a response to the March 17, 2011 announcement by the US Nuclear Regulatory Commission recommending evacuation or taking shelter indoors for US citizens within 80 km of the Fukushima nuclear power plant. In essence, this announcement within a week of the initial disasters marks the beginning of intense international scrutiny of the nuclear situation with particular reference to the spread of radiation, as a number of embassies of foreign governments, including Germany and Canada, quickly followed the American lead in releasing evacuation-related information.

TABLE 6.3 General categorization of disaster-related news items on website top pages

Website	Asahi N (%)	Mainichi N (%)	Yomiuri N (%)	CNN Int'l N (%)	CNN US N (%)
Earthquake/ tsunami					
–March 17	31 (37.8)	19 (27.5)	21 (24.7)	8 (33.3)	6 (35.3)
–March 24	35 (43.2)	13 (22.4)	30 (37.0)	7 (50.0)	6 (33.3)
–March 31	38 (54.3)	12 (25.0)	37 (46.3)	5 (55.6)	4 (66.7)
Nuclear situation					
–March 17	26 (31.7)	21 (30.4)	25 (29.4)	15 (62.5)	9 (52.9)
–March 24	20 (24.7)	13 (22.4)	21 (25.9)	5 (35.7)	11 (61.1)
–March 31	7 (10.0)	6 (12.5)	21 (26.3)	4 (44.4)	2 (33.3)
Lifeline					
–March 17	24 (29.3)	25 (36.2)	34 (40.0)	0 (0.0)	0 (0.0)
–March 24	17 (21.0)	28 (48.3)	26 (32.1)	0 (0.0)	0 (0.0)
–March 31	16 (22.9)	26 (54.2)	12 (15.0)	0 (0.0)	0 (0.0)
Aid/Relief					
–March 17	1 (1.2)	4 (5.8)	5 (5.9)	1 (4.2)	2 (11.8)
–March 24	9 (8.6)	4 (6.9)	4 (4.9)	2 (14.3)	1 (5.6)
–March 31	9 (12.9)	4 (8.3)	10 (12.5)	0 (0.0)	0 (0.0)
Total[1]					
–March 17	82	69	85	24	17
–March 24	81	58	81	14	18
–March 31	70	48	80	9	6

1 Totals differ from Table 6.1 as the totals in this table include special sections as well as photo and video collections containing short news stories.

In the initial week after the disaster, differences in the total amount of coverage devoted to the overall disaster situation started to appear in the Japanese domestic websites and the international websites. In general, among the three Japanese newspaper websites, the *Asahi* website appeared to focus mostly on information concerning the earthquake and tsunami, the *Yomiuri* website appeared to target the nuclear situation, and the *Mainichi* website included the most items overall on the three days regarding lifeline-related information. On the Japanese newspaper websites as well, over time, coverage of the earthquake and tsunami as well as aid/ relief information increased as percentages of total news items related to the disaster, while the percentages of news items related to the nuclear situation and general lifeline information decreased.

TABLE 6.4 News items related to the earthquake/tsunami on the top pages of websites (March 17, 24, and 31, 2011)

Website/News Items	Asahi N (%)	Mainichi N (%)	Yomiuri N (%)	CNN Int'l N (%)	CNN US N (%)
Special section	5 (4.8)	7 (15.9)	5 (5.7)	4 (20.0)	4 (25.0)
Loss of life/missing	6 (5.8)	0 (0.0)	6 (6.8)	0 (0.0)	0 (0.0)
Damage	5 (4.8)	2 (4.5)	10 (11.4)	1 (5.0)	0 (0.0)
Evacuation	3 (2.9)	0 (0.0)	3 (3.4)	1 (5.0)	0 (0.0)
Human interest	15 (14.4)	0 (0.0)	9 (10.2)	1 (5.0)	3 (18.8)
Medical/welfare	9 (8.7)	0 (0.0)	1 (1.1)	0 (0.0)	0 (0.0)
Science/technical	0 (0.0)	3 (6.8)	6 (6.8)	2 (10.0)	1 (6.3)
Economic, business, and politics	32 (30.8)	10 (22.7)	28 (31.8)	6 (30.0)	4 (25.0)
Emperor	4 (3.8)	1 (2.3)	7 (8.0)	1 (5.0)	0 (0.0)
Editorial	6 (5.8)	11 (25.0)	3 (3.4)	0 (0.0)	1 (6.3)
Crime	1 (1.0)	1 (2.3)	2 (2.3)	0 (0.0)	0 (0.0)
Other[1]	18 (17.3)	9 (20.5)	8 (9.1)	4 (20.0)	3 (18.8)
Total	104 (100.0)[2]	44 (100.0)	88 (100.0)	20 (100.0)	16 (100.0)[2]

1 The "Other" category includes items such as event cancellations or postponements, international reaction, education, and hoarding.

2 Rounded to 100.0.

Examining the content of the news-item links in more detail further reveals the extent of the differences in reporting in each of the four categories. For example, the breakdown of the type of stories concerning the focus of coverage on the earthquake and the tsunami (Table 6.4) suggests that the bulk of the coverage concerning the earthquake and tsunami in the Japanese newspaper websites as well as the CNN websites focused on the economic, business, and political repercussions of the disaster. Human interest stories (the *Asahi* and the *Yomiuri*), editorials (the *Asahi* and the *Mainichi*), and "Other" items also figured prominently on the Japanese newspaper websites during this initial three-week period after the disaster. In contrast, in addition to the overall emphasis on the nuclear situation noted earlier, the CNN websites had more links to special sections related to the earthquake and tsunami, as well as high percentages of human interest stories.

In addition to chronological differences, the breakdown of nuclear-related news items on all websites (Table 6.5) clearly demonstrates variations among the Japanese domestic newspaper websites and the international websites.

TABLE 6.5 Number of news items related to the nuclear situation on the top pages of websites (March 17, 24, and 31, 2011)

Website/ News Items	Asahi N (%)	Mainichi N (%)	Yomiuri N (%)	CNN Int'l N (%)	CNN US N (%)
Special section	5 (9.4)	0 (0.0)	3 (4.5)	0 (0.0)	1 (4.5)
Plant damage, evacuation	16 (30.2)	9 (22.5)	19 (28.4)	5 (20.8)	2 (9.1)
TEPCO	0 (0.0)	6 (15.0)	5 (7.5)	1 (4.2)	0 (0.0)
Radiation	14 (26.4)	16 (40.0)	16 (23.9)	5 (20.8)	11 (50.0)
Scientific or technical	2 (3.8)	8 (20.0)	3 (4.5)	3 (12.5)	3 (13.6)
Economy, business, politics	5 (9.4)	0 (0.0)	1 (1.5)	0 (0.0)	1 (4.5)
Other[1]	11 (20.8)	1 (2.5)	20 (29.9)	10 (41.7)	4 (18.2)
Total	53 (100.0)	40 (100.0)	67 (100.0)[2]	24 (100.0)	22 (100.0)[2]

1 The "Other" category includes items such as international reaction, human interest, food safety, and editorials.

2 Rounded to 100.0.

Clearly, coverage overall among all news websites focused on plant damage, evacuation, and radiation, particularly in the *Asahi* and the *Yomiuri* websites, where nearly a third of their nuclear-related coverage was devoted to news items concerning damage to the Fukushima Daiichi nuclear plant and evacuation of the immediate area surrounding the plant. However, in contrast, the *Mainichi* website focused its reporting on news items concerning radiation (40 percent in total for the three days), a figure that was exceeded only by the number of radiation-related stories posted on the *CNN US* website (50 percent).

The overall chronology of the reporting coverage (Table 6.3) and closer scrutiny of the breakdown of nuclear-related news items in Table 6.5 reveals the prominence that the *CNN International* and the *CNN US* websites devoted to the unfolding nuclear situation compared with the Japanese newspaper websites.

For example, one prominent story on the top page of the *CNN International* website on March 17, 2011 (the day that the US Nuclear Regulatory Commission issued its advisory) carried the headline "U.S. Official: Spent fuel rods exposed, raising concerns." In the special section devoted to the Japan tsunami and earthquake on the same date, four out of seven major stories focused on containment, education, and international reaction to the nuclear situation ("Heroes' fight to prevent meltdown," "Q&A: Japan's nuclear crisis," "China freezes nuclear plant approvals," and "Spain orders review of nuclear power").

On the March 24, 2011 *CNN US* website, news items specifically relating to the situation at the nuclear plant ("Work resumes at Japan nuclear plant" was the top story on this date) and radiation levels throughout Japan ("Radiation in Tokyo's tap water plummets to safer levels") as well as overseas ("Radiation found in more U.S. states") were also given prominent attention on the top page.

More detailed analysis of the breakdown of news items on Japanese newspaper websites and their placement within the websites also demonstrates differences in coverage. For example, of the five news-item links on the top page of the March 17, 2011 *Yomiuri* website, one special-section item in the middle of the page (*hibaku taisaku* or radiation measure) linked to a separate page defining key terms concerning radiation and visual explanations, one general item was listed in the prominent general news category (*shakai*) concerning transportation of radiated materials, and three links in the science section (*kagaku*) carried stories about a press conference update of the situation, radiation fallout to other areas in the Kantō region, and measures to reduce radiation damage in the plant itself. The *Yomiuri*'s coverage of the nuclear situation overall continued to expand throughout the month, and by March 31, in addition to three news items directly relating to the radiation situation, 11 items covered reaction by the International Atomic Energy Agency IAEA (three items), international nuclear standards (three items), nuclear-radiation maps and food safety (four items), and international nuclear assistance (one item).

In contrast, on the *Asahi*'s March 17, 2011 website, in addition to three stories specifically targeting the radiation situation, it was the first news website in Japan to directly report on international reaction (five items included in the "Other" column of Table 6.5), and this figure was higher than those directly related to radiation (three items). In fact, on March 24, 2011, out of a total of 20 stories generally related to the nuclear situation, 11 items were directly concerned with the expanding radiation situation. Among the three Japanese newspaper websites, however, the coverage by the *Mainichi* about the nuclear situation (as well as the earthquake/tsunami disasters in general) focused much more on lifeline, aid, and relief (see below).

Owing to geographical relevancy, the websites of the major Japanese newspapers reviewed carried a great deal more information regarding lifeline-related information than the international news websites (Table 6.6).

Here as well, there were certain similarities and differences noted among Japanese newspaper websites. All websites had special sections containing lifeline-related information such status reports, evacuation-related information, and updates concerning medical services. In addition to these special sections, evacuation and safety, transportation, and information relating to the emergency scheduled power outages (*teiden*) were also features common among all websites. As shown in Table 6.6, communications-oriented information, mainly pertaining to mobile phone services, was particularly emphasized in the *Mainichi*'s website. The *Mainichi* website also contained either a graphical display or a direct link to Google's People Finder application, which allowed people to search for missing persons.

TABLE 6.6 News items related to lifeline information on the top pages of websites (March 17, 24, and 31, 2011)

Website/News Items	Asahi N (%)	Mainichi N (%)	Yomiuri N (%)	CNN Int'l N (%)	CNN US N (%)
Special section	4 (7.1)	9 (11.4)	4 (4.9)	0 (0.0)	0 (0.0)
General lifeline	7 (12.5)	9 (11.4)	3 (3.7)	0 (0.0)	0 (0.0)
Medical	1 (1.8)	2 (2.5)	5 (6.2)	0 (0.0)	0 (0.0)
Evacuation and safety	5 (8.9)	9 (11.4)	19 (23.5)	0 (0.0)	0 (0.0)
Transportation	9 (16.1)	5 (6.3)	11 (13.6)	0 (0.0)	0 (0.0)
Scheduled power outages	17 (30.4)	14 (17.7)	18 (22.2)	0 (0.0)	0 (0.0)
Searches for missing or deceased	5 (8.9)	3 (3.8)	6 (7.4)	0 (0.0)	0 (0.0)
Non-Japanese in Japan	1 (1.8)	1 (1.3)	2 (2.5)	0 (0.0)	0 (0.0)
Power conservation (setsuden)	0 (0.0)	1 (1.3)	3 (3.7)	0 (0.0)	0 (0.0)
Communications	1 (1.8)	19 (24.1)	1 (1.2)	0 (0.0)	0 (0.0)
People finder	0 (0.0)	3 (3.8)	0 (0.0)	0 (0.0)	0 (0.0)
Other[1]	6 (10.7)	4 (5.1)	9 (11.1)	0 (0.0)	0 (0.0)
Total	56 (100.0)	79 (100.0)[2]	81 (100.0)	0 (0.0)	0 (0.0)

1 The "Other" category includes items such as communications, power conservation measures, disaster headquarters contact, and public utilities/
2 Rounded to 100.0.

The results for the final category of aid and relief are shown in Table 6.7.

TABLE 6.7 News items related to relief aid and donations on the top pages of websites (March 17, 24, and 31, 2011)

Website/News Items	Asahi N (%)	Mainichi N (%)	Yomiuri N (%)	CNN Int'l N (%)	CNN US N (%)
Special section	0 (0.0)	0 (0.0)	0 (0.0)	2 (66.7)	2 (66.7)
Goods donation (within Japan)	8 (42.1)	3 (25.0)	5 (26.3)	0 (0.0)	0 (0.0)
Money donations (within Japan)	4 (21.1)	8 (66.7)	4 (21.1)	0 (0.0)	0 (0.0)
Volunteer activity	1 (5.3)	0 (0.0)	3 (15.8)	0 (0.0)	0 (0.0)
Other[1]	6 (31.6)	1 (8.3)	7 (36.8)	1 (33.3)	1 (33.3)
Total	19 (100.0)[2]	12 (100.0)	19 (100.0)	3 (100.0)	3 (100.0)

1 The "Other" category includes items such as general international aid, celebrity donations, charities, and charity sports events.
2 Rounded to 100.0.

All newspaper and news-related websites contained links to relief aid and donations, yet the emphasis among the Japanese newspaper websites was clearly different. Among the categories, the *Asahi*'s website carried the most news items concerning donating goods within Japan, either by providing information as to how people could donate goods to people in the disaster-stricken area or by carrying news items about prominent donations (by individuals or corporations) as well as international assistance efforts. The *Mainichi*'s website content in this area mainly aimed at providing information as to how people in Japan could make direct donations to relief funds.

Discussion and conclusion

This exploratory content analysis of the headlines on the top pages underscores the differences between the Japanese domestic and international news websites, particularly in terms of coverage concerning detailed damage reports about the Fukushima nuclear plant and the fears of radiation contamination within Japan and overseas. In addition, these results show that the coverage concerning the damage started to peak approximately one week after the initial earthquake and tsunami. Particularly in the second week, as international news reports appeared to shift focus to the nuclear situation and radiation fears, the focus of certain Japanese newspapers clearly differed.

March 17, 2011 marks a turning point in media coverage of the "triple disasters" when the American government announced an 80 km evacuation zone surrounding the Fukushima Daiichi nuclear plant. One newspaper article in the *Asahi Shimbun* dated March 18, 2011, suggested the rationale for the establishment of the evacuation zone was uncertainty on the part of the American government about the quality of information being obtained from the Japanese government and TEPCO in addition to reports on the difficulties faced by CNN reporters dispatched to Japan in obtaining reliable information (*Asahi Shimbun* 2011). CNN's difficulties might be attributed to the usual problems of "parachute" journalism and accessing and understanding reports from multiple levels of governments and concerned agencies within Japan, but these problematic aspects also seem to have influenced reporting by Japanese media as well.

One further possible explanation concerns differences in interpreting the consequences of the "triple disaster." For the Japanese press, in addition to covering the earthquake, tsunami, and the nuclear plant situation, there could be also an intrinsic sense of responsibility about managing the crisis and not sparking hysteria. In addition the domestic media felt a responsibility to provide information regarding lifeline, support, and aid information to people in the immediate vicinity, those affected by scheduled power outages in the Kantō area, and to the general public. In trying to explain why the Japanese media seemed to put less emphasis on the nuclear accident there is the question if the Japanese press made a deliberate choice or if it was the lack of information regarding the nuclear and radiation problems. This raises further questions about whether the press clubs[2] played a role in news management or whether it was primarily a problem of inadequate information disclosure and transparency by TEPCO and the government.

In conclusion, while there are limitations in this exploratory research project concerning the number of websites reviewed as well as the chronology of events (particularly concerning the nuclear situation in Japan as it unfolded in 2011), this study advances our understanding of how the media covers disaster. Given the major developments in the nuclear story since the end of May when TEPCO belatedly admitted that it knew three meltdowns had occurred soon after the tsunami crippled cooling systems, future analysis of domestic coverage of this story is warranted. Until that time, the domestic media refrained from using the word "meltdown" in describing the crisis. Thus, a major story that emerges from 3/11 is the role of the media and how it has evolved in crisis. The summer of 2011 witnessed extensive media coverage of radiation and food safety issues along with revelations about dubious practices by utilities and government agencies aimed at promoting nuclear energy. The media has played a largely constructive role in helping the public better understand public safety risks associated with the nuclear accident and the pros and cons of renewable energy while also reminding the nation of the ongoing dire situation in tsunami-battered communities.

Notes

1   The Archive-It Public Collection focusing on the Japan Earthquake (available at: www. archive-it.org/public/collection.html?id=2438) is a joint project hosted at Virginia Technical University and is sponsored by Japan's National Diet Library, the Library of Congress, and the Reischauer Institute of Japanese Studies. The archive contains archived replicas of websites, blogs, and other social commentary pertaining to the March 11, 2011 disasters in Japan. Due to the technical construction of the *Mainichi* newspaper website, the Archive-It public collection for its March 17, 24, and 31 versions was used for this analysis.

2   Press clubs are pools of reporters assigned by mainstream media to cover a particular industry or government ministry. In exchange for inside information and privileged access there is a degree of cooptation.

References

Abdul-Mageed, M.M. and Herring, S.C. (2008) "Arabic and English News Coverage on Aljazeera.net," in F. Sudweeks, H. Hrachovec, and C. Ess (eds.), *Proceedings of Cultural Attitudes Towards Technology and Communication 2008* (CATaC'08), Nimes, France, June 24–27.

Asahi Shimbun (2011) "Bei gawa, jōhō kanri ni fushin mo, Fukushima daiichi genbatsu 80 kiro kengai e, jikokumin hinan kankoku," March 18 (Morning edition), p. 5.

Barak, A. (2010) "The Psychological Role of the Internet in Mass Disasters: Past Evidence and Future Planning," in A. Brunet, A.R. Ashbaugh, and C.F. Herbert (eds.) *Internet Use in the Aftermath of Trauma* (Volume 72, NATO Science for Peace and Security Series – E: Human and Societal Dynamics), Amsterdam: IOS Press.

Dimitrova, D.V. and Neznanski, M. (2006) "Online Journalism and the War in Cyberspace: A Comparison Between U.S. and International Newspapers," *Journal of Computer-Mediated Communication*, 12(1), article 13, online, available at: http://jcmc.indiana.edu/vol12/issue1/dimitrova.html (accessed July 15, 2011).

Pew Research Center for the People and the Press (2011) *Public Stays Focused on Japan as Media Turns to Libya*, Pew Research Center for the People and the Press, online, available at: http://people-press.org/files/2011/03/3-30-11-New-Interst-Index-Release.pdf (accessed July 15, 2011).

Schwalbe, C.B. (2006) "Remembering Our Shared Past: Visually Framing the Iraq War on U.S. News Websites," *Journal of Computer-Mediated Communication*, 12(1), article 14, online, available at: http://jcmc.indiana.edu/vol12/issue1/schwalbe.html (accessed July 15, 2011).

Wu, H.D. (2007) "A Brave New World for International News? Exploring the Determinants of the Coverage of Foreign News on US Websites," *International Communication Gazette*, 69(6): 539–551.

PART III

Energy

7

NETWORKS OF POWER

Institutions and local residents in post-Tōhoku Japan

Daniel P. Aldrich[1]

The 11 March 2011 earthquake that struck off Japan's coast epitomized what researchers call a compounded or cascading disaster.[2] While the quake itself caused few direct fatalities, it created a tsunami as tall as 38 m in places, which devastated communities along Japan's eastern coast and swamped backup cooling systems at nuclear power plants in the area. Atomic reactors are designed to automatically shut down in the event of an earthquake, but without batteries and diesel generators to draw away residual heat, the Fukushima's reactors remained hot. Whether the backup systems were damaged primarily by the intensity of the quake or the tsunami has not yet been determined conclusively. Whatever the cause of the problem, the fuel rods in at least three of the six reactors at the Fukushima Daiichi Reactor complex operated by the Tokyo Electric Power Company (TEPCO) melted down after reaching temperatures in excess of 2000°F. Freed from their zirconium cases, the radioactive material tumbled free and likely burned holes through the thick steel plating of the containment vessels. As engineers manually pumped water into the vessels to try to keep the fuel rods and the reactors cooled, the heat released hydrogen gas through oxidation with the zircaloy shell on the fuel rods; the hydrogen ignited and blew off the tops of three of the reactor buildings. Decision makers had to deliberately vent the reactors to reduce pressure, and along with these intentional releases of radioactivity into the atmosphere, the "feed and bleed" process of pumping in water created more than a 100,000 metric tons of contaminated water most of which is being held in temporary tanks (with more than 10,000 tons already dumped into the sea).

As Japan seeks to restore communications, manage daily life with power shortages (as many nuclear power plants remain offline both due to safety precautions and requests from the government that they do so), and find more permanent housing for 80,000 or so residents who fled the area near the Fukushima nuclear plants (some of whom may never return to their houses), observers have raised several critical questions. First, it is important to know why nuclear power plants (all of which have large quantities of fuel rods onsite) were located in such vulnerable areas along the coasts of Japan. Second, many have wondered how Japan developed such an advanced commercial nuclear power program – complete with plans for nuclear fuel recycling, fast breeder reactors, and the use of mixed oxide (MOX) fuel – despite its tragic experiences at Hiroshima, Nagasaki, and the Lucky Dragon incident. Last, observers have asked to what extent the ongoing crisis will alter Japan's plans for nuclear power.

While some have argued that Japan "had no choice" in adopting nuclear energy as a central part of its energy mix because of a lack of natural resources (Harner 2011) or that a lack of institutional access points constrained potential citizen opposition and allowed the growth of its nuclear power program (cf. Cohen, *et al.* 1995), I believe that the answer to these questions comes from the interactions between social networks and institutions. When siting Japan's commercial nuclear reactors, bureaucrats have worked hand-in-hand with the private utility companies to place projects in villages and towns where resistance was seen as less likely. Decision makers looked to localities where horizontal associations such as fishing cooperatives were on the decline and local residents would be unable to mount a defense against the plant.

Once site selection was finished, the Japanese government has used policy instruments to induce public support for a nuclear program based on a top-down, technocratic vision. Targeting specific demographic groups and working to provide financial incentives for otherwise declining, rural, and depopulating areas, the government created organizations to influence local civil society. Despite claims from the government that it is "going back to the drawing board" on the issue of nuclear power, whether or not Japan will remain wedded to nuclear energy remains to be seen. With opinion polls showing shifts towards more negative feelings about nuclear energy among the general population, actual and potential host communities have been less worried about their exposure to radiation in the case of an accident and more concerned about the loss of revenue caused by a termination of Japan's nuclear program. This chapter explores these three issues in sequence and concludes with suggestions for incorporating social capital into the recovery process.

Selecting sites for nuclear power plants

Observers have noted that all of Japan's nuclear power plants are situated along the nation's coastline, with many reactors just tens of meters from the ocean itself. Fukushima Daiichi's location in the coastal villages of Ōkuma and Futaba meant that its seawalls were immediately overtopped and the machinery of the plant itself swamped by the tsunami which reached as high as 38 m in some localities (some 90 percent of the homes in Ōkuma, for example, were reported destroyed by the water). The reactors at Fukushima were built by GE engineers more than four decades ago, and the placement of backup systems in low-lying areas was clearly a mistake (and few would have thought to prepare for such a "black swan" type event). Yet the Agency for Natural Resources and Energy (ANRE), which regulates the electric power sector and the Nuclear and Industrial Safety Agency

(NISA), which regulates nuclear power, sit within METI (the Ministry of Economy, Trade, and Industry; it was the Ministry of International Trade and Industry or MITI until 2001). MITI provided millions of yen in funding for years to utilities such as TEPCO to assist them in mapping out potential locations for nuclear reactors in the early years of nuclear power. Decision makers did not place these projects randomly; they invested planning and effort (and, according to some accounts, illegal donations, see Lesbirel 1998: 78, 138) in selecting towns like Kashiwazaki-Kariwa, Shimane, Tomari, and Ōkuma as host communities.

How to explain why these locations and not alternatives were selected is a matter of strong debate. In North America, for example, researchers have argued that African Americans, Native Americans, and Hispanic Americans live with more proportionally unwanted and dangerous facilities such as Superfund sites, lead smelters, and polluting industries (Bullard 2000). In Japan, while minorities are a very small percentage of the overall nation, there are still recognizable groups, including the Ainu, burakumin, and Koreans (see Tsuda 1998 for a discussion of Japanese-Brazilian immigrants), who have reported prejudice both in the workplace and in social relations (although these groups reside in areas where technical considerations preclude the siting of nuclear power plants). On the other hand, in interviews, engineers and bureaucrats in France and Japan told me that they selected locations for nuclear power plants and other often controversial projects based solely on technocratic criteria. Scholars have described a number of different approaches to the heuristics that can be used by developers and governments in choosing one area over the other; I have detailed six of them in the table below.

TABLE 7.1 Approaches to site selection

Approach	Logic	Key siting factors
Technocratic criteria	Trained experts use specialized knowledge to select locations	Distance to electricity grids, aseismic bedrock, proximity to cooling water
Civil society	Developers avoid locations better able to mobilize	Deep reservoirs of bonding and bridging social capital
Political discrimination	Party in power places unwanted projects in backyards of opponents	Presence of opposition party
Racial/ethnic/ religious discrimination	Dominant ethnic group uses power to place facilities in minority areas	Presence of minorities
Economics	Wealthier localities have resources to fight off unwanted projects	Socioeconomic conditions
Powerful politicians	Politicians with greater resources will intervene to push away or draw in projects	Presence of *daijin* (Diet members who have served six terms or more)

Note: Table adopted from Aldrich (2008).

Under the technocratic approach, civil engineers, meteorologists, and other trained planners work to figure out the "ideal" location based on apolitical premises such as cost-benefit analyses or geographic information systems (GIS) surveys. This approach assumes that the selection takes place above political or local concerns and focuses only on ground water, bedrock type, how far the location is to the existing electricity grid, and so on. A radically different approach based on civil society sees the selection process as one that minimizes risks to the project and maximizes the likelihood that it will come online quickly. To do so, planners must estimate which localities are most likely to cooperate with siting plans and avoid those communities where local civil society groups, such as fishing cooperatives and farming groups, could mobilize to fight the project. This approach, focused on the strength of local bonds and the ability of the group to overcome barriers to collective action, has been cited by many scholars as an accurate representation of the decision heuristics involved in controversial facilities (Hamilton 1993; Clingermeyer 1994; Aldrich and Crook 2008).

Alternatively, many believe that discrimination plays a role. One form of discrimination could be based on race, ethnicity, religion, or caste. In Spain, for example, the Basque have argued that the eventually successful attempts to place nuclear reactors in their territory beginning in the 1970s is due to institutional discrimination against them by the Spanish.[3] Another form of discrimination would be one based on political power; some scholars, for example, argued that the long-dominant Liberal Democratic Party (LDP) in Japan placed nuclear power plants in the backyards of their Socialist and Communist opponents (Ramseyer and Rosenbluth 1993: 129). In the United States, many observers argued that the selection of Yucca Mountain as a site for the nations' only high level nuclear waste repository had much to do with the Republican make up of Congress and the Democratic nature of Nevada. Economists, on the other hand, might argue that local socioeconomic conditions dominate the outcomes of siting processes.

Wealthier communities have less need of any jobs or taxes generated by the plant, and also have more resources (such as time, money, and legal assistance) to fight them. Poorer communities, alternatively, may view these projects as benefits providing an economic lifeline at a time when many rural, depopulating villages had no industries of their own. A final explanation would be based on the political power of politicians, such as Tanaka Kakuei, to pull in "pork barrel" projects they believe will benefit their constituency or push away unwanted projects that they believe will anger them.

To judge which of these theories best explains the placement of reactors in Japan, I analyzed all of the towns and villages throughout the country that had nuclear power plants alongside very similar towns with the same technocratic criteria that did not receive them. In doing so, I was able to untangle the effects of variables such as powerful politicians, economic conditions, civil society (through the strength of local fishermen and farming cooperatives and through the change in population levels), and so forth. The results of my analysis of some 150 actual and potential nuclear power plant communities[4] indicate that the strength of civil society mattered tremendously, even holding all other variables constant.

That is, controlling for the other theories such as economics, political power, and so forth, Japanese decision makers chose locations based on levels of social capital. Interviews with bureaucrats and activists alike confirmed that decision makers often sought to illuminate the strength of local horizontal associations such as the fishermen's cooperatives (*gyogyō rōdō kumiai*) in potential locations. In internal memos, MITI officials regularly discussed whether or not these groups were waxing or waning; these details were critical because of the veto power held by fishing cooperatives over the siting process. In the village of Kaminoseki in Yamaguchi prefecture, for example, the opposition to a planned nuclear reactor complex has been led for decades by a local fishermen's cooperative. S. Hayden Lesbirel discussed a number of siting cases in which siting plans for nuclear plants were derailed by angry local fishermen (1998). My research showed that utilities were much more likely to site nuclear power plants in communities where these groups were on the decline, as opposed to areas where their strength was maintained or increased. Coastal towns and villages like Ōkuma were ones in which the networks best positioned to hold the line against the proposal could no longer do so.

The first stage in handling potential contestation over nuclear power plants is to site them in areas where such resistance is less likely. Once utilities have selected a location for nuclear power plants with the assistance of the government, the next stage in handling this policy is to ensure that the public is onboard.

Manipulating public opinion

Most observers imagine that democratic governments envision public opinion as a guidestar which – at least when public opinion seems relatively strong on an issue – should be taken as a general framework for politicians and decision makers to follow. Normative political theory (Rousseau 1762), studies of the "maternalist" welfare state in the US post-Civil War (Skocpol 1992), investigations of citizen involvement in usually technocratic decision making processes (McAvoy 1999), and more recent arguments for deliberative democracy (Gutmann and Thompson 2004) have all underscored the importance of mandates coming up from the grass roots and being molded into policy outcomes.

However, in the arena of nuclear power, Japanese leaders and civil servants envision public opinion as malleable; in this approach, the people's perspective should be changed to match the perspective of the administration rather than elevated as a guidestar which should be followed (cf. Jacobs and Shapiro 2000). In Japan's Iron Triangle, bureaucrats, politicians, and quasi-government organizations work cooperatively with utility companies to sway the public and emphasize the safety and necessity of atomic energy. While Japan's private regional power utilities, including Tokyo Electric Power Company (TEPCO), Chubu Electric Power Company, and Hokuriku Electric Power Company, are responsible for the design, planning, construction, maintenance, and repairs to reactors throughout Japan, the central government has been far from a passive regulator in the field. Since the mid-1950s, the Japanese government has sought to develop an indigenous source of electricity, and the pressure to do so increased dramatically with the OPEC oil shocks in the 1970s.

Former Prime Minister Nakasone Yasuhiro, for example, recently told a staff writer with the *Asahi Shimbun* (24 May 2011) that he pushed Japan to develop nuclear power because "We had no oil, no gas, and our coal reserves were dwindling." A number of nations around the world lack such resources but have not pursued nuclear energy as strongly as the Japanese government. Ireland[5] and New Zealand, for example, are also "small island nations" with limited resources, but neither has adopted nuclear power in response to geographic conditions (see Eric Dinmore's 2006 dissertation for an exploration of Japan's "resource problems" from the 1920s). Japan's current system is the product of deliberate political will, not merely market decisions in the absence of large reserves of oil and gas. In 1954 Nakasone, then a Diet member with the Lower House from Gunma prefecture, pushed the Lower House Budget Committee to accept a ¥235 million nuclear budget (roughly US$14 million at the time), which they did.[6]

From the mid-1950s Japan's government has continued to press ahead with plans for nuclear power despite opposition both at the local and national levels. Where anti-nuclear contestation and referenda have stopped the use of nuclear power in some European nations (Germany, Switzerland, and Italy have all at one point or another enacted moratoria on nuclear power) and in southeast Asia (where the nations of Thailand and Malaysia, for example, have recently enacted a freeze on nuclear power), Japan has never had such a broad dialogue with civil society on policy. When citizens have been invited to present their pre-screened questions at public meetings on the topic of nuclear power, it is difficult to see where their arguments have been taken seriously in the arena.

Japan's "nuclear village" (as many observers call it) is not comprised solely of pro-nuclear politicians like Nakasone and, later, Prime Minister Tanaka Kakuei (who boasted of bringing home a number of nuclear power plants to his constituency in Kashiwazaki-Kariwa in Niigata prefecture). Bureaucrats within the MITI (now METI) early on recognized the need to gain "public acceptance" of the reactors both in the host communities which have them in their own backyards and in the wider sphere of public opinion. To do so, the central government has created a wide array of policy instruments designed to bring public opinion in line with national ambitions. These tools have included science curricula written by bureaucrats which teach schoolchildren that nuclear power is safe and necessary, awards ceremonies for local mayors and executives who cooperate in siting nuclear power plants in their backyards, and jobs, new markets, and incentives for fishermen and farmers who might fear "nuclear blight" in which consumers shy away from the products created near nuclear power plants (see Aldrich 2005 for a categorization of these tools).

Working with utilities, the Agency for Natural Resources and Energy (ANRE, *Shigen enerugii chō*) has set up three different organizations developed solely to promote nuclear power in potential host communities around the nation.[7] Most extensive of these attempts has been the institutionalized system of compensation and redistribution known in Japanese as the *Dengen Sanpō*, which has used the money generated by a submerged tax on electricity use (charged to both industrial commercial and industrial users of electricity) to funnel millions of dollars a year to rural communities which agree to host nuclear power plants and other generating facilities. In many cases, the chance to bring in tremendous sums of money into otherwise economically dying communities has created a "cycle of addiction" (Hasegawa 2004: 26) and a "culture of dependency" (Fackler and Ōnishi 2011).

Japan's pursuit of nuclear power has been one tied to a technocratic vision of a nation free from entanglements in the Middle East and able to achieve "energy security" (despite the obvious need for oil for manufacturing and automobile needs).[8] The use of a variety of targeted policy instruments since the mid-1970s has dampened the ability of anti-nuclear groups to affect Japan's energy choices. What future does Japan's nuclear program have after the second worst nuclear accident in history?

The future of nuclear power

Decision makers in other nations – especially Italy, Germany, and Switzerland – have seen Fukushima as a worst-case scenario of control over a potentially hazardous technology gone awry, and have begun to curtail their involvement with nuclear power. In Germany, a committee set up by Chancellor Merkel suggested that Germany close its 17 nuclear reactors by 2021 to "fundamentally eliminate risks" (*New York Times* May 11 2011) and she has publicly committed to doing so. In Switzerland, the cabinet has decided to phase out nuclear power by 2034 to move toward a "clean, safe, and secure energy supply" (*Bloomberg News* May 26 2011). Italy's national referendum on the issue in mid-June 2011 allowed residents to speak their minds on the issue; following the Chernobyl reactor meltdown, the nation moved to shut down reactors, but had planned on opening new ones in the coming years. Some 94 percent of the 57 percent of eligible voters who turned up voted against nuclear power in Italy's referendum, essentially closing down the option for the foreseeable future. In Japan, while there have been some moderate demonstrations against nuclear power in the post-3/11 days, there are few signs of broad-based, sustained anger or opposition to nuclear power. Opinion polls show some negative movement among individuals who may have been neutral on the issue before the accident, but overall the main trend remains mixed feelings on the issue.

Scholars have argued that public opinion on issues often follows the government position. In France, for example, where the government has long promoted nuclear power, few individuals identify themselves as anti-nuclear. In the United States, where, despite regular pronouncements about support for nuclear power, the government has been divided and ambiguous on the issue since the 1960s, public opinion is similarly divided (cf. Baumgartner and Jones 1993). In Sweden, where the government adopted a moratorium on nuclear power, the opinions of citizens have become more negative on the issue. James Jasper calls this the "political context" and argues that "public opinion tends to support that [policy] path rather than simply returning to its prepolitical patterns" (1988: 357). In Japan's case, this theory fits the data quite well. While Fukushima is an accident that created environmental and health hazards on a large scale, most Japanese residents seem prepared to maintain the status quo.

Surveys of more than 2000 Japanese respondents in mid-April 2011 by Japanese newspapers (about a month after the accident) showed that roughly half supported nuclear power while one-third opposed it; for another question in the same survey, around 41 percent said that nuclear power should be reduced or stopped. A month later, another survey showed a slight negative tilt, with 43 percent of the respondents in favor of nuclear power and 36 percent against. In the April survey, slightly more than half said that nuclear power should be stopped. The Pew Research Center carried out a different poll over two weeks in April, and found that 46 percent of the respondents wanted to maintain nuclear power at its current levels, while 44 percent sought to reduce it. By June 14, an NHK poll showed that roughly 47 percent of the respondents wanted to decrease the number of nuclear power plants, with an additional 18 percent arguing for their total abolition. But on July 13, *Asahi* reported that 77 percent of respondents favored the gradual abolition of nuclear power with only 1 percent in favor of an expansion. Broader public opinion has swung toward the anti-nuclear side of the spectrum, but this sentiment is not held across the board. While these polls may show a more negative approach to nuclear power, large numbers of residents have not participated in protests or signed petitions against nuclear power. Approximately 15,000 participants showed up for anti-nuclear rallies on April 10 in Kōenji and May 7 in Shibuya, and there have been smaller rallies in and around Tokyo as well which have attracted crowds in the hundreds. These were at best medium-sized rallies for Japan – in previous years more than 90,000 people marched in Okinawa against the presence of US forces there – and did not involve a large percentage of the overall population.

Among the individuals whom we might expect to be most concerned with nuclear power – residents of towns where nuclear power plants are in the process of being planned or constructed – there has been little change in their perspective. While some have expressed concern with the overall safety of nuclear power plants, many local executives seem more concerned about their potential loss of income and incentives should the government stop the nuclear power programs. A one-time opponent of nuclear power told reporters that, "the town knows it can no longer survive economically without the nuclear plant" (quoted in Fackler and Ōnishi 2011). Towns selected as hosts for nuclear power were ones in which well-organized and potentially resistant groups such as fishermen were already on the decline; once money and subsidies begin to flow, their incentives to fight back and ability to recruit allies diminish tremendously. Recent local elections have confirmed that many residents in host or potential host communities continue to see nuclear power positively. Aomori prefecture is host to the Higashidori nuclear complex, and Aomori Governor Mimura Shingo recently won re-election in early June on a pro-nuclear platform, defeating a challenger who endorsed a "freeze" position on nuclear plants (*Yomiuri Shimbun* June 6 2011). Economic dependency and government institutions pushing public support for nuclear power have created an environment in which mass protest against nuclear power is unlikely.

While politicians and bureaucrats in Japan have not taken the drastic steps of their counterparts in Italy, Switzerland, and Germany, decision makers in the government have been willing to alter some aspects of the national energy plan as a result of public unrest. Prime Minister Kan Naoto requested that Chubu Electric Power Company shut down the operational units at the Hamaoka nuclear complex in Shizuoka prefecture that sits atop a subduction zone until lingering uncertainties about its survival in the wake of a very likely earthquake can be resolved. Chubu complied, shutting down reactors 4 and 5 and not restarting reactor 3 (which had been offline for inspection). In a broader response, until the Fukushima crisis, the most recent published energy policy report envisioned nuclear power contributing 50 percent of Japan's energy needs by 2030. By mid-May of 2011, Kan promised that Japan would more vigorously pursue renewable energy sources. He argued that 20 percent of Japan's power could be supplied by solar energy by the year 2020. The current administration has also begun to alter the regulatory framework for the nuclear industry, promising to break off the Nuclear Industry and Safety Agency (NISA, responsible for oversight) from the Ministry of Economy, Trade, and Industry (METI, responsible for promoting nuclear power) in response to criticisms of this potential moral hazard.

Plans for 14 new reactors have been set aside for the time being as well; Kan stated that Japan should "start from scratch" to create a new energy policy that builds on renewable, not just nuclear, sources (*The Guardian* May 11 2011). Officials have said less about Japan's unrealized vision of a closed-fuel cycle, in which fast breeder reactors (such as the experimental Monju reactor), mixed oxide (MOX) fuels, and fuel reprocessing keep highly radioactive wastes to a minimum. Plans made public in 2010 hoped to commercialize the developing technologies of the fast breeder reactors in the next three decades; whether or not this remains realistic has not been mentioned.

Past accidents both at home and abroad – including Three Mile Island, Chernobyl, and the deaths of two workers in September 1999 at the Tokai JCO plant – resulted in short-term suspensions of expansion plans, but did not drastically alter long-term plans or shake up existing government institutions. These past accidents also resulted in what turned out to be short-lived swings against nuclear power; over time, polls showed a return to the pre-accident status quo (see Aldrich 2008: 136–144 for details). Whether or not these are first moves towards decoupling Japan's future from nuclear power or instead a temporary suspension before returning to previously established schemes remains to be seen. Authorities have not discussed ending the use of the various policy instruments designed to alter public opinion detailed above, such as public relations campaigns, Nuclear Power Day, huge subsidies, and pro-nuclear advertisements. In fact, the Japan Times (July 8 2011) detailed how Kyūshū Electric Power Company had its employees send emails from their home accounts supportive of restarting the Genkai power plant to a local television program in an attempt to show broader support for the proposal.

As past research has shown that local residents seem to be increasingly immune to these techniques (Aldrich 2005, 2010), authorities may need to deepen their subsidies and strengthen existing tools to reach a more skeptical public which sees more clearly the potential costs of nuclear power.

Conclusions

This chapter has sought to understand Japan's nuclear power industry from the perspective of local networks and central government policy instruments and institutions. Power utilities such as TEPCO worked with central government planners to map out compliant towns for nuclear power plant facilities. By placing atomic reactors in these rural, depopulating, often poverty-stricken areas where horizontal associations were waning, decision makers hoped to avoid controversy and strife. In doing so, though, they placed all of Japan's reactors on its coasts in areas quite vulnerable to tsunami, and set up the environmental conditions for the ongoing nuclear crisis.

Rather than viewing public opinion on nuclear power as a guidestar to be followed, the central government has worked hard to sway it and bring it in line with national energy goals. Through a variety of policy instruments, including financial incentives, educational curricula for children, "advertorials" in national newspapers, and jobs for fishermen, bureaucrats in the government have sought to induce public acceptance of nuclear power. Finally, I argued that opinion polls have shown movement towards the anti-nuclear spectrum, but there have been few, large-scale, anti-nuclear rallies due to the crisis and actual host communities have not displayed these tendencies. The government's strong pro-nuclear position has been a core factor in this outcome. Pro-nuclear incumbents continue to achieve victory in regional and local elections while local residents in potential host communities have been more concerned with maintaining benefits than setting up a moratorium on nuclear power. The government has promised to deemphasize the role of nuclear power in Japan, plans for new reactors have been temporarily shelved, and one complex has been temporarily taken off line, yet the country still lacks a national debate on the topic and has yet to publicly discuss the costs and benefits in advancing its high level, closed-fuel-cycle nuclear program.

Beyond the nuclear crisis, what will be the next stages in Japan's recovery from the March 2011 tsunami? Comparative research on post-disaster recovery has demonstrated that just as local networks were a critical part of the site selection process, social networks also serve as engines for the recovery process (Aldrich 2010, 2011, forthcoming). The affected areas in the Tōhoku region, though, have measurably lower levels of social capital than their counterparts elsewhere. For example, residents in the prefectures of Fukushima, Miyagi, and Iwate in the Tōhoku region spend less time, on average, engaged in informal socializing, have more single-member households, and are older than residents in Hyōgo prefecture in the Kansai area (Kage 2011). In past disasters, these lower social capital metrics have accompanied slower, less-focused recoveries. Along with more shallow reservoirs of social capital, the Tōhoku areas have fewer financial resources as well compared to other parts of Japan. To ensure that Tōhoku is on the right track, the government can take several steps to ensure that recovery plans strengthen, not weaken, existing ties.

First, authorities should work to keep friends, neighborhoods, and networks intact when placing them in more permanent shelters; this prevents the kind of social isolation that resulted in "lonely deaths" (*kodokushi* in Japanese) following the 1995 Kobe Earthquake. Second, local governments should think about ways of getting home-bound seniors more interaction both with neighbors and visitors, perhaps through funding for homebound visits or support for NGOs and NPOs which take on these tasks. Finally, localities affected by the disaster should engage in policies that promote civic engagement and volunteerism, whether through community currency programs, support for *matsuri* (Japanese festivals) and public events, or funding for new local initiatives. Viewed from the context of the top-down, technocratic nuclear power field, decision makers need to recognize that the process of recovery from the disaster needs to be a bottom-up, resident-driven one in which local needs – not national priorities – drive public policy.

Notes

1   Daniel P. Aldrich is associate professor of public policy and political science at Purdue University, a member of the Mansfield US-Japan Network for the Future, and an AAAS Fellow. He thanks John Ash, Ken Hartman, Eric Dinmore, Jeff Kingston, and Paul Scalise and for their detailed comments and suggestions.

2   The 2011 UN Global Assessment Report on Disaster Risk Reduction labeled the event as a "synchronous failure" involving "a multisectoral systems collapse." Engineers often cite the 2003 blackouts in the United States as a cascading failure, but more important for this paper is the interaction between a "natural" disaster and the sociotechnical environment in which it happened. Hurricane Katrina, for example, was only a category 3 storm when it made landfall in Louisiana, but it interacted with poorly constructed levees, high levels of poverty, racism, and underpreparedness to create a tremendous catastrophe.

3   See www.ezkerabertzalea.info/doku/principlesandwill.pdf for a sample statement from activists who see the nuclear power plants at Lemoiz as another form of prejudice.

4   The results can be found in Aldrich 2008; the complete list of the 500 towns in the full dataset can be found online at: http://dvn.iq.harvard.edu/dvn/dv/daldrich.

5   Ireland – nicknamed the "Celtic Tiger" due to its strong economic growth – has maintained one of the highest levels of GDP per capita growth among the OECD despite the extended economic downturn recently, and was in the top 24 nations according to the 2010 World Bank Development Indicators. New Zealand, while slightly below the OECD average in terms of real GDP per capita as of 2010, has demonstrated an ability to maintain environmentally friendly energy while displaying strong GDP growth over the past two decades. While neither nation has an economy the size of Japan's, both are advanced industrial democracies with strong industrial bases that have pursued alternative sources of energy with more zeal than Japan. In short, geography is not destiny when it comes to power supply.

6   Some have argued that Nakasone and other members of the nuclear lobby emerged out of trans-World War II boosterism for hydroelectricity (personal communication, Eric Dinmore June 2011).
7   METI spun off the Japan Industrial Location Center, Japan Atomic Energy Relations Organization, and the Center for Development of Power Supply Regions to handle public relations and incentives campaigns.
8   Public pronouncements about the need for indigenous sources of electricity predated the mid-1950s, with many politicians in the 1930s arguing for Japan's hydroelectric potential, believing that dams would be the "white coal" that would help solve the "resources problem" (personal communication Eric Dinmore, June 2011).

References

Aldrich, Daniel P. (2005) The limits of flexible and adaptive institutions: The Japanese government's role in nuclear power plant siting over the post-war period, in S. Hayden Lesbirel and Daigee Shaw (eds.), *Managing Conflict in Facility Siting*, pp. 111–136. Cheltenham: Edward Elgar Publishers.

Aldrich, Daniel P. (2008) *Site Fights: Divisive Facilities and Civil Society in Japan and the West*, Ithaca, NY: Cornell University Press.

Aldrich, Daniel P. (2010) Fixing recovery: Social capital in post-crisis resilience. *Journal of Homeland Security*, Volume 6, June, pp. 1–10.

Aldrich, Daniel P. (2011) The power of people: Social capital's role in recovery from the 1995 Kobe Earthquake, *Natural Hazards*, Vol. 56 No. 3 pp. 595–611.

Aldrich, Daniel P. (forthcoming) Social, not physical, infrastructure: The critical role of civil society in disaster recovery, *Disasters: The Journal of Disaster Studies, Policy and Management*.

Aldrich, Daniel P. and Crook, Kevin (2008) Strong civil society as a double edged sword: Siting trailers in post-Katrina New Orleans, *Political Research Quarterly*, Vol. 61 No. 3 September pp. 379–389.

Baumgartner, Frank and Jones, Bryan (2003) *Agendas and Instability in American Politics*, Chicago, IL: University of Chicago Press.

Bullard, Robert (2000) *Dumping in Dixie: Race, Class and Environmental Quality*, Boulder, CO: Westview Press.

Clingermayer, J (1994) Electoral representation, zoning politics, and the exclusion of group homes, *Political Research Quarterly*, Vol. 47 No. 4 pp. 969–984.

Cohen, Linda, McCubbins, Mathew, and Rosenbluth, Frances (1995) The politics of nuclear power in Japan and the United States, in Peter Cowhey and Mathew McCubbins (eds.), *Structure and Policy in Japan and the United States*, New York: Cambridge University Press, pp. 177–202.

Dinmore, Eric (2006) A small island nation poor in resources: Natural and human resource anxieties in trans-World War II Japan, unpublished PhD dissertation for Princeton University, NJ.

Fackler, Martin and Ōnishi, Norimitsu (2011) In Japan, a culture that promotes nuclear dependency, *New York Times* 31 May.

Guttman, Amy and Thompson, Dennis (2004) *Why Deliberative Democracy?* Princeton, NJ: Princeton University Press.

Hamilton, James (1993) Politics and social costs: Estimating the impact of collective action on hazardous waste facilities, *RAND Journal of Economics*, Vol. 24 No. 1 pp. 101–125.

Harner, Stephen (2011) No Alternative to Nuclear Power, *Forbes*, March 23.

Hasegawa, Koichi (2004) *Constructing Civil Society in Japan: Voices of Environmental Movements*, Melbourne: Trans Pacific Press.

Jacobs, Lawrence and Shapiro, Robert V. (2000) *Politicians Don't Pander: Political Manipulation and the Loss of Democratic Responsiveness*, Chicago, IL: University of Chicago Press.

Jasper, James (1988) The political life cycle of technological controversies, *Social Forces*, Vol. 67 No. 2 pp. 357–377.

Kage, Rieko (2011) Comparing the Kobe and Tōhoku Pacific Coast Earthquakes, presentation prepared for conference Trying to Understand the Earthquake at the University of Michigan, March 21.

Lesbirel, S. Hayden (1988) *NIMBY Politics in Japan*, Ithaca, NY: Cornell University Press.

McAvoy, Gregory (1999) *Controlling Technocracy: Citizen Rationality and the NIMBY Syndrome*, Washington, DC: Georgetown University Press.

Ramseyer, Mark and Rosenbluth, Frances (1993) *Japan's Political Marketplace*, Cambridge, MA: Harvard University Press.

Rousseau, Jean-Jacques (1762) *Du Contrat Social, Principes du droit politique*, available in many English translations, including *The Social Contract* (1968), trans. M. Cranston, London: Penguin.

Skocpol, Theda (1992) *Protecting Soldiers and Mothers: The Political Origins of Social Policy in the United States*, Cambridge, MA: Harvard University Press.

Tsuda, Takeyuki (1998) The stigma of ethnic difference: The structure of prejudice and "discrimination" towards Japan's new immigrant minority, *Journal of Japanese Studies*, Vol. 24 No. 2 pp. 317–359.

8

HARD CHOICES

Japan's post-Fukushima energy policy in the twenty-first century

Paul J. Scalise[1]

The 'Great East Japan Earthquake' of 11 March 2011 inadvertently shook more than just infrastructure and private property; it threatened to create what some observers call a subsystem collapse (Baumgartner and Jones 1991). For most of the postwar era, a policy subsystem involving multiple actors evolved to meet Japan's market challenges and industrial development by offering energy diversification, energy efficiency, and finally greater reliance on nuclear power. These efforts risked sudden reversal in a matter of weeks following Japan's unprecedented magnitude-9 earthquake. The resulting 15-meter (49.2 feet) high tsunami flooded the back-up diesel generators cooling the Fukushima Daiichi Nuclear Power Station, owned and operated by Tokyo Electric Power Company (TEPCO). Within hours, the exposed fuel rods overheated leading to a nuclear meltdown (Evans 2011).

Today, this tsunami-induced nuclear disaster has kindled renewed interest in renewable energy development at the expense of nuclear power. On 31 March 2011, Prime Minister Kan Naoto expressed his intention to reconsider Japan's Basic Energy Plan (*Enerugi kihon keikaku* or BEP) and start discussions over from a clean slate (Fackler and Pollack 2011). Twenty-two days later, the entrepreneur, Son Masayoshi—Japan's richest man—presented his idea for an East Japan 'Solar Belt' in which billions of yen would be funneled away from nuclear power towards renewable energy. Speaking at a press conference on 10 May 2011, Kan acknowledged that the nuclear incident coupled with global warming led his cabinet to 'work to ensure an enhanced level of safety for nuclear power, while at the same time more vigorously promoting natural and reusable energy' (Press conference by Prime Minister Naoto Kan 2011). This idea not surprisingly morphed into the premier's desire for a 'nuclear-free society' in Diet hearings held on 13 July 2011 (Demetriou 2011).

As Japan raucously debates the future of nuclear power and renewable energy in both the National Diet and the courtroom of public opinion, some observers have wondered in which direction Japan's once 'quiet politics' of national energy policy, in which highly organized interest groups dominated the policy process in arenas shielded from public view, would take the country now that energy has become a 'high salience issue' (Culpepper 2011). Can Japan achieve a nuclear-free society without risk of rolling blackouts? Are energy security and environmental sustainability fundamentally compatible or mutually exclusive? Is economic efficiency still possible in an energy market that also promotes and subsidizes renewable energy sources?

This chapter seeks answers to these fundamental questions. It begins by discussing the fundamental principles of Japan's national energy policy since BEP in broad strokes – what has changed and how. It then explores the origins and logic of this policy by analyzing the country's electricity sector in cross-national and longitudinal context.[2] The third section of the chapter analyzes the feasibility of BEP pre- and post-Fukushima. It finds that many of the policy goals and aspirations of its political actors to be sometimes vague, contradictory, or logistically difficult given Japan's market structure. The final section discusses the political will and capacity actors have to change Japan's energy policy, concluding that no single actor dominates the process. If a subsystem collapse is imminent, to whom or what can this change be attributed and what lessons can be draw from it?

Basic energy plan: background, structure and targets

Japan's national energy policy, like its electric power regulations, can be described best as reactionary. For much of its post-Meiji history, decision makers lacked a comprehensive energy strategy choosing to rely on an assortment of ad hoc rules, regulations, and laws that were generally wielded in times of national uncertainty and economic crisis (Scalise 2009: 73–106, 148–192). In the postwar era, these measures were adopted often in response to the oil shocks of the 1970s, the 'lost decade' of the 1990s, and the global warming initiatives of the new millennium.

Current national energy policy is broadly outlined in the Basic Act on Energy Policy (*Enerugi seisaku kihon hō*, Act No. 71) of 14 June 2002.[3] It generally sets out to improve what is known as the '3 Es': energy security (Article 2), environmental sustainability (Article 3); and economic efficiency (Article 4). Like most Japanese laws, the Act does not offer much by way of detail and numerical targets. However, under Article 12 of the Act, the BEP diverges from previous policies by authorizing the government to 'formulate a basic plan … in order to promote measures on energy supply and demand on a long-term, comprehensive and systematic basis.' It is reviewed every three years, and revised when needed.

Revisions proved necessary in May 2006. Along with growing resource competition with China and India, the price of imported crude oil rose by almost 400 percent from 1998 ($12.8/barrel) to 2006 ($63.5/barrel) precipitating a re-evaluation of policy (Figure 8.1). The Ministry of Economy, Trade, and Industry (METI) drafted The New National Energy Strategy (*Shin-kokkai enerugii senryaku* or NNES), which established a target for the proportion of nuclear energy in total power generation of 30–40 percent or higher by 2030 (OECD/IEA 2008: 30). In June 2010, this target was raised to 50 percent or higher. Other revisions in 2010 included:

- doubling Japan's 'energy independence ratio' from 38 percent to 70 percent;
- increasing the proportion of renewable energy in total power generation to 20 percent or higher by 2030;
- doubling the zero-emission power source ratio from 34 percent to 70 percent;
- cutting the CO_2 emissions from the residential sector by half; and
- maintaining and enhancing the energy efficiency in the industrial sector at the highest levels of the world.

The energy independence ratio is defined as the sum of its energy self-sufficiency (sources that can be produced domestically) and the purchase of fossil fuels under independent development. Because Japan is resource poor and dependent on 96 percent of its primary energy supply, and especially as it imports virtually 90 percent of its imported oil from the politically volatile Middle East, finding alternatives that shield the country's vulnerability to severe fossil fuel price fluctuations and potential shortages on the world market have become the priority (ANRE 2006; Scalise 2004). In order to reach these new targets, Japan would have been required to increase its share of nuclear power in the generation of electric power from 29 percent to 50 percent while simultaneously raising its share of renewables from 9 percent (of which 8 percentage points are hydro) to 20 percent. Concurrently, fossil fuels would have to have decreased in both absolute and relative terms. According to the Strategic Energy Plan, liquefied natural gas (LNG) would have to fall from 28 percent to approximately 10 percent; coal would fall from 25 percent to 10 percent; and petroleum-based sources would fall from 13 percent to less than 1 percent (METI 2010: 10).

The second broad target, which is related to the first, concerns Japan's zero-emission power source ratio in terms of greenhouse gas (GHG) emissions. The world scientific consensus sees a strong linkage between fossil-fuel burning, climate change, and environmental impacts (Houghton and Intergovernmental Panel on Climate Change. Working Group I. 2001). Because approximately 63 percent of Japan's electric power continues to be generated from fossil fuels, expanding the generation technologies of renewables and nuclear power would help dramatically to reduce GHG emissions (Hoffert, et al. 2002; Service 2005). Consequently, Japan's energy independence ratio would need to correspond to its zero-emission power source ratio in order to achieve success. One of the greatest obstacles is economic.

Japan's energy economics in the twenty-first century

Japan's capital expenditures (*setsubi tōshi*) in the electric power sector have been propelled by cost-benefit considerations, including resource availability, application technology, the useful life expectancy of the generation asset, its utilization rate (how much capacity is used in a given period relative to potential output) and political will. Table 8.1 provides Japan's current energy economics at a glance. As mentioned above, Japan's energy portfolio for electric power generation still predominantly consists of fossil fuels (63 percent), followed by nuclear (28 percent), hydro (8 percent), and other renewables (0. 3 percent).

Historically, Japanese electric power companies have shifted from one power source to another based on cost and value (Figure 8.1). Abundant and inexpensive hydro-electric power gave way to domestic coal production after most appropriate hydro-electric sites were captured, thus slowly increasing political and economic costs to further building large-scale dams in remote locations. Domestically-mined coal gave way to inexpensive and abundant supplies of imported oil following import liberalization in 1961 (Culter 1999). Oil then gave way to a diversified energy portfolio including imported liquefied natural gas (LNG), imported coal, and inexpensive nuclear power in equal measure following the 1973 oil shock. A major shift towards nuclear power was set to become the next phase.

TABLE 8.1 Energy mix (2010)

Fuel	Power generation	Current generation cost	Useful life	Avg. construction cost	Maximum utilization rate	CO_2 emission
Unit	(TWh)	(Yen/kWh)	(Years)	(Yen/kW)	(%)	(CO_2-eq./ kWh)
Coal	237.9 (24%)	6~7.6	30–40	336	85	975.2
LNG	282.4 (28%)	8.4~10.1	30–40	222	68	607.6
Nuclear	279.8 (28%)	5.1~7.4	40–60	368	90	22.1
Oil	101.9 (10%)	9~15	30–40	387	55	742.1
Hydro	79.3 (8%)	8~13	80+	690	85	11.3
Geothermal	2.6 (0.3%)	8~22	20–30	340	85	15
Wind	(Intermittent)	10~15	20	300	30	29.5
Solar	(Intermittent)	30~58.7	20	300	15	53.4

Notes: A kilowatt-hour, or kWh, is the amount of electricity required to power 10 100-watt light bulbs for one hour. A terawatt-hour, or TWh, is one billion kilowatt hours.

Sources: for generation cost per kWh estimates by fuel type, see: Federation of Electric Power Companies of Japan interview (June 2011), based on data from University of Tokyo. For power generation, utilization rates, and useful life, see: *Denki jigyō rengōkai tōkei iinkai, ed. Denki jigyō binran* (Handbook of Electric Power Industry) (2010) Tokyo: Nihon denki kyōkai. For average construction cost per kW, see: *Denryoku shinsetsubi yōran* (Survey of New Electric Power Facilities) (2006) Tokyo: Ministry of Economy, Trade, and Industry. For CO_2-equivalent per kWh by fuel type, see: Communications Office (2003) "Nuclear Power Generation and the Nuclear Fuel Cycle," in *Energy in Japan*, edited by Agency for Natural Resources and Energy. Tokyo: Ministry of Economy, Trade, and Industry.

Japan's policymakers originally chose nuclear power as a strategic necessity in order to enhance national energy security, buffer the economy from energy shocks, and perhaps even serve as an important export product (Kim and Byrne 1996). Japan's unique lack of natural resources justified not only nuclear power, but also a commitment to plutonium fueled fast breeder reactors (Byrne and Hoffman 1996). This extensive support was tacitly based on a 'lesser of two evils' rationale in which the risks posed by fossil fuels outweighed the risks posed by nuclear power. In his chapter, Daniel Aldrich discusses the ways in which authorities mapped out locations and used policy instruments to induce public support in order to complete this technocratic vision – a task that became increasingly difficult over time.

Activists, students, and policy entrepreneurs have long debated the political economy of competing energy sources to replace nuclear power since the events of Three Mile Island in 1979. Nuclear power's positive media image characterized as 'atoms for peace' (jobs, economic growth, and abundantly cheap and clean power) slowly shifted towards a negative image consisting of mushroom clouds,

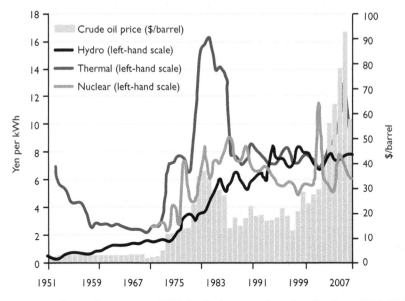

FIGURE 8.1 Generation cost per kWh by fuel type and crude oil prices, 1951–2010 (sources: for generation cost per kWh by fuel type, 1951-2000, see: *Kantō no denki jigyō to tōkyō denryoku* (Electric Power Industry and TEPCO in the Kanto Region), CD-ROM (2000) Tokyo: Tōkyō Denkryoku. For generation cost per kWh by fuel type, 2001–2010, see: *Yūka shōken hōkokusho* (Annual Report – various years) Tokyo: Tokyo Electric Power Co. For historical crude oil prices, see: EDMC 2010).

Notes: actual power generation costs fluctuate depending not only on the operating period but also on the load factor, imported fuel costs, weighted average cost of capital, and other fixed costs. Decommissioning and reprocessing of irradiated fuel are included in nuclear power's generation cost per kWh, pre-Fukushima.

radioactive waste, nuclear fallout, and the like. Yet despite this negative image, clear trade-offs have prevented decision makers from placing all of Japan's eggs into another energy basket. Fossil fuel-powered generation (coal, natural gas, and oil) continues to be among the most cost competitive and reliable electric power sources in Japan, but rising imported fuel prices coupled with a high carbon footprint and death toll linked to its extraction, operation, and maintenance make it politically and environmentally unattractive.[4] By contrast, solar power is quiet and clean, but its prohibitive cost per kWh and low utilization rate ensure its marginalization for energy-intensive industries requiring stable 'baseloads' to operate efficiently during business hours. Wind power is far less costly per kWh, and offers a slightly higher utilization rate, but its unreliability requires increasing fossil-fuel back-up sources while the windmills pose a danger to avian wildlife. Hydroelectric and geothermal power – both called 'mature' renewable energy sources – show strong promise on economic and environmental grounds, but face political opposition from activists and small business owners alike who disapprove of flooded valleys, alterations to the ecosystem, and unpredictable exploration prospects in environmentally fragile locations (sometimes national parks) where, for example, it is hot enough to produce geothermal steam close to the surface.

Because new renewables are relatively high-cost and intermittent (Table 8.1), support mechanisms such as feed-in tariffs, green certificates, premiums, and production tax credits are still needed to induce residential and industrial support. The *political* support for and the inducement policies towards increasing renewable energy, however, began long before the events of 11 March. One such example is the Special Measures Law Concerning the Use of New Energy by Electric Utilities (*Denki jigyōsha ni yoru shin-enerugii nado no riyō ni kansuru tokubetsu sochi hō*, Act No. 62), which the National Diet passed in 2002 and implemented in 2003 reinforcing renewable energy promotion measures. The eponymously named 'Fukuda Vision' announced by the former premier in response to growing concern in Japan about climate change is another such example. Following a speech entitled 'Action Plan for Achieving a Low-carbon Society' on 29 July 2008 (GWPH 2008), a series of policy measures were implemented by the government to counter GHG emissions. On the residential front, starting in January 2009 METI provided subsidies and tax credits for the installation and renovation of solar panels on residential homes. On the industrial front, METI encouraged the beginnings of a feed-in tariff that required electric power companies to buy surplus solar power from residential homes at ¥50 per kWh until at least 2020.

Feasibility and performance: whither Japan?

Speaking at an energy symposium in Chino, Nagano prefecture, on 31 July 2011, Prime Minister Kan argued that Japan 'cannot take a risk [with nuclear power] that could destroy the Earth even if it is a one in a hundred million chance… Renewable energy will lead to Japan's new industrial revolution' (Kyodo 2011). Such rhetoric aside, one of the most important questions to analyze is the feasibility of the national energy policy in a post-Fukushima Japan. Notwithstanding the technological constraints and innovations of new renewables versus nuclear power, one should consider underlying supply and demand for electric power in cross-national context – two sides of the same political and economic coin.

In fiscal year 2010 (ending March 2011), almost 1,112 terawatt-hours of electricity were generated in Japan, a 4 percent increase from 2000. The Japan Center for Economic Research forecasts 1.1 percent growth in GDP in 2000–2025 for its positive case. If GDP growth leads to increased consumption of electricity in Japan as econometric studies have suggested (Cheng 1998; Lee 2006), new renewables would need to increase by seven to eight times to achieve the 20 percent generation target and the 70 percent targets for energy independence ratio and zero-emission generation sources, respectively. Yet, this increase of seven or eight times assumes no growth in conventional fossil-fuel generated sources or nuclear power. Moreover, should Japan's 54 nuclear power plants gradually be decommissioned without further nuclear build – as Kan and others have suggested should happen – these targets will be extremely difficult to reach.

About 18.8 gigawatts (GW) of generating capacity are currently under construction with most being gas-fired and coal-fired power plants. A further 30.8 GW is planned, including 42 megawatts (0.1 percent) of new renewables, by 2015. If Japan hopes to achieve its GHG emission target reductions, it will depend greatly on the amount of renewable energy and nuclear power it can commercially introduce over the next 20 years. As of August 2011, these prospects appear dim; only 19 of Japan's 54 nuclear reactors (35 percent) are on-line with political pressure to maintain the status quo until safety assurances are met (JAIF 2011a).

TABLE 8.2 International comparison, 1990 vs. 2010

	Industrial tariff (¢/kWh)		Residential tariff (¢/kWh)		Reserve Margin (%)	New Renewables (%)		
	1990	2010	1990	2010		1990	2000	2010
Denmark	7	12.6	20.9	36.6	120	3.1	15.5	27.5
Germany	4.9	10.9	13.6	16.7	85	0.3	2.4	13.2
Iceland	n/a	n/a	n/a	n/a	100	6.7	17.2	27.1
Japan	11.5	16.8	17.4	24.8	10	1.4	1.6	2.2
Spain	4.8	10.3	11.4	21.2	20	0.4	2.8	15.8

Notes: 'New renewables' excludes hydroelectric and includes geothermal, solar photovoltaic, solar thermal, biomass, liquid biomass, biogas, wind, tide, wave, ocean, and municipal waste. The reserve margin is the percentage of installed capacity in excess of peak demand. Tariff data for Iceland are unavailable.

Sources: OECD/IEA 2003, 2006, 2007, 2008, 2009, 2011.

Virtually all OECD countries provide 'new renewable' generation at some level. However, geography, market structure, and government policy determine the quantity. Denmark (wind), Germany (solar), Iceland (geothermal), and Spain (wind/solar) provide 15~30 percent of their total generated electricity from new renewables. In contrast with Japan, however, all four leading countries in renewable energy had relatively low electricity prices in 1990 *before* the introduction of feed-in tariffs. In addition, electricity capacity reserve margins – a common metric for surplus capacity – indicated percentages well above 20 percent (Table 8.2). This pre-existing oversupply prevented the intermittent supplies generated by new renewables from risking blackouts as surplus back-up power existed in the event that solar, wind, and other renewables were unable to meet peak demand.

With Japan's national reserve margin in the low 10 percent range and falling year-on-year (Scalise 2011a, 2011b), rolling blackout risk places renewed emphasis on rapid investment from stable sources with relatively quick lead times in the siting, licensing, and construction of new generation capacity. The Ministry of Environment (MOE) has already granted TEPCO a special exemption from conducting environment impact studies before expanding and building fossil-fuel power plants in the Kantō region, thus highlighting how economic realities continue to trump environmental concerns (Nikkei 2011). This economic reality militates against strong support for new renewables among industry and the incumbent suppliers in the short- to medium-term as TEPCO and Tōhoku EPCO struggle to bring capacity back online.

On the demand side of the equation, Japanese industry continues to be the largest consumer of energy as well as the largest producer of CO_2 emissions by sector at 46 percent and 34 percent, respectively. Yet from 1990–2008, they also made the strongest improvements in both energy efficiency and reduced CO_2 emissions by sector, thus creating further challenges as *setsuden* (energy conservation) becomes more important in Japan (EDMC 2010: 38, 47). With *Keidanren*, the principal industrial peak association for virtually all big businesses and companies in Japan, quite vocal in its opposition to higher electricity prices from the introduction of feed-in tariffs and other austerity measures sacrificing business productivity, a larger share of the burden will need to be carried by the largely inefficient residential and commercial sectors if the goals of the BEP and NNES are to be met.

Is a subsystem collapse imminent?

A fundamental move away from nuclear power towards renewable energy sources would require more than just technical blueprints and economic incentives to surpass Japan's structural challenges analyzed in previous sections of this chapter; it would require a shift in actor perceptions and policy images that form what some observers call 'policy whirlpools,' 'iron triangles,' or 'subsystem politics' (Griffith 1939; Heclo 1978; Redford 1969). This phenomenon characterizes several actor interests that come together in certain political venues for the purpose of compromise and coordination. Consequently, success or failure of Japan's national energy policy partially rests with the level of support from Japan's decision makers at local, prefectural, and national levels in these policy venues.

Since the Fukushima disaster, public opinion polls indicate a gradual souring towards nuclear power in the 13 prefectures that host nuclear plants. Telephone surveys conducted by the *Asahi Shimbun* in the months of April, May, and June 2011 suggest diminishing support for nuclear power in Japan. In its April 2011 survey, the newspaper found that 32 percent disapproved of nuclear power while 50 percent were in support. One month later, the same newspaper recorded a slight increase in disapproval while support levels dropped to 43 percent. By June 2011, the situation reversed: disapproval was almost half of respondents while approval for nuclear power fell to only 37 percent (JAIF 2011b). This political souring has forced most prefectural governors to refuse permission to restart those that are offline until they have convincing assurances of their safety.

It remains to be seen if this gradual shift in voter perceptions will materially impact the political arena. The Democratic Party of Japan-led government, once a vocal supporter of lowering Japan's GHG emissions by 25 percent from 1990 levels by 2020 under the Hatoyama cabinet, began to backtrack on renewable energy development and their emission targets as soon as the party encountered industry opposition and conflicting budget priorities in 2009–2010 (Hughes 2009; Scalise 2010). If the Kan cabinet, and its successors, hope to promote a shift towards new renewables, they will need to take stock of the political landscape.

There are ten major electric power corporations (EPCOs, *ippan denki jigyōsha*) in Japan: TEPCO, Kansai (KEPCO), Chubu (CEPCO), Tōhoku, Chūgoku, Kyushū, Hokuriku, Shikoku, Hokkaido, and Okinawa. All nine EPCOs except Okinawa own and operate nuclear power plants. Organizing their common interest via the Federation of Electric Power Companies of Japan (*Denki jigyō rengōkai*, hereafter FEPC), they are the most obvious of the agenda setters though not necessarily the most powerful. Their relative size, de facto monopoly status, relationship with wholesale suppliers, privately owned assets, and control of pricing information is stronger than that of almost any other developed nation, yet evidence of direct linkages with the political process is circumstantial, at best. Despite the roughly 70 known electricity suppliers in Japan's nationwide market that range from joint-ventured electric power utilities (JVs, *kyōdō karyoku hatsuden denki jigyōsha*) to municipal utilities (*kōei denki jigyōsha*) to larger wholesale electric-power suppliers (*oroshi denki jigyōsha*), none of the ten major EPCOs have made (reported) cash contributions to any of the major political parties since 1977 (Scalise 2009: 57–62, Tatsuru 1983: 81–84). Only an occasional donation from one of the JVs or regional municipals can be seen over time, and such donations are relatively small.

There are several reasons for this lack of overt political maneuvering. One is size. The Japanese companies are among the largest in the world, measured in terms of kilowatt-hours and installed capacity. TEPCO, for example, remains the largest privately owned electric power company in Japan, and is surpassed worldwide only by the State Power Corporation of China, EDF, and E.ON. We should stress the word *private* in this context. The sheer size of such electricity sales and installed capacity suggests a lucrative market for potential new entrants should full liberalization occur. Moreover, because of the size of the industry, we should consider the various corporate linkages and political aspects of employment – areas of concern that directly and indirectly affect more than just the EPCOs.

Leaving aside the political and economic question of new entrants into the electricity market, there is a stable number of suppliers and growing number of generators in postwar Japan. Based on these initial figures, one could easily mistake this seemingly fragmented market as conducive to greater price competition under more liberalized market conditions. However, appearances can be deceiving. Since their 1951 postwar reorganization into the nine regionally independent vertically integrated utilities, the incumbent suppliers have predominantly controlled the means of electricity generation as well as its transmission and distribution to the vast majority of end users. This 'vertically integrated' structure has led to nine regional de facto monopolies on power.[5]

Their regulator, METI (formerly MITI), takes a decisively pro-business approach in their dealings with the electric power companies and their competitors. In recent years, the MOE has competed with METI for the upper hand in the regulatory control of the sector (Peng Er 2010). While the MOE takes an actively pro-environment approach for obvious reasons of self-interest and preservation, the political necessity (mentioned above) of maintaining a stable supply of power in Japan sometimes forces the MOE to turn a blind eye to certain environmental regulations in the name of economic efficiency and stability. Some observers argue that the government-business relationship is theoretically strengthened via *amakudari* (literal translation: 'descent from heaven'). If ministerial career advancement seems unlikely between the ages of 45 and 55, ministry officials usually 'descend' into either a private sector position or politics. *Amakudari* is an omnipresent phenomenon in the electric power sector; all major listed utilities have at least one former career bureaucrat sitting on the board of directors (*yakuinkai*) and elsewhere, though their exact purpose, connections, and usefulness is debatable.[6]

It remains to be seen if politicians will adopt a similar 'pro-stability' tack in the coming years. All draft bills concerning the economic development of the electricity industry and regulatory matters related therein fall under the purview of the Commerce and Industry Committee (*Shōkō i'inkai*, hereafter CIC) in the postwar period, later renamed the Economy, Trade and Industry Committee (*Keizai sangyō i'inkai*) in 2000.[7] The Lower House's CIC is comprised of 40 members, and the Upper House's CIC is comprised of 20 members; it is one of the larger standing committees in the Diet and one of the most active. Historically, the LDP occupied the majority of seats on both CIC with a smattering of opposition parties thrown into the fray. In 1999, for example, LDP members held 23 out of 40 or 58 percent of the Lower House's CIC seats versus 10 out of 21 or 48 percent of the Upper House's CIC. The number of bills brought before a given committee range widely in any given year. The figure can be as low as one to as high as 16.

Some observers have argued that the Diet is a mere rubber-stamping organ of the bureaucracy (Johnson 1982: 48–49; van Wolferen 1990: 44). Yet, politicians have the legal authority either to reject or revise draft bills at their discretion.[8] In the case of energy, postwar politicians have been known to attack bills drafted by the METI bureaucracy when they either failed to support political expectations or did not stand up to scrutiny during standard question-and-answer periods. One appropriate example in recent years dealt with partial revisions to the laws regulating the electric power industry and nuclear waste from reactors (*Denki jigyō hō oyobi genryō busshi, kakunenryō busshi, oyobi genshiro no kisei ni kansuru hōritsu no ichibu o kaisei suru hōritsu*). In November 2002, the Lower House CIC voted to revise the bill (and again in the plenary session) after several tense questioning bouts revealed serious safety flaws in the proposed bills overlooked by both the *shingikai* (advisory councils) and the bureaucracy. Such an occurrence has been commonplace in the postwar period. One scholar found that of the 9,135 draft bills presented to the Diet in 1947–2001, 1,811 (or 20 percent) were revised significantly before passage at the instruction of the standing committees (Masuyama 2003: 35).

The extent to which *zoku* ('policy tribes') set the agenda in Japan's government-business relationship surrounding energy policy is debatable, of course. These *zoku* are politicians who are actively involved in the jurisdictional activities of one particular ministry, acquire a level of expert knowledge in that area, and then represent (i.e. lobby for) the interests of that industry in the Diet (Curtis 1999: 53–55; Inoguchi and Iwai 1987; Ishikawa 1990) As a result, area specific *zoku* tend to build close relationships with the bureaucracy.

There is no specific electricity industry *zoku*. The closest equivalent is either the energy *zoku*, which oversees the activities of METI regarding basic energy policy and strategy, or the commerce and industry *zoku*, which by definition covers a much broader range of industries. These two groups have never publicly championed the interests of the EPCO as a business. Indeed, the energy *zoku* under the leadership of Toshizuku Kanei in the Research Commission on Oil, Resources and Energy (*Sekiyutō shigen enerugi chōsakai*) are primarily concerned with the problems associated with electricity supply and demand. In particular, these energy *zoku* concern themselves with long-term strategies not only to meet the demand, but also to secure its supply through the further implementation of nuclear power. Electric power restructuring is not considered relevant.

Individual politicians might have a special interest. Tokio Kanō (LDP) is a former TEPCO vice president, serving his second six-year term as a member of the House of Councilors. As of 2003, he sits as vice chairman of the influential House of Councilors' Economy, Trade, and Industry Committee (*Keizai sangyō i'inkai*). Mr. Kanō makes thinly veiled pro-EPCO statements by advocating the importance of energy security and stability over greater competition and has the full support of the incumbent EPCOs ('*Chū, in tono kankei hatten ga jūyō* [it is important for Japan to develop relations with China and India]' 2006). Kiyoshi Hasegawa (DPJ) is a former TEPCO employee and Vice President of the Electric Power Labor Federation (*Denryoku roren*). Like Mr. Kanō, he served two six-year terms in the House of Councilors' Economy, Trade, and Industry Committee before retiring from politics in 2004. Mr. Hasegawa's interests rest firmly with those of organized labor, as evinced by his induction into the SDPJ in 1992 – a party that received large cash contributions from organized labor and held clear pro-labor platforms. Finally, Masashi Fujiwara (DPJ) might also have a special interest. A former KEPCO employee and active labor union leader for over thirty years – first for KEPCO and later for *Denryoku Sōren* as vice president – Mr. Fujiwara was elected to the House of Councilors in 2001. It is possible that all three of these politicians received funding from the electricity industry, though nothing in this investigation was conclusive in that respect.

To be sure, the presence of such an ambiguous force may present another obstacle to the implementation of a new and successful energy policy as '[T]he active presence of *zoku* [makes] it more difficult' for politicians to coordinate policies (Schoppa 1991).

Conclusions

This chapter has sought to elucidate the broad evolution of energy policy in postwar Japan, how it has changed and why; to explain the nature of policy change more generally, in particular the role of framing; to analyze the economic and technical realities of Japan's energy market in cross-national context as decision makers apply foreign roadmaps to their country's policies; and finally to learn about the capacities of various interest groups in Japanese democracy, who can create policy changes and who cannot.

To be sure, Japan's national energy policy is at a crossroads. In the short span of four months, public opinion soured towards Japan's nuclear power program as TEPCO failed to contain the nuclear crisis at Fukushima Daiichi Nuclear Power Station. What was once the domain of consummate insiders has now spread to a public increasingly apprehensive about nuclear safety. Re-election minded politicians, career-minded bureaucrats, energy-intensive industries concerned about high prices, eco-entrepreneurs and beleaguered power companies now jockey for position in the courtroom of public opinion.

How did all of this occur and what does it teach us about the future? This chapter argues that Japanese national energy policy is a fragile consensus that unravels once the underlying assumptions surrounding the policy's purpose change; that external shocks tend to provoke crises that force decision makers to import workable blueprints of sector reorganization. The energy diversification and demand management programs that emphasized nuclear power set in place following the 660 percent rise in imported oil prices in 1973–1981 continued uninterrupted for two decades despite eroding power company profit margins, high electricity prices, and declining shareholder value. Following the relative failure of electricity liberalization and the neo-liberal ideas that propelled it in the 1990s, Japan embarked on the next great wave of sectoral re-organization in the midst of resource nationalism, the meteoric rise of China, global warming initiatives and the Kyoto Protocol, and final the *coup de grace*: renewed oil price spikes in 1998–2008. 'Energy security,' not 'energy efficiency,' became the political mantra that produced the 2002 BEP and the 2006 NNES.

If the latest shock to the system provokes an increasingly anti-nuclear backlash, the lack of nuclear power to meet demand will certainly place further risk on electric power companies struggling to maintain a secure, stable supply of electricity. Such a political environment would almost certainly force decision makers to abandon their ambitious GHG emission targets by increasingly resorting to conventional thermal fossil fuel generation. *Setsuden* (energy conservation) might be one of the policy tools needed in curbing future blackout risk in Japan, but the more conventional power used to replace nuclear power opens renewed threats to volatile imported fossil fuel prices.

Today, the question of which paradigm will dominate public discourse – energy security and economic efficiency (nuclear power) or environmental sustainability (renewable energy) – plays out in the National Diet and the media. Japan struggles to implement public policies once again to counter recurring external shocks reinforced by the latest incident at Fukushima, but faces technological uncertainties and economic risks. As overseas renewable energy policies – feed-in tariffs for all new renewables in particular – are the latest subject of interest, many observers wonder if Japan's democracy will produce suitable answers. High cost and unreliability could make new renewables a hard sell to a country that values stability and certainty. The manufacturing sector and electric power utilities, which prioritize stability in energy prices and supply, will oppose pro-renewable energy proposals that risk even higher electricity prices. Yet politicians will come under growing anti-nuclear pressure as the full costs of the Fukushima disaster, and the real costs and risk of nuclear energy, emerge and many businesses seek new opportunities in renewable business opportunities.

Notes

1 Paul J. Scalise is JSPS Postdoctoral Fellow at the Institute of Social Science, University of Tokyo, and Non-Resident Fellow at the Institute of Contemporary Asian Studies, Temple University, Japan Campus. The author would like to thank Naomi Fink, Tai Inada, Taro Ishida, Jeff Kingston, Samuel Lederer, and Ikuo Nishimura for their helpful comments and suggestions.

2 This chapter focuses exclusively on the issue of electric power generation and its spillover effects. It will not discuss energy policy as it pertains to upstream fossil fuel exploration and its downstream distribution businesses.

3 An English-language translation of this bill is available at: www.japaneselawtranslation. go.jp.

4 According to a study commissioned by the Swiss Federal Office of Energy, there were a recorded 4,290 energy accidents worldwide, 1,943 defined as severe, between 1969 and 1996. The number of corresponding energy-related fatalities were 19,650 (coal), 12,638 (hydro-electric), 15,257 (oil), 3,236 (LPG), 1,375 (natural gas), and 33 (nuclear). See Hirschberg, *et al.* (1998).

5 Okinawa EPCO was established with full government funding on 15 May 1972. The company was privatized after 16 years of public control on 1 October 1988 becoming

the tenth privately owned EPCO. In this chapter, any general reference to 'EPCOs' alludes to all ten companies unless stated otherwise.

6   The exact definition of *amakudari* varies from author to author. For a thorough empirical analysis of *amakudari* and its various theories and hypotheses in English, see: Colignon and Usui (2003).

7   Rules of the House of Representatives 1947, Section 5, Article 92, Clause 9. Tokyo: EHS Law Bulletin Series; Rules of the House of Councilors 1947, Section 4, Article 74, Clause 9, subparagraph 7. Tokyo: EHS Law Bulletin Series.

8   The Diet Law (Law No. 79, 1947), Ch. 6, Article 56, paragraphs 3 and 4. Tokyo: EHS Law Bulletin Series; Rules of the House of Representatives 1947, Section 5, Article 143. Tokyo: EHS Law Bulletin Series; Rules of the House of Councilors 1947, Section 5, Article 125. Tokyo: EHS Law Bulletin Series.

References

ANRE (2006) *Energy in Japan 2006: Status and Policies*, Tokyo: Ministry of Economy, Trade, and Industry.

Baumgartner, F.R. and Jones, B.D. (1991) 'Agenda dynamics and policy subsystems,' *The Journal of Politics*, 53(4): 1044–1074.

Byrne, J. and Hoffman, S.M. (1996) 'The ideology of progress and the globalization of nuclear power,' in: Byrne, J. and Hoffman, S.M. (eds.), *Governing the Atom: The Politics of Risk*, London: Transaction Publishers.

Cheng, B.S. (1998) 'Energy consumption, employment and causality in Japan: A multivariate approach,' *Indian Economic Review*, 33(1): 19–29.

'Chū, in tono kankei hatten ga jūyō [it is important for Japan to develop relations with China and India]' (2006) *Denki Shimbun*, January 1.

Colignon, R.A. and Usui, C. (2003) *Amakudari: The Hidden Fabric of Japan's Economy*, Ithaca, NY: ILR Press.

Culpepper, P.D. (2011) *Quiet Politics and Business Power: Corporate Control in Europe and Japan*, New York: Cambridge University Press.

Culter, S. (1999) *Managing Decline: Japan's Coal Industry Restructuring and Community Response*, Honolulu, HI: University of Hawaii Press.

Curtis, G.L. (1999) *The Logic of Japanese Politics: Leaders, Institutions, and the Limits of Change*, New York: Columbia University Press.

Demetriou, Danielle (2011) "Japan should aim to become nuclear free society, says prime minister," national edition, *The Daily Telegraph* (London), 13 July, p. 17, online, available at: www.telegraph.co.uk/news/worldnews/asia/japan/8634755/Japan-should-aim-to-become-nuclear-free-society-says-prime-minister.html [accessed 13 November 2011].

EDMC (2010) *Energuii keizai tōkei yōran [Handbook for Energy and Economic Statistics]*, Tokyo: The Energy Data and Modeling Center.

Evans, M. (2011) 'Japan nuclear crisis: Timeline of official statements,' *The Telegraph*, 15 March, online, available at: www.telegraph.co.uk/news/worldnews/asia/japan/8383473/Japan-nuclear-crisis-Timeline-of-official-statements.html [accessed 27 July 2011].

Fackler, M. and Pollack, A. (2011) 'Disaster overturns Japan's nuclear program; Prime Minister shelves reactor plans and vows new focus on renewables,' *The New York Times*, 11 May.

Griffith, E.S. (1939) *The Impasse of Democracy: A Study of the Modern Government in Action*, New York: Harrison-Hilton Books.

GWPH (2008) 'Action plan for achieving a low-carbon society,' online, available at: www.kantei.go.jp/foreign/policy/ondanka/final080729.pdf [accessed 2 July 2011].

Heclo, H. (1978) 'Issue networks in the executive establishment,' in Beer, S. H. and King, A.S. (eds.), *The New American Political System*, Washington, DC: American Enterprise Institute for Public Policy Research.

Hirschberg, S., Spiekerman, G., and Dones, R. (1998) 'Severe accidents in the energy sector', *Comprehensive Assessment of Energy Systems*, Villigen: Aul Scherrer Institut, online, available at: http://manhaz.cyf.gov.pl/manhaz/szkola/materials/S3/psi_materials/ENSAD98.pdf.

Hoffert, M.L., Caldeira, K., Benford, G., Criswell, D.R., Green, C., Herzog, H., Jain, A.K., Kheshgi, H.S., Larkner, K.S., Lewis, J.S., Lightfoot, H.D., Manheimer, W., Mankins, J.C., Mauel, M.E., Perkins, L.J., Schlesinger, M.E., Volk, T., and Wigley, T.M.L. (2002) 'Advanced technology paths to global climate stability: Energy for a greenhouse planet,' *Science*, 298(5595): 981–987.

Houghton, J.T. and Intergovernmental Panel on Climate Change, Working Group I (2001) *Climate Change 2001: The Scientific Basis – Contribution of Working Group I to the Third Assessment Report of the Intergovernmental Panel on Climate Change*, Cambridge/New York: Cambridge University Press.

Hughes, L. (2009) 'Climate change and Japan's post-Copenhagen challenge,' *Brookings Northeast Asia Commentary*, Washington, DC: Brookings Institution.

Inoguchi, T. and Iwai, T. (1987) *Zoku gi'in no kenkyu [A Study in 'Policy Tribe Members']*, Tokyo: Nihon Keizai Shimbunsha.

Ishikawa, M. (1990) 'Medea—kenryoku he no eikyoryoku to kenryoku kara no eikyoryoku ['Media's impact: "to the powers that be" to "from the powers that be"],' *Leviathan, tokushu: Masu medea to seiji (Special Issue: Mass Media and Politics)*, Tokyo: Kitakyushu.

JAIF (2011a) 'Operating records of nuclear power plants in June 2011,' 1 July, online, available at: www.jaif.or.jp/english/news_images/pdf/ENGNEWS02_1310368183P.pdf [accessed 18 July 2011].

JAIF (2011b) 'Trend of public opinions on nuclear energy after Fukushima accident (March 11) in Japan,' online, available at: www.jaif.or.jp/english/news_images/pdf/ENGNEWS02_1312778417P.pdf [accessed 5 July 2011].

Johnson, C.A. (1982) *MITI and the Japanese Miracle: The Growth of Industrial Policy, 1925–1975*, Stanford, CA: Stanford University Press.

Kim, J.D. and Byrne, J. (1996) 'The Asian atom: Hard-path nuclearization in East Asia,' in Byrne, J. and Hoffman, S.M. (eds.), *Governing the Atom: The Politics of Risk*, London: Transaction Publishers.

Kyodo (2011) 'Kan repeats pledge to reduce reliance on nuclear power,' *Nikkei.com*, evening, online, available at: http://e.nikkei.com/e/ac/tnks/Nni20110731D3ZJF357.htm [accessed 31 July 2011].

Lee, C.-C. (2006) 'The causality relationship between energy consumption and GDP in G-11 countries revisited,' *Energy Policy*, 34(9): 1086–1093.

Masuyama, M. (2003) *Gikai seido to nihon seiji [Agenda Power in the Japanese Diet]*, Tokyo: Bokutakusha.

METI (2010) 'The strategic energy plan of Japan: Meeting global challenges and securing energy futures (revised in June 2010),' online, available at: www.meti.go.jp/english/press/data/pdf/20100618_08a.pdf [accessed 4 July 2011].

Nikkei (2011) 'TEPCO gets pass on impact studies for power plant expansions,' *Nikkei.com*, 5 April, online, available at: http://e.nikkei.com/e/fr/tnks/Nni20110404D04JFA18.htm [accessed 4 July 2011].

OECD/IEA (2003) 'Japan: 2003 review,' *Energy Policies of IEA Countries*, Paris: International Energy Agency.

OECD/IEA (2006) 'Denmark: 2006 review,' *Energy Policies of IEA Countries*, Paris: International Energy Agency.

OECD/IEA (2007) 'Germany: 2007 review,' *Energy Policies of IEA Countries*, Paris: International Energy Agency.

OECD/IEA (2008) 'Japan: 2008 review,' *Energy Policy of IEA Countries*, Paris: International Energy Agency.

OECD/IEA (2009) 'Spain: 2009 review,' *Energy Policies of IEA Countries*, Paris: International Energy Agency.

OECD/IEA (2011) 'Energy prices and taxes: Quarterly statistics (first quarter 2011),' *IEA Statistics*, Paris: International Energy Agency.

Peng Er, L. (2010) 'The Hatoyama administration and Japan's climate change initiatives,' *East Asian Policy*, 2(1): 69–77.

Press conference by Prime Minister Naoto Kan (2011) *Cabinet Office*, Tokyo: States News Service.

Redford, E.S. (1969) *Democracy in the Administrative State*, New York: Oxford University Press.

Scalise, P.J. (2004) 'National energy policy: Japan,' in Cleveland, C. and Ayres, R.U. (eds.), *Encyclopedia of Energy*, Boston, MA: Elsevier Academic Press.

Scalise, P.J. (2009) *The Politics of Restructuring: Agendas and Uncertainty in Japan's Electricity Deregulation*, D.Phil. doctoral dissertation, University of Oxford.

Scalise, P.J. (2010) 'Out of gas: Rethinking Hatoyama's energy policy,' *The Oriental Economist*, 78(5): 9–11.

Scalise, P.J. (2011a) 'Can TEPCO survive?' in Kingston, J. (ed.), *Tsunami: Japan's Post-Fukushima Future*, Tokyo: Foreign Policy.

Scalise, P.J. (2011b) 'Looming electricity crisis: Three scenarios for economic impact,' *The Oriental Economist*, 79(4): 8–9.

Schoppa, L.J. (1991) 'Zoku power and LDP power: A case study of the zoku role in education,' *Journal of Japanese Studies*, 17(1): 79–106.

Service, R.F. (2005) 'Is it time to shoot for the sun?' *Science*, 309(5734): 548–551.

Tatsuru, S. (1983) *Denryoku sangyō no atarashii chōsen [The New Challenges to the Electric Power Industry]*, Tokyo: Nihon Kogyo Shimbunsha.

Van Wolferen, K. (1990) *The Enigma of Japanese Power: People and Politics in a Stateless Nation*, New York: Vintage Books.

9

FUKUSHIMA AND THE POLITICAL ECONOMY OF POWER POLICY IN JAPAN

Andrew DeWit, Iida Tetsunari, and Kaneko Masaru

Throughout the summer following the March 11 magnitude 9 earthquake and massive tsunami, Japanese politics and energy policy continued to reel from the shock of nuclear meltdowns at the Fukushima-Daiichi reactor complex. Confusion is of course to be expected in the wake of such an enormous tragedy. But it is being exacerbated by vested interests that seek to stymie fundamental reforms to the energy sector involving the generation and transmission of electrical power. Tokyo Electric Company's (TEPCO) ruinous reactors in Fukushima are the most visible legacy of these vested interests' dominance of Japan's energy policy. Key actors in this "nuclear village," as it is now widely known, are TEPCO and the nine other monopolized regional utilities that divide the country into their respective fiefs. They cooperate closely with bureaucrats in the Ministry of Economy, Trade and Industry (METI) and elsewhere in the state, as well as with a broad swath of the political class. Management and labor in some of Japan's blue-chip firms, including power-unit builders Toshiba, Hitachi and Mitsubishi, are part of the village. So too are a host of figures positioned at the uppermost ranks of media, academia and elsewhere. Collectively, they are a textbook case of the problem of concentrated benefits and dispersed costs. Their tightly focused rent-seeking drove Japan to bet heavily on nuclear power; and though the risks of this policy are now clear, they are determined to preserve as much of the status quo as they can while passing on its burgeoning costs.

The most salient political economy question after Fukushima is the degree to which vested interests can shift its costs to taxpayers and utility ratepayers while minimizing reform to the energy economy and its policymaking institutions. It is impossible to project the outcome of this battle, which will continue to unfold over the coming months and years. The nuclear village will almost certainly be rocked by yet more scandals and revelations of the costs of Fukushima, further infuriating public opinion and increasing politicians' incentives to support change.

The village may even be ousted from its pole position in energy policy by the popular, powerful and expanding wave of opposition centered in regional and local governments, innovative capital, a host of nonprofit organizations (NPOs), small and medium enterprises (SMEs) and other disparate actors. While the outcome is unclear, the stakes in this contest are enormous. We argue that they include Japan's ability to revitalize domestic demand as well as lead the global community towards smart communities and sustainable growth.

The incumbent versus emergent interests

Japan's 54 nuclear reactors are the nuclear village's key asset in a regionally centralized power production and transmission network. Japan's ten regional electrical utilities were established in the wake of the Pacific War. Path dependence afterwards saw Japan's power market remain balkanized in ten districts, each with its own monopolized electrical utility. Moreover, these monopolized, vertically integrated electricity firms dominate their respective regions' power generation, transmission, distribution and sales. In other words, regional monopolization is matched by functional monopolization.

The latter part of the 1990s saw movement towards regulatory relaxation and liberalization. And though there was indeed some progress on this front, the dual regional and functional monopolization escaped reform. This dual monopolization is not seen elsewhere among developed economies, and is highly unusual even when compared with developing countries (Iida 2011). Japan's utilities are so ensconced in their regional fiefs that they do not bother to build power-sharing infrastructure among themselves let alone develop a suitably diverse power supply. The International Energy Agency (IEA) Director Tanaka Nobuo (a former METI bureaucrat) laments that they shrugged off the IEA's advice to expand inter-regional networks by arguing that it would be cheaper simply to install more nuclear capacity (Nikkei Business 2011a).

This monopolized power industry operates the world's third largest nuclear generation capacity, a complex strikingly vulnerable to Japan's frequent earthquakes and accompanying tsunamis. The industry has been regulated by the largely captured Nuclear and Industrial Safety Agency (NISA), which oversees regulatory compliance from within METI. The regulator was thus an arm of the government agency – METI – most committed to expanding nuclear power.[1] This organizational design encourages moral hazard and undermines accountability, as was abundantly clear to informed observers even before the Fukushima crisis.

The nuclear village's capacity to buy support and spread its costs has become staple fare in the mainstream media and also in blogs and social media such as Twitter. Even so, the nuclear village holds many advantages in the post-Fukushima contest over energy reform. For one thing, they are well organized and compact, and they dominate policymaking in the central government, the peak business association of Keidanren, and elsewhere. The nuclear village also has the financial heft of ¥16 trillion in annual power sales, additional trillions of yen in power-unit and ancillary investment, ample public-sector subsidies, as well as other lucrative benefits to spur on their efforts. Moreover, it is motivated by the need to protect tens of trillions of yen worth of sunk costs in plant and equipment. These pecuniary incentives are reinforced by the socio-psychological returns of being center-stage in energy and associated policymaking in the world's third largest economy (*Daiyamondo* 2011).

Energy is the biggest and most strategic sector in the economy, as it literally drives all the other sectors. Controlling the electric power economy gives the utilities enormous influence over policymaking. As the battle over reform heats up, it is clear that the nuclear village's main strategic advantage is that it only needs to defend the status quo, one that is widely supported by the Establishment. Opponents of the village have a much tougher task: they need to overturn the conventional wisdom on nuclear energy that has prevailed for the past four decades, and they also have to present a credible alternative that appeals to key policymakers. With the Diet effectively deadlocked and members of the ruling Democratic Party of Japan (DPJ) divided over their ties to the village, there is no clear political leadership in the central government. Instead, a policy war is being waged in committees and corridors. In this fluid context, METI's strong support for retaining nuclear energy is an asset of incalculable worth precisely because it controls national energy strategy.

The nuclear village's disadvantages largely stem from the radioactive ruins up in Fukushima. The shocking meltdowns have generated an increasingly detailed debate over the enormous costs of the status quo and an examination of other policy options. And that debate has engaged an increasingly wide range of interests that normally ignore, or are excluded from, energy policymaking. Should the Fukushima disaster slide from public consciousness, the nuclear village would surely retain the upper hand in this contest because significant change in any policy realm is always difficult. But the scale of the Fukushima disaster, and its collateral damage, continues to surprise much expert opinion and impress itself on public perceptions about nuclear safety. Hitherto hidden costs are now becoming visible in the fiscal process as well as in daily life. Among other things, the health threat of irradiated food products probably ensures that the late July Kyodo poll showing 70 percent opposition to nuclear power is not a peak (Reuters 2011).[2]

Public outrage at the establishment's efforts to obfuscate the facts on radiation and other aspects of the crisis is impossible to suppress or ignore as the mainstream media pulls back the veil and social media foster a vigorous civil society. The startling shift in public opinion, from disinterest in energy to strong opposition to nuclear power, has put the nuclear village on the defensive. In addition, until his resignation on August 26, Prime Minister Kan Naoto took a leading role in voicing doubts about the safety of nuclear energy and endorsing a shift to renewable energy. He deployed the available policy levers to impede the nuclear village's capacity to regroup and railroad the policy agenda. Kan's approach was very different from a year before, as he cooperated with the nuclear village after taking office in June of 2010. But after March 11, his incentives to cooperate weakened greatly as he became a lightning rod for discontent about the crisis and its mounting costs. As civil society increasingly rejected the nuclear-centered energy policy, Kan seized the opportunity to cultivate a new base of popular support.

Kan's post-Fukushima incentives were also shaped by the rapid rise of a credible movement for an alternative energy economy. Organized by Son Masayoshi, CEO of Softbank and the richest person in Japan, fully 35 of Japan's 47 prefectures have signed onto a drive for renewable energy. A larger constellation of interests is more or less strongly allied in this effort. NTT Docomo, Mitsui and other firms announced their intentions to enter the power-generation business, taking away some of the lucrative gains currently monopolized by the nuclear village. Many firms in renewable energy equipment, construction, finance and other sectors are also looking forward to benefiting from renewables. Also among the nuclear village's antagonists are other bureaucratic agencies, such as the Ministry of Farms, Fisheries and Forests, whose areas of jurisdiction have been ravaged by the meltdowns. They want a seat at the table determining new energy policy, where they can represent farmers and other interests whose livelihoods have been severely damaged and who would benefit from the distributed economic opportunities of an energy shift.

As one might expect, these disparate interests have trouble reaching a common agenda. Rather than defend the concrete and institutionalized reality of the present, they seek to build out a new energy economy. One problem is that there are many different routes to attaining that goal. For some actors, it is enough to champion reduced power consumption and greater efficiency. This option certainly has significant scope, as Japan is for example considerably behind European and Scandinavian counterparts in the deployment of district heating systems that capture waste heat from power generation and use it to heat and cool buildings and in other applications (IEA 2008). Other actors argue that conservation is not enough, and point to Japan's rich options in wind, solar, geothermal and other renewable power generation. Renewables have been kept at bay by the strategies of the nuclear village (DeWit and Iida 2011), so there is plenty of low-hanging fruit. Reaching a common agenda and holding to it has taken some time. But developing a viable policy alternative has played a significant role in shaping disparate groups into an increasingly coherent political force. As we shall explain in more detail below, they appear to be uniting behind deregulating the power sector, building the smart grid, and augmenting Japan's feed-in tariff. These policies are aimed at encouraging the deployment of renewables and thus distributing power-generation opportunities across regions and socioeconomic groups.

Back to the drawing board

Let us briefly review how Japan slid into this fast-moving and pivotal contest over energy policy. The Fukushima disaster derailed a nuclear-centered energy policy that was running at full speed. The past decade's surge of fossil-fuel prices and geopolitical risks saw Japan's imports of these resources climb from about 1 percent of GDP in 2003 to 4.8 percent in 2008. Rising prices and worsening instability helped the nuclear village secure a national commitment to nuclear power as the only real energy alternative to fossil fuels. Pre-3/11, Japan got close to 30 percent of its electricity from nuclear reactors. It's 2010 Basic Energy Plan sought to raise this share to about 50 percent of electricity by 2030. The Plan was to construct nine new nuclear plants by 2020 and at least 14 by 2030. Longer-term goals include the ambitious target of securing 60 percent of all energy needs, not only electricity, from nuclear sources by 2100. That would be a six-fold increase over the present 10 percent. The target was touted as critical for cutting Japan's CO^2 emissions by 90 percent from 2000 levels (DeWit and Iida 2011).

With the juggernaut of the 2010 Basic Energy Plan stopped in its tracks by the Fukushima meltdowns, Japan's entire energy policy is being reconsidered. Nuclear energy's proponents acted quickly in order to minimize change. The May 6 edition of the *Tokyo Shimbun* thus noted that METI drafted an internal document entitled "Safety Declaration" aiming to maintain power production from the existing nuclear reactors. METI sought to get in front of public outrage at TEPCO and the Fukushima disaster with the target of achieving "the world's safest nuclear energy" between 2030 and 2050. But still, the shock of the reactor meltdowns also compelled METI to back off from its aggressive nuclear construction plans and downgrade the role of nuclear power from the center of the "energy best mix" to one among three pillars. It described the first pillar as solar power and other renewables, while expressing concerns about their costs. The second pillar emphasizes conservation by reforming lifestyles and the industrial structure to achieve lower energy consumption. The third pillar is "the world's most secure nuclear power" (*Tokyo Shimbun* 2011a).

In May the struggle between the premier and the nuclear village, a fight at the heart of the central state, began to intensify. On May 6, Prime Minister Kan Naoto requested that Chubu Electric, the monopoly utility in Japan's Kansai area (which includes Osaka) shut down its Hamaoka nuclear plant in Shizuoka prefecture. The reactor complex is in an area likely to be hit by a massive earthquake in the not too distant future, so Kan asked that the reactors be taken off-line until adequate safety measures could be installed. This high profile measure raised questions about nuclear safety and was widely supported by the public. On May 10, Kan upped the ante by announcing that Japan would be adding "renewable and natural energy sources such as solar, wind and biomass power ... to our core energy sources" and to increased conservation. In addition, he mooted the idea of deregulating the utilities in terms of splitting power generating from transmission, a key to facilitating growth in renewables. On May 17, his cabinet formally decided on a thorough review of energy policy, and on May 19 he sought to concentrate that review in the Council on the Realization of the New Growth Strategy, which he chaired as premier. Kan was clearly trying to weaken METI's control over energy policymaking (*Asahi Newspaper* 2011).

When Kan began visibly to distance himself from the nuclear village in early May, it seemed the best outcome incumbent interests could hope for would be no further downgrading of nuclear power's status in the revised Energy Plan. But then the nuclear village opted to play a major role in the June 2 effort to remove Kan from office by a no-confidence vote in the Diet, an effort that failed (*Tokyo Shimbun* 2011b). That gambit further weakened Kan's incentives to try to cooperate with them. Against this backdrop, Kan used policy measures to put off the nuclear village's efforts to restart nuclear reactors taken off-line for maintenance and safety checks. Salient among these measures are the "stress tests" that appear likely to keep these reactors shut down until at least the end of 2011 (*Nikkei* 2011).

Then Kan ramped up his activism in June and July. His repeated overtures to public opinion were so successful that by late July over 70 percent opposed nuclear power. He also began articulating a policy of gradually shifting away from nuclear energy, and in its place encouraging the diffusion of renewable power. Salient among the measures to achieve that massive shift in energy policy, he emphasized the role of the feed-in tariff (FIT). As we explain in more detail below, the FIT is a policy mechanism aimed at stimulating investment in renewable energy by guaranteeing the market for renewably produced power. The FIT does this by specifying the length of time (usually 15 to 25 years) during which utilities are obligated to purchase electricity generated by various categories of renewable energy, and pass the extra costs onto consumers through a modest increment in their monthly utility bill. The FIT also sets the prices for the various types of renewables (i.e. wind, solar, biomass, geothermal), taking into account their relative cost-competitiveness with conventional power generation as well as the need to incentivize cost reductions and technological advances.

The great irony in Kan's championing the FIT is that it had been designed by METI, which thought it could control the policy and preserve the pole position of nuclear energy. But Kan, strongly encouraged by emergent renewable energy interests, recast the FIT as a tool to displace the nuclear village from the center of the energy economy.

METI's core objective in the midst of all this ferment was to keep energy policymaking within its jurisdiction, allowing it to shape the range of debate and policy options. The originally scheduled spring 2013 revision of Japan's Basic Energy Law has been moved up to 2012, highlighting the urgency of the situation. The ongoing rethink of energy policymaking may lead to a weakening of METI's role, but it is a skilled and powerful infighter and will not concede its turf without a no-holds-barred fight. If its control over energy policy is diminished, however, it is possible that the revision could include a formal commitment to gradually phasing out nuclear power, deregulating the utilities, and otherwise unbundling the nuclear village.

The real cost of power

Japan's energy policy is dominated by the "3 Es": efficiency, economy and environment. The nuclear village had managed to portray nuclear power as best satisfying these conditions among the range of fossil-fuel and renewable alternatives. The Fukushima incident has, of course, brought home the fact that there are tremendous risks entailed in the nuclear option. Desperate to depict mounting concern as mere emotionalism, the nuclear village and its allies overseas argue that no one has died from the accident. But this is disingenuous, as cancers take time to develop. What is known for certain at present is that tens of thousands of Fukushima-area residents have been displaced, radioactive contamination is widespread, and Japan's reputation and industries have taken an enormous blow. And that hardly exhausts the toll of the damage to the Japanese people and their political economy.

More specifically, Fukushima has focused attention on the factors underlying electricity prices as well as the means through which nuclear power has been subsidized through the public sector budget. The nuclear industry and its supporters still routinely assert that nuclear power costs only between ¥5–7 per kilowatt hour. But it is becoming clear in public debate that these quoted costs do not include a number of important elements. Many direct and indirect subsidies and other measures are omitted, in what even the mainstream business press regards as an orchestrated and misleading effort to portray nuclear as the low-cost power alternative (*Nikkei Business* 2011b).

Accurately assessing the costs of nuclear energy in Japan should include:

1. Government electricity allocation funds amount to ¥1.2 trillion per annum, and there is also a development fund that amounts to about ¥3 trillion. These monies are used to defray construction and associated costs of nuclear plants in local communities that host reactors. Both of these funds are financed from taxes, but neither is included in the quoted cost for nuclear power.
2. Nuclear power costs are estimated by assuming that the operating rate of Japan's nuclear reactors is between 70 to 85 percent. In reality, this level is not achieved and in 2007 was only 60.7 percent. In the wake of the Fukushima incident, only 12 of Japan's 54 nuclear reactors were on-line as of September and the operating rate dropped to 20 percent of capacity.
3. Japan is subject to significant seismic action and tsunamis, realities that the nuclear village played down as it sought to cluster capacity in risky areas. For nuclear power in Japan to have a hope of surviving this crisis, the disaster preparedness of Japan's nuclear plants will have to be significantly enhanced. The Chubu reactor is, for example, to be protected by an 1.6 km long, 18 meter high tsunami wall that is projected to cost ¥100 billion (about US$ 1.2 billion). The very significant burden for retrofitting plants and remedying the currently inadequate safety standards are not reflected in the quoted price of nuclear power.
4. The ¥19 trillion "backend" cost for dealing with spent fuel and retired reactors is also not included in the quoted price. The use of nuclear fuel eventually produces dangerous nuclear waste, but the in-country facilities for treating it are inadequate. This problem has simply been kicked into the future with the expense kept out of the estimates for generating power.

5. The Japan Center for Economic Research's May 31 projected ¥6 to 20 trillion cost of decommissioning the Fukushima reactors, a process that will take decades, is also omitted from the cost calculation. There are also 100,000 tons of highly irradiated water to treat and massive quantities of irradiated soil to be cleaned. These expenses are part of the real cost of nuclear energy, but are not included in official estimates.

6. The compensation claims from the Fukushima incident are also not part of the quoted figure. Projecting the final tally with precision is difficult at present, but Bank of America's Merrill Lynch unit assessed damages as perhaps reaching ¥11 trillion. The only thing that we can reasonably conclude at present is that the compensation claims will be large, taxpayers and energy consumers will foot most of the bill and that, here too, the official cost of nuclear energy is vastly understated (Kaneko 2011: 98–102).

Well before the Fukushima incident, Ritsumeikan University energy specialist Ōshima Kenichi perused public financial documents and determined that nuclear power costs are more than double the ¥5–6/kWh estimate used by some state agencies and other elements of the nuclear village. Ōshima calculated the true cost of nuclear power in Japan at ¥12.23/kWh compared to ¥9.9 and ¥7.26 for thermal power and hydro respectively (*Japan Times* 2011). His figures for nuclear energy costs do not, however, include the indirect subsidy of a de facto state guarantee of compensation costs as well as the enormous burden of the clean-up. Nor does it include the losses suffered by Japan as a whole as its food exports and inbound tourism decline by double digits and the "Japan Brand" itself gets tarnished, perhaps indelibly.

Comparative cost estimates for renewable projects in Japan peg solar at ¥47/ kWh, wind ¥11/kWh, small hydro ¥8–20/kWh, biomass ¥12.5/kWh, and geothermal ¥12–20/kWh (*Tōyō Keizai* 2011). These costs will almost certainly continue their striking rates of decline as the renewable capacity diffuses and technology advances. Photovoltaic module prices, for example, have shown cost reductions of 22 percent for each doubling of cumulative capacity (*Renewable Energy World* 2011). By contrast, the costs of fossil fuels as well as nuclear power will almost certainly continue to increase.

Moreover, these numbers for comparative power generation prices are at present under study by Japanese government committees charged with providing credible estimates for power options for the revised energy policy. It remains to be seen how accurate the reassessment of costs will be, since so many interests within the central state have a stake in maintaining the status quo.

The sustainable option

Japan's current policy conflict has global implications. For well over a decade, Japan has been portrayed as a dwindling has-been, its political economy a model of what not to do in the face of financial and other crises. Its response to this energy crisis will be equally instructive, and what Japan chooses may also help reshape the world.

Still the world's third richest nation, with the third largest electricity market, Japan possesses abundant human, financial and technical resources to devote to its post-Fukushima power crisis. It needs new power generating capacity and transmission infrastructure to replace what has been wrecked. Heading towards the slated redraft of the Basic Energy Policy, a crucial question for Japanese energy policymakers is what kind of generating capacity that should be and how it should be integrated into the national grid. The reformists argue that now is the time to deregulate the utilities and foster green growth. The need to reconstruct some part of the grid opens the possibility of doing it "smart" and distributed rather than conventional and centralized.

The monopolized utilities have been working behind the scenes over the past two years to impede domestic progress on installing smart grids and develop smart city urban forms. The nuclear village continues to argue that their centralized, nuclear-centered power economy is cheaper and more reliable than its distributed alternative. It also warns that not sticking with allegedly low-cost nuclear power will lead to lower growth and competitiveness and a shift of investment and jobs overseas.

In spite of this argument from the business establishment, the distributed and sustainable energy policy option is rapidly moving to the center of the Japanese public debate. Public opinion polls routinely show that large majorities are in support of the FIT and renewable power, even if it costs more than conventional power (*Sankei Shimbun* 2011). Moreover, the debate in the reconstruction councils and elsewhere increasingly stresses that the centralized system focused on nuclear power is too costly and dangerous and proceeds from there. Information on energy and power-infrastructure alternatives is becoming more broadly diffused.

In consequence, large swathes of the political, business, academic and media communities that shape Japan's public debate understand that highly complex, centralized systems per se are inherently and disastrously vulnerable to shocks, something as true of financial regimes and supply chains as of power generation and transmission. They are also learning that Germany and a host of other countries and regions emphasize sustainable energy as industrial policy, and are building competitive and rapidly growing "green" industries. These countries distribute increasing amounts of small-scale generating capacity among the myriad rooftops, yards, rivers and open fields of households, small businesses, farmers and local communities. This strategy spreads the wealth and political influence created by growing the energy economy. This is hardly a radical way to use the public sector: Texan Governor Rick Perry, a staunch Republican, has presided over that state's emergence as America's leading wind producer, bringing wind from sparsely populated and low-income West Texas to its cities in the East and passing on to utility ratepayers a roughly US$5 per month cost for new power lines (Galbraith 2011). Moreover, especially critical in Japan, distributed power also renders the generating network more disaster resilient because it is not concentrated and so vulnerable to earthquake and tsunami.

Key in Germany and elsewhere are policies that defray and drive down the cost of making the transition to sustainable energy. The declining costs of renewables worldwide are in large measure thanks to their diffusion via the feed-in tariff (FIT). As noted earlier, the FIT is largely a bridging mechanism that overcomes the problem of renewable energy's higher cost or uncertain markets versus coal and other conventional forms of power generation. The FIT provides renewable energy producers a guaranteed market and price, usually through adding a small charge to the consumer's electricity bill. The FIT thus encourages the diffusion of renewable energy generation.

Diffusion is key in bringing down the costs of renewable energy. As with any technology, such as the personal computer and the mobile telephone, wind turbines, solar panels and geothermal facilities achieve cheaper per-unit costs the more widely they are deployed. Moreover, the greater the demand for renewable energy technologies, the greater is the incentive to innovate and further bring down costs. Consider, as a comparison, that in 2000 DVD players cost an average of US$345, but in 2011 have dropped to US$40. And in 2004 the Treo mobile phone cost about US$399, but by 2010 the price for an iPhone 3G was down to US$49 and by 2011 mobile phones were becoming a freebie with a purchase of phone service (Farooq 2011). And consider, too, that ten years ago virtually no one could have imagined the mobile phone becoming a combined handheld computer, camera, stereo and credit card.

The FIT at present fosters 75 percent of global solar and 50 percent of global wind in no fewer than 85 national and subnational jurisdictions. The UN, the IEA, Deutsche Bank, the US National Renewable Energy Laboratory and a range of other organizations and agencies have determined the FIT to be the most effective and efficient means of diffusing renewable power (DeWit and Yamazaki 2011). In Germany, where renewables have tripled over the past decade to provide over 20 percent of electricity by mid-2011, the FIT costs German households about €3 per month (roughly the price of a loaf of bread).

Japan's FIT

Japan adopted a FIT on November 1, 2009 (DeWit and Iida 2011). But this was a deliberately hobbled version that the nuclear village hastily drafted and got passed soon after the 2009 Diet election. The nuclear village moved quickly in order to pre-empt the DPJ election manifesto promise of a German-style comprehensive FIT, one applying to all renewables. Yet even the nuclear village's hobbled FIT, one that applies only to solar and with plenty of restrictions, saw Japan's solar market take off in 2010. In that year, Japan installed 990 megawatts of new capacity after long being eclipsed by the Germans and then the Chinese. The Unit One reactor at Fukushima Daiichi, by comparison, supplied 460 megawatts before melting down soon after March 11.

The scale of Japan's latent demand for solar energy extends to other renewable power sources. Japan's farmers, local communities, construction firms and other interests are increasingly enthusiastic about geothermal, wind, biogas and other power generation. They see these businesses as a chance to enhance income and local energy security, and to contribute to the fight against climate change. Added into the bargain of sustainable energy choices are reduced dependence on unstable and increasingly costly foreign fossil fuels as well as none of the risks of nuclear power (Kaneko 2011: 165–170).

Japan's new FIT legislation, passed by the Diet in August 2011, encourages geothermal, wind, small hydro and biogas from July of 2012. The revised FIT, as legislated, is quite different from the draft version. The latter included a host of restrictions and other limitations that the nuclear village forced over the objections of experts, local communities and other interests that sought a more robust, comprehensive FIT. Ironically, the draft version received cabinet assent on March 11, just hours before the earthquake. The main problem with the FIT revision (as tabled) was that the levels of subsidy for generation other than solar were to be set at virtually uniform rates of ¥15–20/kWh. To be viable, there should be higher levels of support for less-competitive renewables such as geothermal relative to such relatively mature technologies as wind power. The point of a FIT is to create appropriate incentives to diffuse a variety of power alternatives. Given the crisis, the FIT represents a policy opportunity for diffusing alternative power as rapidly as possible, thereby contributing to the resolution of Japan's power needs as well as strengthening its position in the global competition to promote green businesses.

The nuclear village, however, looks at this policy opportunity rather differently, viewing it as a threat. Former Prime Minister Kan focused public attention on the FIT when he promised to resign once the Diet passed it (and two other measures). The FIT is troubling to the nuclear village because instead of just promoting select renewables to lessen reliance on fossil fuels, it is now aimed at cutting dependence on nuclear energy. Hence, when the FIT bill was being reshaped by Diet committee, the nuclear village fought to restrain the growth of renewables through tight caps on incentives (*Asahi Shimbun* 2011). But caps were kicked out and LDP pressure saw price-setting per se removed from METI's grip and left to a third-party committee (*SankeiBiz* 2011). The FIT passed by the Diet on August 26 was thus a major improvement on the 2009 legislation as well as the draft assented to by the cabinet on March 11. The nuclear village is, of course, now desperate to fill the ranks of the new, price-setting committee with its sympathizers. But that may prove to be difficult due to this cross-party agreement as well as the degree of attention focused on the FIT and the lucrative opportunities it opens to rural politicians and business interests.

The policy shapes politics

Softbank CEO Son Masayoshi understands how important the FIT is to achieve a transition towards a sustainable energy economy. Starting in mid-April of 2011, Son began giving numerous well-publicized talks and writing several articles for high-profile media about renewables and argued persuasively for an energy shift driven by the FIT. In May, he also met at length with Prime Minister Kan to talk about energy policy. On May 25, he was able to build on previous strong subnational interest in renewables and secure 19 prefectures' agreement to set up a renewable energy council. The council's goals include building ten large-scale solar plants with a capacity of 50 million kw and eventually enough to replace the capacity of 50 nuclear power plants. This group has since expanded to 35 prefectures.

Son advocates gradually shifting away from nuclear energy by ramping up renewable capacity. He long believed in official estimates that nuclear power cost only ¥5–6/kWh, but now argues that after examining ancillary charges as well as contemporary generation costs, the real cost is at least triple that. He concedes that the cost of solar and most other renewables is still higher than nuclear power, but stresses that the FIT can be the key mechanism in driving diffusion, cost reductions and the distribution of economic opportunity. The nuclear village has sought to call his motives into question, clearly attempting to personalize the issue and undermine public support for an energy transition and the FIT. However, Son's organization of prefectural governments and the movement of well-known Japanese firms into the renewable space has expanded policy momentum and maintained strong public support.

This rapid, post-Fukushima rise of a sub-national movement towards renewables, spearheaded by Japan's innovative business elite, is also backed by central government agencies such as the Ministry for Agriculture, Forestry and Fisheries (MAFF). It also has significant political support, as we see in the August passage of the FIT. Indeed, over 200 Diet members came to see Kan and Son speak on the FIT at a special June 14 meeting of the all-party "Energy-Shift" study group. And as of July 8, 225 Diet members declared themselves in favor of the expanded FIT. Among them is Kōno Tarō, a prominent Liberal Democratic Party politician, who has emerged as a vocal critic of vested energy interests. Kōno, challenging his own party's line and legacy of building the nuclear village, stresses the role of the FIT and other policies to phase out nuclear energy and achieve 100 percent renewables by 2050.

The political center now features venerable NHK, the national broadcaster, running investigative programs on why Japan – ostensibly a powerhouse of green – lags so far behind the Europeans and others in deploying its abundant renewable energy resources and manufacturing capacity for renewable devices. As the political debate centers on the FIT, the mainstream media is coming to understand its central role in driving renewable revolutions in Germany, Spain and elsewhere. The FIT is thus gaining recognition as key to contemporary green industrial policy rather than being yet another "window-dressing" initiative in the face of climate change.

The scale of green growth potential

The intersection between policy and finance is the crucial nexus where possibilities get transformed into reality. At the global level, "hundreds of billions of investment dollars, if not trillions, from pension funds, private equity investors, sovereign wealth funds and hedge funds are waiting on the sidelines" while energy interest groups fight to shape public policy. Policies like the FIT are seen as key to opening the road to sustainable investment because they offer "transparency, longevity and certainty" (Platt 2010). This backdrop of latent financial power waiting in the wings for a strong policy signal is especially true of Japan. Banks in Japan have remained shy of lending, save to the state, even two decades after the 1980s bubble's collapse. Borrowers for new business also remain scant because domestic business prospects are unattractive, depressing domestic consumption and maintaining Japan's excessive and increasingly risky reliance on exports. A green energy policy at the core of a smart post-3/11 reconstruction could create robust and sustainable demand in Japan's domestic economy, opening up lucrative opportunities and generating both electricity and jobs.

There is indeed significant evidence that the global energy economy is at a very critical turning point, where financial flows are following smart policy. For example, the United Nations Environmental Programme's July 2011 release of "Global Trends in Renewable Energy Investment 2011" showed that global renewable investment for 2010 totaled US$211 billion. This was fully one-third higher than the previous year's US$160 billion, and a staggering 540 percent increase since 2004. The report also showed that small-scale, distributed investment in renewables had risen 132 percent in Germany to US$34 billion and by 59 percent in Italy to US$5.5 billion, while the cost of solar modules had fallen by 60 percent since mid-2008. The UN study also indicated that wind turbine costs had dropped by 18 percent per megawatt over the previous two years (UNEP, 2011).

More broadly, from 2007 to the second quarter of 2011, private-sector spending on smart city, smart grid, green construction, renewable energy, and other elements of the sustainable economy reached a cumulative US$2.4 trillion. Projections suggest this spending will expand to US$10 trillion by 2020 (Ethical Market Media 2011). In September of 2010, Japan's *Nikkei Business* estimated that the energy-related aspects of the smart city market were ¥45 trillion in 2010 and likely to grow to ¥180 trillion by 2020. The domestic returns from these infrastructure investments are potentially very high. The US Electric Power Research Institute estimates that a smart grid for the US would cost about US$477 billion over the next 20 years, but deliver three to six times that in benefits (EPRI 2011). In Japan, Nomura Securities Financial and Economic Research Center estimates the grid would cost roughly ¥12 trillion through 2030. A smart reconstruction offers Japan the opportunity to become a leading player in these fields, using the domestic market to ratchet down production and other costs as well as foster more rapid technological progress.

The point here is to highlight the pace, scale and potential returns from the green revolution that is already underway. Nicholas Stern, the author of the October 2006 *Stern Review on the Economics of Climate Change*, now refers to the above developments as an industrial revolution, one China is leading (Stern 2011). China's incentives are now so robust that in mid-2010 it leapt to the top of Ernst & Young's quarterly "Renewable Energy Attractiveness Index," outpacing all competitors, including aggressive US states such as California. As for Japan, in the

August 2011 index, it dropped to nineteenth place from eighteenth the previous May.

Japan clearly has enormous potential and incentives to move up the ranks in this race. As we have argued, however, it is handicapped by the opposition of vested interests to changes in the status quo. The current policymaking watershed involves a choice to continue along the path set by the nuclear village, with all the attendant risks, or opting to shift energy policy in favor of ramping up renewables. The costs of nuclear policy are already enormous and growing, explaining why there is growing support for a phased withdrawal over coming decades. This gradual shift away from nuclear energy would boost Japan's competitiveness in renewable power, smart-grid and smart-city markets, but the nuclear village still holds trump cards in the fight over Japan's energy and economic future.

Either of the nuclear and renewable options requires increasing state-sector support in the short run, but their outlooks diverge over the medium and long run. Nuclear is much more expensive than official estimates if waste reprocessing, decommissioning and compensation are factored in. New capacity for nuclear power also appears to be getting very expensive, especially where safety is stressed (Mason 2011). Despite scaremongering by the nuclear village about the dire consequences of phasing out nuclear energy, continued reliance on nuclear energy therefore implies high risks and increased costs. In contrast, the track record of subsidizing renewable strategy is one of often dramatically declining prices. Moreover, opting for renewables brings the added fillip of encouraging elements of the nuclear village to expand into rapidly growing markets at home and overseas. Even the big nuclear-reactor builders Toshiba, Mitsubishi and Hitachi have signaled their intentions to shift more towards green markets (Fairley 2011).

Japanese public opinion has clearly voiced its majority desire to grow renewable, distributed power. The vast majority of Japan's prefectural and big-city governments have chosen this route as well, and are working with the most innovative elements of Japanese capital. To achieve this post-Fukushima reboot of the power economy requires smart energy policy, centered on a robust FIT, as well as a strong dose of deregulation and competition for the monopolized utilities. Whether the central government's policymaking process will deliver remains to be seen.

Notes

1   In response to widespread criticism of this conflict of interest, NISA and other relevant organizations will be consolidated and reorganized as the Nuclear Safety and Security Agency (NSSA) under the aegis of the Environment Ministry as of April 2012.

2   A mid-July *Asahi* poll showed 77 percent opposition while after Prime Minister Kan resigned at the end of August, polls showed 66 percent wanted his successor Noda Yoshihiko to embrace Kan's vision of gradually phasing out nuclear energy.

References

Asahi Newspaper (2011) "Kan bent on taking down utility interests with him," June 29, online, available at: www.asahi.com/english/TKY201106280233.html.

Asahi Shimbun (2011) "Saisei ene hōan wo hihan" (Criticism of the renewable energy bill), July 29, online, available at: http://mytown.asahi.com/shiga/news.php?k_id= 26000001107290001.

Daiyamondo (2011) "Genpatsu: kane, riken, jinmyaku (Nuclear power: money, interests, networks), May 21, pp. 26–59.

DeWit, Andrew and Iida, Tetsunari (2011) "The power elite and environmental-energy policy in Japan," *The Asia-Pacific Journal*, 9(4), January 24, online, available at: www. japanfocus.org/-Andrew-DeWit/3479.

DeWit, Andrew and Yamazaki, Yukiko (2011) "Smart Policy and the Renewable Energy Revolution: the Feed-in Tariff," *Rikkyo Economics Research*, 64(4): 25–47, online, available at: www.rikkyo.ac.jp/eco/research/pdf/papar/no64/p025_047_2_64_4_ DeWit_Yamazaki.pdf.

EPRI (2011) "Estimating the costs and benefits of the smart grid: A preliminary estimate of the investment requirements for a fully functioning smart grid," Electric Power Research Institute, online, available at: http://my.epri.com/portal/server. pt?Abstract_id=000000000001022519.

Ethical Market Media (2011) "Green Transition Scoreboard, August 2011 Update," August, online, available at: www.ethicalmarkets.com/wp-content/uploads/2011/09/Green-Transition-Scoreboard-August-2011.pdf.

Fairley, Peter (2011) "Japan faces post-Fukushima power struggle," *IEEE Spectrum*, August, online, available at: http://spectrum.ieee.org/green-tech/solar/ japan-faces-postfukushima-power-struggle.

Farooq (2011) "Solar price drops mirror high tech consumer goods," *Solar Energy – The Future* (blog), July 13, online, available at: http://solarenergy-thefuture.blogspot. com/2011/07/solar-price-drops-mirror-high-tech.html.

Galbraith, Kate (2011) "In Texas, Perry has presided over wind, gas booms," *The Texas Tribune*, August 21, online, available at: www.texastribune.org/texas-politics/2012-presidential-election/texas-perry-has-presided-over-wind-gas-booms.

IEA (2008) "CHP/DHC Country Scorecard: Japan," IEA, June, online, available at: www. iea.org/g8/CHP/profiles/japan_jun08.pdf.

Iida, Tetsunari (2011) "Country perspective: Japan," in *The End of Nuclear Energy? International Perspectives after Fukushima*, Nina Netzer and Jochen Steinhilber (eds.), Bonn: Friedrich Ebert Stiftung, July, online, available at: http://library.fes.de/pdf-files/ iez/08289.pdf.

Japan Times (2011) "38 years of nuke profit up in smoke," June 28, online, available at: http://search.japantimes.co.jp/cgi-bin/nn20110628x2.html.

Kaneko, Masaru (2011) *Datsu Genpatsu Seichouron: Atarashii Sangyou Kakumei He (Getting Out of Nuclear-Centered Growth and Into A New Industrial Revolution)*, Tokyo: Chikuma.

Mason, Rowena (2011) "EDF's reputation faces risk of meltdown," *The Daily Telegraph*, July 25, online, available at: www.telegraph.co.uk/finance/newsbysector/ energy/8658298/EDFs-reputation-faces-risk-of-meltdown.html.

Nikkei (2011) "Japan to start nuclear stress tests as early as this week," July 21, online, available at: http://e.nikkei.com/e/fr/tnks/Nni20110721D21JF314.htm.

Nikkei Business (2011a) "Ima ga seisaku saikō no kōki" (Now is a good time to rethink policy), July 11 p. 40–41.

Nikkei Business (2011b) "Genpatsu ga mottomo yasui no uso" (The lie that nuclear power is the cheapest), July 11 p. 29.

Platt, Gordon (2010) "Paying for the Green Revolution," *Global Finance*, February, online, available at: www.gfmag.com/archives/113-february-2010/9986-cover-story-paying-for-the-green-revolution.html#axzz1TJGNJDZl.

Reuters (2011) "Japanese support PM's desire to do away with nuclear power – poll," July 24, online, available at: http://af.reuters.com/article/worldNews/idAFTRE76N0RN 20110724.

Renewable Energy World (2011) "Technology cost review: Grid parity for renewables?" September 2, online, available at: www.renewableenergyworld.com/rea/news/article/2011/09/technology-cost-review-grid-parity-for-renewables.

SankeiBiz (2011) "Saisei ene, tokusohō shūin tsūka de fukyū zenshin (An advance for diffusing renewables via passage of the special bill by the House of Representatives), August 24, online, available at: www.sankeibiz.jp/macro/news/110824/mca1108240501001-n1.htm.

Sankei Shimbun (2011) "Yoron chōsa: Posuto-Kan jirihin no shushō kōhotachi" (Poll: the poverty of post-Kan candidates for PM), July 25, online, available at: http://sankei.jp.msn.com/politics/news/110725/stt11072520520009-n1.htm.

Stern, Nicholas (2011) "China risks overtaking Europe in green economic revolution," *Financial Times*, July 4, online, available at: http://blogs.ft.com/the-a-list/2011/07/04/china-risks-overtaking-europe-in-green-economic-revolution/#axzz1 ThfZMAfL.

Tokyo Shimbun (2011a) "Keisanshō: genpatsu jūshi no hōshin kenji" (METI sticking fast to its commitment to nuclear power"), May 6.

Tokyo Shimbun (2011b) "Kan oroshi ni genpatsu no kage" (The shadow of nuclear power behind the movement to dump Kan), June 3.

Tōyō Keizai (2011) "Saisei kanō enerugii dengenbetsu kosuto" (The cost of renewables energy by power source"), *Weekly Tōyō Keizai*, July 30, pp. 49–50.

UNEP (2011) "Global investments in green energy up nearly a third to US\$ 211 billion," UNEP News Centre, July, online, available at: http://www.unep.org/newscentre/default.aspx?DocumentID=2647&ArticleID=8805.

PART IV

History and politics

10

DEALING WITH DISASTER

Peter Duus

While history may repeat itself, it does not always do so, as Karl Marx once said, first as tragedy, then as comedy. Anyone who watched the unfolding of the 2011 Tōhoku disaster on the television screen will feel a shock of recognition when looking at the photographs of the 1891 Nōbi Earthquake or newsreels of the 1923 Kantō Earthquake. One sees the same desolate landscapes, the same shattered structures, the same rising columns of smoke, the same piles of splintered wood and rubble, and the same dazed and frightened faces. The visual evidence vividly illustrates how often history as tragedy has repeated itself.

The Japanese are peculiarly susceptible to this kind of tragedy. The country is at constant risk of catastrophic disaster. It sits atop the intersection of four major tectonic plates; it is crisscrossed by hundreds of active geological fault zones; its landscape is dotted by over a hundred active volcanoes; its riverbeds are steep, shallow and given to overflowing; and it lies in the path of destructive seasonal typhoons. According to one estimate, if a catastrophic disaster is defined as one in which more than 1,000 people die, then the Japanese have experienced nearly a hundred in the last 1,400 years – or about one every fifteen years. The last two centuries have been particularly lethal, with death counts rising into the thousands and tens of thousands (Usami 2002: 799).

Just as catastrophic disasters have repeated themselves, so have the ways that the Japanese reacted to them. If one looks back in time, a repetitive pattern of response is easy to recognize. This, I suppose, may be a result of the frequency of the lesser floods, quakes, typhoons, landslides and tsunamis that occur between the catastrophic ones. Disaster is always within living memory. A generation or two can pass between catastrophic disasters, but the lesser ones occur every few years. The consequence is the development over time of an institutional or cultural memory about dealing with disaster. This memory is not perfect, nor does it prevent mistakes from being made, but it does mean that the Japanese are never completely unprepared for yet another collision between the natural environment and its human inhabitants.

The pattern of reaction to catastrophic disaster can be broken down into several overlapping phases: blaming, coping, hoping, learning and forgetting. This pattern may not be unique to Japan, and as the new fields of disaster history and disaster science grow – a sign of the times? – perhaps similar patterns will be discovered elsewhere. But the frequency of disaster, and the voluminous documentary and visual archive it has engendered, makes the pattern easier to discern in Japan.

Blaming

The first impulse of Ishihara Shintarō, governor of Tokyo, who shocked critics in the 1950s with novels about his self-indulgent generation, was to attribute blame for the Tōhoku disaster. "Japan's identity is greed," he told a news conference a few days after the quake, as widely reported. "We should avail of this tsunami to wash away the greed. I think that it is divine punishment." He retracted his remark a day or two later. The aging population of rural Tōhoku, traditionally a low-income region, hardly seemed guilty of avarice or hedonism, and a Tokyo metropolitan election was just around the corner soon. Many voters were likely to be upset by the incumbent's mean-spiritedness.

Ishihara was not alone in attributing blame. Journalists, pundits and politicians began the search for the culpable almost immediately. The conservative opposition party, the Liberal Democratic Party, demonstrating a singular lack of imagination, trotted out a slogan it had been using for months. It accused the incumbent Prime Minister Kan Naoto of lacking "leadership" in responding to the disaster, and eventually it proposed an ultimately unsuccessful no-confidence resolution to bring his government down. Other domestic and foreign observers raised questions about inadequate bureaucratic disaster management, voiced suspicions of government cover-ups and deliberate disinformation, called attention to the cozy relationship between the nuclear power industry, and questioned the very technology of nuclear power generation. While not all these observers were equally well informed, their allegations certainly provided fodder for legitimate debate, but the blaming impulse itself conformed to the experience of earlier disasters.

It is not surprising to find that dispensing blame is one of the first reactions to catastrophic disaster. When a tragic event occurs our impulse is to explain it rationally. Unable to accept the idea that tragedy may simply be a senseless caprice of nature or human fallibility, we want to find a cause that makes sense of things. (My own reaction to the death of President Kennedy, for example, was to make an irate phone call to the John Birch Society headquarters, the only group I could imagine as sponsor for the assassination. Others may have shared my impulse. The line was busy for hours, and I never got through.) This desire to make sense of things is often tinged by anger, fear and distrust. It generates an impulse to strike back and to make someone or something to pay for the death, suffering, injury that the disaster has wrought. The impulse is usually temporary, eventually overcome by the need to cope with the tragedy and begin rebuilding. But if the level of panic is high enough, the urge to blame is not merely cathartic. It may be acted out violently. And as the experience of New Orleans after the Katrina hurricane suggests in some societies lawlessness often follows in the wake of disaster.

In the late Tokugawa era blame for disasters usually focused on nature itself. It was generally thought that the forces of nature were tightly bound in a causal relationship with divine and human order. Common sense dictated that catastrophic disaster be explained as a reaction to human behavior. The Ansei Earthquake that hit Edo, the *shogun*'s capital, in 1855 came less than a year after an earlier quake struck western Japan along the Tōkai plate and caused a deadly tsunami that swept along the Pacific coasts of Shikoku and Honshū. Nature appeared to be gravely out of joint. *Kawaraban* broadsheets, the tabloid news sheets that reported on the quake within a few days, often linked the Edo quake to the earlier disasters and pointed to nature's agency in bringing them on (Kitahara 2000: 80–99).

Namazu-e ("catfish pictures"), published either as *kawaraban* illustrations or as separate prints, drew on a popular local folk belief that attributed Edo Earthquakes to the movements of a gigantic catfish buried under the city. The catfish was sometimes singled out for blame, but so was the negligence of the deity at Kashima Shrine, who was supposed to keep the catfish pinned down with a rock. Whether this explanation was meant to be taken literally or whether it veiled a critique of the political authorities is difficult to say. It might well have been both. But *kawaraban* also suggested that the quake resulted from immoral, licentious, extravagant or selfish human actions that created an imbalance between *yin* and *yang* forces, and that an over-accumulation of *yang* literally upset the natural world. After all, the most heavily hit commoner neighborhood was the Yoshiwara licensed brothel quarter, where prostitutes, female entertainers and others perished in post-quake fires. In fact, many women found it hard to escape fires because brothel owners limited the number of exits to thwart runaways but their deaths were seen by the *kawaraban* as punishment visited on the unrighteous (Smits 2006; Noguchi 2004: 205–218).

Many in the ruling elite reacted to the disasters much as Governor Ishihara later did, reading it as a divine warning or divine punishment (*tenbatsu*) to the country's leadership. Confucian metaphysics linked the moral behavior of rulers to the occurrence of natural anomalies and interpreted earthquakes, floods and droughts as divine messages intended to bring them to their senses. In 1855 heavy physical damage was visited on the *shogun*'s castle, the mansions of the vassal *daimyo*, and the residential districts of the *shogun*'s direct retainers. It was not difficult for malcontents to argue that they were the target of divine punishment. The fact that the 1854 tsunami and the 1855 earthquake came in the wake of Commodore Perry's disruptive intrusion only confirmed that. The arrival of the foreigners was at least a symptom if not a cause of divine punishment.

By the time of the Nōbi Earthquake of 1891, an event with an epicenter in the Nōbi Plain that rocked central Japan from Osaka to Tokyo, Confucian metaphysics had been substantially supplanted by a modern scientific worldview. Nature was stripped of its agency, and the catfish theory became folk superstition – folklore rather than folk wisdom. But the quake came at the end of two decades of intense Westernization as nativist revival was beginning to take shape. Not surprisingly, the Japanese press, reacting to reports that the earthquake had brought down modern brick-built factories in Osaka and Nagoya while traditional structures like castles and temples remained intact, initially fixed blame for the death and destruction on Westernizing architects, engineers, and government officials who had introduced brick-and-mortar construction techniques into the country.

Indeed the blame sometimes was extended to other kinds of Western technology that failed – well-water pumps that were clogged by the tremors or kerosene lamps that toppled over and started fires. And lurid woodblock prints showed railroad trains plunging off cliffs or dead bodies scattered about the wreckage of an overturned locomotive and carriages (Clancey 2006: 114–116) This hysteria tapered off, however, when it was discovered that in rural villages nearer to the epicenter more than 7,000 had died, tens of thousands had been injured, and over 100,000 had been made homeless when their traditional thatched wooden houses collapsed.

Oddly enough, the notion of "divine punishment" was resurrected during the Kantō Earthquake of 1923. This time, however, blame was placed not on the ruling elite, but on a new urban culture and lifestyle emerging in the country's prosperous cities, particularly Tokyo, where tens of thousands had died. In this view, material progress in the cities had brought with it moral decline. As one scholar has put it succinctly, "To many observers, Tokyo had become a center of hedonistic consumer culture, entertainment, decadence, political unrest, and labor agitation and a breeding ground for dangerous thoughts and questionable behavior" (Schencking 2008: 323). The city itself was the most ominous signifier of a society that was abandoning traditional values.

Indeed, a week or so after the earthquake the Taishō emperor issued an imperial rescript that called for a restoration of these values.

> In recent years much progress has been made in science and human wisdom. At the same time frivolous and extravagant habits have set in, and even rash and extreme tendencies are not unknown. If these habits and tendencies are not checked now, the future of the country, we fear, is dark, the disaster that has befallen the Japanese being severe.
>
> (Naimushō 1924: 5–7)

In short order middle class academics, politicians, economists, scholars, philosophers, journalists, military officers and social reformers hopped on the imperial bandwagon, railing against materialism, capitalism, consumerism, urbanism, movies, Ginza cafes or whatever their pet social grievance happened to be as the ultimate cause of widespread destruction and suffering.

There was also a more sinister side to the blame game after the 1923 earthquake, which generated an unusual degree of fear and panic. More than 100,000 were dead or missing, several hundred thousand houses and other structures were flattened, water lines and telephone lines had been cut, and the municipal authorities, including the police, were overwhelmed. The central government, decreeing martial law immediately, deployed army troops throughout the city to check disorder. Rumors scapegoating "lawless Koreans" spread rapidly. Neighborhood watch groups, some armed with clubs and swords, sprang up almost immediately and contributed to the spread of disorder rather than to its containment. Hundreds of Koreans – and many Chinese – died in attacks by crowds, by police and by the vigilante groups who feared they were poisoning wells, starting fires and setting off dynamite explosions (Allen 1996).

Attacks like those on Koreans in 1923 have been rare in the history of recurring disasters in Japan. To be sure, in 2011 rumors about "gangs of foreigner robbers" and "widespread rapes" in devastated areas circulated in Sendai, but so did less virulent and more plausible rumors that electricity would not be restored for the next few years or that no temporary shelters would be provided for disaster victims (*Asahi Shinbun*, March 26, 2011). Rumormongering, however, seems to have been kept to a minimum by 24/7 television news coverage. The rhetoric of blame, moreover, was not as extreme as in 1923 nor did it involve a generic critique of the whole society. Rather it focused on particular actors – Tokyo Electric Power Company (TEPCO), the Kan cabinet, the Nuclear and Industrial Safety Agency (NISA), and so forth – that could plausibly be held responsible for post-quake distress. But there was an undercurrent of anxiety that the disaster would further weaken a society that many thought had lost its vision. In a sense, at some level, the disaster was seen as a test of whether the tragedy would reverse or intensify the malaise that had overtaken the country during its "lost decades" since the early 1990s.

Coping

Obviously the first concern in the wake of disaster is the restoration of order and stability as quickly as possible – coping with the dead and injured, providing relief for the homeless and the hungry, cleaning away the rubble and so forth. Often family and community networks are the primary source of refuge and relief for disaster victims. Personal trust, shared suffering, physical proximity and long-standing social ties offer a ready-made foundation for cooperation. Certainly this appears to have been the case in 2011 when firemen who had lost their families joined the search in the rubble for other dead, not just their own; when small businessmen kept their employees on the payroll until their workshops or warehouses could be rebuilt; and members of a fishing cooperatives who decided to spend their reserve funds to buy new boats and share profits until everyone was back on their feet. ("We are *nakama* [buddies]," the cooperative director said on television.) While it is difficult if not impossible to document or quantify the impact of such activities, they were surely important to disaster victims.

But there was also an expectation that government would provide collective help for disaster victims and play a central role in the restoration of normality.

Indeed, there was a long tradition of such interventions. Like the monarchies of early modern Europe the Tokugawa ruling class understood the connection between a state's legitimacy and the welfare of its subjects. Confucian political ideology postulated that an "honorable lord" had a moral duty to protect the people not only from bad harvests and famines but other disasters as well. Fire was a central concern of the Tokugawa shogunate. The constant recurrence of conflagrations in Edo made officials attentive to the necessity of handling disasters quickly and efficiently. After the great Meiroku Fire of 1657 burned half the city, for example, they opened up firebreaks around the *shogun*'s castle, encouraged the *daimyo* to build secondary mansions on the outer edges of the city, mandated the use of ceramic roof tiles instead of wooden shingles and encouraged the building of substantial plastered structures.

As in Europe, management of fire, a common but avoidable disaster, paved the way for management of other natural disasters – earthquakes, flood, tsunamis. In 1855, for example, long experience with disaster relief allowed the authorities to spring into action very quickly, setting up relief facilities to attend to the needs of the injured or homeless and dealing with other hardships faced by the rest of the commoner population (Kitahara 2000: 251–269). The goal was to reestablish normal routines, normal commercial traffic, and normal daily life as quickly as possible. To be sure, rapid response was also probably prompted by a desire to forestall social unrest. The 1830s and 1840s had been marked by repeated peasant risings and urban riots brought on by poor harvests and widespread famine.

Within a few days of the quake, shelters for the homeless or distressed were thrown up in public gathering places in Asakusa, Ueno, Fukugawa and elsewhere; rations of cooked or raw rice were distributed to the hungry, particularly the indigent; the dead were recovered and counted; the injured were treated; and merchants were enjoined not to take advantage of scarcities by hoarding or raising prices for rice and other daily necessities. All these were standard practices, regularly deployed earlier in times of fire or famine. Constables attached to town magistrates' offices joined in the relief efforts but much of the work was done by local neighborhood officials. The burden of reconstruction lay in the hands of the city's merchants and land holders, whose interests were best served by speedy recovery. Conventional wisdom held that if a shopkeeper was not back in business within three days he would never recover. The task of coping thus relied on the undocumented labors of ten thousands of townspeople anxious to rebuild their lives.

Private acts of generosity, springing from pure altruism, community bonds, or status seeking also supported relief efforts. As Kitahara Itoko has pointed out, Tokugawa authorities encouraged voluntary charity and mutual aid by well-to-do commoners; they rewarded donors to relief efforts by publicly posting the names of donors. Money contributions in times of distress had become a kind of social obligation – as well as a mark of social status. In 1855, for example, 250 or so wealthy townsmen donated 15,000 *ryo* – roughly the annual income of a small *daimyo* lord – to the relief efforts, and others inside and outside the city contributed needed daily consumption goods – rice, *umeboshi*, cooking bowls, pickled *daikon*, and the like (Kitahara 2006: 227–228).

How the city was reconstructed is not so clearly documented. Certainly no overall plan was in place, nor was the city itself a unified entity. It was divided between the *samurai* quarters, where nearly half the population lived, usually on a temporary basis; and the commoner neighborhoods, where the other half lived. Official reconstruction focused on public infrastructure and favored the interests of the wealthy and/or powerful, i.e. the *daimyo* and the *samurai*. *Daimyo* lords brought materials and workmen from their own domains to rebuild their mansions and compounds, often financing reconstruction with loans from "privileged merchants" (*gōyō shōnin*) to whom they were already deeply in debt. The shogunate gave priority, and deployed its own funds to support, its direct retainers as well the dozen or so *daimyo* lords who controlled the *shogun*'s administrative structure. Although the shogunate slowly restored water mains, roads, and bridges the commoner neighborhoods were largely left to fend for themselves.

These coping practices carried over into the modern era but the institutional setting of disaster relief had changed significantly. Whereas disasters, even catastrophic disasters, are inherently local, affecting only a small proportion of the population, the creation of the national state as an "imagined community" vastly expanded a public sense of involvement in disaster. The Meiji government, a modern centralized state with fiscal resources and political control vaster than the Tokugawa shogunate, took as a given its need to respond promptly and generously to disaster. To provide relief after the Nōbi Earthquake in 1891, for example, the national government drew on a sinking fund established in 1880 by setting 3 percent of annual tax revenues for general relief purposes; and the new Imperial Diet appropriated relief funds from the national budget. In a sense, modernization had nationalized the coping process. Indeed, relief donations by the Meiji emperor, drawn from the huge imperial household budget, marked this symbolically by establishing the nation's ruler as the nation's prime charitable giver.

Newspapers, another new institution, also played a role in soliciting private relief donations. In 1891 contributions amounted to ¥900 million, and private donors also provided substantial supplies of material goods. Growing national consciousness posited that the nation, not simply kin or neighbors, was the community to which everyone belonged; and established the notion that the national public had a responsibility, if not an obligation, to aid local disaster victims. Within a few days of the 1923 Kantō Earthquake, for example, prefectural governors in the Kansai region mobilized a movement to provide earthquake victims with money, manpower and medical supplies. Relief and reconstruction were financed not only by funds from the national budget and the sale of public bonds but also by an outpouring of private donations. The imperial family, of course, donated ¥10 million to the relief effort, but private donations came to another ¥21 million.

Dreaming

If one immediate reaction to disaster is to seek blame, another is to imagine that something better might come next. A disaster is sometimes taken to be a signal that society is on the verge of great change. Hope, after all, is a much more comforting response to disaster than blame. Indeed, it is difficult to imagine recovery from disaster without its buoying promise. Disaster thus becomes a moment of potential transformation that will right the world and make it even better than before. An opinion survey in Japan a month or so after the 2011 quake, for example, revealed an interesting mixture of optimism and pessimism. While a little over half the respondents anticipated that economic conditions would worsen in the coming year, nearly 58 percent thought the disaster would make the country stronger. The prediction of worsening economic conditions seems obvious but the confidence that the country would become stronger seems less so – unless one appreciates the importance of hope for the restoration of normality.

It appears that popular sentiment after the 1855 earthquake was equally ambivalent. While *namazu-e* portrayed the earth-shaking giant catfish wreaking havoc on merchants and entertainers who catered to hedonistic pleasure-seekers, they also showed a divine surrogate like Daikoku, a symbol of good fortune, bestowing prosperity on day laborers, lumber wholesalers, roof tile merchants, and artisans like carpenters, plasterers and masons, who would profit from rebuilding the city.

Some historians even argue that in the popular view the earthquake was a "world-renewing" event (*yonaori*), opening a bright future by righting social wrongs and by leveling class differences. (Minami 1999: 10–34; Smits 2006) It seems doubtful, however, that these views were shared by the ruling elite, whose debates over the future revolved around the shogunate's response to foreign pressure.

The 1923 earthquake, on the other hand, gave birth to hope that Tokyo would be rebuilt as an ideal city. As the Christian socialist Abe Isoo noted, "When we stand among the desolate ruins and imagine the birth of a new, ideal capital, we cannot help but feel inspired" (Schencking 2008: 307). His own scheme involved curbing urban hedonism by curbing ladies' fashions, outlawing the production and consumption of alcoholic beverages, and closing down the country's red light districts. But urban planners, urban bureaucrats, and social reformers saw the massive destruction of the city as a rare opportunity to rationalize the urban grid, beautify the cityscape, expand social service institutions, and enhance the city's economic efficiency.

The grandiose reconstruction plans of Home Minister Gotō Shimpei, technocrat extraordinaire (and later first Chief Boy Scout of Japan), illustrate how high hopes could rise. He proposed a reconstruction plan that involved a government buy-out of all the devastated districts in the city, construction of a modern government center with magnificent new buildings, a new road network with broad boulevards and green zones, upgraded water, sewer and mass transit systems, and expanded social welfare facilities – all at an estimated cost of ¥4 billion, an amount twice the size of the national budget. In a sense, it was the culmination of several decades of dreaming about making Tokyo into a modern world capital that began with the building of the red-brick Ginza district after a fire in the early 1870s (Sorenson 2002: 125–131).

Like those earlier dreams, Gotō's collapsed when confronted with fiscal and political realities. Fiscal conservatives like Finance Minister Inoue Junnosuke, objected to any massive increase in government expenditure; and just as rural interests had opposed the government's heavy investment in the Ginza district, rural representatives in the Imperial Diet objected to spending so much money on the capital city at a time when the rural economy was suffering from a long-term structural recession. The budget was whittled down to ¥470 million, and execution of the plan met resistance from the city's landowners, who did not want to part with their property, no matter how good that might be for reinvigoration of the city.

Reconstruction of the city instead followed a pattern evident in the aftermath of the 1855 earthquake: it placed a heavy emphasis on infrastructure; and it envisaged a distribution of resources that favored the powerful. What emerged was not the shiny new city that visionaries like Gotō hoped for but a slightly streamlined version of the existing city. Downtown residential areas were rationalized through land adjustment agreements, new and straighter streets and roads (including broad avenues like Shōwa-dōri) were laid out, large new public parks and several dozen smaller ones were created in downtown areas, elementary schools were rebuilt, and hundreds of bridges (including six major ones) were built or restored. However, the old cheaply built rental housing for working class and middle class tenants that had been destroyed by the quake was simply replaced by newly built cheap residential housing. Indeed, the reconstruction may have made housing conditions in the city worse as many displaced inhabitants of the inner city moved into new unplanned and underdeveloped suburban communities on which postwar urban sprawl expanded. (Hanes 2000) Disaster relief had become nationalized by the 1890s, but post-disaster reconstruction had not.

Although reconstruction planning remained in flux for several months after the Tōhoku Earthquake, it seemed likely that the national government would subsidize rebuilding in a variety of ways. Given the rural character of the devastated areas, and the economic marginality of the northeastern region, however, it also seemed unlikely that something new and better will be built there. The precarious financial situation of the national government will probably constrain reconstruction efforts, and so will depopulation of the region as younger inhabitants who have lost families and/or jobs have left for other labor markets and as fears of contamination in the districts nearby the Fukushima nuclear plants inhibit in-migration. In any case, hopes and dreams seem to be in scarcer supply than in the past. The reconstruction process will be one of restoration rather than innovation, and perhaps limited restoration at that.

Learning

The Swiss disaster historian Christian Pfister has argued European societies, and perhaps all societies, go through a collective learning process as the result of dealing with disasters, especially recurring disasters. However deadly and disruptive a natural disaster might be, it is possible to imagine that if the proper steps are taken, a similar event can be contained or defeated the next time. As a matter of survival, disaster-prone societies therefore seek to find ways to mitigate the effects of disaster if not to completely avoid them. Natural disasters are important because they test a society's ability to learn from collective experience (Pfister 2009).

Although the Tokugawa authorities learned how to cope with disaster, it is probably safe to say that by the mid-nineteenth century the Japanese had reached the limits of their technological ability to deal with disaster, whether flood, fire or earthquake. The opening of the country to new knowledge from the "civilized" West in the 1860s spurred a sudden leap in their learning curve. The transfer of technology brought in new techniques and new strategies to prevent or reduce disaster damage. By the 1890s, for example, the use of modern firefighting equipment – portable water pumps and urban water delivery systems – substantially reduced damage from fire in cities like Tokyo and Osaka; and with less success new dam and levee construction techniques from the West were imported to contain flooding rivers.

The 1891 Nōbi Earthquake mobilized a cohort of young civil and mechanical engineers, architects and other scientists trained abroad or at the government's Imperial Engineering College (Kōbu daigakkō) to deal with earthquake disasters. As Gregory Clancey has pointed out, by the turn of the twentieth century, the Japanese were global leaders in the field of seismology. Indeed, three foreign teachers at the college developed the first seismograph, and their students pioneered new ways of measuring and tracking earthquakes. The 1891 earthquake was the first one systematically surveyed in Japan, and it led to the creation of a network of seismic reporting stations to track and report on local tremors (Clancey 2006: 151–179). Japanese seismologists were most interested in earthquake prediction. Identifying where and when an earthquake might take place was essential knowledge for country that faced such risk perennially. In the search for the signals that would predict earthquake, early Japanese seismologists left few stones unturned: they explored the significance of climate and weather change; they examined the peculiar behavior of eels, catfish, pheasants and other living creatures; they pursued theories linking earthquake to magnetic activity; they compiled a monumental archive of historical evidence to understand the periodicity of earthquakes; and they conducted field research to identify fault lines. In the end, of course, no reliable signal system was developed, but seismologists acquired a better sense of where earthquakes were likely to occur.

Since seemingly invulnerable Western-style buildings had proven susceptible to damage in the 1891 quake, the Japanese also began to study ways of strengthening residential, industrial and commercial structures. In the 1890s architects experimented with techniques to make brick-and-masonry buildings more earthquake resistant by reshaping bricks into interlocking elements like Lego pieces or advocated the use of Western carpentry techniques like trusses and nails instead of joinery (Clancey 2006: 180–211). The most important breakthrough, however, was the introduction of ferro-concrete construction of large urban buildings, such as the downtown business center the Mitsubishi interests built in the Marunouchi section of Tokyo. The construction industry, however, had little or no interest in residential structures, which were still built by traditional craftsmen, so cities like Tokyo and Osaka remained vulnerable to post-quake fires as well as wartime incendiary raids.

While some local governments like Osaka developed building codes earlier, it was only in 1919 that the first national urban building standard code was established. It set limits on building heights but did not mandate seismic standards. That changed after the 1923 Kantō Earthquake when seismic design standards for large buildings such as seismic co-efficients and maximum ground acceleration were introduced (Sorenson 2002: 85–108). After World War II, in the 1950s, and again in the 1980s, more elaborate regulatory codes were issued as new risk calculations were made and new construction technologies were developed. During the boom years of the 1980s and 1990s the Japanese construction industry devised ways to improve the earthquake resistance of high rise buildings, including dampers that allowed buildings to sway with tremors rather than resist them. This aspect of the learning process appears to have paid off. In 1995 the Kobe Earthquake, for example, inflicted much lighter damage to buildings constructed after 1982 than on older ones.

Learning how to manage disaster has required the conjunction of local knowledge and advanced technology, but in the final analysis learning has its limits. At best, it can reduce but not prevent the loss of human life. Nor does the knowledge that is useful to withstand one kind of disaster necessarily work well in the event of another kind. A classic example is the damage suffered by commoner sections in the 1855 earthquake. Well-to-do merchants built thick-walled masonry storehouses to protect their goods and treasures against the ever-present threat of fire, but the quake crumbled 1,400 of them while more flammable structures survived. And prevention measures sometimes makes disasters worse – witness the levees and dikes the Army Corps of Engineers built to protect the city of New Orleans.

The main lessons likely to be learned from the 2011 disaster will have less to do with damage done to its victims in the Tōhoku region than with its impact on the whole society. To be sure, there will be efforts to find better ways of protecting coastal communities from tsunamis, for example by relocating them to higher ground, but the most heated debate underway at the moment is about the necessity and viability of nuclear power generation. The outcome of this debate, however, will not simply determine whether the next disaster will be less disastrous; it will affect how the country will generate electrical energy in the future, an issue central to economic development. In that sense the impact of the Tōhoku disaster on the learning process has far broader implications than that of previous disasters. Indeed, it has had an impact not only on Japan but on the outside world as well. In a sense, the events of 2011 internationalized the country's disaster, prompting debate in the United States, Europe and elsewhere on the wisdom of using nuclear power generation to produce clean energy.

Forgetting

There is no question that cumulative experience over the past century has made Japanese better at dealing with major disasters. Had it not been for the extraordinary height and power of the tsunami in 2011, and the location and management of TEPCO's nuclear power plants, relief and recovery might have proceeded more smoothly than they have. In Tokyo, buildings forty stories tall survived as they would not have without the new building codes and technologies; subway passengers would have been injured or suffocated had it not been for sensor devices that brought them to a halt at the first sign of a tremor; and the discipline – and forbearance – that the tens of thousands of Tokyo workers displayed on the day of the disaster would not have been so visible had it not been for years of drills and schoolroom instruction about what to do in an earthquake.

But there is no guarantee that was has been learned will not be forgotten. It is interesting that we find it easier to remember human disasters like wars and other forms of human violence than disasters wrought by natural forces. An enemy is tangible and persistent in a way that a tornado, a tsunami and an earthquake is not; and natural disasters last for hours, days and weeks whereas wars can last for years or even decades. War monuments and national holidays constantly remind us of when and why they happened but there are few monuments for disasters. And school history textbooks do not cover disasters with the detail that they cover wars.

To be sure, the Japanese are less apt to forget the ever-present risk of natural disaster than other societies. Japan is probably the only country with an official Disaster Day, established in 1960 to commemorate the 1923 disaster. (Even Governor Ishihara shows up for rescue and recovery drills decked out in appropriate work jacket.) And in every Japanese city one is reminded of the ever-present risk of disaster by signs demarking evacuation areas. A 2010 Cabinet Office opinion survey on disaster prevention indicated that 83.6 percent of the respondents said that they felt "anxiety" about harm from a natural disaster, and 75 percent said that they had prepared themselves for a disaster by making an evacuation plan and keeping a radio, flashlight, medications, stores of food and water on hand.

But even if the possibility of disaster may not be forgotten, not everyone remembers how best to deal with the risk. The coastal area of the Tōhoku region is dotted with steles warning against building below the high water marks of the tsunamis of 1896 and 1933. Some inhabitants remembered and acted accordingly; others forgot as local population grew and building lines moved closer and closer to the shore. Remembering saved many from the impact of the 2011 tsunami, but forgetting doomed others. Perhaps in this day and age, when the ability to accumulate and store information has metastasized, one can hope that what has been learned will be remembered more easily. But optimism may not be warranted. Only 4 percent of the respondents to the survey mentioned above said they planned to reinforce their houses to better withstand an earthquake. Indeed 47 percent said that they did not intend to, principally because of the cost. In the end, despite all that has been learned from the past, and despite all the advances in technology, not everyone can prepare for every contingency. Sadly history will once again repeat itself as tragedy, and so will the cycle of response.

References

Allen, J. Michael (1996) "The Price of Identity: The 1923 Kantō Earthquake and Its Aftermath," *Korean Studies*, 20: 64–93.

Cabinet Office (2010) Survey, online, available at: www8.cao.go.jp/survey/tokubetu/h21/h21-hinan.pdf.

Clancey, Gregory (2000) "The Meiji Earthquake: Nature, Nation, and the Ambiguities of Catastrophe," *Modern Asian Studies*, 40(4): 909–952.

Clancey, Gregory (2006) *Earthquake Nation: The Cultural Politics of Japanese Seismicity, 1968-1930*, Berkeley, CA: University of California Press.

Hanes, Jeffrey (2000) "Urban Planning as an Urban Problem: The Reconstruction of Tokyo after the Great Earthquake", *Seisaku kagaku*, 7: 123–136.

Kitahara, Itoko (2000) *Jishin no shakaishi: Ansei daijishin to minshū*, Tokyo: San'ichi shobo.

Kitahara, Itoko (2006) *Nihon saigaishi*, Tokyo: Yoshikawa kōbunkan.

Minami, Kazuo (1999) *Bakumatsu isshin no fūshiga*, Tokyo: Yoshikawa kōbunkan.

Naimushō (1924) *The Great Earthquake of 1923 in Japan*, Tokyo: Shakaikyoku.

Noguchi, Takehiko (2004) *Ansei Edo jishin: Kasai to seiji kenryoku*, Tokyo: Chikuma shobō.

Pfister, Christian (2009) "Learning from Nature-Induced Disasters: Theoretical Considerations and Case Studies from Western Europe," in C. Mauch and C. Pfister (eds.), *Natural Disasters, Cultural Responses: Case Studies Toward a Global Environmental History*, Lanham, MD: Lexington Books, pp. 17–40.

Schencking, J. Charles (2008) "The Great Kantō Earthquake and the Culture of Catastrophe and Reconstruction in 1920s Japan", *Journal of Japanese Studies*, 34(2): 295–331.

Smits, Gregory (2006) "Shaking Up Japan: Edo Society and the 1955 Catfish Pictures", *Journal of Social History*, 39(4): 1045–1078.

Sorenson, Andre (2002) *The Making of Urban Japan: Cities and Planning from Edo to the Twenty-First Century*, London: Routledge.

Usami, Tatsuo (2002) "Historical Earthquakes in Japan," *International Handbook of Earthquake and Engineering Seismology, Volume 81 A*, International Association of Seismology and Physical Earth's Interior, London: Academic Press, pp. 799–802.

11

THE POLITICS OF DISASTER, NUCLEAR CRISIS AND RECOVERY

Jeff Kingston

The fiercely partisan politics of the complex Tōhoku catastrophe has slowed action on recovery and discredited politicians of all political stripes.[1] The public views Diet members with growing contempt because too many politicians seem to have prioritized petty party politics over reconstruction. In early June 2011, while nearly 100,000 evacuees languished in evacuation centers, and with relatively little progress towards recovery in many battered coastal communities or managing the nuclear meltdown at Fukushima Daiichi, the Diet devoted its energy to a no-confidence motion to oust Prime Minister Kan Naoto. Naturally, the public was dismayed by this unproductive vendetta at a time when the nation was looking for substantial emergency measures. Polls taken at the time of the no-confidence motion showed that a vast majority of Japanese did not think ousting Kan was a pressing priority even though he was unpopular. In the court of public opinion, the verdict on national politicians is dereliction of duty.

On the eve of 3/11, Prime Minister Kan looked to be on his way out as scandals sullied his administration and he plunged in public opinion polls. In the wake of the disasters, Kan enjoyed a brief bounce in public support and a lull in the escalating vilification by the media and political opponents in the Diet. Within a month, however, this fragile solidarity unraveled and it was back to politics as usual featuring internecine sniping by the Ozawa Ichiro wing of Kan's Democratic Party of Japan (DPJ) and shrill criticism coupled with stonewalling of many legislative initiatives by the Liberal Democratic Party (LDP).

Gridlock and the blame game

Over the long years of LDP dominance of Japanese politics since 1955, policies and legislation were worked out in negotiations within the party's Policy Affairs Research Council (PARC) and between PARC and bureaucrats in the ministries rather than in open parliamentary compromise. As a result, the habits of compromise in the Diet were stunted. The emergence of a "twisted" Diet (the lower and upper houses controlled by different parties) since 2007 has lead frequently to legislative gridlock with both main parties adopting scorched earth tactics. According to Aurelia Mulgan-George, "This situation has not been conducive to nurturing a 'loyal opposition', meaning the main opposition party holds the ruling party accountable and debates policy, but allows effective government rather than obstructs the legislative process as a means to discredit the ruling party" (personal communication August 6, 2011). The Kan Cabinet lacked a two-thirds majority in the Lower House so could not override Upper House vetoes and also faced sabotage from within orchestrated by Ozawa Ichiro who lost the DPJ presidential election to Kan in 2010 and was subsequently sidelined by the premier.

On March 18, Prime Minister Kan invited LDP opposition leader Tanigaki Sadakazu to join his government, but this offer was spurned and ongoing polarization in the "twisted" Diet lead to a slow-motion response to the crisis. The LDP used its control of the Upper House to tie up key legislation passed in the DPJ-controlled Lower House, slowing progress on recovery. This does not mean legislative paralysis as many important bills eventually got passed, such as the $50 billion emergency disaster relief budget approved by the Diet on May 2. However, it was not until June 20 that the Upper House finally enacted a basic law on reconstruction of the devastated Tōhoku region. While a similar bill for the Kobe quake recovery in 1995 passed within a month, it took 102 days for the 2011 Diet to hammer out an accord. Disagreements over the powers and functions of a planned reconstruction agency lay at the heart of this impasse and finally the DPJ capitulated to the LDP's views, sparing the Diet further indignity. This dawdling response reinforced negative perceptions of politicians among the public and, more importantly, left devastated communities feeling hostage to irrelevant political battles. The Diet session was extended until the end of August over the objections of the LDP, a stand that drew considerable public censure given the need for urgent action on pressing national issues such as relief and recovery measures, tax reform, rising public debt, renewable energy policy, and the troubled nuclear industry.

In early June, the LDP tabled a no-confidence motion that Kan survived only by implying he would step down. What exactly he promised at that time remains a matter of dispute, but Kan publicly set conditions on June 28 for his departure, requiring the LDP to cooperate in order to be rid of him. His most controversial demand was that the Diet pass a comprehensive feed-in-tariff (FIT) aimed at stimulating expansion of renewable energy capacity.[2] This is the third rail of nuclear-dominated energy politics and explains why powerful vested interests rallied against Kan.

The Ministry of Economy, Trade and Industry (METI) drafted the FIT bill and the cabinet approved it on March 11, but in the wake of Fukushima the implications changed dramatically. Initially, METI envisaged renewable energy replacing fossil fuel-fired power generation, but suddenly it became apparent that the Fukushima crisis would ratchet up pressure for renewable energy sources displacing nuclear energy. After Kan requested Chubu Electric to shut down the Hamaoka nuclear power plant in May because of its high-risk location on a major active fault line, the "nuclear village" (pro-nuclear advocates in utilities, METI, business federations, the LDP, media, and academia) pressed hard for his ouster. Also in May, Kan declared that Japan would boost renewables to 20 percent of its electricity generating energy mix in the 2020s up from about 1 percent (*Japan Times* July 24, 2011).[3] Kan represented a serious threat to nuclear energy interests in Japan and they fought back. There are certainly other reasons why the no-confidence motion was tabled, but Kan's inclination to hit the reset button on national energy strategy and target bureaucratic and utility interests related to nuclear energy put him on the village's hit list.

In many respects, Prime Minister Kan was an inept politician and his cabinet team lurched from gaffe to gaffe, provoking general dissatisfaction and a media feeding frenzy. There are very good reasons why very few people in Japan thought that the Kan cabinet was on top of things and dealing effectively with the crisis. Part of the problem was mixed messages, as the prime minister, cabinet ministers and spokesmen had difficulty staying on the same page or even convincingly conveying empathy. Matsumoto Ryū, for example, resigned in early July only a week after being appointed Reconstruction Minister following his arrogant and insensitive remarks to politicians from the devastated Tōhoku region. Mostly, however, there was deep frustration about the slow pace of progress on mitigating the human misery unleashed by the tsunami and the nuclear meltdowns.

Kan was a convenient lightning rod for this frustration, and because he stepped on powerful toes in the "nuclear village," there was an orchestrated campaign to oust him. For example, twice TEPCO spread false information that was aimed at tarnishing Kan, only to recant. TEPCO claimed that Kan's visit to the stricken reactors on March 12 was the reason why venting did not proceed, thus causing the hydrogen explosions on March 12, 14 and 15. Later it turned out that the utility was divided over venting and argued all night, not obeying instructions from the government to proceed with venting[4] (*Mainichi Daily News* July 4, 2011). When the utility did try to vent, the system did not function because it depended on the same electricity sources that had failed and caused the crisis. Nobody at Fukushima Daiichi had any experience with manually operating the vents and so the manual had to be retrieved from the radiation-contaminated control room, delaying the response. In the event, this also proved ineffective, but TEPCO had planted the disinformation in the public mind that somehow Prime Minister Kan was responsible.

The second attempt to discredit Prime Minister Kan backfired when TEPCO leaked information to the LDP blaming the meltdown on Kan because he had ordered the cessation of pumping seawater to cool the fuel rods. Later it was reported that Kan did not issue any such order. Rather it was a TEPCO employee serving as liaison with the prime minister's office who called the Fukushima plant manager and said that the "mood" in the prime minister's office was in favor of stopping the pumping of seawater and thus it should be stopped. Subsequently it was established that the Fukushima Daiichi plant manager did not follow his colleague's order to stop the pumping of seawater since under international protocols it is the onsite manager's call (*Japan Times* May 27, 2011). Kan may have been exonerated, but both cases ignited a furor in the media and Diet that tarnished his credibility. The blame game for Fukushima is a very high stakes battle helping to explain these efforts to discredit Kan by spreading malicious disinformation.

Crisis response

Overall, Kan probably deserves more credit than most observers are willing to give him. Under the dire circumstances of a complex catastrophe involving the triple whammy of an unprecedented earthquake, tsunami and nuclear crisis, Kan managed the initial relief operations reasonably well. A lot depends on the yardstick against which he is measured. Compared with other leaders dealing with natural disasters – think Katrina, the 2004 tsunami in Aceh and Sri Lanka, and the earthquakes in Kobe 1995, Sichuan 2008 and flooding in Europe in 2010 – Kan's response was not that bad. Having witnessed the bungling response to the Kobe quake I am impressed by how much better the Kan government's initial disaster response was, although follow-up was slow because disaster-hit areas have been held hostage to party politics. This is scant consolation to evacuees, but failure to meet public expectations or assuage frustrations does not mean Kan was doing a lousy job.

Much of the public dissatisfaction expressed by citizens outside Tōhoku stems from the Fukushima accident. TEPCO bears primary responsibility for this catastrophe along with METI for failing to properly monitor the nuclear industry, a pattern established under LDP rule. Prime Minister Kan established an independent panel to probe the causes of the nuclear accident at Fukushima. It remains to be seen how independent and aggressive the panel will be and to what extent officials will cooperate with the investigation. An interim report is expected in December 2011 and, whatever its conclusions, it will lead to intensified political maneuvering over national energy policy.

Where the government is perhaps most at fault is in its negligence over radioactive contamination and food safety issues. The government was slow in taking measures to prevent contamination of the nation's food supply, for example failing to ban shipment of rice straw from contaminated areas that was sold as cattle feed to ranchers throughout the country. Agriculture Minister Kano Michihiko conceded the government did not foresee this problem. In addition, the government first relied on voluntary beef shipment bans in contaminated areas, only to discover local authorities and the media reporting the presence of unsafe levels of cesium in beef on supermarket shelves in Tokyo and elsewhere. Only then did the government act belatedly to ban beef shipments from designated prefectures. This government negligence imperiled consumer's health while destroying trust in upscale *wagyu* beef brands carefully nurtured over several years. The lack of a national system for checking radiation contamination in food left the task to the initiative of local authorities, supermarket chains, slaughterhouses and farmers conducting voluntary tests.

Parents of children are also incensed that the government has not done more to deal with radiation affecting schoolyards while there are broader anxieties that many hot zones lay beyond the 20 km evacuation zone. The brisk sales of personal Geiger counters reflect apprehensions about government failures to keep the public informed about radiation risks. The government does have a system for assessing where winds would carry radiation, but this information was not made public during the initial days after the meltdowns and subsequent explosions spewed radiation into the air.[5] As a result, many residents and evacuees were exposed to radioactive contamination because they were not given vital information (*New York Times*, August 8, 2011).

Many farming communities have been ruined by the contamination and are impatiently awaiting compensation for the fallout from Fukushima, an accident people believe was triggered by nature, but compounded by human error. They, like the 80,000 evacuees who once lived in the 20 km evacuation zone, are waiting for answers about when their land will be inhabitable and they can resume their livelihoods. In August the government finally announced that the land in some affected areas might not be habitable for decades to come. The political fallout is diffuse, with a gathering collapse of faith in the powers that be.

Returning to the initial rescue and relief operations, Prime Minister Kan immediately mobilized 100,000 troops and accepted international offers of assistance in stark contrast to the fumbling response to the 1995 Kobe Earthquake by the LDP-dominated coalition government. Tsunami disaster relief was reasonably fast and effective under difficult circumstances and evacuees received basic needs. Certainly they had reasons to be frustrated with the pace of relief and recovery, but it is hard to imagine any government performing better given the devastation of ports and other infrastructure and the sheer scale of the disaster. Opposition politicians churlishly criticized the government for not meeting its target of building 30,000 temporary houses for evacuees by June, but it managed to build 27,200 units, an impressive performance in ten weeks given shortages of building materials, difficulty in finding suitable sites and damage to transport networks. By comparison, in Tamil Nadu (India) nearly seven years after the devastating 2004 tsunami, the government only managed to build a total of 7,800 units. Kan's efforts also compare favorably to the American debacle with trailer housing after Hurricane Katrina in 2005.

Despite deficient political skills, Kan demonstrated a surprising level of leadership at least in terms of energy issues. When it became apparent that TEPCO could not be relied on to provide accurate information in a timely manner, Kan spoke for the nation in dressing down the company on the day after the accident and also called on the US Nuclear Regulatory Commission and US military assets in Japan to get better information on the expanding crisis. He rejected TEPCO's early demand to evacuate all staff from Fukushima Daiichi and ordered them to stay at the site to try to restore cooling functions and bring the situation under control (Fuji TV

September 12, 2011).[6] He launched an independent investigation of the Fukushima meltdown, pressured Chubu Electric to shut down its vulnerable Hamaoka nuclear plant, hit the reset button on the national energy strategy, called for splitting the Nuclear Industrial Safety Agency (NISA)[7] that oversees the nuclear plants from pro-nuclear METI, advocated splitting power generation from transmission to promote renewable energy and submitted comprehensive feed-in-tariff legislation to facilitate rapid expansion of renewable energy. Assertive as these plans were, Kan was widely derided in the media for failing to lead while popular frustration with the prolonged nuclear crisis translated into falling support in public opinion polls.

One of the key problems exposed by the crisis is the vacuum of power at the center – the prime minister does not have very much power and is at the mercy of parliamentary politics, especially problematic given the divided Diet where the opposition LDP controls the Upper House and his own party was deeply fractured. Another key problem is inter-ministerial bickering and turf fighting as dysfunctional politics synergizes with a dysfunctional bureaucracy. The media dwelled on Kan's lack of leadership qualities without really delving into the institutional reasons for why it is difficult for Japanese leaders to lead and Japan is so hard to govern. One official involved with the nuclear crisis told me,

> Battles won in one ministry had to be fought all over again in another. The amount of time and energy spent on smoothing inter-ministerial rivalries and ruffled feathers was enormous and unproductive, hugely slowing the government's response. These bureaucratic spats were a constant source of frustration for everyone who wanted to tackle the crisis and help.

Certainly Kan also deserves blame for his isolation and unpopularity. His go-it-alone, improvisational style sidelined his cabinet on key decisions, alienated party members and was prone to mistakes and subsequent zigzagging that discredited his initiatives. This was also an unorthodox style in a nation where consensus is valued and in any country bold policy initiatives are resisted by vested interests.

Prioritizing consensus, however, does not make for bold and timely action, especially when it challenges a pre-existing consensus. To create a new consensus is time consuming and risky because it forces supporters of the existing consensus to reconsider their assumptions and change their longstanding views, ones that are tied to powerful institutional interests in the case of nuclear energy. As the *Mainichi* notes, a wide network of powerful interests support and depend on the nuclear industry: "Heavy machinery manufacturers are snuggled right up against them. Banks favor deep-pocketed power utilities as safe, high-interest borrowers, as do trading firms who find they can sell fuel to utilities at high prices" (*Mainichi* July 18, 2011).

Ignoring consensual politics helped Kan bypass vested interests and act boldly; perhaps this was his only option in taking on the nuclear village and their insidious influence that even extended into his cabinet, but in doing so he alienated his own party. Moreover, realizing his disaster agenda, especially on energy issues, was very difficult because he also could not count on key bureaucrats as most of them were eager for him to fail. His talent for making enemies and disinclination to reach out and cultivate support undermined his effectiveness. In addition, the media often trivialized his initiatives, portraying them as gambits to extend his tenure rather than delving into the policy details and implications.

Arthur Stockwin, a specialist on Japanese politics at Oxford University, explains,

> Perhaps the best hypothesis might be that he has, like many of his predecessors, faced the problems of a highly dysfunctional system, and despite the inevitable appearance of incompetence that this brings (because the media always focus on narrow personal failures – gaffes etc.), he has been feeling his way round the system, acting in unorthodox ways because he has little chance of making progress through "normal channels". This does not seem to me particularly untypical of Japanese prime ministers, though of course some have simply resigned themselves to exercising little influence. Kan may not be a political genius, but the magnitude of the crisis has stimulated some interesting resourcefulness on his part.
>
> (personal communication, July 20, 2011)

Nuclear politics

The prime minister called for rethinking the national energy strategy, and cancelling plans to ramp up Japan's nuclear power generation to 53 percent of Japan's total electricity generating capacity by 2030 (up from 29 percent pre-3/11). In early July, the government announced that all 54 of Japan's reactors would be subject to two-stage stress tests, ensuring that most of Japan's nuclear power plants would remain off-line for several more months until certified safe. This abrupt decision to follow the EU example on nuclear reactor stress tests came after METI Minister Kaieda Banri had assured the public on June 18 that the nuclear plants had been checked and deemed safe as part of a PR campaign to convince local mayors and prefectural governors to approve restarting idled reactors. Also in June, Kaieda visited local politicians in Kyushu to reassure them about the safety of two reactors in Genkai, Saga prefecture in order to gain approval for restarting them, a move that advocates hoped would give momentum to their efforts to overcome widespread public anxieties and restart idled reactors all over Japan (at that time only 19 of Japan's 54 reactors were online).

The darkest moment came on June 26 when METI arranged a public forum in Genkai aired on Internet and cable television. On this program, officials briefed local residents about safety measures and received online comments ostensibly representing local opinions about restarting the reactors. However, Kyūshū Electric later admitted that it asked related companies and subsidiaries to request their employees to post comments in favor of restarting the reactors and the utility helpfully gave examples of what sorts of reasons should be given by these "citizens" in support of resumption of operations, i.e. warning that blackouts might cause old people and children to suffer heatstroke, businesses to suffer and electricity bills to rise[8] (*NHK TV News* July 14, 2011; *NHK TV News* July 30, 2011).

Revelations about this orchestrated campaign to fabricate local support indicates just how worried the utility is about public sentiments, something that has not previously been a problem in local communities hosting nuclear plants because of the economic benefits lavished on them for doing so[9] (*Mainichi Daily News* July 5, 2011). It had been assumed that local towns would remain supportive even after Fukushima because of their "subsidy addiction." Previously poor communities that agreed to host nuclear plants suddenly enjoyed a vastly improved standard of living and steady jobs, but they also acquired expensive and extensive facilities and infrastructure beyond local means that could only be maintained by continued subsidies from the central government and utilities operating reactors in their towns[10] (*New York Times* May 30, 2011; *Japan Times* July 14, 2011; *Mainichi Daily News* July 5, 2011).

This dependence on nuclear plants means host communities have few options, but times are changing and local support is not nearly as firm as it once was because everyone can see how the lives of those living within 20 km of Fukushima Daiichi were devastated and how little help they received. On August 4, Minamisōma town in Fukushima where there had been plans to build new reactors announced that it will no longer accept subsidies normally given to projected host sites by the utility, although given the prefecture's newfound nuclear allergy, cancellation of the project was already a foregone conclusion (*NHK* August 4, 2011). *NHK* reported that other projected host sites may follow suit. More importantly, in October 2011 *NHK* conducted a poll among mayors of all the nuclear reactor hosting communities and found that 80 percent opposed restarting idled reactors following the reactor stress tests, reflecting widespread doubts about longstanding reassurances concerning plant safety and skepticism that the stress tests will be rigorous and reliable (*NHK* October 9, 2011). Distrust of the utilities has grown considerably all over Japan and in the towns with the most at stake it is understandable that they wonder if the results of the checks conducted by the utilities themselves can be trusted given their vested interest in resuming operations. In the end many of these towns may capitulate to pressure, blandishments and payoffs, but the *NHK* poll is remarkable because it shows how these "captive" communities are not nearly as resigned and quiescent as observers assumed.

In the wake of the sham forum scandal, METI and Kaieda saw their PR campaign implode as the mayor of Genkai withdrew his support for restarting the reactors. Kyūshū Electric lost all credibility and inadvertently stoked local opposition because of its high-handed deception. Nearly one-half of the "votes" in favor of restarting the reactors came from the sham supporters (130 out of 286) so that in fact a narrow majority of local citizens (163) opposed plans by Kyūshū Electric and the government to bring Genkai's two reactors back online (*Yomiuri* July 14, 2011). This was a public relations nightmare for the nuclear industry, a self-inflicted wound that amplified public apprehension and fueled distrust. Matters worsened on July 29 when utility executives claimed that NISA had been orchestrating other town hall meetings in Shizuoka (2007) and Kagoshima (2011) in favor of nuclear energy, a startling revelation that the government asked them to stage-manage support (*NHK News* July 29, 2011). Further revelations suggest that fabricating public support for nuclear energy has long been standard operating procedure for the nuclear watchdog agency. (*Japan Times* August 4, 2011). Aside from sowing further doubts among the public about nuclear energy, and the professionalism and ethics of watchdog agency officials, the spreading scandal indicated that solidarity within the nuclear village was unraveling as power companies claimed they were not acting on their own and implicated METI and NISA in the bogus schemes.

The *Mainichi* compares Japan's current commitment to nuclear energy with the Imperial Navy's ill-fated wartime commitment to battleships, stating,

> sticking to something that we knew to be flawed led to our demise. During the Pacific War, Japan knew that it had entered the age of aerial warfare, and yet clung to its "taikan-kyoho shugi" ("big-ship, big-cannon policy"), focused on naval gunnery contests between battleships, ultimately losing the war.
>
> (*Mainichi* July 18, 2011)

In the same opinion essay, Naval strategist Minoru Genda who served on the Imperial Navy General Staff, is quoted as follows,

> Changing military policy was not just about changing one's weapons, but about changing an entire organization that had been built upon the "big-ship, big-gun policy." That's a difficult thing to do considering the nature of Japanese people, who easily give in to sentiment and are reluctant to make waves.

Regarding nuclear energy, the Mainichi concludes, "So we apparently know what we're doing is wrong, but keep doing it anyway."

Shifting public opinion

Initially, public opinion polls conducted in mid-April following the accident at Fukushima Daiichi did not show a significant decline in support for nuclear energy, but over the next two months there was a significant shift against nuclear power in various polls (JAIF 2011). The *Asahi* reported that support for nuclear power declined from 50 percent in mid-April to 43 percent in May and to 37 percent in June 2011. Over the same period, opposition to nuclear power increased from 32 percent to 42 percent. Various public opinion surveys asked about the future of nuclear power in Japan. In April, those in favor of increasing nuclear energy ranged from 4 percent (*Sankei*), 5 percent (*Asahi*), and 7 percent (*NHK*) to 10 percent (*Yomiuri*). By June, the *NHK* poll reported this figure declined to 1 percent. The *NHK* poll also reported that between April to June support for maintaining the status quo on nuclear energy declined from 42 percent to 27 percent while support for decreasing nuclear power rose from 32 percent to 47 percent. In the *NHK* poll, those in favor of abolishing nuclear power increased from 12 percent in April to 18 percent in June.

The *Mainichi Shimbun*'s nationwide opinion poll in mid-May found that 66 percent supported Kan's initiative to shut down the Hamaoka nuclear power plant while 25 percent opposed. It also reported that 31 percent responded that nuclear power is unavoidable, down from 40 percent in April.

In a mid-June poll, the *Asahi Shimbun* asked:

Do you support a policy to phase out nuclear power with a goal to abandon it?
    Agree 74 percent; Disagree 14 percent.

Do you think natural (renewable) energy will be an energy source which will replace nuclear energy?
    Yes 64 percent; No 24 percent.

Given efforts by the utilities and government over the years to reassure the public about the safety of nuclear power, and the necessity of relying on it, not only for energy security, but also to reduce carbon emissions, it is surprising that public attitudes shifted so far and so quickly. It appears that the late-May revelation by TEPCO that it had misled the public about the scale of the crisis by not acknowledging that there had been three meltdowns until then undermined public faith in the utility and nuclear energy. This admission of intentionally deceiving the public was a PR fiasco and was seen as damage control before an International Atomic Energy Agency (IAEA) team was arriving to conduct an investigation.

Over the summer of 2011, prominent political leaders outside Tokyo also expressed doubts about nuclear power. Niigata Governor Izumida Hirohiko announced that he would not allow the restart of reactors in his prefecture even after the stress tests which he dismissed as, "only meant to make people feel better" (*Yomiuri* August 9, 2011). He said he intends to withhold approval for restarting idled reactors in Niigata, including TEPCO's massive complex at Kashiwazaki that was struck by a powerful earthquake in 2007, until the crisis is sorted out in Fukushima. The mayors of Hiroshima and Nagasaki also weighed in on the August anniversaries of the atomic bombings of their cities, questioning the safety of nuclear power and urging a shift towards renewable energy.

Renewable politics

On July 13, Prime Minister Kan announced his vision of gradually phasing out nuclear energy. This would mean abandoning current plans to build 14 new reactors by 2030 and thus overturn the current national energy plan that calls for nuclear reactors to generate more than one-half of Japan's electricity by 2030. Expressing his personal views, Kan stated,

It was when I considered the scale of such risks arising from the nuclear incident that I realized that it would no longer be possible to conduct policy on the basis of ensuring safety alone, which was the conventional wisdom until the incident. I was made keenly aware of the type of technology nuclear power actually is.

These thoughts led me to conclude that with regard to Japan's future nuclear power policy, we should aim to achieve a society that is not dependent on nuclear power. In other words, we should reduce our dependence on nuclear power in a planned and gradual manner and aim to realize a society in the future where we can do without nuclear power stations. I have come to believe that this is the direction that Japan should pursue

(Prime Minister's Office 2011)

Kan's spokesman clarified that Kan's bombshell was not national policy, but on July 29, the government officially shifted its energy policy away from nuclear energy and backed Kan's call for reducing reliance on atomic power (*Japan Times* July 30, 2011). This interim report raises, without quite endorsing, Kan's proposal for splitting electricity generation from transmission and also advocates a public debate aimed at bridging the gap between public sentiments and "expert's judgments," implying disingenuously that all experts are pro-nuclear. There is no such doubt about public sentiments; an *Asahi* poll in mid-July found that only 1 percent of respondents favored expanding nuclear power while 77 percent favor gradually abolishing it.[11]

Advocating a separation of nuclear watchdog responsibilities from the purview of METI (Ministry of Economy, Trade and Industry), something that the IAEA supports, Kan said, "We must fundamentally review the way nuclear power has for many years been administered. The regulatory body and the functions to promote nuclear energy have been under the same government ministry" (Kan 2011). Kan also supported separating the power transmission business from the ten regional power-generating utilities as a way of giving renewable energy providers access to the energy-generating market. Such a move would help boost prospects of renewable energy, but is fiercely resisted by the utilities. So too was Kan's plan for a comprehensive feed-in-tariff.

Kan's renewable offensive was opposed by the LDP, the party that oversaw the expansion of Japan's nuclear industry, and also by the leading business federations, Keidanren and Keizai Doyukai, the ten utilities, and METI, the ministry that has promoted the nuclear industry. But there are signs that the nuclear village faces formidable challenges as prominent executives and corporations jump on the renewables bandwagon. Son Masayoshi, CEO of Softbank telecommunications, unveiled plans to invest $1 billion in ten massive solar farms, but this ambition hinges on a comprehensive FIT and agreement by the ten regional utilities to buy the electricity generated. Son has already convinced most of the governors of Kansai (western Japan) to jump on board the renewables bandwagon, a rather remarkable achievement given that Kansai is so heavily dependent on nuclear energy (50 percent) and hosts so many nuclear plants. Son also established the

Renewable Energy Council in cooperation with 35 prefectural governments on July 13 to lobby for the FIT legislation, and a smart grid next-generation electricity transmission and distribution network designed to manage renewable energy and lessen dependence on nuclear energy. Significantly, Son exercises considerable influence as he is an iconic figure and an alpha blogger with millions of loyal fans on social media. In addition, another high profile business executive known for his innovative thinking, Mikitani Hiroshi, president of Japan's leading online retailer Rakuten Inc., quit Keidanren in protest over the its support for the energy status quo. Moreover, blue chip firms like Sharp and Mitsui, and even nuclear power giants such as Toshiba and Hitachi, are also eyeing profits in renewables, indicating that Japan, Inc.'s consensus in favor of nuclear energy may be unraveling and is certainly under siege.

In July, Kan stated that he would not hold a snap election as a referendum on nuclear energy policy. This made sense because the DPJ did not want to risk its majority in the Lower House; the DPJ is unpopular and has a miserable record to run on. Kan, however, positioned his party to reap the green, anti-nuclear vote whenever the elections are held, a strategy that recognizes the vulnerability of the LDP due to its long-standing support for the nuclear industry.

LDP advocacy for the utilities has been richly reciprocated as 72.5 percent of total individual donations to the political fund management body of the LDP in 2009 came from former and current executives of TEPCO and eight other utilities (*Mainichi* July 23, 2011; *Japan Times* July 24, 2011). A stunning 92.5 percent of executives at the nine utilities made such donations, indicating just how close ties are between the LDP and the power companies and why the LDP strongly opposes Kan's goal of phasing out nuclear energy.[12] The revelations about the utilities donating nothing to the DPJ and considerable sums to the LDP reinforces perceptions about shady and collusive relations that place the nuclear village's interests ahead of public safety.

One of the enigmas of post-Fukushima politics is why Kan was not able to capitalize on the dramatic shift in public sentiments away from nuclear power to renewables given that he demonstrated leadership on this very issue. While support ratings for the Kan cabinet sank to 15 percent in a mid-July *Asahi* poll (from 22 percent in June), and the disapproval rating rose from 56 percent to 66 percent, support for his energy policies was strong as more than three-quarters of Japanese agreed with his goal of gradually phasing out nuclear energy. Oddly, among proponents of phasing out nuclear energy, only 15 percent supported the Kan cabinet, showing just how hard it was for him, in the face of media headwinds, to translate a popular policy into political popularity. Media coverage insisted that getting rid of Kan was essential to recovery, but his successor, Noda Yoshihiko, inherits the same problem of a divided Diet and an LDP eager to precipitate early elections by handcuffing and discrediting whoever is premier.

Prime Minister Noda, like Kan, has indicated that he does not support building any new reactors, does not favor extending the operating licenses of aging plants beyond their original life spans and supports a gradual phasing out of nuclear energy, but overall seems more ambivalent about the issue than his predecessor. He states that nuclear energy remains important to Japan's economy and intends to restart reactors following stress tests. Given the long time-frame for phasing out nuclear energy, the nuclear village will be biding its time and wait for the LDP to resume governing and/or a possible shift in public sentiment stemming from conservation measures, possible blackouts, higher electricity costs, flight of business overseas and higher carbon emissions as utilities switch to more oil and coal. Can the anti-nuclear movement survive these stress tests? Much depends on how the media frames the debate.

Transparency, collusion and complicity

The Fukushima meltdown is the second largest nuclear accident ever, and has become Japan's Chernobyl. On May 24, more than two and a half months after the event, TEPCO acknowledged that there had been a meltdown of the cores at three of the reactors at the Fukushima Daiichi complex within the first few days after the tsunami. Until then, TEPCO downplayed the severity of the crisis. This tardy nod towards transparency exposed the fact that TEPCO was misleading the public about the extent of the crisis from the beginning.

According to TEPCO, some of the damage at Fukushima may have been caused by the earthquake, counter to initial reports that the reactors had withstood the tremors and were only overwhelmed by the "unexpected scale" of the tsunami. Belatedly TEPCO admitted that the earthquake may have damaged the High Pressure Core Flooder (HPCF) that supplies coolant water to reactor cores during an emergency to prevent overheating and meltdown. The revelation that the damage to HPCF piping might have been caused by the earthquake carries safety implications for quake resistant designs at Japan's other nuclear reactors (Adelstein and McNeil 2011).[13] The costs of retrofitting all nuclear plants to improve quake resistance on top of building higher tsunami walls would be enormous if not prohibitive.[14] It has also emerged that the government and TEPCO were warned that assumptions about the maximum height of a projected tsunami at Fukushima were overly optimistic. In the wake of all this damning news, on May 22 the *Japan Times* editorial stated that the past half century of nuclear power, "worked for a while, until, of course, it no longer worked. Now is the time to begin the arduous process of moving towards safer, renewable, and efficient energy sources."

There has been pointed, if not belated, media criticism about the lack of transparency and inadequate information disclosure by TEPCO and the government. This dissatisfaction stems largely from TEPCO's failure to provide accurate information in a timely manner, a view shared by the International Atomic Energy Agency (IAEA 2011). Moreover, the company president Shimizu Masataka disappeared, right after the disaster, staying MIA for nearly a month, fueling public anger and irresponsibly tarnishing the company's image.

The domestic media, however, never mentioned the "m" word (meltdown) until the end of May when TEPCO admitted, despite previous denials, that there had in fact been a meltdown soon after the tsunami struck. TEPCO knew about the meltdowns and that radiation leaks peaked in the initial days following the hydrogen explosions, but did not divulge this information and was not pressed to by journalists. Why was the media so inhibited and reluctant to press TEPCO on key questions and issues? The nuclear village is extremely influential and the media rarely confronts the Establishment until it inevitably must. The utilities not only have networks of power at their disposal, they command a massive advertising budget that gets the attention of media executives and makes them think twice before taking them on. In addition, the *kisha* club (press clubs) for utilities exerts a powerful influence on how the news is presented and what is covered because only members can attend industry press conferences and editors usually defer to their judgment. These press clubs are co-opted by, and are often deferential to, the organizations they cover, gaining insider access and information in exchange for soft handling (Hall 1997; Freeman 2000; Pharr and Krauss 1996). Since the late May revelations, however, the media turned up the heat on the utilities, raising questions that were not asked for too long about nuclear safety and government oversight.

The media is drawing attention to the cozy and collusive relations between government and the nuclear industry, and how the former has not properly monitored the latter. The practice of *amakudari* (descent from heaven) involves bureaucrats taking up positions in companies that they formerly regulated, while industry officials are regularly represented on influential government advisory panels that shape policy in their area (Colignon and Usui 2003; Amyx 2004). Like the revolving door in the US, there is considerable connivance between business and government in Japan. It seems that this pattern of interaction and the fixed mindset within the incestuous nuclear village has controlled Japan's energy policy and ignored contrary views (*New York Times* April 26, 2011). Courts have also helped by usually rejecting plaintiffs' claims about unsafe sites, seismic science or design flaws. Any victories in the lower courts are overturned on appeal, most embarrassingly involving the Kashiwazaki plant that was shutdown in 2007 by a magnitude 6.8 earthquake that exceeded design specifications. This occurred not long after an appeal court sided with TEPCO in dismissing a suit claiming that the site was unsafe because the world's largest nuclear power complex was built on top of a fault line (Kingston 2011: 152–153).

The nuclear industry is heavily regulated, but critics assert that the regulations are not effectively enforced as the layers of decision-making and cumbersome bureaucratic procedures insulate TEPCO and other utilities from robust supervision, leaving them to their own devices (*New York Times* June 21, 2011; Kaufmann 2011; McCormack 2011). Critics maintain that NISA regulators exercise their supervisory duties in a perfunctory "go along, get along" manner. In 2001, for example, TEPCO estimated that the maximum tsunami at the Fukushima plant would be 5.7 meters, but did not submit any documentation supporting this estimate. NISA never questioned this estimate or asked for any documentation backing it up. In the event, the 3/11 tsunami was more than twice as high as this calculation. It is also troubling that nuclear safety measures tend to be more reactive than proactive, and rely on optimistic assumptions that downplay risks. Given that so many of Japan's reactors are aging (three are over 40 years old and another 16 are over 30 years old) with the attendant risk of metal fatigue, and revelations of systematic falsification of repair and maintenance records in 2002, the stress tests imposed by Prime Minister Kan will be subject to careful scrutiny, especially as they are being administered by the utilities under the supervision of the Nuclear Safety Commission, headed by nuclear advocate Madarame Haruki.

Rebuilding

The politics of rebuilding Tōhoku over the next decade are complex as the central, prefectural and local governments seek common ground and stake out turf while allocating responsibility and authority. The stated ideal is reliance as much as possible on local initiatives and preferences. However, central planning and control, especially over budgets, is the established practice. Moreover, given that the capacity of many local governments has been weakened by the disaster, it is hard to imagine that there will be a profound shift in this pattern; authority will remain highly centralized while responsibility will be widely shared. In addition, the massive reconstruction budget draws interest from the usual confluence of pork barrel interests representative of the *doken kokka* (construction state) (Kingston 2004: 122–156). The politics of reconstruction means it is not just about what gets done, but also who gets what and how the slices of the pie get allocated.

Funding the estimated $210 billion recovery is also subject to intense political battles because it will determine who will pay.[15] Some advocated issuing special reconstruction bonds, but Japan already has a public debt to GDP ratio of 210 percent and there is resistance to further mortgaging the future. Others call for temporary hikes in various taxes while the Ministry of Finance is trying to push through its long-standing agenda of boosting the consumption tax. Prime Minister Noda is known to favor increasing taxes, but faces stiff resistance within his party. Opinion polls show the public is evenly divided on the issue.

The two initial emergency relief budgets totaling $77 billion provided support for local governments, compensation for those affected by the nuclear accident and relief for tsunami affected families and businesses. On July 29 the government unveiled plans to spend a further $167 billion for reconstruction over the next five years, and in August authorized deficit bonds to pay for it. The new spending will focus on rebuilding ports and roads, allocating support to fisheries and farming while providing incentives for businesses to rebuild rather than relocate factories overseas. It also emphasizes housing and relocation assistance for the region's displaced elderly.

While recovery funding is a crucial battle, the fundamental problem so far is too little, too late as the wheels of government move far too slowly for people who have lost everything and are now losing hope. Reconstruction politics is unfolding as the central government seeks to translate the guidelines and principles set out in the Reconstruction Design Council (RDC) Report submitted June 25 into practical policies. The report concludes that it is not possible to rebuild in ways that eliminate risk, instead calling for a reconstruction design that acknowledges Japan's vulnerability to natural disasters and plans accordingly: "Based on the premise that earthquakes and tsunami remain an ever-present threat for the future, we will advance a concept of 'disaster reduction'" (RDC 2011: 49). This approach focuses on minimizing the impact of future disasters through improved infrastructure and emergency preparedness training in order to nurture a "disaster resilient nation."

Some survivors remain keen to rebuild their communities as they were, protected with higher sea walls, partly because of their attachment to their ancestral homes and to the communities that once thrived in their towns, but also because land is the single most important asset of most households. Many face the problem of outstanding mortgages on destroyed properties and need to borrow more to restart their lives and businesses. There is also an inclination among some survivors not to give in while many depend on the sea for their livelihoods and living nearby is convenient. One problem is that many of these coastal towns are located on narrow flat terrain between mountain and ocean, so finding sufficient elevated ground for relocating communities is not easy. In some cases this might mean relocating communities some distance from their original sites, always a thorny issue. Implementing land use regulations that restrict rebuilding in vulnerable areas makes sense, but will face some local resistance and entails the politics of compensation, i.e. the government acquiring land with little utility value.

The RDC favors integrating sparsely populated towns into compact towns in safer inland locations where it would be possible to provide improved social services for elderly residents. The government is also keen to restore livelihoods, another policy arena with political implications. For example, there are plans to consolidate more than 200 small fishing ports on the devastated coastline into a few large modern facilities with integrated processing facilities and transport linkages, but achieving consensus on such a plan will not be easy. Clearly, one size does not fit all situations and there is a tangle of legal and political issues to deal with before creating a consensus on the way forward, especially since many residents have their eyes firmly on the rear-view mirror when it comes to rebuilding; recreating the familiar is preferable to the unknown.

The RDC also weighs in on renewable energy, suggesting that this could be a mainstay of the Tōhoku economy, not only in terms of generating electricity, but also in terms of jobs, research, development and production of renewable energy equipment. Furthermore, the RDC advocates a comprehensive feed-in tariff in order to facilitate a shift to renewable energy (RDC 2011: 40). Commenting on the Fukushima accident, the RDC rebukes the nuclear village, stating, "people were told only about the myth of the 'safety' of nuclear power and the doubting voices also tended to get drowned out" (RDC 2011: 37).

Conclusion

Political vision starts with giving hope about overcoming existing problems. GNPism, the unifying and motivating ideology of the post-World War II era, targeted recovery from the war and redefined national identity. Japan's biggest problems today are the aging population, economic stagnation, tsunami devastation and the nuclear crisis. Bold moves on these issues could capture the public's imagination. Renewable Energy Superpower might resonate among the Japanese, but it remains to be seen if the backlash against nuclear power will survive the stress tests of conservation, higher electricity costs and rising CO_2 emissions. The nuclear village will lobby forcefully and persistently because it has so much at stake and is politically more vulnerable than it has ever been. The consensus that it nurtured over the years about the safety and necessity of nuclear power has never been so challenged as it is now. The village is desperate and has enormous power to influence public discourse and politics, so it is too early to suggest that the opinion polls mean that Japan is phasing out nuclear energy. Ramping up renewable energy capacity will take many years and in the meantime there will be many opportunities for reversing the reversal; the battle has just begun.

There are influential businessmen, firms and politicians betting, however, that renewable energy is the future and that nuclear energy, and the ways and means of the nuclear village, will join the list of jettisoned legacies from the twentieth century. There is also a citizens' campaign lead by Nobel Literature laureate Oe Kenzaburo, among other luminaries, to collect ten million signatures for an anti-nuclear petition. It is striking that this campaign drew a crowd of up to 60,000 to an anti-nuclear energy rally in Meiji Park on September 19, 2011, the largest demonstration in Tokyo since the 1960s. It is equally remarkable that NHK, located just across the street from this large demonstration, did not even mention it on that day's main evening news program. The demonstration was not ignored by the media, but given the size of the crowd, the pointed criticism of Japan's national energy strategy and the risks of ongoing radiation contamination caused by the March meltdowns, the story was not given very prominent or extensive play. This minimal coverage is significant given the media's powerful role in shaping public discourse and opinion, especially as the political battle heats up over national energy strategy and the role of nuclear power and renewables.

The great risk Japan faces is not failing to recover from 3/11, or taking on too much debt, but rather pursuing a recovery that looks too much like the past. If the nation only recovers to regain the level of stagnation and inertia that prevailed pre-3/11, it will be an indictment of the ruling elite and a negative barometer for Japan's future. Alas, looking at the disarray of political forces gathered in Nagatacho and the methodical mandarins in Kasumigaseki, it is hard to be optimistic about the prospects for bold action. One could put a bright face on it and make a convincing argument that what good that has occurred in the past two decades has been despite incompetent politicians and plodding governance, but this holds out little hope for concerted action on urgently needed reforms.

Notes

1 The following essay summarizing post-Fukushima political developments through the end of August 2011 draws heavily on mass media reports that are widely available online. I am grateful for comments and suggestions by Rod Armstrong, Gerald Curtis, Andrew DeWit, Mure Dickie, Alexis Dudden, David Leheny, Aurelia Mulgan-George, Richard Samuels and Arthur Stockwin.

2 At the end of August the Diet passed the FIT, facilitating Kan's resignation.

3 If large-scale hydropower is included, renewables account for 9 percent of Japan's electricity generating capacity as of 2010.

4 The Associated Press detailed the first 24 hours of the nuclear crisis including the venting problem.

5 System for Prediction of Environmental Emergency Dose Information (Speedi). The information from Speedi was first released on March 23.

6 Corroborated by personal communication from US Embassy staff April 2011. Had he not ordered TEPCO to stay the crisis would certainly have become worse, possibly involving a meltdown at the fourth reactor where the spent fuel pool contained recently removed material. An explosion there might have forced the evacuation of Greater Tokyo.

7 NISA and other relevant bodies will be reorganized and consolidated into the Nuclear Safety and Security Agency (NSSA) under the Environment Ministry by April 2012. The NSSA will regulate the nuclear industry and conduct radiation monitoring. The Environment Ministry has been pro-nuclear energy as a means to reduce carbon emissions.

8 Subsequently Saga Governor Furukawa Yasushi admitted it was inappropriate that he told Kyūshū Electric executives before the forum took place that it would be important to solicit views from pro-nuclear voices in the business community to counter widespread anti-nuclear sentiments.

9 In Genkai, 60 percent of the town budget comes from hosting the nuclear power plant. Between 1975 and 2010, Genkai received ¥26.5 billion in subsidies and grants and one-sixth of local jobs are at the plant or related enterprises.

10 There are numerous news reports about communities hosting nuclear power plants receiving lavish subsidies and becoming dependent on them.

11 *Asahi*, July 13, 2011.

12 The systematic pattern of donations, clustered in December with strikingly similar amounts donated by executives of similar rank, suggests that they are in fact corporate donations disguised as individual contributions. Corporate donations by utilities were officially ended in 1974 due to public criticism about cozy relations between power companies and the LDP. Industry executives' donations accounted for 63.5 percent of individual donations to the LDP in 2007 and 70.1 percent in 2008. In 2009 presidents each donated ¥360,000, vice-presidents ¥240,000 and other executives ¥100,000.

13 Interviews with onsite TEPCO workers confirm that the earthquake caused damage that precipitated the nuclear crisis.

14 Chubu Electric unveiled plans for building an 18 meter seawall and other measures to protect the Hamaoka plant from tsunami that will cost an estimated ¥100 billion.

15 Regarding compensation for the Fukushima accident, the government is providing public funds covering TEPCO's exposure to claims estimated at some $50–100 billion, a politically unpopular move that bails out the utility at taxpayer expense.

References

Adelstein, Jake and David McNeill (2011) "Meltdown: What Really Happened at Fukushima?" *Atlantic Wire*, July 2, online, available at: www.theatlanticwire.com/global/2011/07/meltdown-what-really-happened-fukushima/39541(last accessed July 22, 2011).

Amyx, Jennifer (2004) *Japan's Financial Crisis*, Princeton, NJ: Princeton University Press.

Colignon, Richard and Usui, Chikako (2003) *Amakudari: The Hidden Fabric of Japan's Economy*, Ithaca, NY: Cornell University Press.

Freeman, Laurie (2000) *Closing the Shop*, Princeton, NJ: Princeton University Press.

Hall, Ivan (1997) *Cartels of the Mind*, New York: W.W. Norton.

IAEA (2011) *Preliminary Summary (June), International Fact Finding Expert Mission of the Nuclear Accident Following the Great East Japan Earthquake and Tsunami, Tokyo, Fukushima Dai-ichi NPP, Fukushima Dai-ni NPP and Tokai NPP (2011) Japan, May 24–June 1*, online, available at: www.iaea.org/newscenter/focus/fukushima/missionsummary010611.pdf.

JAIF (Japan Atomic Industrial Forum), Dept. of International Affairs (2011) *Trend of Public Opinions on Nuclear Energy after Fukushima Accident (March 11) in Japan*, June 16, online, available at: www.jaif.or.jp/english/news_images/pdf/ENGNEWS02_1312778417P.pdf.

Kan, Naoto (2011) "Kan suggests severing NISA from industry ministry," May 18, *NHK World*, online, available at: www3.nhk.or.jp/daily/english/18_36.html.

Kaufmann, Daniel (2011) *Preventing Nuclear Meltdown: Assessing Regulatory Failure in Japan and the United States*, Brookings Institution, April 1, online, available at: www.brookings.edu/opinions/2011/0401_nuclear_meltdown_kaufmann.aspx.

Kingston, Jeff (2004) *Japan's Quiet Transformation*, London: Routledge.

Kingston, Jeff (2011) *Contemporary Japan*, Oxford: Wiley-Blackwell.

McCormack, Gavan (2011) "Hubris Punished: Japan as Nuclear State," *The Asia-Pacific Journal*, 9(16): Article 3, April 18, online, available at: www.japanfocus.org/-Gavan-McCormack/3517.

Pharr, Susan and Ellis Krauss (eds.) (1996) *The Media and Politics in Japan*, Honolulu, HI: University of Hawaii Press.

Prime Minister's Office (2011) *Statement*, July 13, official translation, online, available at: www.kantei.go.jp/foreign/kan/statement/201107/13kaiken_e.html.

Reconstruction Design Council (RDC) (2011) *Towards Reconstruction: 'Hope beyond the Disaster' – Report to the Prime Minister's Office in Response to the Great East Japan Earthquake*, June 25, online, available at: http://reliefweb.int/sites/reliefweb.int/files/resources/Full_Report_1670.pdf (last accessed July 19, 2011).

12

FRIENDS IN NEED

"Operation Tomodachi" and the politics of US military disaster relief in Japan

Chris Ames and Yuiko Koguchi-Ames

Since World War II, Japan has been accustomed to providing international disaster relief rather than accepting it. After the 1995 Kobe quake, the Japanese government refused foreign government offers due to national pride, bureaucratic hurdles and putative Japanese exceptionalism (Fukushima 1995). Despite several major earthquakes since 1945 when US military basing began in Japan, these resources have never been used for earthquake relief. In an about face, after the 2011 Tōhoku Earthquake, Japanese leaders immediately requested assistance from Australia, New Zealand, South Korea and the United States, including from the United States Forces Japan (USFJ) (Reuters 2011). USFJ has nearly 40,000 troops and billions of dollars of assets on Japanese soil. Arguably, it took a Chernobyl-level nuclear disaster at Fukushima—an event clearly beyond domestic expertise and control—for Japan to call upon the USFJ for support. Critical as it was, the nuclear disaster was not the only factor influencing Japanese leaders to seek foreign assistance. As business scholar Erik Werker suggests, international disaster relief is heavily influenced by the disaster-stricken nation's domestic politics (Werker 2010). The scale of the tsunami damage, changes in the role of Japan's Self Defense Forces (SDF), instability in the domestic political climate, and simmering bilateral tensions over realignment of US bases in Okinawa were all factors in the decision to seek US military support. In retrospect, Japan's acceptance of this support might turn out to be a bellwether of significant changes in Japan's self-image on the international stage. On pragmatic grounds, even the harshest critics of US military disaster relief after the Tōhoku quake face difficulty suggesting that Japan, and residents of the quake stricken area in particular, would have been better off without it.

Paul Wilcox, a US military retiree serving as the Japan Country Director at the Northeast Asian Policy Division of the US Pacific Command Headquarters in Hawaii, reportedly came up with the operation's name, calling it Operation Tomodachi, *Tomodachi Sakusen* in Japanese, meaning "Operation Friends,"

(*Yomiuri Shimbun* 2011b). On 12 March 2011, US marines departed from Marine Corps Air Station (MCAS) Futenma in Okinawa aboard cargo aircraft loaded with relief supplies, heading for Tōhoku, inaugurating the massive relief effort. At its peak, approximately 20,000 US troops, 140 aircraft and 15 ships participated. Major accomplishments included donation and delivery of logistical support, including 189 tons of food, 7,729 tons of fresh water and large amounts of fuel delivered to disaster-stricken areas by US aircraft carrier-based helicopters and other airlift. US assets also supported search-and-rescue operations sustained by the SDF and Japan Coast Guard. In addition, American military landing craft were used to transport SDF personnel and vehicles directly to hard-hit locations. Marines, soldiers and airmen worked to restore the devastated Sendai Airport, the regional hub closest to the epicenter, to operational status. US naval floating crane vessels were deployed to locations along the coast to clear ports of debris. Marines worked alongside Japanese schoolchildren in Miyagi prefecture to clear their secondary school of debris. Perhaps the most critical role for the USFJ and specialized US civilian teams was addressing the nuclear crisis at Fukushima. The US donated 100 radiation suits and two fire trucks to Tokyo Electric Power Company (TEPCO) as well as two barges loaded with fresh water. American surveillance aircraft provided information and analysis of radiation levels in addition to aerial photographs of the ailing power plants. Also, the US dispatched 150 marines specializing in radiation disasters as members of the Chemical Biological Incident Response Force (CBIRF) (*Asahi Shimbun* 2011b).

In the most gripping moments of the crisis, US military expertise seemed crucial as it became clear that the Japanese government and TEPCO were not in control of the unfolding nuclear crisis in Fukushima. In those dark hours, Japanese Internet blogs teemed with occult explanations and conspiracy theories, ranging from numerological associations between 3/11 and the US terrorist attacks of 9/11, to right-wing Tokyo Governor Ishihara Shintarō's 14 March statement that the tsunami was "divine punishment" (*Yomiuri Shimbun* 2011a). Operation Tomodachi fuelled the fires of conspiracy and nationalist indignation as well as simultaneously fostering hope. Japanese Prime Minister Kan Naoto stated that the quake and its aftermath were "the most severe crisis in the 65 years since the war" (*Sankei Shimbun* 2011a). Kan's comparison with the end of World War II obliquely referenced the image of the US military as paternalistic savior, an image historian John Dower (1999) found to be salient in his study of how the Japanese dealt with both defeat and the US Occupation. The US military has held a kind of mythological power, particularly for older Japanese, derived from defeating the supposedly invincible Japanese during World War II, and from its use of the seemingly supernatural atom bombs at the war's end. Executive Director of the Asian Development Bank and political scientist, Robert M. Orr, Jr., served as a relief volunteer after the 1995 quake in Kobe, where he experienced this mythology firsthand, recalling:

I went into one evacuee center and was treated somewhat like a soldier from the American occupation period. As I came in with a back-pack, an elderly lady looked up and with tears in her eyes declared to her relatives that there was nothing to worry about now, the Americans had arrived!

(Orr 1995)

Attention to Japanese historical memory regarding the war and Occupation, as well as later decades of contestation over US military bases is critical for understanding Operation Tomodachi. The multi-vocal, symbolic resonances of the US military's images in Japan are complicated and seemingly contradictory; Japan, a polytheistic culture not separating good and evil into binary categories, grapples with the legacy of its relationship with its foe/friend amid a gargantuan crisis, replete with the historic associations of war, the US military, radiation and natural disaster. Historians Haruko Taya Cook and Theodore F. Cook isolated a singular underlying pattern of how Japanese they interviewed recalled their wartime experiences. The historians noted that "the most common feeling we encountered ... was a sense among those we interviewed that the war, like some natural cataclysm, had 'happened' to them, not in any way been 'done' by them" (Cook and Cook 1992: 3). As Dower (1999) and others have argued, the US Occupation supported such interpretations of the war by placing most of the blame for it on the "Class A" war criminals. This served the goals of the US Occupation as it worked to place the war in the past, providing an opening for the US military to be perceived as a friend in the postwar period, relegating the foe role to history, a process that remains incomplete and contested as evident during Operation Tomodachi.

After receiving comparatively little attention early in the crisis, Operation Tomodachi eventually yielded widespread praise as well as criticism throughout Japan. US military efforts benefited from being under the direction of the SDF, which was ostensibly organized from its establishment in the 1950s to provide disaster relief and to keep domestic order. The SDF's relief role in the Kobe quake of 1995 resulted in an improved public image as well as easier recruitment. Throughout the 2011 earthquake crisis, public confidence in the SDF exceeded the Japanese government or TEPCO by far (Pew Research Institute 2011). *Newsweek* reporter Yamada Toshihiro, who accompanied US marines on a mission in Miyagi prefecture, credited the decision to cast US troops in a support role for the SDF as a reason for positive reception among the public and the media (*Newsweek* 2011). A Pew Research Institute study conducted in May, 2011 found that 57 percent of the Japanese public surveyed said the US had done "a great deal" to help Japan after the quake, 32 percent said a "fair amount," 7 percent said "not very much" while 1 percent said "nothing at all" (Pew Research Institute 2011). Only 17 percent responded that the European Union contributed "a great deal" towards relief efforts (ibid.) While noting the public relations benefits for the USFJ, Yamada was most impressed with the sincerity and "true friendship" extended by the marines to local victims of the disaster. Robert Eldridge, a scholar of US-Japan relations and United States Marine Corps (USMC) official, witnessed tremendous enthusiasm for Operation Tomodachi among Marines in Okinawa, remarking

"You basically had to tie Marines down because everyone wanted to go. It had nothing to do with PR, it was all about helping people out" (Eldridge 2011).

In personal interviews, several US military participants confided to us feeling that they had made significant contributions to earthquake victims as well as the general situation in Japan. US Army Non-Commissioned Officer (NCO) SSgt Tim Smith (pseudonym) participated in efforts to clean mud and debris from a school in Tōhoku and previously served in the Iraq and Afghanistan wars. He reflected on the place of Operation Tomodachi in his military career, saying, "Over in the desert we all wondered if we were helping anyone or even why we were there. But in Operation Tomodachi we knew we were doing something good." This comment was echoed by others (anonymity protected): "After going up there, I realized that this (disaster relief) is why I joined up," and "the Japanese have been so kind to my family in the years we've been stationed here, it was nice to feel like I could give back something in their hour of need." There is little doubt that the participants in Operation Tomodachi felt their mission was both worthwhile and appreciated. Some GIs noted in recent interviews that the mission was disorganized and that the SDF did not always seem to know what to do with the US troops and material. After expressing such misgivings, however, two Marine Corps NCOs concluded by saying "well, at the end of the day, it was just a mess up there, but what can we expect from a joint mission in a disaster zone?" Imperfect as Operation Tomodachi was likely to be, considering the circumstances, US troops felt they made direct contributions to people losing their loved ones, their homes and their towns.

One of the most sensitive topics was how US military personnel would handle finding dead bodies. Japanese officials worried that foreigners might not understand Japanese mourning practices or be sufficiently sensitive to the many bereaved persons in the quake zone. Inevitably, US troops did encounter dead bodies among the mountains of debris they were working to clear. In those cases, the SDF and Japanese police were summoned. In the end, no problems were reported (Eldridge 2011). Amid such sensitivities, it is a mark of success for Operation Tomodachi that some municipalities requested US troops return to continue relief work after the mission had been concluded, leading to an extension of operations in some areas even as late as mid-July (*Stars and Stripes* 2011c). Many US missions were not exclusively composed of US military or even joint USFJ-SDF personnel. Military members even worked alongside Japanese civilian volunteers at some sites. Typically, interpersonal interaction between USFJ personnel and ordinary Japanese citizens tends to take place in areas near US bases, but Operation Tomodachi created unprecedented opportunities for Japanese from elsewhere to meet and work with American military members. This, too, is likely to contribute to greater awareness of the USFJ and its mission throughout Japan.

Erik Werker notes that while "most disaster relief is simply to help disaster victims," it "also happens to be a very easy way to earn goodwill internationally" (Werker 2010). There appears to be a rough pattern in which Operation Tomodachi supporters emphasize the image of US troops providing help on the ground while, conversely, critics focus on government or military political uses of the goodwill garnered through relief efforts. Clearly, the USFJ as well as the US and Japanese governments did not object to the operation receiving positive press. Both governments hoped an improved public image would strengthen the alliance and demonstrate tangible benefits of USFJ to the Japanese public (*Stars and Stripes* 2011a).

Critics of Operation Tomodachi assert that USFJ support is not only an effort at garnering PR, but also a self-serving attempt to continue receiving billions of dollars in host nation support (*omoiyari yosan*) from Japan, asserting that ultimately, the estimated US$80 million cost of Operation Tomodachi will be shouldered by Japanese taxpayers. The *Weekly Post*, a right-leaning magazine, pointed out that prior to Operation Tomodachi, members of the ruling Democratic Party Japan (DPJ) were reluctant to extend the generous levels of USFJ host nation support being debated in the Japanese Diet. On 31 March, however, the Diet passed the renewal of the funding, leading the magazine to assert that funding was a quid pro quo for Operation Tomodachi (*Weekly Post* 2011b). On the left, similar charges were made in a full-page advertisement in the *Asahi Shimbun* on 15 May 2011 entitled *Nuchi du Takara* ("Life itself is a treasure"), a phrase in Okinawan dialect made famous by the late Ahagon Shoko, an anti-base peace activist often called Okinawa's Gandhi (*Asahi Shimbun* 2011c). The ad featured the names of 4,214 individuals and questioned whether an Operation Tomodachi ultimately paid for by Japanese taxpayers is "truly a good neighbor policy," concluding that Operation Tomodachi is unnecessary (*tomodachi sakusen wa iranai*) and that the host nation support money would be better used for reconstruction (ibid.). Since Operation Tomodachi had more or less been completed by 15 May – the anniversary of the end of the US Occupation of Okinawa in 1972 – the ad's assertion that the operation "is unnecessary" in the present tense makes it ambiguous whether or not the signatories would have preferred no US military assistance. The present tense might also be aimed at avoiding offending disaster victims. The ad also called for the removal of the MCAS Futenma base and the US Marine Corps from Japan, signaling local sentiments about whether Operation Tomodachi would quiet anti-base sentiments among Okinawans. For more than a decade, US-Japan relations have been strained over local opposition to the concentration of US bases on Okinawa Island, where roughly half of the US troops and two-thirds of USFJ facilities in Japan are stationed on an island with 0.3 percent of Japanese territory. US bases use nearly 20 percent of Okinawa Island's total land area. Any nuanced understanding of Operation Tomodachi must be situated within the triangulated historical relationships among mainland Japan, Okinawa and the United States.

Debates over Operation Tomodachi, significant portions of which were based out of Okinawa, brought into relief a perception gap between mainland Japan and Okinawa concerning the USFJ. In 1995, three US servicemen in Okinawa abducted and raped a 12-year-old Okinawan girl (*The Japan Times* 2008). This crime shook the foundation of the US-Japan security treaty. Later that year, roughly 80,000 Okinawans gathered to protest not only the crime, but also historical mistreatment both by the United States (Okinawa's Occupation lasted two decades longer than the mainland's) and by Japan. Many Okinawans resent that Tokyo used Okinawa as a sacrificial pawn towards the end of World War II and subsequently burdened the island with a majority of the USFJ. Waves of protest in Okinawa following the 1995 incident resulted in a US-Japan agreement to reduce the footprint of US bases in Okinawa. The centerpiece of this agreement was the relocation of MCAS Futenma, which is an airstrip surrounded by densely populated municipalities. The original plans called for it to be moved between 2001 and 2003, but relocation plans had stalled for more than a decade when the Tōhoku quake hit. Fears that aircraft from the base might crash in surrounding communities were realized in 2004, when a helicopter crashed on the campus of Okinawa International University. Since the agreement to relocate the base, a political debate has raged over the slated relocation of the functions of the base to a less densely populated, but environmentally fragile, location in the northern part of Okinawa Island. Many Okinawans and their elected representatives have argued that the base should be moved to mainland Japan or overseas.

Most recently, the US Senate Committee on Armed Services called for integrating MCAS Futenma into nearby US Air Force Kadena Air Base, rather than creating a new facility (*Stars and Stripes* 2011b). Inability to move forward on the issue is widely credited with leading to the resignation of former Prime Minister Hatoyama Yukio, whose DPJ took power in 2009 after almost uninterrupted rule by the conservative Liberal Democratic Party during the postwar period. Prime Minister Kan Naoto, head of the DPJ and premier during the 2011 earthquake, succeeded Hatoyama, but was also unable to break the MCAS Futenma deadlock.

MCAS Futenma played a major role in Operation Tomodachi, leading US commanders to emphasize its importance in the overall USFJ mission (*Asahi Shimbun* 2011a). An editorial in the *Okinawa Times* newspaper, likened these US military statements to using the disaster for political purposes and suggested that military leaders making such comments were violating the principle of civilian control over the military. The editorial asserted that such politicizations of humanitarian assistance are disrespectful to the troops providing the relief since it would make them akin to "looters after a fire" (*Okinawa Times* 2011). The conservative mainland newspaper, *Sankei Shimbun*, was critical of the *Okinawa Times* and the other Okinawan newspaper, the *Ryūkyū Shimpō*, for playing down the contributions of Operation Tomodachi (*Sankei Shimbun* 2011b).

Such accusations from the political right in Japan have their counterpart on the left in Okinawa, where the two local newspapers have long criticized mainland Japanese media for not reporting problems related to the massive concentration of US bases in Okinawa. Sociologist Kozy Amemiya likens the US bases in Okinawa to a natural disaster, asserting "Okinawa's hurricane is the US military bases, and Okinawa has had numerous Katrinas, the latest one of which was the crash of a US military helicopter on the campus of Okinawa International University in August 2004" (Amemiya 2005). She continues:

It was only luck that there was a fraction of the usual number of people on the campus on that day due to the summer vacation. Nonetheless, the crash once again laid bare Okinawans' fear of living under constant threat to their lives by having US military bases on their island. It also revealed the imbalance of burden-sharing between Okinawans and Japanese, and yet the Japanese media remained indifferent. The two main Okinawan newspapers issued an extra edition without delay to report the crash. On the same day the major Japanese newspapers also issued an extra edition, but not about the crash; it was about the retirement of an owner of one of Japan's professional baseball teams. The Japanese media treated the crash in Okinawa as minor news.

(ibid.)

Amemiya is a founding member of the group Okinawa Women Act Against Military Violence (OWAAMV), which has mobilized opposition to US military bases in Okinawa and strives to create worldwide awareness of the challenges the bases present to Okinawans through research, media and political advocacy. Fellow OWAAMV leader and Naha City Assemblywoman Takazato Suzuyo contends that the words "Operation" and "Tomodachi," when used in relation to the US military, tend to be contextualized historically in a different manner in Okinawa than they are in mainland Japan (Takazato 2011). Okinawa was the only home island in Japan with a civilian population that experienced a land battle in the Pacific War. The US military invaded the island on 1 April, 1945 in "Operation Iceberg," which claimed the lives of more than 100,000 civilians, an equal number of Japanese troops, 12,500 American combatants as well as smaller numbers of other nationals. The incomprehensible human tragedies of the battle have been likened to genocide by former Prefectural Governor and historian Ōta Masahide, who called the invasion a "Typhoon of Steel" (*tetsu no bōfū*), drawing on the image of the war as natural disaster. Through this historical experience, many Okinawans harbor an aversion to war and military matters that transcends the anti-military "allergy" common in the mainland.

Since 1995, Okinawan leaders, who sometimes assert themselves as a distinct ethnic group called *Uchinanchu*, have redoubled their efforts to get mainland Japanese and the national government in Tokyo to understand the challenges their prefecture faces economically, historically and psychologically due to the war and the subsequent concentration of US forces on their island. Ironically, the 2011 earthquake may be viewed as reversing the direction of empathy seeking. After the temblor, it is mainland Japanese who began seeking understanding from Okinawans. Differential views of Operation Tomodachi in Okinawa and mainland Japan are consistent with this pattern. However, it should be noted that neither mainland Japanese nor Okinawans are monolithic in their views of the USFJ, the SDF and the value of Operation Tomodachi. Many Okinawans not only donated generously to relief for the earthquake victims, but also highly praised the contribution made by the USFJ via Operation Tomodachi, much of which involved US marines based out of Okinawa. Okinawan officials, local media and anti-base activists, on the other hand, have been vocally critical of Operation Tomodachi, using the national attention garnered from the event as an opportunity to remind the nation of their island's prolonged struggle.

Kevin Maher, a US diplomat in charge of Japanese affairs and former head of the US consulate in Okinawa, increased tensions between the United States, Japan and Okinawa markedly when it was reported, just days before the earthquake, that he had told a group of students that Okinawans are "masters of manipulation and extortion" who are "lazy" (*The Japan Times* 2011). The US State Department apologized to the Okinawan people and removed Maher from his post the day before the earthquake. Although Maher subsequently contested the allegations about what was said, significant damage had already been inflicted on bilateral relations.

Leftist, anti-base activists and anti-alliance rightists are not uniform in their opinions, of course, but the confluence of a national disaster and mobilization of the USFJ for support raises hackles for all varieties of nationalists. In addition, leftist, anti-base activists are not limited to Okinawa. There are also significant anti-base movements centered on mainland facilities such as Camp Zama, Naval Air Facility Atsugi, Yokosuka Naval Base in Kanagawa Prefecture and MCAS Iwakuni in Yamaguchi prefecture. However, these bases, as well as relatively tension-free ones, such as Misawa Air Base in northern Aomori Prefecture and Sasebo Naval Base in Nagasaki prefecture, tend to be joint bases which share SDF and USFJ components, minimizing local anger since the base also host local sons and daughters in uniform. A senior US military officer speaking off the record suggested that most US bases in Japan, including Okinawa, will eventually become joint bases due to the increasingly positive profile of the SDF as well as long-standing objection to the US presence.

USFJ personnel and their SDF counterparts have been training together for decades, but Operation Tomodachi was the first instance in which they conducted joint operations (Nishihara 2011). Among the many "firsts" inaugurated by Operation Tomodachi is the fact that the USFJ was under the SDF as part of a "Joint Support Force" rather than the more equitable "Joint Task Force" (ibid.). Throughout the history of their relationship, it has always been the USFJ that has taken the lead, both de facto and symbolically. In a recent ethnography of the Ground-Self Defense Force (GSDF), anthropologist Sabine Frühstück described SDF members as "uneasy warriors" (Frühstück 2007: 80). Frühstück notes that the power relations between the two forces are perceived within the SDF as weighted heavily in favor of the USFJ. She concluded that GSDF "service members use the notion of an American military manhood as a foil against which they measure their own organization, their level of professionalism" (ibid.). If, as Frühstück asserts, the SDF uses its relationship with the USFJ to achieve viability and self-respect as a uniformed force, being in command over the USFJ during Operation Tomodachi marks not only the maturation of USFJ-SDF cooperation, but also signifies the emergence of a more confident SDF. A qualitative shift in the SDF's role appears to be underway, which is likely to correspond to changes in the structure of US basing in Japan over the long term. Additional roles for the SDF were inaugurated in 2011, setting up its first full-fledged, forward-deployed base overseas with the opening of an anti-piracy base in Djibouti aimed at supporting US counterterrorism operations and future activities of the SDF abroad.

Since its inception, at the behest of the US, the constitutionality of the SDF has been subject to vigorous political debate in Japan, whose pacifist constitution, penned under US Occupation guidance in 1947, expressly forbids the maintenance of a standing military. The presence of the USFJ has allowed Japan to achieve several key objectives in the postwar period including creating a bulwark against Communist expansion in East Asia, reassuring other Asian countries that Japan will not invade them again, keeping open sea lanes so resource-poor and export-dependent Japan can prosper, and as well as providing high "bang for the buck" defense capability. The SDF was created under the Self-Defense Forces Law of 1954 as an auxiliary to the USFJ, responsible for domestic stability amid disasters and invasions. Since the mid-1970s, the SDF has been expanding its capabilities, including the acquisition of power-projection assets such as AWACS (Airborne Early Warning and Control) aircraft as well as participating in UN-sponsored Peace-Keeping Operations abroad. Such expansion led the development of new defense guidelines in 2004, edging the SDF ever closer to becoming a bona fide military, which has at times appeared to be supported by the US. Domestically, the debate has focused on whether Japan should become a "normal" country with a standing military, but Article 9 of the Constitution forbids this and public opinion is divided. Already, SDF's annual budget is greater than that of the United Kingdom's military. The SDF has maintained and expanded its mission and training for disaster relief, not only providing for domestic but also international disasters, including the Southeast Asia tsunami of 2004 and Haitian earthquake of 2010. Due to what has been called an allergy toward military matters, the Japanese public has long been ambivalent about the SDF.

High-profile disaster relief efforts and a public relations campaign during the 1995 Kobe earthquake improved the SDF public image significantly. SDF relief efforts in the March 2011 quake are the largest operation in the SDF's 56-year history, eventually involving almost half of the entire SDF (Nishihara 2011). Changes in public opinion appear to be underway. The Pew Research Center conducted a survey in Japan that concluded: "More than nine-in-ten (95%) say the SDF has done a good job responding to the crisis, including 62% who say the force has done a *very* good job" (Pew Research Center 2011). The high marks for the SDF contrast markedly with opinions about other actors with only 20 percent saying the national government did a good job, 19 percent praising Prime Minister Kan, and only 11 percent supporting TEPCO. The media also earned praise as 54 percent said the news media did a "good job" in the crisis. The survey also found the highest level of positive perceptions of the United States since Pew began conducting such surveys in 2002, jumping to 85 percent from 66 percent in the previous survey in 2010 (ibid.).

Operation Tomodachi not only provided much needed relief, but it also brought the operations of the USFJ and SDF closer together. A pragmatic view of

Operation Tomodachi presents a hopeful scenario for disaster relief in future events within Japan as well as in other Asian nations. It is not a question of if another major earthquake will strike in Japan and surrounding areas, but when it will happen. Seismologists estimate that there is an 87 percent chance that the next Tokai Earthquake, a.k.a. the "big one," arising from the same fault that caused the devastating earthquake that struck Tokyo and surrounding areas in 1923, will occur within the next couple of decades (*Yomiuri Shimbun* 2011b). This event could potentially cause casualties ranging in the millions and damages exceeding US$1 trillion (Popham 1985). Accordingly, Japan's need for disaster relief and planning is acute and, driven by the Tōhoku disaster, is likely to expand.

Large earthquakes are also anticipated elsewhere in Asia along the "Ring of Fire" that extends from the American West Coast to Alaska and Siberia down through Japan to Southeast Asia. Robert Eldridge believes that the USFJ and SDF can help a lot of people not only in Japan, but throughout Asia in future disasters. Yet, the politicization of international disaster relief presents hurdles for such plans. USFJ and the SDF have public image problems that militate against maximizing their utility in international disaster relief operations, with the USFJ facing issues in Japan and the SDF elsewhere in Asia. Considering this problem, Eldridge, along with former Commanding General US Marine Corps Pacific Wallace Gregson and former Center for Naval Analyses Representative III MEF James North foresaw a need for USFJ-SDF cooperation on humanitarian assistance and disaster relief as early as 2008, when they published a ground-breaking proposal on this topic in Japanese journals in both English and Japanese. The authors suggested that it might be easier for disaster-stricken nations to accept a joint USFJ-SDF relief team that is ship-based, conducting "a particular humanitarian assistance mission and returning to the sea base quickly," allowing the mission to avoid being "perceived as militarily provocative or politically sensitive" (Gregson *et al.* 2008). In light of the success of Operation Tomodachi and the USFJ-SDF ties it engendered there may be an opening for realizing such disaster relief cooperation.

Eldridge has endeavored as a senior community-relations leader for the USMC in Okinawa to prepare agreements between local communities and the military bases there in case a natural disaster strikes the island. Base assets and personnel would be made available to local community members under the plan. Unfortunately, the proposals have not moved forward. The political climate in Okinawa makes it difficult for cooperation between local authorities and the US bases. Although the threat of a major disaster occurring in Okinawa is significantly less than in the Tokyo area, the archipelago *has* been hit by devastating tsunamis nine times over the past four hundred years, including the 1771 Meiwa tsunami, which was one of the most destructive in Japanese history (Tsuchiya and Shuto 1995).

Heavily politicized as USFJ involvement in disaster relief operations may be, the operation did help individuals and communities in desperate situations. Operation Tomodachi is only one facet of foreign assistance in Japan after the Tōhoku disaster, but the mainly positive publicity it received and the success of USFJ-SDF cooperation suggests there is scope for the USFJ to expand its role in disaster relief in Japan. The openness of the Japanese government to foreign assistance in 2011 is a positive sign about the emergence of a more open and multi-culturally astute Japan that contrasts with refusal of foreign governmental assistance following the 1995 Kobe quake. Yet some nationalists such as Kobayashi Yoshinori, a popular right-wing manga artist and xenophobic pundit, believe the lesson of the disaster is that Japan needs to become more self-reliant and guard against depending on foreign assistance such as Operation Tomodachi, lest the SDF become "simply a rescue squad" rather than an "armed force" (*Weekly Post* 2011a; Kobayashi 1998). For those unfamiliar with Kobayashi's oeuvre, he justifies the Imperial Armed Forces actions during World War II and also actively promotes Japan waging future wars.

Since Japan's modernization in the nineteenth century, self-reliance has been perceived as a hallmark of achieving first-rate status among nations. As humanity faces shared challenges presented by natural and human-made disasters, global warming, globalization, expanding populations and dwindling natural resources, however, it must also actively support common solutions and develop mechanisms of mutual assistance. The Tōhoku disaster and Operation Tomodachi demonstrate the value of cooperation and the need to nurture such mechanisms of mutual assistance in preparing for the next disaster. This should be a high priority regional endeavor in a high-risk zone where global interests are at stake.

References

Amemiya, K. (2005) "Japan's 'New Orleans'," *JPRI Critique*, 12(6), online, available at: www.jpri.org/publications/critiques/critique_XII_6.html (accessed 29 July 2011).

Asahi Shimbun (2011a) "U.S. military providing huge disaster relief effort," 24 March, online, available at: www.asahi.com/english/TKY201103230212.html (accessed 29 July 2011).

Asahi Shimbun (2011b) "Beigun ni yoru omona Kyōryoku," 30 April, morning edition, p. 3.

Asahi Shimbun (2011c) "Nuchi du Takara" (advertisement), 15 May, morning edition, p. 19.

Cook, H.T. and Cook, T.F. (1992) *Japan at War: An Oral History*, New York: The New Press.

Dower, J. (1999) *Embracing Defeat: Japan in the Wake of World War II*, New York: Norton.

Eldridge, R. (2011) personal communication, 24 June 2011.

Frühstück, S. (2007) *Uneasy Warriors: Gender, Memory and Popular Culture in the Japanese Army*, Berkeley, CA: University of California Press.

Fukushima, G.S. (1995) *The Great Hanshin Earthquake*, Japan Policy Research Institute Occasional Papers No. 2, March, online, available at: www.jpri.org/publications/occasionalpapers/op2.html (accessed 29 July 2011).

Gregson, W.C., North, J., and Eldridge, R. (2008) "Responses to humanitarian assistance and disaster relief: A future vision for U.S.-Japan combined sea-based deployments," *Kokusaikokyoseisakukenkyu*, 12(2): 37–47.

Kobayashi, Y. (1998) *Sensō-ron*, Tokyo: Shōgakukan.

Newsweek (2011) "The A-Team: Hisaichi de mita 'Tomodachi Sakusen'," 30 March (Japan edition), pp. 36–39.

Nishihara, M. (2011) "How the earthquake strengthened the Japan-US alliance," *East Asia Forum*, 29 June, online, available at: www.eastasiaforum.org/2011/06/29/how-the-earthquake-strengthened-the-japan-us-alliance (accessed 29 July 2011).

Okinawa Times (2011) "'Shinzai Futenma PR' seiji riyō ni Kenshiki o utagau," 22 March, online, available at: www.okinawatimes.co.jp/article/2011-03-22_15716 (accessed 29 July 2011).

Orr, R.M. (1995) *The Relief Effort Seen by a Participant*, Japan Policy Research Institute Occasional Papers No. 2, March, online, available at: www.jpri.org/publications/occasionalpapers/op2.html (accessed 29 July 2011).

Pew Research Institute (2011) "U.S. applauded for relief efforts: Japan resilient, but see economic challenges ahead," 1 June, online, available at: www.pewglobal.org/2011/06/01/japanese-resilient-but-see-economic-challenges-ahead/#prc-jump (accessed 29 July 2011).

Popham, P. (1985) *Tokyo: The City at the End of the World*, Tokyo: Kodansha.

Reuters (2011) "Japan requests foreign rescue teams, U.N. says," 11 March, online, available at: www.reuters.com/article/2011/03/11/us-japan-quake-aid-refile-idUSTRE72A71320110311 (accessed 29 July 2011)

Sankei Shimbun (2011a) "Kanshusho 'Sengo Mottomo kibishii kiki,' Keikaku teiden ryōsho," 13 March, online, available at: www.sankei.jp.msn.com/affairs/news/110313/dst11031322220121-n1.htm (accessed 29 July 2011).

Sankei Shimbun (2011b) "Okinawa, Beigun e no Kyōkan jiwari Jimotoshi wa 'Futenma Mondai ni Riyō' Shuchō," 7 April, online, available at: http://sankei.jp.msn.com/affairs/news/110407/dst11040700390001-n1.htm (accessed 16 November 2011).

Stars and Stripes (2011a) "Japanese PM thanks U.S. troops during visit to devasted region," 10 April, online, available at: www.stripes.com/news/japanese-pm-thanks-u-s-troops-during-visit-to-devastated-region-1.140688 (accessed 29 July 2011).

Stars and Stripes (2011b) "Top senators call U.S. military plans in Japan unworkable, unaffordable," 12 May, online, available at: www.stripes.com/news/top-senators-call-u-s-military-plans-in-japan-unworkable-unaffordable-1.143371 (accessed 29 July 2011).

Stars and Stripes (2011c) "Seabees still working in tsunami-ravaged northern Japan," 16 July, online, available at: www.stripes.com/news/seabees-still-working-in-tsunami-ravaged-northern-japan-1.149403 (accessed 29 July 2011)

Takazato, S. (2011) personal communication, 24 May.

The Japan Times (2008) "U.S. military crime: SOFA so good?" 26 February, online, available at: www.japantimes.co.jp/cgi-bin/fl20080226zg.html (accessed 29 July 2011).

The Japan Times (2011) "U.S. sacks Maher, apologizes for remarks," 11 March, online, available at: www.japantimes.co.jp/cgi-bin/nn20110311a1.html (accessed 29 July 2011).

Tsuchiya, Y. and Shuto N. (1995) *Tsunami: Progress in Prediction, Disaster Prevention, and Warning*, New York: Springer.

Weekly Post (2011a) "Kobayashi Yoshinori-shi Jieitai wa Kazai Resukyū-tai de wa nai to Ninshiki o," 22 April, online, available at: www.news-postseven.com/archives/20110414_17367.html (accessed 29 July 2011).

Weekly Post (2011b) "Tomodachi Sakusen no Mikaeri wa Omoiyari Yosan1880 Oku-en x 5 Nen," 29 April, online, available at: www.news-postseven.com/ archives/20110419_17830.html (accessed 29 July 2011).

Werker, E. (2010) "Disaster politics: International politics and relief efforts," *Harvard International Review*, 23 August, online, available at: http:hir.harvard.edu/disaster-politics?page=0,1 (accessed 29 July 2011).

Yomiuri Shimbun (2011a) "Ishihara Chiji: Tsunami wa Tenbatsu, Gayoku o araiotosu hitsuyō," 15 March, online, available at: www.yomiuri.co.jp/politics/news/20110314-OYT1T00740.htm.

Yomiuri Shimbun (2011b) "Beigun 'Tomodachi Sakusen' taieki gunjin ga Meimei 'Masaka no Tomo koso Shin no Tomo'," 20 May, online, available at: www.yomiuri.co.jp/ feature/20110316-866918/news/20110520-OYT1T00187.htm (accessed 29 July 2011).

PART V

Recovery and reconstruction

13

THE ECONOMIC FALLOUT

Japan's post-3/11 challenges

Kenneth Neil Cukier

On the morning of March 11 the *Nikkei*, Japan's business daily, reported that Tobishima, a construction company living off public works projects, was cutting roughly a quarter of its workforce, about 380 employees. Another article explained that Sojitz, a big trading house, was preparing to export farmed bluefin tuna to China, targeting its newly wealthy consumers. A third piece discussed the failure of fathers to take paternity leave: in Sweden more than 90 percent take time off from work, in Japan only 1 percent do.

The snapshot of what the country's major newspaper deemed important that day neatly sums up the concerns of Japan more broadly before the disaster: the economy was ailing, increasingly dependent on China and in certain ways out of step with global trends. The earthquake, tsunami and nuclear catastrophe changed many things about Japan, but once the immediate crisis is over and reconstruction is well underway, the Japanese economy will simply return to where it had been: stuck in the doldrums.

Prior to March 11 many Japanese and foreigners privately hoped for some sort of crisis, believing that only a major shock might jolt the country out of its two decades of torpor. Even the global recession following the Lehman Brothers bankruptcy was not enough to spur Japan to reform. Yet despite destruction on a biblical scale, substantial changes have not happened. The Japanese public shows a willingness to make sacrifices, from favoring higher taxes (according to opinion polls) to sweating during the summer due to energy-saving measures. But the same spirit for change has not been matched by Japan's most powerful actors: politicians, bureaucrats and *Keidanren*, Japan's business lobby, have done more to preserve the status quo than promote an agenda of serious reform.

It is not a very optimistic starting point with which to consider the extraordinary challenges facing Japan. In the aftermath of the disaster, industry bounced back at a prodigious pace, non-governmental organization did extraordinary relief work, the Self-Defense Forces showed themselves to be extremely competent and able, while the Japanese public impressed the world by sticking together amid the tragedy and radiation worries. Yet the failure of the leaders to use the crisis to push through much-needed and long-overdue economic reforms marks a missed opportunity to improve the long-term prospects of the Japanese economy.

The result is that Japan seems more likely to change at the pace it usually has, slowly and haltingly, which although better than nothing is so at odds with global trends that the practical effect is meager. The disaster exacerbates long-standing economic worries, from the failure to deregulate large parts of the economy, negotiate free trade agreements and revise tax and social security policy. It also means that if Japan continues to sidestep the tough medicine of fiscal constraint, it could walk into a financial meltdown of its own making.

Reconstruction costs are estimated as high as ¥50 trillion (around US$650 billion), which amounts to 10 percent of gross domestic product. The 1995 quake in Kobe, by contrast, was one-fifth that sum. Damage from radiation contamination, securing the food-chain and compensation could raise the bill higher still. Superficially, and perhaps with twisted irony, Japan's gross domestic product (GDP) will grow at a perky pace. Though the economy was walloped in the first half of the financial year, it will pick up in the second half once reconstruction spending kicks in. And GDP is forecast to exceed 3 percent in 2012, a rate not seen since the 1980s. But this is deceptive: GDP measures flows, not stocks. It is not a true economic expansion but merely replacing what was destroyed with money Japan does not have.

This essay is an overview of the impact of 3/11 on the Japanese economy. First, it examines what happened: how the economy was jolted, and in particular, the damage to firms that led to a supply shock felt worldwide, and how firms bounced back more quickly than expected. Second, it considers the effect of the power shortages, the debate over energy market deregulation and discussions in the business community to move operations overseas, in part for reliable, low-cost energy. Third, it looks at the initial reconstruction plans and what it means for Japanese public debt and tax policy. Lastly, it places these issues in the context of Japan's long-standing economic concerns, and notes how the failure of the political and business leaders to rise to the challenges of 3/11 may lock Japan into a third lost decade.

The macro equation

The quake and tsunami wiped out cities and villages all along the coast for hundreds of kilometers. The government put the damage at ¥16– 25 trillion (around $200–$300 billion), or 3 percent to 5 percent of GDP (Cabinet Office 2011). Private economic forecasts place the total nearly twice as high, since the official figure only accounts for the damaged infrastructure and not costs from lost business activity, nor does it include indirect damage, such as the evacuation, cleanup and compensation costs related to the meltdown at the Fukushima Daiichi nuclear power plant. Yet from the natural disaster, a cascade of other economic problems followed.

First, there was a severe gas shortage throughout the entire northeast that stretched for weeks. As far away as Niigata and Aomori, cars waited at gas stations for hours, in lines stretching for miles. Gas was usually rationed at 10 kiloliters or ¥1,000-worth – not much at all. Throughout the region, factories that were able to restore service had trouble operating because employees lacked fuel to drive to work. This was due to the trade ministry's mishandling of the situation. Immediately after the quake the government ordered the private sector to release three days' worth of fuel from the roughly 70-day supply in its mandatory stockpiles. It was only ten days later that the amount was increased to 25-days' worth of gas. Even then, most of the oil in stockpiles is unrefined: reasonable if it is intended as a cushion against a supply disruption, but useless for responding to a natural disaster that knocked out many refineries.

A second problem was radiation worries. In the first few weeks, some countries turned away Japan-made products due to contamination fears, and overseas consumers stopped buying certain products, particularly food. In early April (months before the food scare over contaminated beef erupted domestically in July), as many as 30 countries and territories imposed restrictions on Japanese imports. America, which buys 15 percent of Japanese farm exports, put products from Fukushima and three other prefectures on a watch list requiring certification that it is radiation-free. The European Union established a watch-list of 12 prefectures that stretched even farther south than Tokyo. In China, where relations with Japan have long been strained, the government seemed to rejoice in banning imports from 12 prefectures. Certificates attesting to the location of origin were required by importers, and checks were conducted.

The fears, exhibiting more emotion than sense, made a small dent in trade but damaged "brand Japan." Radiation checks were required for electronics that came from inside a clean room. Precision machine parts headed to China were turned away at the border. New cars that were kept outside in large parking lots before they were shipped were exposed to minute amounts of radiation. A trade official, in an interview with the author in May 2011, remained at ease. The cars can be decontaminated by washing, he said. And the half-life of iodine-131 is only eight days, so it would have been less potent by the time the ships arrive at foreign ports. It was not exactly the most encouraging remedy, albeit scientifically sound. Nissan had two massive car-carrying ships boarded by US Customs before it arrived at the Port of Los Angeles to conduct inspections. Cars would drive through radiation monitors when they left the ship onto land, I was told in July 2011 by a Nissan official.

A third setback was consumption. The 78-year-old governor of Tokyo, Ishihara Shintarō, called for *jishuku* (self-restraint) on the part of the Japanese people just as Japan's famous cherry trees started blossoming across the country, which usually signals a start to festive office parties under the petals. Though other politicians including the prime minister urged citizens to rein in their self-restraint for the good of the economy, the sentiment did not ebb until Golden Week in late April. Household consumption fell by around 2 percent in both April and May compared with the year earlier (Van de Putten 2011). The effects of *jishuku* particularly hit restaurants and entertainment.

Meanwhile, the number of overseas visitors dried up as vacations were canceled due to fears over radiation, power shortages, or simply wanting to avoid a place where *jishuku* had become a new watchword. The amount of foreign travelers fell by 60 percent in April, 50 percent in May and 35 percent in June, according to the Japan Tourism Agency (*Nikkei* 2011a, 2011c). By July, around 700,000 hotel bookings had been pulled in Fukushima prefecture alone (*Yomiuri Shimbun* 2011).

Importantly, these immediate problems have not fully run their course even by the second half of the fiscal year. Tourism remained lower; the initial shortage of fuel had abated only to be replaced by fears of insufficient electricity (discussed later in this chapter). Worries over radiation contamination spread to the food supply after the rice-straw feed for cattle was found to have excessive levels of radiation that put the meat many times over the legal limit. The government had not thought to ban the sale of the contaminated feed, nor introduce widespread testing. It only formally banned the sale of cattle temporarily from the affected area (rather than the previous voluntary withdrawal) after outcry in the press. The contamination problem was uncovered piecemeal by local authorities, not the national health ministry in charge of food safety.

Demand picked up in the second half of the year, as was forecast. Although by August only a fraction of the reconstruction funds had been spent, it nevertheless boosted consumption. Where in the first half of 2011 nominal GDP fell around 2 percent, the second half was estimated to increase by about 1 percent compared with a year earlier (UBS 2011; Goldman Sachs 2011). Yet it was no cause for celebration, since the modest pick-up was mainly replacing what was lost.

One smooth response to the disaster, albeit perhaps on too modest a scale, was by the central bank. The Bank of Japan flooded the banking sector with liquidity and increased the sorts of collateral it would accept in its policy of mild quantitative easing. Also, it offered hyper-low interest rates of 0.1 percent (the same as the policy rate) to encourage banks to lend in the stricken areas. It even sent massive amounts of yen in cash to Tōhoku within days of the quake, knowing that there would be a shortage of banknotes just as everything else. This was a particular concern for the region: Tōhoku people are notoriously distrustful of banks and their branch infrastructure was underdeveloped. Many people kept cash under the mattress even more than elsewhere in Japan. So survivors who lost their homes had much of their life savings washed away as well.

The global supply chain

The most noticeable effect of the quake was on the global supply chain. The Tōhoku region is not a major economic area. Prior to March 11 most people considered it a backwater with a fishing and agriculture industry, and many elderly since younger people were steadily moving away. The perception was not wrong: the area is home to around 5 percent of the Japanese population and accounts for 4 percent of its GDP. Thus it came as a surprise to many just how important the region was for the global economy. Many firms produced items that were critical inputs for other products; when factories were disrupted and various high tech widgets and specialty products became unavailable, global supply-chains went into spasms.

For years, Japanese companies have watched rivals steal their market share – and national pride – for items like televisions and cars. But under the hood and behind the casings, Japanese firms still dominate the parts inside, upon which businesses everywhere depend. Renesas, a semiconductor company, had eight factories in the area damaged on March 11, including one in Hitachinaka that handles around 40 percent of the microcontrollers used in cars for running everything from dashboard electrons to anti-locking brakes. When it could not fulfill orders, the assembly lines of Toyota, Nissan and others ground to a halt (*The Economist* 2011a).

The pain was felt as far away as Volvo in Europe and a General Motors truck factory in Louisiana. Immediately after the quake, Nissan placed 40 suppliers on a watch-list for disruptions. Toyota expected a dearth of 500 components made from rubber, plastics and electronics. Merck, a German chemicals company (unrelated to the drug firm), had its factory in Onahama damaged, cutting production of Xirallic, a metallic paint pigment. This alone forced car dealers in America to suspend sales of the color "Tuxedo black" until production was restored (*The Economist* 2011a). Prior to March 11, foreign critics and Japanese businessmen complained that the country's economy was over the hill and less integrated into the global economy than it ought be. Though there is much truth to that, the supply chain shudders served as a powerful rebuttal to such criticisms.

The region was an under-appreciated hub for certain industries. Most of the country's celebrated specialized materials hail from Kyoto and many precision parts come from the Osaka region. Yet Tōhoku enjoyed a dominance in certain semiconductors and electronics. The factories of Shin-Etsu and Sumco – which control around 25 percent of the world's production of 300-millimeter silicon wafers – were damaged and production suspended. Mitsubishi Gas and Chemical and Hitachi Chemical, which together hold about 90 percent of the market for bismaleimide-triazine resin used to bond parts of a microchip in smartphones, had to suspend operations (CLSA 2011). The compact battery in Apple iPods relies on a polymer made by Kureha, which holds 70 percent of the market, but whose factory in Iwaki was temporarily shut down (*Wall Street Journal* 2011). Fujitsu had nine factories and Sony had ten facilities damaged in the quake.

South Korean and American carmakers temporarily benefited from their Japanese rivals' travails. Hyundai and Kia's American sales in April were up by 40 percent and 57 percent, respectively, from a year earlier (though the strong yen also was a factor). Detroit's big three carmakers gained 3.2 percentage points in market share in April compared with the previous month. The Japanese carmakers between them shed a massive 4.5 percentage points of market share.

Source: METI, UBS

FIGURE 13.1 Industrial production index and inventory (source: data from METI; Aida *et al.* 2011).

However, business was restored far sooner than predicted. In early April, Toyota said it expected its factories to run at around 50 percent capacity until June, but in that month assembly lines were already running at 90 percent capacity (*The Oriental Insider* 2011a). Nissan's recovery was even quicker. Data on industrial production shows how manufacturing immediately fell 15 percent, but returned to 90 percent of its pre-quake capacity after three months (see Figure 13.1) (*The Oriental Insider* 2011a; *The Economist* 2011b).

In a show of classic Japanese corporate solidarity, numerous car companies and Renesas's parent companies (Hitachi, Mitsubishi Electric and NEC Electronics) sent 2,500 employees to Renesas factories to help it restart. At a factory of TDK in Kitakami, Iwate that makes electronic capacitors, Toyota employees arrived unannounced a few days after the quake to talk with managers about plant restoration and production. They were driving throughout the area visiting all their suppliers, and their suppliers' suppliers. After getting a quick update on the state of things, they hit the road – but not before leaving a precious cache of dried food for factory employees.

The filial links among companies in Japan may lead to a certain degree of underperformance in good times, by letting inefficiencies linger and sustaining relationships as much based on old loyalties as business sense. But in times of trouble, these same relationships lead to extraordinary performance in restoring operations. Japanese executives look upon it as a source of pride – and competitive advantage.

Despite the speedy recovery, Japan's exports fell dramatically. Worse, the need to import fuel to make up for the energy shortfall due to idle nuclear reactors helped to bring Japan's trade balance into the red in April and May, a very rare occurrence. At the same time, suppliers were forced to diversify their operations to protect against production outages. So ironically, the very evidence of Japan's continued importance in global supply chains is also accelerating corporate Japan's march out of Japan.

Power and hollowing out

Japan's power supply has become one of the chief factors influencing economic growth after the quake. The country imports nearly all of its energy. About one-third of Japan's electricity supply comes from nuclear. Prior to the quake, the trade ministry planned to increase it to half of Japan's electricity generating capacity by 2030. Yet after Fukushima, public sentiment turned against nuclear power. In the months after the quake, prefectural governors did not approve the restart of reactors that had been suspended for scheduled maintenance. Of the nation's 54 reactors, more than two-thirds were off-line five months after the quake. Because reactors shut down for maintenance roughly every 13 months, the media warned of blackouts and business flight overseas. Some even forecast that all the reactors would be shut down by mid-2012.

This alarmed the business community. They had already faced the threats of rolling blackouts due to a power shortage at peak times during the summer. The president of one large chemical factory in the Tōhoku region explained in an interview with the author early in April that although the plant was totally restored it remained idle due to potential rolling blackouts that were being considered by the regional energy utility. His factory's machines and processes depend on continuous power. Unless the supply is assured, he explained, it did not make business sense to start them up. The same concern holds true for semiconductor manufacturing, where factories happened to be spread abundantly throughout Japan's northeast. Any interruption of power, even if planned, can be harmful to the operations. Factories run non-stop not for economic efficiency, but technical precision: it may take hours just to re-calibrate the equipment if it ever needs to be restarted.

The business sector responded to the threat of power outages with characteristic discipline. Heavy users changed their operations to begin earlier in the morning or shift work to the weekends, to smooth out usage. The entire car industry agreed to take Thursdays and Fridays off and work Saturdays and Sundays. In the end, the initial estimates of a power shortfall were revised upward due to idle or partially operating fossil-fuel plants being called back into service, and summer outages did not occur. Yet questions over the reliability and cost of energy forced corporate boards to reconsider the risks of keeping operations in Japan. Japanese business had been on a march to move operations overseas anyway because of the strong yen, the declining population, lackluster domestic growth and to be closer to fast-growing markets.

Amid the uncertainty over the power supply, on July 13, Prime Minister Kan Naoto made a stunning announcement. He stated: "we should aim to achieve a society that is not dependent on nuclear power. In other words, we should reduce our dependence on nuclear power in a planned and gradual manner" (Kantei

2011). Within two days Mr. Kan had characteristically backpedaled and described his prepared remarks at an official press conference as merely his "personal views" (*Asahi Shimbun* 2011). Even his own cabinet ministers openly criticized his comments. But it raised expectations in the public that a national dialogue was underway on the viability of nuclear energy in the world's most seismically active nation.

As an alternative to nuclear energy, Mr. Kan pointed to green technologies like solar. As one of the conditions for resigning, he insisted that the Diet pass legislation supporting renewable energy which it did in August. In May, sales of energy-saving LED lights exceeded those of incandescent bulbs for the first time (*The Oriental Insider* 2011c). Son Masayoshi, the entrepreneurial president of Softbank, a big mobile phone company, established ties with some 20 prefectures potentially to build ten solar power plants. Converting one-fifth of Japan's unused farmland to solar would generate 50 million kilowatts, argued Mr. Son – an amount that is equivalent to the entire peak power supply of TEPCO, the Tokyo regional utility that operates the Fukushima plant (*The Economist* 2011b). A Silicon Valley-based dot-com millionaire, Elon Musk (who co-founded PayPal and Tesla Motors), donated $250,000 for solar power projects in the Fukushima area.

Some government officials whispered about energy deregulation and separating the transmission and power generation businesses of the utilities as a first step to encourage competition, which is common in liberalized energy markets in the West. The legislation outlining the plan by which TEPCO could compensate victims of the nuclear disaster was seen as a mechanism to put that goal into place, by setting up the financial structure to buy and sell the power company's assets. But the forces of the Japanese establishment that supported TEPCO seem to have quashed such ambitions. The law, passed on August 3, in essence rewarded TEPCO by keeping it intact. There has barely even been a management reshuffle.

The *Keidanren*, Japan's influential big business lobby, spoke out forcefully against deregulation – a strange case of major energy users rallying to prevent competition that might lower prices and improve services. (This reactionary response inspired Mikitani Hiroshi, the founder of Rakuten, a big online shopping mall, to resign from the group – a rare public snub.) But such is the off-kilter variant of Japanese capitalism. The country's business sector has long operated as one large "protection racket" to maintain economic privileges for large firms at the expense of smaller ones and of consumers. The business leaders perhaps knew that undermining the monopoly rents of the utilities might eventually winnow their own oligopolistic industry structures.

Another reason for resisting deregulation may be because the utilities are big customers of Japanese businesses and pay premium prices for everything. As state-sanctioned monopolies, the utilities' profitability is overseen by the trade ministry based on a complex formula. Among the only way they can increase their earnings is to increase their costs and so they are profligate, explained Koga Shigeaki, a trade ministry official, who in spring 2011 decided to break the institutional silence about such dubious practices. Also, the *Keidanren* and its regional subsidiaries were founded by the utilities and are still heavily supported by them with funds and personnel. Advocating energy deregulation would be tantamount to betrayal. And unlike in the West where rivals would welcome entering the market, in Japan the other regional monopoly-utilities would refuse, since it would only invite competition into their market too.

For years, a lens to consider modern Japan was the "construction state" due to the massive public works that propped up the economy. But a better optic post-3/11 is the "TEPCO state," since its influence is extraordinary. The utilities sponsor much research by academia and think-tanks, which is seen as a way to win supporters. Despite being a monopoly they are large advertisers of public-interest ads and regularly take media leaders on travel junkets, which is seen as a way to bring the chattering classes to their side. (On the day of March 11, TEPCO's chairman Katsumata Tsunehisa was in China with a group of retired journalists, which emphasizes the close ties among the utilities and the media.) So a rigorous consideration of energy deregulation has barely appeared in academe and the press. One ranking trade ministry official who produced economic studies on the energy sector during the reformist period of Prime Minister Koizumi Junichirō in 2001–2006 saw his promising career sidelined when the tide shifted, akin to East European intellectuals ensnarled in Soviet purges after the Prague Spring.

According to the Japan Center for Economic Research (JCER), if idle nuclear power plants are not restarted in 2011 Japan's GDP would fall by 1.4 percent, even if other power sources pick up the slack. If all are shuttered in 2012 then it predicts the economy will shrink by a further 2.2 percent (*The Oriental Insider* 2011b). Yet some of the forecasts have been open to suspicion because of the influence of the power companies, who are the major funders and sometimes sit on their boards.

Still, the need for stable, low-cost power is cited by companies as a reason to move operations overseas. A poll by the *Nikkei* in July found that 40 percent of companies expect to shift some operations overseas within three years unless the operating environment in Japan improves. Topping the list of requirements is the need for "a comprehensive energy policy, including measures to help alleviate power shortages" which was cited by 51 percent of executives (followed by "lower corporate tax rate" by 37 percent of respondents and free-trade by 35 percent of them) (*Nikkei* 2011b). A separate poll by the trade ministry showed that 69 percent of companies surveyed said it was possible they may transfer at least some of their operations overseas to diversify risk in case of disasters (*The Oriental Insider* 2011d).

Numerous companies have raised the likelihood of moving production abroad. Nomura finds that Japanese overseas factories are almost as technically efficient as domestic ones, and always more profitable (Nomura 2009, 2010). Hitachi Metals in June said it would shift 30 percent of its car parts manufacturing to South Korea and the US by 2013, citing energy supply concerns. The most promising destination is South Korea, says a director who serves on numerous Japanese corporate boards. It is close to Japan, is easier to operate in than China, has highly-skilled workers and Koreans make excellent partners. In addition, unlike China, it also respects intellectual property rights (interviews with the author in March and August 2011).

Most importantly, South Korea boasts numerous free-trade agreements that lower the costs of exports to Southeast Asia, America and Europe. Japan, meanwhile, suspended its inter-ministerial discussions after the quake on whether to simply consider joining the negotiations for a regional free-trade pact called Trans-Pacific Partnership. So the prospect of Japan entering into new free-trade deals in the short-term is small. This hurts Japanese industry, which faces duties of 12 percent on televisions exported to Europe, 25 percent on cars to China and 22 percent for transportation equipment to Vietnam (UBS 2011).

The dual-edged sword for Japan in the post-3/11environment was the yen. On August 19 the currency broke through an historic, post-World War II high on a nominal basis of around ¥76 per US$1 (though in real terms, when adjusted for Japan's mild deflation and the rest of the world's inflation, it was still slightly below its 25-year average). This also pushed exporters to considering moving operations overseas, even though it helped companies who import materials and fueled an overseas mergers and acquisitions boom by Japanese firms. Moreover, it helped the country pay for more energy from overseas suppliers, notably liquefied natural gas from Russia. The strength of the currency was not a vote of confidence in Japan, but a reflection that it looked better than the rest: America's recovery was soft and its pristine AAA debt rating was downgraded, while Europe faced the prospect of a euro zone collapse, following troubles in Greece, Ireland and Spain.

Reconstruction, debt and taxes

On June 25 the Reconstruction and Design Council, appointed by the prime minister, unveiled its 74-page report entitled "Hope Beyond Disaster." Like previous government-sponsored reports over the past 20 years, it was long on ambitions but short on implementation. Most of the ideas were extremely sensible, from raising taxes, fostering renewable energy and improving the efficiency of the agriculture and fishery sectors. It called for the creation of special economic zones to bypass stifling regulation on the national level and giving local leaders more autonomy. For example, in early April the cost for rebuilding homes in Miyagi was estimated as being twice as high as should be, according to the president of a local construction company, because of barriers to importing cheap wood from Taiwan, a long-standing sop to domestic producers.

But some of the Council's points were naively optimistic. Small businesses? "A variety of assistance measures of a sufficient scale must be ensured," the report urges. Science and technology? "Set up new world-class businesses through collaboration," it trumpets. And it calls for encouraging global companies to set up R&D headquarters in Tōhoku – apparently unaware that even chic Tokyo cannot attract multinationals anymore.

The mayor of Rikuzen Takata, a small city utterly washed away, suggested literally moving a mountain to raise the city's ground level higher. Prime Minister Kan and others speak of elevating entire communities when rebuilding. Yet few voices dared suggest that there may be better ways to respond to those rare tsunamis that only occur once in a thousand years – otherwise Japan risks going bankrupt over the next 999 years trying to protect against them.

The government has thus far unveiled three emergency relief budgets. The first supplementary budget of ¥4 trillion passed on May 2 aiming to get aid to victims quickly. The second package of ¥2 trillion passed on July 25, and was meant to support longer-term aims such as compensation and reconstruction assistance. The third supplementary budget, proposed in August, is pegged as high as ¥10 trillion for vast port and road infrastructure programs.

Financing this relief and recovery spending is difficult. Japan already faces serious public debt concerns. During the 20 years of economic stagnation since the bubble burst in 1989, Japan's public debt has steadily grown while income from taxation has continually declined (see Figure 13.2). Today, government spending is about a third of its GDP, which is roughly the same as in the US and other advanced economies. However, around half of the budget comes from debt, an extraordinarily high figure. One-fifth of the budget is simply to service the existing debt, which at a little over 1% says a lot. Indeed, if the Japanese economy were to grow, it would put upward pressure on bond yields and risk sparking financial havoc.

Taken together, Japan's public debt amounts to two times the size of its GDP, the highest in the OECD and almost twice as much as America's. To be sure, 95 percent of the debt is owned domestically, so the government has lots of policy options on how it wants to deal with it. Yet the perilous fiscal situation was an invisible Sword of Damocles during discussions on financing reconstruction. On August 24 Moody's downgraded Japan's debt rating one notch to Aa3 because of its huge size and the chaotic politics. It followed a move at the very start of the year, on January 27, by Standard & Poor's to downgrade Japan's government debt to AA-, its fourth-highest ranking. The agencies had placed the ratings outlook on review after the quake. During this all, the markets barely took notice. But that, again, is because the rest of the world's economy looked worse, not because they felt Japan was safe.

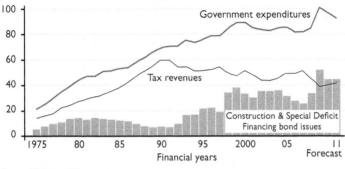

Source: Ministry of Finance

FIGURE 13.2 A downgrade two decades in the making (source: Ministry of Finance: *Japanese Public Finance Fact Sheet (FY 2010 Budget – supplementary data)*, February 2011).

To finance the plans, one idea is to issue special "reconstruction bonds" carrying terms of five or ten years, funded directly by earmarked income or special corporate tax increases. But more debt, simply renamed, is only part of the story. Taxes are the next mechanism to pay for reconstruction. Within weeks of the disaster, a previous plan to lower the corporate tax rate from a maximum of 40 percent (the highest in the OECD) to 35 percent was rescinded. It makes it harder for Japanese firms to compete with South Korea where firms pay a maximum rate of 24 percent. Meanwhile, the government unsuccessfully pushed to raise the consumption tax from 5 percent (the lowest in the OECD) to the still-low 10 percent, earmarked for social security outlays. For comparison, Britain's VAT is 20 percent.

The opposition LDP only supports tax increases if the DPJ dilutes main portions of its campaign platform, such as giving an allowance of ¥312,000 per year for children under age 15 regardless of family income, and plans to eliminate a ganglion of fees imposed on students attending public high school that amount to ¥160,000 per year. It already had forced the DPJ to drop a plan to eliminate highway tolls. Though the LDP demands seem like an austerity measure, they actually harm long-term economic prospects, since the costs of rearing and educating children are the principle reasons for the country's low birth rate.

Lastly, the government is considered selling its shareholdings in the former monopoly telecoms carrier NTT, in which it holds a 34 percent stake, as well as Japan Tobacco, of which it owns half, to raise funds. Also on the block may be the state's stake in Tokyo Metro and other property holdings. Together, the government estimates it can raise as much as ¥7 trillion. This figure is hardly enough relative to the scale of the crisis, and its costs, but if it sets in motion greater privatization and boosts the stock market by bringing new shares to the public, that may be a thin silver lining.

Land of the setting sun

In the midst of the financial crisis in 2008, President Obama's chief of staff Rahm Emanuel remarked: "Never let a serious crisis go to waste. What I mean by that is it's an opportunity to do things you couldn't do before" (*Wall Street Journal* 2009). The same sentiment was held among many Japanese who looked at the disaster and optimistically saw a moment where long-overdue changes were possible. But Japan squandered the moment. The political and business class failed to establish a fresh vision for the country and lead the public towards it. Anachronistic facets of the Japanese post-war state that were long overdue for reform – and even contributed indirectly to the disaster – were not expunged even though there were stirrings for change.

We could have seen a modern regulatory system and fewer institutional conflicts of interests. We could see the abolition of *amakudari*, whereby retired bureaucrats work for firms they previously supervised. We could have seen the elimination of the press club system – which is an "information cartel" that neuters the media, and prevents it from performing its societal function as a check on power. Despite a legacy of a half-century of one-party rule, we could have seen political parties collaborate, and the government support more disclosure and accountability. Yet there was little appreciation among politicians and business leaders that these features of contemporary Japan may have contributed to the inadequate crisis-management plans at Fukushima before the disaster and the inefficient response afterwards, aspects that the Japanese people now recognize.

While the country is bouncing back from the disaster in impressive ways, it appears to be returning to the funk it had been in pre-3/11. Ultimately, the biggest challenge facing Japan is one of identity. Will the country play a greater global role or turn its attention inward? Prior to the disaster, Japan was already in retreat. Fewer people spoke English or studied and worked overseas, among other things. A post-crisis Japan could help the world define robust standards for nuclear safety, crisis management, supply-chain resilience and renewable energy – just as it offered valuable lessons during the 2008–2009 financial crisis, based on its experience a decade earlier. But Japan may choose differently, and the process of domestic rebuilding may only reinforce its insularity, making Japan less relevant globally.

It is vital that Japan constructs the future, not simply rebuilds the past. For this to happen, perhaps the old practice of *gaiatsu*, or "outside pressure," can be of help, whereby foreigners support the bold and innovative Japanese in positions of influence to see that their vision of a modern Japan is achieved. Such certainly was the case prior to the Meiji Restoration (1868) and during the US Occupation (1945–1952), instances where Japan reinvented itself. In both cases, the nation faced an existential crisis. But the nightmare of 3/11 was largely confined to Tōhoku, while national politicians, business leaders and energy utilities act as if nothing has changed. So Japan's economic future may look a lot like it did on the morning of March 11, when newspaper headlines informed salarymen that the economy was sick, reliant on China and out of step with global trends. It does not have to be so bleak, but it might become so if Japan's capacity for inaction exceeds its willingness for reform.

References

Asahi Shimbun (2011) "Kan says call to end nuclear power was only a personal view," July 15.

Aida, T., Umetsu, C.N., and Aoki, D. (2011) "Steady progress towards a recovery," UBS, July 8.

Cabinet Office (2011) *Economic Impact of the Great East Japan Earthquake and Current Status of Recovery*, May 30, Government of Japan, online, available at: www.meti.go.jp/english/earthquake/recovery.

CLSA (2011) "Ripples Across Asia," March 27.

The Economist (2011a) "The global car industry: After the quake," May 20.

The Economist (2011b) "New Japan v old Japan: Stepping out," June 24.

Goldman Sachs (2011) *Japan Economics Analyst*, Issue No: 11/08, June 10.

Kantei (2011) "Press Conference by Prime Minister Naoto Kan," July 13.

Nikkei (2011a) "Foreigners key to Japan growth but hurdles remain," July 29.

Nikkei (2011b) "'Going abroad' in the cards, say 40% of major companies: Nikkei survey," July 18.

Nikkei (2011c) "Foreign visitors down 36% in June," July 14.

Nomura (2009) "Still going global," by Takahide Kiuchi, May 8.

Nomura (2010) "Growing integration into Asian economy should help revitalize Japan's economy," by Takahide Kiuchi, April 28.

The Oriental Insider (2011a) "Economy: Good news and bad," by Richard Katz, June 10.

The Oriental Insider (2011b) "What if no Japan nukes are online in 2012, Part 1," by Richard Katz, June 20.

The Oriental Insider (2011c) "Shift to LED bulbs," July.

The Oriental Insider (2011d) "Hollowing out, Part 1," by Richard Katz, July 28.

UBS (2011) "Japan Economics Perspectives," by Takuji Aida, July 8.

Van der Putten, R. (2011) "Japan: Diminishing effect of jishuku on consumer spending in May," Paris: BNP Paribas, July 1, online, available at: http://research.bnpparibas.com/applis/www/RechEco.nsf/EcoFlashByCountryEN/A3BA425A3E884037C12578C0004005B1/$File/EcoFlash190_english.pdf?OpenElement.

Wall Street Journal (2009) "A 40-Year Wish List," unsigned editorial, January 28.

Wall Street Journal (2011) "Chemical reaction: iPod is short key material," by Mariko Sanchanta, March 29.

Yomiuri Shimbun (2011) "Over 680,000 hotel bookings canceled," July 30.

14

AGEING SOCIETY, HEALTH ISSUES AND DISASTER

Assessing 3/11

Ōtani Junko

Introduction

The Tōhoku Earthquake and tsunami were devastating overall, but disproportionately affected the elderly, raising awareness about emergency disaster public health issues in an ageing society. This chapter assesses the consequences of 3/11, and draws comparisons with the 1995 Great Hanshin Earthquake, in terms of Japan's ageing society and health issues. I also consider long-term challenges in terms of mental health and psycho-social support.

The 2011 Tōhoku Earthquake and tsunami

The overwhelming destruction of the 1995 Kobe Earthquake was often compared with the heavy bombing towards the end of World War II especially among older people in the affected areas (Ōtani 2010). Few people were expecting that an even more devastating cataclysm would hit Tōhoku in 2011 on a scale again reminding us of wartime devastation.

The 3/11 Tōhoku Earthquake and tsunami is often said to be the worst catastrophic disaster Japan has experienced since World War II (Nagamatsu *et al.* 2011). Learning lessons from the 1995 Kobe Earthquake, the government organized and deployed approximately 700 medical teams specialized in disaster management within the first 72 hours, a critical window for rescuing survivors. The Internet, which was not common in Japan in 1995, facilitated communication among clinicians and enabled them to promptly identify the needs of the affected hospitals and deliver necessary supplies to the extent possible given extensive damage to the transport infrastructure. Medical professional societies took the initiative in the logistics of transferring victims away from the disaster zone.

TABLE 14.1 Medical professionals dispatched by Ministry of Health, Labour and Welfare

	Currently working as of August 5, 2011	Accumulated number (AN) as of August 6, 2011
Medical team	42 staff (10 teams)	AN: 11,806 staff (2,493 teams) Iwate: 8 staff, 2 teams Miyagi: 30 staff, 7 teams Fukushima: 4 staff, 1 team
Pharmacists	0	AN: 1,915 staff
Nurses	0	AN: 1,394 staff Fukushima: 5 persons
Dentists	0	AN: 307 staff
Physical therapists	10 staff	Accumulated number 146 staff Iwate: 6 staff Miyagi: 4 staff
Public health physicians, public health nurses, Nutritionists	145 staff (56 teams)	AN: 9,472 staff Iwate: 45 staff, 16 teams Miyagi: 73 staff, 29 teams Fukushima: 27 staff, 11 teams
Kokoro-no-Care team (mental health and psycho-social support)	27 staff (9 teams)	AN: 2,931 staff (204 teams) Iwate: 21 staff, 6 teams Miyagi: 6 staff, 3 teams Fukushima: 0 staff, 0 teams
Radiation physicians for screening to ease anxieties about radiation exposure	2 staff (1 team)	AN: 413 staff (38 teams) Fukushima: 2 staff (1 team)
MHLW officials	125 staff	AN: 2,960 staff Iwate: 26 staff Miyagi: 65 staff Fukushima: 34 staff

Source: Ministry of Health, Labour and Welfare homepage at: www.mhlw.go.jp/jishin/joukyoutaiou. html [accessed August 6, 2011].

As a result of the 2011 Tōhoku Earthquake and tsunami, 80 percent (300) of the 380 hospitals in Iwate, Miyagi and Fukushima prefectures were completely or partially damaged and destroyed (11 were completely destroyed and 289 partially) (*Yomiuri Shimbun* June 9, 2011). Half of the hospitals reported troubles in coping with the volume of out-patients after 3/11. Two months after the earthquake, 10 percent of the hospitals reported that they had not yet resumed normal operations.

Without in any way diminishing the suffering of people in the devastated areas of Tōhoku, it is fair to say that all Japanese suffered from a certain degree of post-3/11 depression. The media reported the traumatic stories non-stop in the days and weeks following March 11. It is indicative that the national suicide rate for May 2011 rose 20 percent from the same month in 2010 (McCurry 2011). The Japanese government announced that 16 people committed suicide in June 2011 due to the disasters out of a total 2,985 suicides nationwide. Out of 45 suicides in Miyagi, eight cases were identified as earthquake-related cases, three out of 36 in Iwate, and two out of 50 in Fukushima. Other cases were identified in other prefectures such as Ibaragi, Saitama and Tokyo. Of the disaster-related suicides eight out of 16 involved people who lost their homes and work places, two were living in evacuation centers and one in a temporary shelter. Out of the 16, 11 were male and five were female and eight were over age 60, five were in their 50s, two in their 20s, and one was younger than age 20 (*Nikkei Shinbun* August 6, 2011; *Yomiuri Shimbun* August 6, 2011). It is still too early to make a conclusive analysis based on this data, but the elderly did account for one-half of disaster-related suicides in June 2011.

The country was swept by gloom fed by relentless reporting of post-3/11 personal tragedies and hardship. Japanese everywhere knew that they too might someday suffer the same fate as the people in Tōhoku, living as they do in one of the most disaster-prone countries in the world. So when the underdog Japanese women's team won the FIFA Football World Cup in July 2011, overcoming what seemed insurmountable odds, the nation was overjoyed, a rare piece of uplifting news. The gritty determination of the team and their teamwork seemed to epitomize Japanese strengths and encouraged survivors struggling to overcome unprecedented adversity.

The 1995 Kobe Earthquake hit mainly urban areas of metropolitan Kobe-Osaka, but subsequently affected newly developing suburban areas outside Kobe with the building of temporary shelters and relocation of permanent housing and communities. In comparison, the 2011 Tōhoku Earthquake hit more remote, rural areas away from big cities, along five hundred kilometers of coastline. This means that evacuation points were scattered over mountainous areas adjacent to the Sanriku Coast, rendering access and assistance much more difficult than in the aftermath of the Kobe Earthquake where staging areas for rescue and relief operations were relatively intact. This made a huge difference in reaching survivors in a timely way. The 2004 Niigata Earthquake and 2007 Chūetsu Offshore Earthquake in Niigata also affected remote, rural mountainous areas and the differences with the 1995 Kobe Earthquake were similarly marked. But the scale of destruction caused by the massive tsunami was far greater and much more widely dispersed.

One of the major features of 3/11 was that it hit areas with a high level of elderly population. Nearly two-thirds of the recovered bodies were 65 years and older and one-quarter of the victims were in their 70s suggesting that age was a critical factor in survival as less mobile people could not escape in time. Due to regional demographics there was also a high proportion of older people among survivors and evacuees, translating into a high demand for routine medications in evacuation centers when many elderly ran out of medicine. The spectrum of causes of death is distinct between the earthquakes of 1995 and 2011. In Kobe, many victims died from fire-related causes and trauma, including being crushed by buildings and debris, while delays in providing hemodialysis or kidney dialysis contributed to additional deaths. Many of the Kobe survivors had serious injuries while in Tōhoku drowning caused most deaths and relatively few survivors had serious injuries (Nagamatsu *et al.* 2011). This reflects what happens during a super-tsunami.

The scale of death was also vastly different with about 6,400 deaths in Kobe versus over 20,000 dead and missing in Tōhoku. Regarding the elderly, in Kobe most died because they were sleeping on the ground floor and injured by falling furniture and collapsing walls. On the other hand, during 3/11, many older people survived the earthquake, but were unable to escape the tsunami and drowned while younger, more vigorous people were able to evacuate in time.

Tsunami lung and hypothermia

The Kobe quake provided insights on dealing with crush-related injuries, lessons that were useful for Japanese medical teams responding to the 2008 Sichuan Earthquake in China. In 3/11, there was a high incidence of tsunami lung, a necrotizing pneumonia that was also common among survivors of the Indonesia-Thailand tsunami on Boxing Day, 2004 (Allworth 2005; Chierakul *et al.* 2005; Kongsaengdao *et al.* 200; Potera 2005). In addition, many survivors of 3/11 suffered from hypothermia as temperatures remained wintry for several weeks afterward. Some survivors were floating in the cold water for several hours before they got rescued so that their body temperature was very low (27°C), triggering a series of symptoms.

Ageing society

One of the major features of this disaster was that it hit areas with a high level of population ageing (Yamamoto *et al.* 2011). In Iwate, 26.8 percent of the population was 65 years old and over in 2009[1] and this proportion is projected to rise to 37.5 percent by 2035. At the evacuation center served by the Nagasaki University medical relief team, out of 221 evacuees on March 28, 84 (38 percent) were aged 65 years and over.

TABLE 14.2 Demographic composition of the disaster-affected prefectures, as of October 1, 2009

Age range	0~14	15~64	65 and over	
				(of which, 75 and over)
All Japan	13.3	63.9	22.7	(10.8)
Iwate	12.6	60.6	26.8	(13.8)
Miyagi	13.4	64.5	22.1	(11.0)
Fukushima	13.8	61.5	24.7	(13.1)
Tokyo	11.9	67.3	20.9	(6.4)

Source: Statistics Bureau, Ministry of Internal Affairs and Communications: www.stat.go.jp/data/jinsui/2009np/pdf/gaiyou.pdf#page=4 [accessed August 5, 2011].

In Kobe, more than half of those who died were aged over 60 and 60 percent were women (Tanida 1996). All of the most common injuries and earthquake-triggered illnesses were reported disproportionately among people aged over 65.

The proportion aged over 65 for all Japan in 1995 was 19.6 percent, 22.7 percent in 2000 and is projected to reach 36.3 percent by 2025 (Ōtani 2010: 3). People aged over 60 years made up 17.8 percent of the population in Kobe 1995 (Ōtani 2010: 14). The overall proportion of people aged over 65 in temporary shelters in Hyōgo prefecture was 30.3 percent in February 1996, one year after the earthquake (Ōtani 2010: 84). However, in some compounds the proportion reached as high 44.2 percent reflecting priority allocation for the elderly (Ōtani 2010: 84, 90–91).

We do not have data for the proportion of older people in Tōhoku temporary shelters, only five months after the earthquake, as they are still building temporary shelters, behind schedule, and still in the process of allocating units to applicants. Yet the stage varies across the vast disaster-affected areas. Some areas are lagging in meeting shelter targets as it is both difficult to locate suitable land sites and to reach agreement with landowners. The media reports that there is a high proportion of older people in some Tōhoku temporary shelters. For example, in Yamamoto village in Miyagi, 31 percent of temporary shelter residents are aged 65 and over.[2] It is also reported that a community center built there (Yamamoto) for 50 households is not yet utilized well, but this is not unusual in disaster-stricken areas where it takes some time to resume normal activities.

The Ministry of Health, Labour and Welfare (MHLW) requested elderly nursing care homes in each prefecture to accept those in need of such care from disaster-affected areas. It also requested each prefecture to dispatch nursing care staff to institutions and evacuation centers. Other prefectures indicated that they could dispatch a total of 7,719 staff, but as of August 5, 2011 such dispatched staff totals 1,531.

TABLE 14.3 The number of elderly nursing care-givers dispatched to an elderly home in the disaster-affected prefectures

		Accumulated number (AN)	Staff currently working
Iwate	• Elderly Nursing homes	283	12
	• Disabled homes	19	6
Miyagi	• Elderly Nursing homes	999	3
	• Disabled homes	62	10
	• Consultation support center for the disabled	12	4
Fukushima	• Elderly Nursing homes	104	0
	• Disabled homes	52	31

Source: Ministry of Health, Labour and Welfare homepage, at:
www.mhlw.go.jp/jishin/joukyoutaiou.html [accessed August 5, 2011].

MHLW announced that it aims to establish elderly nursing centers in at least 100 temporary shelter compounds (*Yomiuri Shimbun* April 19, 2011). This is to prevent *kodokushi* (dying alone) and older people from becoming bed-ridden. This is an unprecedented initiative to establish elderly nursing care facilities at disaster temporary shelters, a sign that the government is concerned to address age-specific needs of evacuees. The government plans to budget ¥7,000 million (US$87.5 million) in 2011 to build such facilities in nine prefectures: Aomori, Iwate, Miyagi, Fukushima, Ibaragi, Tochigi, Chiba, Niigata and Nagano. This includes prefectures not affected by the natural disasters where temporary shelters are being built. An additional budget of ¥1,000–1,500 million (US$12.5–18.75 million) will be allocated to the heavily damaged prefectures of Iwate, Miyagi and Fukushima.

Changing living patterns in rural Japan

By the time of the 1995 Kobe Earthquake, the proportion of older people who lived in two- or three-generations households was declining rapidly, although it was still high (33 percent in 1995 and 21 percent in 2005) compared to other developed countries (Ōtani 2010: 8–10). In contrast, in the 3/11 devastated areas there was a higher proportion of three-generation households, many of them engaged in family businesses such as fisheries and farming. The proportion of nuclear family households is low in Fukushima, 52.3 percent (ranked 39 out of 47 prefectures), compared to 57.9 percent in Japan in 2005. On the other hand, the proportion of the households with someone aged 65 and over is higher in Fukushima, 43.9 percent (ranked 11 out of 47 prefectures), compared to 35.1 percent nationwide (MIAC[3]).

Post-3/11 many of these multi-generation families now live separately, another traumatizing experience for survivors. The older generation does not want to be a burden for their sons and daughters in this difficult time, helping to explain the erosion of multi-generation family living arrangements. The loss of cross-generational cohabitation and the mutual support this allows is another health risk factor.

The younger and middle-aged generations have moved to other areas searching for jobs and cash income to support their extended families during this crisis. Children who lost their schools, in some cases moved to another town for their

TABLE 14.4 Three-generation households

Ranking (out of 47 prefectures)	Prefecture	Proportion of three-generation households (%)
6	Fukushima	17.78
7	Iwate	17.28
18	Miyagi	13.48
	Japan	8.64

Source: Statistics Bureau, Ministry of Internal Affairs and Communications: www.pref.fukushima.jp/ toukei/data/hitome/2010/ken/014.pdf [accessed August 6, 2011].

education. Older people are sometimes left alone in the original house or in the evacuation centers as families scramble to adjust to loss of housing, jobs and income. Following the 1995 Kobe Earthquake, family structure and living arrangements reportedly changed due to the earthquake. Older people were often sent to stay with relatives outside the prefecture or were institutionalized (Ōtani 2010: 86–88). The temporary shelters were too small for a big family to live together, especially under such stressful conditions (Ōtani 2010: 127). Subsequent permanent reconstruction housing offered larger-size dwellings, but not necessarily in desirable locations. As a result, the Kobe Earthquake influenced family living arrangements and a reduction of three-generation households. This new housing was often built in areas remote from the city and it was not convenient for younger and middle-age family members to commute to their jobs. In addition, in many cases younger family members could not afford to house their impoverished parents because they themselves lost everything and they preferred leaving their aged parents in the evacuation center where they could be fed and receive medical services (Ōtani 2010: 89). The middle generation often suffers under the burden of double loans, paying off mortgages on destroyed housing while borrowing more money to restart their lives. This dire financial situation is also evident in Tōhoku where housing and livelihoods were swept away by the tsunami. The *Yomiuri Shimbun* reported in early August 2011 about the case of Mr. Ishii (45) in Fukushima who had to move three times following the tsunami. It calculated the total financial burden of his evacuation (not loss of housing or possessions) including costs of new household furniture, sundries and appliances, transportation, moving expenses, rent, utilities, his reduced salary and loss of wife's part-time income. The total comes to ¥2.49 million or about US$30,000 to which he adds compensation of ¥2.84 million (US$35,000) for mental stress. His point is that the ¥1 million ($12,000) of interim subsidies he has received does not begin to cover actual costs (*Yomiuri Shimbun* August 6, 2011). Apparently, his experience of having to relocate repeatedly is common and makes evacuation unexpectedly expensive.

Vulnerability

Natural disasters tend to highlight the needs of the poorest and most vulnerable groups in society, ones that are usually neglected: orphans, elderly and the disabled (Ōtani 2010: 18). They make visible the previously invisible in the everyday world (Ōtani 2010: 18, 31; Varley 1994). Morrow (1999) sees the vulnerability of victims to disasters as socially constructed. She identified, using Hurricane Andrew as a case study, the poor, the elderly, women-headed households and new migrants as the categories of people at greatest risk during a disaster response (Ōtani 2010: 31).

Post-3/11, the most vulnerable groups are the elderly and children. First of all, the elderly constituted a high proportion of causalities: 65 percent of those who died were over 60 years old and 92 percent of deaths were due to drowning caused by the tsunami. Surviving elderly have reportedly suffered difficult conditions in evacuation centers where there is little privacy, very basic amenities and few comforts. As in Kobe, elderly medical conditions have deteriorated following the disaster.

Dementia among elderly was reportedly triggered or worsened following the tsunami similar to the experience in Kobe (Ōtani 2010). Sudden disruption of life routines and the horrific experiences traumatized many elderly and contributed to a rise in dementia among them.

Children have also been affected badly as they lost friends, relatives and the reassuring routines of school and play. The lack of normal activity combined with relentless media coverage of destruction they experienced firsthand, has amplified anxieties and lead to metabolic syndrome among evacuees.

Life at evacuation centers

Health care and medical support at evacuation centers leaves much to be desired even if they do provide shelter and sustenance. Common basic issues are privacy, hygiene and nutrition. Many survivors are located in large facilities with little privacy, with families divided by cardboard boxes in crowded school gyms. Emergency toilets are often built outside the buildings in open-air places.

It was also cold for some time post-3/11 and heating was limited. As summer became hot, the lack of air conditioning made conditions uncomfortable. In the cold weather many people, especially older people, restricted their eating and drinking because they did not want to wake up in the middle of night to walk to the outdoor toilets. This caused many to suffer from dehydration and malnutrition as in Kobe (Tanida 1996; Ōtani 2010: 21).

The potential for infectious disease outbreak was a major concern, but so far this has been avoided. Tap water and sewage systems were destroyed, and evacuees were advised to wrap their stools in newspaper and place them in a plastic bag. But when patients with acute gastroenteritis suggestive of norovirus infection were found at an evacuation center in Iwate, the medical relief team facilitated improvement of hygiene measures, introduced chlorine-based disinfectants, and promoted accurate knowledge of virus transmission (Yamamoto *et al.* 2011).

The immediate threat of an epidemic of diseases associated with poor hygiene and sanitation has been averted with no serious large-scale outbreak, but malnutrition has affected some survivors. At many scattered evacuation places where distribution was inadequate, even more than one month after 3/11, only small quantities of bread and *onigiri* (rice balls) were delivered and people had to live without fresh vegetables and fruit for a long time. The situation was so dire that some NGOs started to charter helicopters to drop vegetables to areas inaccessible by road. In addition, cooperatives and commercial delivery firms such as Yamato and Sagawa helped deliver necessary items and ease shortages in areas accessible by road. In contrast, after the 1995 Kobe earthquake, people might have had to survive on bread and *onigiri* for only two or three days, but soon were able to eat more balanced meals thanks to efficient aid distribution, again reflecting the relatively intact transportation infrastructure.

FIGURE 14.1 Temporary toilet set up by Ministry of Land, Infrastructure, Transport and Tourism (MLIT) at evacuation center (Kesennuma Gym). Infectious disease control sign put up by public health nurse: "If diarrhea, see medical staff," April 14, 2011 (taken by author).

Lack of physical activity by those living at evacuation centers is also a health risk. Deprived of their daily routines and chores, older people started to suffer from economy class syndrome – blood clots associated with long distance airline travel. This can be life threatening. Medical teams regularly visit evacuation centers to check blood circulation of older people, especially their legs and massages are often provided by public health nurses who also distribute long stockings that help keep feet warm in the cold weather and also improve blood circulation.

Despite the challenging conditions, people have worked tirelessly. Yamamoto (Yamamoto *et al.* 2011), who has worked in other countries such as Haiti, reports that it is extremely impressive that evacuees at the shelters organized functional communities. Representatives met every night to discuss the shelter's rules. People shared the chores of serving meals and cleaning the living spaces and toilets, and took routine physical exercise together. This kind of autonomous function is a key for successful external support and interventions (Ōtani 2010). A healthy functioning community is crucial for developing a safety net in communities and planning public health interventions.

FIGURE 14.2 Oral health care: how to clean your teeth without a toothbrush. Newspaper ad by Sunstar, *Kawanishi Shinbun* (local/regional paper), April 14, 2011.

Public health issues

Since the tsunami swept away everything, people at evacuation centers lacked basic necessities such as toothbrushes for daily oral care. Public health practitioners cooperated with leading oral hygiene firms such as Sunstar to teach evacuees how to clean and brush their teeth without toothbrushes and toothpaste. Signs were put up at evacuation centers and also advertisements were placed in newspapers.

Emergency temporary toilets were also set up at evacuation centers to stop the spread of infectious diseases. Evacuees kept them clean while public health nurses raised awareness by putting up signs like: "If diarrhea, see medical staff."

Public health nurses' heroic post-3/11work has earned them well-deserved kudos. Immediately after the earthquake, many public health nurses went searching for survivors, usually older people they had been regularly visiting, to make sure they were okay. They carried out their duties even though they themselves lost family members, and suffered damage to their housing and workplace, often not sleeping for days right after the earthquake. In many towns, records were destroyed but the public health nurses continued to serve the community under trying circumstances and then extended their mission by delivering aid and improving health conditions at evacuation centers. As in Kobe, they will continue to play a critical health role in the temporary shelters for quite some time. Minsei-iin (welfare-commissioner who is not paid – voluntary work – but has long established trusted position in Japanese society) also played a critical role in several communities in Kobe as they are doing so in Tōhoku (Ōtani 2010: 36). Public health officials and volunteers used the Internet and Twitter to cope with public health issues by gathering information about needs and directing deliveries of food, clothing, blankets, children's books and other sundry items such as sanitary pads and diapers to where they were needed.

Mental health care

Public health authorities in Kobe early on focused on addressing various mental health issues. The Hyōgo Prefecture Department of Health public health survey for earthquake-affected households was conducted every year from 1996 to 1999. The survey collected data that enabled public health authorities to identify increased problems of alcohol dependency, in addition to nutrition and diet issues (Ōtani 2010: 73). Some people died of malnutrition that was triggered and accompanied by alcohol dependency.

Since Kobe, Kokoro-no-care, a concept encompassing mental health care and psycho-social support, has become a watchword for helping post-disaster communities recover. International media coverage drew attention to post-3/11 mental health problems and inadequate attention by Japanese public health authorities (McCurry 2011). However, this criticism drew a sharp response from Japanese experts because it did not adequately reflect the capacity of Japan's health system and the lessons it learned from the 1995 Kobe and 2004 Niigata Earthquakes.

These previous disasters provided training opportunities for traumatic stress counseling and national guidelines for post-disaster mental health over the past few years (Suzuki and Weissbecker 2011; Kim and Akiyama 2011). McCurry's suggestion that Japan was completely ill-prepared to provide mental health support for disaster survivors was overstated and sensationalist. Certainly many people are suffering from staggering personal and material losses that would tax the capacity of any nation's mental health services, but resources and counseling are available and public health officials are very sensitive about this issue. They have learned from previous disasters and have prepared so that they can provide support for those who need it, although this might not always be sufficient. Tōhoku will be another learning experience to improve preparation for future disasters; it is always possible to find shortcomings, but emergency disaster preparedness is cumulative, incrementally improving, adjusted for each situation and unfortunately never fully comprehensive.

PTSD (post-traumatic stress disorder)

PTSD is usually associated with war, but is equally common in disaster situations as people become overwhelmed by what they have experienced. (Kutchins and Kirk 1997: 102; Ikeno chapter in Kwansei Gakuin University COE Disaster Reconstruction System Research Working Group 2005). Ikeno (ibid.) introduced concepts based on the 1995 earthquake such as counter-transference, burnout, secondary traumatization and vicarious traumatization. Anecdotal reports and preliminary observations suggest that these problems are observed widely among people affected by 3/11, including those who worked in rescue and relief operations.

Those who survived, but lost family members and/or friends express their pain. A schoolgirl said that class was going out for recess and she asked her friend to wait for her in the classroom while she went to the toilet. When she returned, the tsunami had swept her friend away causing her to feel guilty that she caused her friend's death. Many other survivors suffer from this "survivor's guilt." Firemen also blame themselves for not saving more people, wondering if they could have done more. Overall, the heroic actions of firemen have earned them considerable praise in the media, but preliminary reports indicate that many firemen in the disaster-affected areas are suffering mentally and some express their wish to leave the occupation. One can also imagine that members of the SDF who served for prolonged periods in the disaster zone and were engaged in the grim task of recovering bodies must also be suffering to varying degrees from PTSD.

Religion and post-disaster prayers

Religion plays a critical role in disaster-affected areas. Often it is the elderly who are most observant and find greatest solace in religious devotion. It is a source of hope for those living with despair. Postwar Japanese society is known for not being very religious, mostly involving ritualistic observance of Buddhism and Shintoism during life-cycle celebrations and commemorations. However, religious associations have national networks that can help channel practical and emotional/spiritual support in the disaster-affected areas. Local temples and shrines have community networks that facilitate relief activities especially in rural areas. Christian groups in Kobe went to a completely destroyed area in Iwate in order to erect a cross where there had been a church, thereby giving encouragement and hope to parishioners, letting them know they were not alone and could rely on a wider community of believers. International Christian religious networks have also been active in Japan, raising money and supporting relief activities while a Korean Buddhist group worked in disaster affected areas.

Health hazards

Asbestos was a popular building material in the twentieth century because of its fire retardant and insulation qualities. It was discovered, however, that asbestos causes lung cancer and it was banned in many countries. Japan did not impose such a ban until 1995, meaning that older buildings damaged by the earthquake and tsunami in 2011 pose a serious threat to public health. In the weeks following 3/11, clouds of dust whipped up by strong winds enveloped many devastated communities and thus there is considerable concern that many survivors and rescue workers have been exposed to asbestos. SDF members were issued special masks, but many people used simple paper masks during clean-up operations that might not have been effective in blocking the asbestos particles.

Radiation is another major health hazard that is arousing public anger and concerns about food safety and the well-being of children. In Fukushima, another prefecture with many elderly, the evacuations of households within 20 km of the plant has caused extensive disruption and spread uncertainty. There is no clear timetable for their return. Many farming households in neighboring rural communities have been ruined by radioactive contamination because of bans on shipping of their produce or livestock. The capacity for older farming households to hang on and recover from this major setback is doubtful, suggesting the government needs to fine-tune its compensation and relocation policies in Fukushima and other affected regions.

It is indicative of altruistic spirit that a group of more than 200 pensioners all over the age of 60 volunteered to participate in tackling the nuclear crisis at the crippled Fukushima power plant. This Skilled Veterans Corps gathered retired engineers and others with relevant professional expertise who offered to face the dangers of radiation to spare younger workers from exposure that might cause long-term health consequences. The government expressed gratitude for this selfless offer but declined to take them up on it. Yamada Yasuteru, leader of this silver corps, explained, "We are not kamikaze. The kamikaze were something strange, no risk management there. They were going to die. But we are going to come back" (BBC 2011).

Building temporary shelters

The government had promised to build 52,000 temporary homes in the region by August 2011, but by the middle of June, only about half had been completed (McCurry 2011). This process was slower than expected given Japan's accumulated know-how. When the 2005 Fukuoka Earthquake occurred in Kyūshū, temporary shelters were built much more rapidly than in 1995 Kobe, suggesting a greater level of preparation (Ōtani 2009). Following the May 12, 2008 Sichuan Earthquake, the Chinese government was very quick to build temporary shelters drawing on experiences abroad, mainly Japanese, and drew up a plan only one week after the earthquake. They actually started to build on May 19, and survivors started moving into temporary shelters by May 29, 2008 (EERI 2008: 10; Ōtani 2009). In Kobe, by contrast, it took three months to get started building temporary shelters. In Kobe, we learned it is important to pay special attention to elderly and disabled in both allocation and design of temporary shelters. The shortage of common space, green areas and adequate living facilities can have an adverse impact on the mental health of residents and in building a sense of community (Ōtani 2010: 97; Hirayama 2000).

The government has been criticized for its slow response to 3/11 in general, but despite considerable obstacles it did manage to build over 27,000 units by the end of May, only ten weeks after the disaster struck. Flat, high ground not too far from devastated communities was limited and transport infrastructure was badly damaged. A surprising development is that many of the temporary units went unoccupied even after being allocated because evacuees who left the evacuation centers faced loss of critical government financial and nutritional support as well as

FIGURE 14.3 Temporary shelters being built at Kesennuma middle school ground, April 14, 2011 (taken by author).

access to timely information on post-disaster life recovery and thus could not afford to relocate. There were TV interviews with elderly who have refused to move and they complained about the rigid rules that deprive them of benefits and the possibility of being separated from their communities.

Elderly in disaster

One of the major features of this disaster was that it hit areas with a high level of population ageing (Yamamoto *et al.* 2011). More than 30 percent of evacuees are aged over 65 and many suffer chronic diseases such as hypertension, diabetes and heart disease. One of the major challenges for health providers was to identify the medicines that patients had been taking. Frequently, older patients do not remember the names of their pills and pharmacy records were often lost in the tsunami. Pharmacists, working closely with evacuees, played a crucial role in the identification and selection of pills and alternatives.

Previous experiences indicate the need to pay special attention to older survivors and take care not to leave them in isolation, especially those lacking extended family support (Ōtani 2010: 132). *Kodokushi* (dying alone) became a major issue following Kobe as the media covered the plight of lonely elderly living in isolation without the mental or physical resources to cope with such a traumatic disruption of their lives on their own (Ōtani 2010: 39).

To prevent isolation, it is critically important to design common space that facilitates daily interaction. So it is not just a case of numbers of units or seismic strength, but also creating aesthetically attractive compounds with barrier-free design for the elderly and the disabled. Yet news reports from Tōhoku pointed out that temporary shelters in Ishinomaki were built with a 14 cm gap in the floor heights so that going to the bathroom is unsafe for older people.[4]

The lessons of Kobe also suggest the need to rethink "temporary" as many residents remained in these compounds for three years. The types of amenities and facilities should reflect the reality that many evacuees may end up staying for considerable period of time in these temporary compounds.

Enhancing older people's post-disaster life at temporary shelters

At temporary shelters, as learnt from the Kobe experience, it is important to create an environment that does not leave older people alone. The increasing risk of *kodokushi* (dying alone) has been a concern for government, media and volunteers. Location of temporary shelters is important as older people (many of whom have physical weakness or disability) need to do daily grocery shopping and be able to see a doctor and friends. In addition, it must be a place where public health nurses and volunteers can reach – this has been a challenge in Tōhoku as the disaster area is vast in a mountainous coastal zone and the evacuation sites are scattered widely. Compounds should be designed to promote communication between neighbors while maintaining a degree of privacy. The lack of privacy has been one of the problems at the evacuation centers. The hardware (temporary housing units) of recovery needs to be complemented by appropriate software (services and sense of community) that nurtures life support networks. The building of temporary compounds must serve this function and given the high proportion of elderly evacuees there needs to be an emphasis on community building and bonding to prevent loneliness and isolation. In addition to regular visits to monitor well-being, it is important to organize community events that bring people together such as holding regular tea parties in the community center or establishing clubs for karaoke, Japanese chess, cooking, etc. and to stage seasonal festivals that will appeal to different types of older people. When assigning people temporary shelters, the Kobe experience suggests the government needs to be careful about creating the right demographic mix. In Kobe, by giving priority to older people, the temporary shelter compounds had only old frail people in need of care with little community support. In addition, it is important to assign units in light of the frailty of the elderly and ensuring that access to transportation and shopping is not difficult and placing them close to the entrance of the compound. In such ways it is possible to enhance the life of the elderly at temporary shelters.

Conclusions

While international aid and media attention may peak in times of disaster, they are not usually sustained for long after the emergency while many survivors have a great need for long-term support (Ōtani 2010: 18). Challenges remain long after international attention fades away. As to medical and health impact, experts suggest that it is necessary to keep monitoring the disaster-affected cohorts, for example, for mental health issues such as PTSD (Takei, N. *Asahi Shimbun* August 5, 2011). Providing accommodation and job opportunities are a foundation of post-disaster life reconstruction. Providing temporary shelters is not simply a matter of building shelters to meet numerical targets, but also must serve the needs of the residents. On the other hand, infrastructure alone cannot relaunch the life of survivors. It is a combination of hardware (facilities) and software (services) adjusted to specific needs that are crucial to establishing an effective community-care system. The community creation process can be difficult and labor intensive, requiring significant resources to help ensure success, including time, money and people (Ōtani 2010: 141). There is a process of trial and error to see what works best and what needs to be modified. Accommodating the special needs of the elderly is important in what can be long-term "temporary" housing and also in designing more permanent resettlement solutions. The lessons of 3/11 for other nations with large ageing populations are still emerging, but the high percentage of elderly victims suggests the need to modify disaster emergency procedures in light of their vulnerability to disaster.

Notes

1   Cabinet Office, Government of Japan, *Ageing Society White Paper 2011*, p. 7, online, available at: www8.cao.go.jp/kourei/whitepaper/w-2011/zenbun/pdf/1s1s_2.pdf [accessed July 21, 2011].

2   *Kahoku Shinbun* June 25, 2011, online, available at: www.kahoku.co.jp/spe/spe_sys1071/20110625_01.htm [accessed August 6, 2011].

3   Ministry of Internal Affairs and Communications, Statistic Bureau homepage, online, available at: www.pref.fukushima.jp/toukei/data/hitome/2010/ken/014.pdf [accessed August 6, 2011].

4   *Kahoku Shinbun* June 25, 2011, online, available at: www.kahoku.co.jp/spe/spe_sys1071/20110625_01.htm [accessed August 6, 2011].

References

Allworth, A.M. (2005) "Tsunami lung: a necrotizing pneumonia in survivors of the Asian tsunami," *Medical Journal of Australia*, 182(7): 364.

BBC (2011) "Japan pensioners volunteer to tackle nuclear crisis," May 31, online, available at: www.bbc.co.uk/news/world-asia-pacific-13598607.

Chierakul, W., Winothai, W., Wattanawaitunechai, C., Wuthiekanun, V., Rugtaengan, T., Rattanalertnavee, J., Jitpratoom, P., Chaowagul, W., Singhasivanon, P., White, N.J., Day, N.P. and Peacock, S.J. (2005) "Melioidosis in 6 tsunami survivors in southern Thailand," *Clinical Infectious Diseases*, 41(7): 982–990.

EERI (Earthquake Engineering Research Institute) (2008) *Special Earthquake Report: The Wenchuan, Sichuan Province, China, Earthquake of May 12, 2008*, October, online, available at: www.eeri.org/products-publications/eeri-newsletter.

Hirayama, Y. (2000) "Collapse and reconstruction: Housing recovery policy in Kobe after the Hanshin Great Earthquake," *Housing Studies*, 15(1): 111–128.

Scandinavica, 93(6): 477–481.

Kim, Y. and Akiyama, T. (2011) "Post-disaster mental health care in Japan," *The Lancet*, July 23; 378(9788): 317–318, online, available at: www.thelancet.com/journals/lancet/article/PIIS0140-6736%2811%2961169-0/fulltext.

Kongsaengdao, S., Bunnag, S. and Siriwiwattnakul, N. (2005) "Treatment of survivors after the tsunami," *New England Journal of Medicine*, 352(25): 2654–2655.

Kutchins, H. and Kirk, S.A.(1997) *Making Us Crazy – DSM: The Psychiatric Bible and the Creation of Mental Disorders*, New York: The Free Press.

Kwansei Gakuin COE Disaster Reconstruction System Research Working Group (2005) *Disaster Reconstruction*, Kwansei Gakuin University Press [in Japanese].

McCurry, J. (2011) "Japan's slow recovery," *The Lancet*, July 2, 378(9785): 15–16.

Morrow, B.H. (1999) "Identifying and mapping community vulnerability," *Disasters*, 23(1): 1–18.

Nagamatsu, S., Maekawa, T., Ujike, Y., Hashimoto, S., Fuke, N. and The Japanese Society of Intensive Care Medicine (2011) "The earthquake and tsunami – observations by Japanese physicians since the March catastrophe," *Critical Care*, June 28, 15(3): 167.

Ōtani, J. (2009) "Issues in modern China highlighted by the 2008 Sichuan earthquake with reference to the 1995 Great Hanshin-Awaji earthquake and the 2005 West Off Fukuoka earthquake," *Bulletin of Kyushu University Asia Centre*, 3: 23–37 [Japanese with English abstract].

Ōtani, J. (2010) *Older People in Natural Disasters*. Kyoto: Kyoto University Press/Melbourne: Trans Pacific Press.

Potera, C. (2005) "In disaster's wake: Tsunami lung," *Environmental Health Perspectives*, 113(111): A734.

Suzuki, Y. and Weissbecker, I. (2011) "Post-disaster mental health care in Japan," *The Lancet*, 378 (9788): 317, online, available at: www.thelancet.com/journals/lancet/article/PIIS0140-6736%2811%2961168-9/fulltext.

Tanida, N. (1996) "What happened to elderly people in the Great Hanshin Earthquake?" *British Medical Journal*, 313(7065): 1133–1135.

Varley, A. (ed.) (1994) *Disasters, Development and Environment*, Chichester: John Wiley & Sons.

Yamamoto, T., Kato, M. and Shirabe, S. (2011) "Life, health, and community in a tsunami-affected town," *The Lancet*, July 23, 378(9788): 318.

15

THOUSAND-YEAR EVENT

Towards reconstructing communities

Riccardo Tossani

Five months after the devastating earthquake and tsunami the Japanese public remains largely discontent with the pace of reconstruction progress and the national government's response to the dire needs of the multitude of communities heavily impacted by the disaster. Frustration grew to outright dismay when Matsumoto Ryū, the minister responsible for leading reconstruction in the devastated northeast coast resigned in early July, just nine days in the job, over a scandal in which he was videotaped berating the governor of one of the worst hit prefectures for arriving a few minutes late to a meeting to discuss the recovery effort. Accompanied with threats to the local media not to print the altercation, Matsumoto sealed his fate and added further complications to the Kan government's efforts to accelerate progress in dealing with the displaced and dispossessed (Nakamoto 2011). An impatient construction industry is also decrying the slow pace of reconstruction, blaming local governments for delaying efforts to draw up plans for housing and social infrastructure projects, the surplus in construction materials inventory and postponement of the much anticipated reconstruction-led boom (*Nikkei* 2011).[1]

Events such as this understandably feed the impression of a lack of seriousness on the part of the government to deal with the problem of not just rehousing tens of thousands of refugees but of rebuilding the towns and villages along the northeastern coast of Tōhoku that were either erased or critically impacted by the tsunami. While there has been scant public evidence of substantive action or long-term planning, efforts are nevertheless underway at all levels of government to relieve the considerable stress in the affected areas while proposing rational plans and procedures for their reconstruction. It is the goal of these plans to enable the prompt rebuilding of devastated communities, and of equal importance to reduce the magnitude of life and property loss when similar events occur in the future. The plans will necessarily contain an approach to urban planning and evacuation procedures that will inform existing communities of equivalent vulnerability elsewhere, and in so doing will be influential on the character of future development as well as the life safety of citizens throughout Japan.

It behooves us then to pay close attention to the quality of strategies being formulated by the branches of government responsible for the direction of billions of dollars in reconstruction funds, and to examine the design thinking that has been put forward in recently released case studies as well as the Reconstruction Design Council report.

In any fair evaluation of the timeliness of the government's response or the effectiveness of their reconstruction proposals, one must grasp the nature and scale of the March 11 twin catastrophic events as well as the geographic magnitude of the forces responsible for the disaster. This lends understanding to the breadth of effort required to rebuild vast areas of infrastructure, residences, industry and public amenities, in short recreating from seemingly endless fields of mud and rubble the thriving, multifaceted organic communities that sustained for generations the singular, integrated way of life that is so distinctively Japanese.

We must understand that this event, as catastrophic and historic as it was, had nevertheless been fully anticipated by those whose professions require understanding and foreseeing natural disasters. What is more, the earthquake and tsunami could both correctly be considered as precursors of more of the same in the very near future, as underlying tectonic stresses gravitate southwards along the Japan Trench, barely 150 km off the coast, towards Tokyo, not diminishing but in fact increasing the likelihood of a similar event impacting coastal communities in central and southwest Honshū. At greatest risk is Tokyo, the world's largest city with 30 million people living within 2 m of sea level (Bilham 2011).[2]

Lessons learnt from the great Tōhoku quake and tsunami should have direct bearing on the state of preparedness of communities around Japan, as well as those low-lying coastal areas elsewhere in the Pacific Basin prone to similar geological events. This will be made possible as national leaders recognize the nub of the problem and commission Japan's not inconsiderable intellectual resources, together with specialists from around the world, to create and implement effective policy and planning. While potentially politically risky in the short term, thoughtful and properly informed proposals of real substance are more likely to result in fewer lives lost in the next event, as well as the preservation and enhancement of the most treasured characteristics of Japan's complex cultural and environmental resources.

Early warning

Cell phones, television sets and community emergency services received broadcast earthquake automatic advance warning signals within 30 seconds for localities closest to the epicenter such as Fukushima, to 100 seconds for Tokyo. This was made possible by a national array of seismometers, strain gauges and tidal gauges designed to detect the fast moving "P Waves" radiating outwards at four meters per second. What followed as predicted were the slower and more destructive "S Waves," causing the ground to swell, buckle and crack in a continuous rolling motion. The 9 Richter scale temblor struck, lasting an unprecedented and unimaginable five-minutes plus, with a force five hundred times more powerful than the devastating 2010 Haiti Earthquake. Bridges, roads and buildings heaved and swayed endlessly, products flew off store shelves, furniture toppled and televisions, books, plates and loosely stored artifacts were thrown across rooms to the basso-sound of a passing freight train. Sidewalks and pavements heaved and split revealing fissures that alternately expanded and contracted, spewing water and sand, creating mud volcanoes as the soil below liquefied under pressure of the rising water table, reducing the bearing capacity of structural foundations to the strength of molasses.

Buildings became boats on a mud lake, and parked cars on pavements over landfill such as at Tokyo Disneyland in Urayasu (Chiba prefecture) sunk to their chassis. It did not end there. Five hundred aftershocks were felt and detected in the following week alone, dozens measuring in excess of 6 on the Richter scale and a handful over 7.

Stringent Japanese national building and fire codes, disciplined engineering processes, deep subterranean piles and expensive shoring under city buildings, bridges and elevated highways as well as honest development and construction practices resulted in negligible loss of life or property, an outcome unthinkable even in developed industrialized communities outside of Japan. The advance warning system coupled with the high structural integrity of both public and private buildings allowed occupants, far enough away from the epicenter, time to evacuate to safe areas. Power, light, water and essential utilities remained functional in most places, a testament to the advanced state of preparedness cultivated by the national government following a history of admittedly lesser seismic events. Train services came to a standstill as tracks were inspected for damage. While phone lines were jammed from over-use, the nation's fiber-optic, broadband network remained operative allowing text and even Skype-voice communications from handsets appropriately equipped, reducing the load on emergency services and easing collective anxiety and panic.

It is difficult to imagine a country better prepared for a seismic event of such magnitude, but the tsunami that followed very soon after eroded all confidence in the Japanese government's ability to properly anticipate and react to natural disasters.

Failure of imagination?

Thirty two kilometers below the surface of the Pacific Ocean, just 70 km east of the Fukushima shore, a section of the Eurasian Plate upon which the Japanese archipelago rides like the prow of a cresting ship had for the last 200 years been snagged on the Pacific Plate below, pressing against it and building up energy suddenly released in a seismic event that raised alarms at the Pacific Tsunami Warning Center in Hawaii 3,800 km away. This quick vertical snap thrust a 7 km-high column of water upwards. The subsequent collapse of this water dome generated high-energy ripples that raced across the deep Pacific at over 800 km per hour. Moments later, the first of these gathered in a rising swell above an increasingly shallower seabed, piling up to become a monstrous tidal wave overwhelming shallow bays and breaching 14 m seawalls with ease (Bilham 2011).

The tsunami, backed by an estimated 10 billion tons of water mowed relentlessly through coastal forests, crushing buildings and flinging ships, buses, cars and, of course, people about like so much flotsam, accumulating the detritus of its destruction in a four-story debris glacier against which little could stand. This black swirling wall of liquefied rubble pushed deep inland until exhausted against higher ground. Channeled and focused by valleys and structures, waves reached as high as 38 m (Hongo 2011).[3]

The vast expenditure of tax revenues in disaster prevention measures including tall seawalls has helped earn Japan the moniker of "The Construction State." Yet even this zeal to buttress the island-nation against the brutality of nature did not appear to anticipate the forces unleashed on March 11, 2011. The devastating tsunami impacted over 500 km of coastline, reaching as far as 5 km inland, submerging entire towns and villages in their wake, destroying 48,747 homes and 56 bridges, inundating 23,600 hectares of farmland, mostly rice paddies, with seawater, leaving salt in the soil that could adversely affect rice crops for years in an area that accounts for 3–4 percent of Japan's rice production (Martin 2011).

Receding waters caused further damage in their backward flow out to sea, bearing millions of tons of rubble and detritus which the Pacific Research Center in Hawaii predicts will begin washing up on the beaches of those islands within a year, continuing on to the shores of British Columbia, down against the states of Washington and Oregon all the way to the tip of Baja California by 2014, before bouncing back toward Hawaii for a second impact (Walker 2011). Left behind in the place of preexisting coastal towns from Iwate to Fukushima prefectures was an estimated 25 million tons of debris, only 3.5 million tons of which had been removed by mid-May (Cabinet Office 2011).[4]

The unfathomable magnitude of destruction lends some credence to the idea that the degree of destruction is in some part due to an understandable failure of imagination and foresight. An expert panel under the government's Central Disaster Prevention Council, in an interim review of countermeasures for earthquakes and tsunami in the wake of the catastrophe concluded that Japan's disaster measures did not anticipate the scale of the twin calamities of earthquake and tsunami, "a failure that may have exacerbated the resulting damage" (Kyodo 2011a).[5] This self-criticism acknowledged that, to date, the council had based its recommendations solely on historic data from earthquakes that had occurred repeatedly over the past several hundreds of years and thus likely, from a scientific standpoint, to reoccur. Acknowledging this error of judgment, the Council held the massive Jogan Earthquake of 869 as an event "to reflect upon" while compiling new countermeasures. Prior to 3/11 many experts had questioned the adequacy of the countermeasures, but their criticism was brushed aside. The Council report concludes "it is necessary to compile better antidisaster steps on the use of land and the designation of evacuation sites, while not over relying on levees" (ibid.).

Independent critics of the country's preparedness also make a strong argument that the record history of killer waves visiting the Pacific northeast coast should have been enough precedent to ensure appropriate preparedness in the form of coastal defenses and evacuation infrastructure. In addition to the 869 Jogan Earthquake, devastating tsunami in 1611, 1869 and as recently as 1933 are well documented. The 1896 tsunami took 22,000 lives with analogous forces including the 38.2 m wave that destroyed the Iwate city of Ōfunato, following an 8.5 magnitude temblor.

However, the geotechnical facts of this latest event might suggest a tragic irony: as in the past, there was little that could be done to protect coastal communities on low-lying land from the onrushing wave, and as intimated by the Central Disaster Prevention Council a dependency on seawalls promotes a false sense of confidence and dangerous hubris that could potentially cost thousands of lives.

As is typical with seismic events of such magnitude, the March 11 earthquake resulted in tectonic shifts of the earth's crust over an area of 500 km in length and 200 km in width, with parts of the coastline including Ōshika Peninsula shifting eastwards by 5.3 m and, more significantly sinking by 1.2 m (*Architectural World* 2011). Fourteen-meter-high seawalls were effectively reduced to inadequate 13 m barriers with little hope of holding back 15 m waves. Seawalls have gates for sea access requiring in most cases manual closure procedures following tsunami warnings. This dangerous task is not always possible at short notice, as evidenced by the tragic death of seven volunteer firemen in Ōtsuchi town who had 18 minutes to close 14 gates, and completed 12 before drowning in the attempt. An eighth volunteer is still missing while the body of another volunteer who stayed behind to manually ring the warning bell was recovered. He had chosen to do so because a power outage had silenced emergency alarms (Ogawa 2011).[6]

How high is high enough?

Echoing the findings of the Central Disaster Prevention Council, an Aomori prefectural official challenging the effectiveness of state funded disaster countermeasures asked, "Should we build a seawall that can withstand a tsunami as high as 20 meters or focus more on aspects such as strengthening our measures for evacuation?" (Kyodo 2011b). This poignant question suggests that engineered structures, even those so extensive in scale that state funding is required for their erection, are nevertheless fallible.

Coastal protection has been one of the driving forces behind disaster-prevention public works in Japan, and no doubt will be a component of any reconstruction planning. However, how high a sea wall must a community build for defense against the forces of nature, even those we can reasonably predict, that have consistently overcome a nation's best efforts? Height, while an important safety factor may realistically not be enough to guarantee effectiveness for major events.

Seawalls were breached not only due to operational or design and structural inadequacy, but arguably due to conceptual irrelevance. Walls may not in fact be the answer. The solution, if there is one, may reside in a broad-based rethinking about the overlay of populations on vulnerable geography, in other words, a deeper study of appropriate land use and habitation patterns in addition to evacuation procedures.

Cry wolf

There is much truth in the commonly held belief that the only way to survive a tsunami is to get to higher ground before it reaches you. This axiom presupposes that there is high ground to get to, but tall and appropriately resistant structures would clearly serve the same purpose of refuge. Japan's coastal prefectures designate evacuation sites and escape routes. Evacuation procedures and drills are common in waterfront communities. Local students in Kamaishi, Iwate prefecture had good disaster education in their schools and had completed an evacuation drill just eight days earlier, following designated routes up to the mountains, so most students evacuated safely while some 1,300 residents of the city either died or remain missing (Singer 2011). With only minutes of advance warning, those that failed to get to higher ground were typically the elderly and infirm lacking means or wherewithal to travel a significant distance quickly. Many others were lost trying to help them. Those with means to travel were in many cases confused or unsure, with even the more determined wasting precious minutes putting on extra layers of clothes, collecting "essentials" such as bank books, cash and their official seals (used for transactions in the place of signatures). Loaded down with food items in backpacks many failed to outrun the wave front. Those with cars found themselves in slow-moving traffic, on congested narrow roads in the company of dazed and timid drivers, trapped in cars that were no match against the force of the debris glacier. Sadly, many victims simply chose to ignore the warnings, having grown accustomed to the "crying wolf" of tsunami alarms, putting undue faith in their monumental seawalls.

Tragically, disaster preparedness measures focusing on evacuation sites were far from infallible. The tsunami swept away more than 100 evacuation sites designated by local governments, including 12 above 6 m in Miyagi prefecture's Onagawa (Kyodo 2011c).[7] These included temples, schools and government buildings, such as a town hall located several kilometers inland in Minamisanriku, Miyagi prefecture, where a young public employee broadcast urgent evacuation orders to local residents until the tsunami hit, drowning her, the evacuees and submerging the town hall itself. In Ishinomaki, Miyagi prefecture, 74 of 108 children at an elementary school designated as an evacuation site were killed. Parents who collected their children from the school immediately following the quake to take them home met with the same tragic fate. According to Rajib Shaw, a specialist in disaster and environmental management and associate professor at the Graduate School of Global Environmental Studies at Kyoto University, most of the communities in the prefecture made hazard maps showing areas at risk from 4 and 8 m tsunamis. Because local governments lacked the resources necessary to take specific actions called for by the identified 8 m areas, local residents may have only received the 4 m hazard map (Singer 2011).

A lack of specific information on the risks present in individual localities as well as ineffective escape procedures and rational designation criteria for evacuation sites due to limited community financial and technical resources may well have contributed to the staggering casualty figures, some 20,000 dead or missing.

In Japan regional governments create their own disaster-preparedness plans based on central government basic outlines, prepared by the Ministry of Land, Infrastructure, Transport and Tourism (MLIT). These outlines or guidelines have been necessarily general in nature and include seismic and tsunami hazard maps of a national scale published every year. However since 1979, earthquakes causing ten or more fatalities have occurred in places the MLIT had designated as low risk, and the March 11 tsunami saw massive loss of life in areas designated safe according to the outlines published at the national level. The adequacy of those maps and outlines have now been brought into question by regional governments, with some prefectural officials calling for the national government to take the lead in mapping out new and more adequate guidelines as there are practical limits as to what localities can do on their own.

By the end of April, the much-anticipated revised guidelines had yet to be issued, and prefectural officials were losing patience and threatening to take matters in their own hands and create their own. An exasperated Fukui prefectural official noted: "We cannot just wait. We will start with what we can do" and proposed that local governments review the evacuation manuals of coastal municipalities, requiring those without a guideline to compile one promptly (World Bank 2011). Some regional governments and municipalities have in any case taken the initiative to revise their guidelines independently of the MLIT, such as Oita prefecture's coastal town of Usuki, which faces a bay, now reassessing its disaster measures based on a scenario for a 10 m high tsunami as opposed to the 3 m wave in the current MLIT plan.

Danger zones

In mid-July, the Land Ministry announced plans for "an initiative on building safety under which local governments would designate tsunami danger zones and regulate construction of public and commercial facilities in these areas accordingly." (*Nikkei* 2011). The new regulatory scheme, a component of legislation on tsunami safety in urban planning slated to go before the Diet this year proposes setting the guidelines for designating tsunami danger zones at the national level, with the at-risk category to include areas where existing seawalls were inadequate protection against the largest tsunami on local record, and where evacuation routes and shelters are lacking. The proposal is for maintaining the procedure of local governments to follow these guidelines in the regulation of shopping centers, municipal offices, emergency shelters and "other buildings in the danger zones as needed by specifying such precautions as making buildings at least 20 meters tall and using steel reinforced concrete."[8]

The variegated nature of Japan's coastal topography coupled with the complex fluid dynamics of jet-speed tidal waves over varying ocean and shoreline depths would suggest that a comprehensive identification of at-risk areas would involve an analysis far beyond the scope and capability of local communities and probably prefectural governments. Our nature is to contemplate solutions at a scale comprehensible to individuals and communities. But as we have seen the tectonic forces unleashed by the March 11 event were far from localized and in fact continental in nature, with impacts to the earth's crust so vast that Honshū is measurably closer to California (Chang 2011).

Just as the scale of devastation transcends prefectural boundaries, so must be the response in terms of leadership, economic and technical initiatives and reconstruction planning, drawing on the best scientific, professional and intellectual resources available at a national if not global level.

While the state is in a position to marshal the resources necessary for such a task, it is difficult to imagine meaningful implementation without the close cooperation and participation of prefectural communities. In short, any effective action to designate truly meaningful tsunami danger zones and create new zoning controls and urban planning schemes in reconstruction areas together with viable evacuation measures must necessarily involve an iterative back-and-forth exchange of knowledge and resources between all levels of government, the community and specialist professions. While less a hierarchical or linear process than those customarily followed in bureaucratic Japan, and certainly more time consuming, the parallel actions of local, prefectural and national governments, with assistance from academic and professional institutions is more likely to evolve effective measures for minimizing loss of life in future catastrophes of this nature.

A case study

As suggested by the Central Disaster Prevention Council, prefectural officials and professional observers, seawalls can only do so much and should be considered merely a first line of defense. More comprehensive life-safety measures can be better served by land use zoning that acknowledges the inherent risk of specific local environments and mitigates that risk through strategic urban planning. A damage assessment report published by the Tōhoku Chapter of the Architectural Institute of Japan (AIJ) which studied the impacts to buildings by the March 11 earthquake and tsunami, concluded that "damage to buildings by ground shaking was quite small in the region where tsunami waves did not attack; on the other hand most houses were totally lost in the region of tsunami wave attacks" (Architectural Institute of Japan 2011).

The AIJ report studies in detail the relationship between buildings and terrain from seashore to hilltop on a cross section of the National Route 45 coastal highway along the Ōtani coast, south of Kesennuma City in Miyagi prefecture. In this case study low-lying land immediately behind the seawall (Zone C) is occupied only by coastal forests, a slightly elevated railway and concrete industrial structures, or the bases of tall buildings that rise above the C Zone and well into Zone B. In this case Zone B includes the National Route 45 at 17 m elevation above sea level, behind which residential structures on 3.5 m high concrete bases occupy higher ground of around 20 m and more. With simple summary diagrams the report divides cross-sectional development areas into three zones of distinct levels of vulnerability contingent on the building site elevation above sea level. Zone A is the highest, typically on a hill or high solid ground where no damage results from either tsunami or seismic motion. Zone B is at a height affected by only the top 1–3 m of the tsunami waves, where some buildings did and others did not suffer damage. Zone C is the lowest lying land where buildings could not resist tsunami "wave attacks and were completely destroyed and washed away."

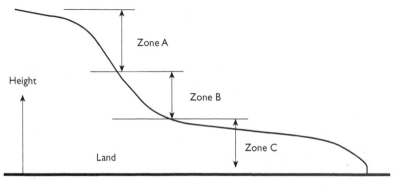

Tsunami Damage Zones   Sea shore

Source: Tohoku Chapter, Architectural Institute of Japan, Reconnaissance Report (12) on Tsunami,
The 2011 off the Pacific Coast of Tohoku Earthquake
Released on April 3, 2011, Disaster Committee, Tohoku Chapter (Dr. Reiji Tanaka, Mr. Ryota Yamaya)

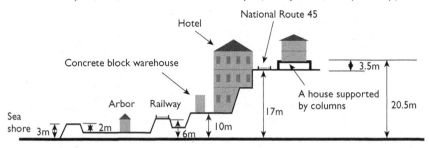

Cross section of the land from sea shore to the hill

Source: Tohoku Chapter, Architectural Institute of Japan, Reconnaissance Report (12) on Tsunami,
The 2011 off the Pacific Coast of Tohoku Earthquake
Released on April 3, 2011, Disaster Committee, Tohoku Chapter (Dr. Reiji Tanaka, Mr. Ryota Yamaya)

FIGURE 15.1 Tsunami damage zones and damage assessment study section (a) tsunami damage zones, (b) cross-section of the land from seashore to the hill (source: AIJ 2011, Dr. Reiji Tanaka and Mr. Ryota Yamaya).

Expanding upon this logic as a founding principle behind new land use zoning and urban planning, a reconstruction master plan was drafted for Onagawa, Ōshiki district in Miyagi prefecture (Onagawa Town Reconstruction Planning Committee 2011a). Framed by green hills and steep valleys, this port town nestled against a picturesque bay facing eastwards to the rich oyster, scallop and salmon fishing grounds of the Pacific was protected by breakwaters at the harbor mouth tipped with an avant-garde red lighthouse. On March 11, with few minutes warning much of the town was obliterated by the estimated 15 m high tsunami.

Home to 6,000 residents and a popular destination for its fish market, restaurants, shops and hot springs, Onagawa's mix of schools, houses, hotels and commercial activities made for a typically integrated Japanese community aggregated along a bustling shoreline. The tsunami plowed through the crescent of buildings huddled helplessly around the bay, sweeping boats, cars, trees and people into a debris glacier that relentlessly drove 2 km deep inland along a mountain stream and residential vales, tearing buildings off their footings and crushing everything in its way. No structures were left standing or undamaged as the receding waters swept out to sea the remnants of a once-thriving village, and the breakwaters and little red lighthouse disappeared.

FIGURE 15.2 Aerial photo: Onagawa, Miyagi prefecture, after March 11, 2011 (source: ©Google Earth July 25, 2011, Google Earth Placemark: Minamisanriku, Motoyoshi District, Miyagi Prefecture.kmz).

FIGURE 15.3 Onagawa port (photographer: Jeff Kingston).

FIGURE 15.4 Onagawa: parking lot at 14 m above sea level (photographer: Jeff Kingston).

Similar wreckage and decimation of waterfront communities occurred up and down the coastline across three prefectures. Just 26 km due north of Onagawa the port town of Minamisanriku saw the tsunami carve a path of destruction up river valleys as far as 3 km from the waterfront, erasing 95 percent of its buildings and leaving 10,000 people, half its population, dead or missing. The tsunami eradicated the infrastructure of cottage as well as regional industries, destroying or rendering unusable 17,000 fishing vessels in Tōhoku and 263 fishing ports in the prefectures of Iwate, Miyagi and Fukushima, where 75 percent of fishermen were elderly with no successors. Like so many coastal communities, Onagawa lost far too many of its citizens together with most of its built environment. But with a stoicism characteristic of the Japanese people, the survivors typically refuse to even contemplate permanent relocation and insist on rebuilding their lives in what is left of their former charming port town.

The Onagawa Plan

On this tragically blank slate the Onagawa Reconstruction Master Plan proposes a phased rebuilding of the community according to an idealized land use zoning which relocates residences, schools and hospitals to the equivalent of the AIJ "Zone B and C" higher ground. Industry, markets, uninhabited tourist amenities and non-dormitory functions, including police stations and sports facilities are relegated to the lower "Zone C" elevations along the shoreline and river valleys. Parks are constructed as landscaped buffers between these zones, with a "memorial" park lining a raised seafront behind taller reconstructed seawalls. Designated evacuation sites are scattered about at much higher elevations, within easy reach of rebuilt roads which double as escape routes. A new train station and town hall, both lost in the tsunami are rebuilt on higher ground.

The plan, drafted by the Onagawa Town Reconstruction Committee at the request of the Miyagi Prefecture Reconstruction Policies and Affairs Division, and issued on May 9, 2011, at first glance appears sound in its adherence to the simple logic of vertical stratification as inferred (but not explicitly recommended) by the AIJ damage assessment report. It responds to first-blush common sense notions as expressed on April 1 by Prime Minister Kan who said the "one key reconstruction goal for the Tōhoku region will be creating coastal areas with high ground for relocating neighborhoods to prevent further damage from the sea" (Hongo 2011). The Plan calls for raising vast swaths of low-lying ground with berms built from the extensive rubble and debris left by the receding waters, supplemented with mass excavations of adjacent hillsides for the remaining required fill.

Remarking on Kan's strategy to create such high ground, former University of Tokyo Professor of Volcanology Morimoto Ryōhei commented: "It sounds like a bad idea to me" (ibid.). Referencing the seismic phenomenon mentioned earlier in this chapter of "mud volcanoes" and solid foundations turning into quicksand as tremors force the water table upwards, Morimoto points out that "Liquefaction was a major issue in the city of Urayasu (Chiba Prefecture) following the March 11

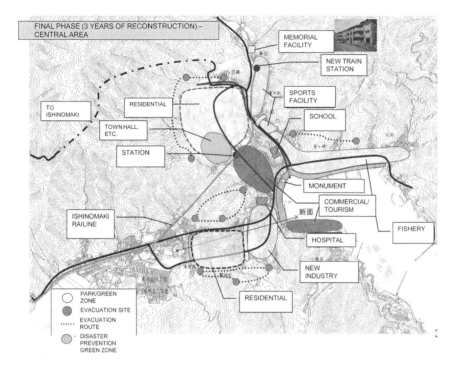

FIGURE 15.5 Onagawa Reconstruction Master Plan, concept draft (source: Onagawa Town Reconstruction Planning Committee (2011a) Appendix 2-2, p. 3, translation by author).

earthquake, which proves landfill and man-made ground are extremely vulnerable to earthquakes ... I feel that lessons aren't being learned" (Singer 2011). The extent of proposed landfill in the Onagawa plan is so vast that one has to question the plan's economic feasibility. It is of course possible to build structures with adequate seismic resistance on landfill, but the cost of piling, shoring and geotechnical countermeasures can easily add 20 percent to the building cost, a premium not necessarily commercially viable in small rural fishing communities, and certainly a great cost burden for public and institutional building programs.

Economic logic might dictate a different approach to reconstruction land-use zoning, urban land planning and structural and building design that obviates the need for expensive landfill, without compromising safety. These considerations may be beyond the skill set of the 14 committee members and advisors who drafted the Onagawa plan, amongst which only one, a professor at Fukushima University, has regional planning, housing and regional policy listed as an area of expertise. In fairness to the intended process, the plan is an early iteration slated for review later in 2011 at the Miyagi Prefecture Reconstruction Conference, and might ultimately manifest more depth of thinking than that possible by its current authors, a cross-section of the community including the chairmen of the Onagawa Chamber of Commerce as well as the Onagawa Women's Association.[9] Not included in this critical town-planning exercise is the expertise usually associated with qualified architects and urban designers. In truth, relevant expertise even in these professions is rare, but it exists in Japan and can be found easily if the net is cast further afield.

Other initiatives built into the Onagawa Plan include those contingent on quarrying hillsides for landfill and relocating residences to undeveloped high ground, which may include tracts set aside for preservation of natural habitat and beauty. Apart from the obvious potential environmental damage that accompanies heroic earth-moving activities, the issue of appropriate land use and land rights comes forward as a profound concern, made more poignant by members of the prime minister's Reconstruction Design Council who advocate changes to land-use policy and the deregulation of land use in regions affected by the disaster (Hirano and Yoshihara 2011).

With the exception of agricultural land, Japan imposes virtually no regulations on land sales, and land-use regulations are quite loose in practice. Coupled with the fact that the national cadastral survey (to determine and register the area, boundaries and ownership of all the nation's land) is still only 49 percent complete, the opportunity for squandering public assets through poorly conceived rezoning is very real. As stated by Hirano and Yoshihara of The Tokyo Foundation in a June 15, 2011 article entitled *Protecting Our Land from a Post-Quake Fire Sale*

> despite its importance as a public good, any given tract of land (or national territory) may change hands and undergo commercial development at any time without so much as a legal determination of its boundaries, as long as the seller and buyer agree on the terms.
>
> (Hirano and Yoshihara 2011)

The strained relationship between Japanese communities and their natural environment is an historic phenomenon which on the upside gives us exquisite manufactured gardens and landscape design, recognized as national treasures and celebrated worldwide. On the downside, we have monumental engineered structures holding up mountains, taming formerly wild rivers and keeping, with tragic exceptions, the sea at bay. This respectful distrust of nature legitimizes an approach to development in bucolic Japan that has resulted in countless examples of building structures of a scale completely inappropriate for their localities in picturesque natural contexts. High-rise hotels in Arcadian valleys and concrete multi-story condominiums on pastoral hillsides are all too common in Japan's otherwise idyllic mountainous landscapes, and largely due to "loose" land-use policy and rapacious or ignorant development practice. Amplify this accepted tendency by the imperative to rebuild communities with the zeal and purpose exhibited in postwar Japan and it is not difficult to imagine the vast tracts of natural landscape, already in short supply, being sacrificed to the dictates of post-tsunami reconstruction. With legislation likely to promote greater permissiveness through deregulation, the importance of intelligent, well-informed comprehensive urban planning becomes paramount, and the right balance of priorities (humanitarian, environmental, political and economic) will necessitate leadership and guidance from individuals or entities with a great deal of relevant knowledge and maturity.

The right DNA

An additional concern of no less importance than those discussed so far is the plan's logic of geographic stratification and the purposeful functional specificity evident in the Plan's proposed land use zoning. This zoning by definition geographically separates dormitory areas, where residents and visitors live and sleep from places of work, recreation and commerce. As evidenced by many New World communities, this stratification propagates the need to commute between specific and disparate parts of the city, exacerbating traffic congestion, time wastage and social dislocation while eroding any sense of community and collective ownership of the public realm, a feature so notably strong in traditional Japanese urban communities. This is particularly true in rural fishing towns such as Onagawa where, as aforementioned, the demographic is typically biased towards the elderly amongst whom this collective sense of belonging is more acute.

The demographic characteristics of these coastal communities would also suggest a planning and design response that puts less rather than more dependence on roads as escape routes, and reducing dependence on automobiles by providing more proximate and numerous designated evacuation areas, enabling the high proportion of elderly residents who typically still work to more easily find safe haven.

Japan's urban fabric, as with many places in Asia where towns and cities aggregated organically in dense clusters over time, evolved from the architectural common denominator that is the traditional shop-house. This iconic urban component is derived from the highly efficient vertical relationship between home and workplace, obviating the need for commuting infrastructure while reinforcing community ownership and pride. This residential model has been variously modified in modern Japanese cities, but its DNA is still the basis for community structures and neighborhood precincts throughout Japan.

Tokyo, the most populous city on the planet, has social and community characteristics more akin to a village. Without sacrificing vitality or diminishing the energetic potential of its urban streets and spaces, the city's residents have a quality of life and level of security unparalleled in the industrial world. While the reasons for this are more complex than just the character and texture of Japanese urban fabric, urban society and its physical manifestations are mutually reinforcing phenomena that simultaneously define, and are defined by, their host culture. The trace DNA at the root of Japanese urban society is missing in the urban planning scheme put forward for Onagawa's reconstruction. The reliance on "common sense" logic of geographic stratification as evidenced by the similarity of cross-section between Onagawa's proposed Master Plan and the AIJ diagrams misses the complex reality of what constitutes a vital and functional urban cultural agglomeration. The simple cross-sectional relationships along a coastal highway have little to do with the sectional relationship between the vital parts of the complex human organism we call a town.

Save the baby

The considerations raised above would suggest a more sophisticated, multi-layered approach to master planning in Onagawa and the multitude of analogous communities that require virtually complete reconstruction. The bathwater is gone but we could still throw out the baby, and unless urban planning evolves quickly from simplistic, albeit well-intentioned diagrams that forsake long-term social and environmental substance for short-term political gain and illusions of expediency, we could eventually lose everything that we hold dear and create a multi-generational monster. As indicated earlier, the skills and intellectual resources necessary for such thoughtful planning are most likely beyond the reach of provincial entities, rapidly assembled and nobly charged with the vital task of envisioning a future form for diverse coastal communities. This resource deficit, in the light of a multiplicity of considerations essential to reconstructing entire communities from the ashes of destruction, has been acknowledged by the members of the Reconstruction Design Council, as evident in their widely anticipated report submitted 106 days after the disaster.

Towards a Reconstruction Master Plan

On April 11, 2011, precisely one month after the disaster now commonly referred to as the Tōhoku Earthquake, the Reconstruction Design Council (RDC) was established by cabinet fiat to "formulate a 'blueprint' for reconstruction that would be a source of hope for people in both the disaster areas and the other areas of the nation for the future" (Cabinet Secretariat 2011). What followed were 12 meetings of the 16 Council members, led by Chairman Iokibe Makoto, President of the National Defense Academy, supported by Vice-Chairman and architect Ando Tadao. This group includes specialists from various fields of expertise as well as a philosopher whose role is Special Advisor and Honorary Chairman. Bringing up the rear is a 19-member "Study Group" with representatives in various disciplines including law, policy, finance, art and sciences, engineering and urban design.[10] The Council engaged in spirited debates in which "heated discussions ensued, sometimes drawn out to well over six hours per session," culminating in a multifaceted report submitted to the prime minister on June 25 (Ministry of Foreign Affairs 2011).

As the opening salvo to an extraordinarily difficult challenge, the report lists seven "principles" upon which, with considerable articulation, it presents a wide range of recommendations. These include promises to both memorialize and understand the disaster, drawing from it and sharing lessons to be passed down to posterity, to have the national government support community-focused "reconstruction through general guidelines and institutional design," to tap into

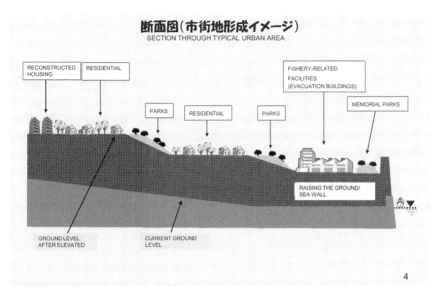

FIGURE 15.6 Typical section: Onagawa Reconstruction Master Plan, concept draft (source: Onagawa Town Reconstruction Planning Committee (2011a) Appendix 2-3, p. 2, translation by author).

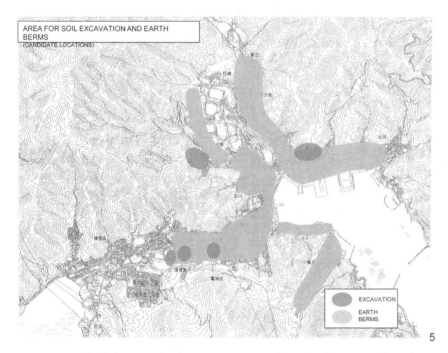

FIGURE 15.7 Earth berm and soil excavation areas: Onagawa Reconstruction Master Plan, concept draft (source: Onagawa Town Reconstruction Planning Committee (2011b) Appendix 3-2, p. 5, translation by author).

the region's latent strengths and develop its socioeconomic potential, to construct "disaster resilient" safe communities, and to revitalize the economy and "pursue reconstruction with a spirit of solidarity and mutual understanding" (RDC 2011: 2).

Echoing themes raised by critics and media, the report openly questions past reliance on pork barrel construction projects including sea walls and coastal dikes, taxpayer funded on the loose promise of providing communities with immunity from natural disasters. "Disaster reduction" is proposed as a more realistic aspiration, and puts forward abstract ideas founded on the concept of "self-aid," where individuals are responsible for their own survival, assisted of course by initiatives designed to create an augmented physical infrastructure lubricated with rational new policies and guidelines. With candid and touching self-reflection, the report asks "is it not rather the case that we have studiously avoided such initiatives, continuing to take refuge in the myth of safety that the benefits of post-war peace have provided?" (RDC 2011: 11). This thinly veiled criticism of notorious public-works practices sets the tone for the report, authored by a group that scrupulously avoided – earning much open criticism – the inclusion of entrenched state bureaucrats. This may well have provided the Council with the political independence necessary for unblinkered observation and criticism, a prerequisite for the formulation of intelligent proposals and meaningful recommendations.

The report covers much ground, providing "blueprints" for revitalizing the Tōhoku region's economy and boosting employment, for developing health and welfare services, for dealing with the aftermath of the Fukushima disaster, for reviving a variety of devastated industries including agriculture, fisheries and tourism, for promoting renewable energy usage and energy efficiency, the utilization of information technology, and most pertinent to this chapter the replanning and rebuilding of towns and communities.

Acknowledging the impossibility of preventing disasters, the report focuses on initiatives to minimize casualties and property damage. While recommendations toy with the questionable viability of raising land on "man-made earthworks, where areas, routes and buildings for evacuation can be developed," it allows that economic feasibility must apply as "projects should be assessed from their planning stages from the perspectives of cost-vs.-effect and efficiency to ensure that only the projects that are truly necessary and effective will be implemented" (RDC 2011: 12, 13). A strict adherence to this dictate, should it survive the evolution and staffing of review organs yet to be formulated, would almost certainly result in a substantial reconfiguration of the Onagawa Reconstruction Master Plan as described above.

Checks and balances

The dialectic of contradictory priorities ever-present in the report and inherited from the intellectual diversity of its authors is intended to infiltrate the implementation process, ensuring ongoing debate and the balancing of opposing needs by judicial entities correctly equipped for the task. And therein lies the challenge, also addressed by the report that acknowledges the imperative of providing the necessary knowledge and skills to the process by creating "an inclusive structure that draws on the knowledge of urban planners, architects, attorneys and government officials" (RDC 2011: 12).

A process properly equipped in terms of intellectual horsepower and professional experience and foresight could contain the checks and balances for the more problematic recommendations that would result in the geographic segregation and dislocation of residents from places of work and leisure. These promote the concentration of land use type according to topographical condition, a simple logic that results in functional specificity as opposed to a more desirable organic diversity, as discussed earlier. Typical planning tendencies are counterbalanced in the same report by an acknowledged need to "capitalize on local ecosystems" and preserve cultural vitality and community identity. The report even goes so far as to recognize the importance of preserving iconic micro-cultural characteristics, from dialects to local festivals, a need made more acute for these aging provincial communities that were already in decline prior to a disaster that resulted in further depopulation.

The report discusses land rights with respect to public works projects, recognizing the problems inherent in a public body purchasing disaster-affected land with little utility value at taxpayer expense, the necessity to transfer land use from residential to agricultural use with commensurate loss of entitlements, and the need to develop mechanisms that can facilitate these kinds of adjustments and transfer processes in an equitable manner.

A key component of the report and its recommendations is its emphasis on "municipality-led processes" which engage "the residents who are closest to their communities and understand local characteristics best" (RDC 2011: 18). Avoiding too great a deviation from bureaucratic tradition, the report maintains the role of national government, like Moses on the Mount, dispensing only visions and ideals for reconstruction communicated through general guidelines and outlines for development to the prefectures. These by definition will fail to delve into the distinctive environmental specifics of localized reconstruction challenges. The implied bargain therefore is for prefectures to establish "town and village community development associations" composed of local representatives engaged in the planning process, conducted at presumably the municipal level, while in exchange the national government will provide "advisor" support "including town planners, architects university scholars and attorneys." Expert personnel thus will be dispatched to provide technical support to local government reconstruction plans and project implementation.[11]

Recognizing the difficulties municipalities might face recruiting expert personnel to formulate plans and implement projects, the report encourages national and prefectural governments as well as newly minted and mandated agencies to cast their net further and "build networks as a means of utilizing the skills of such experts from Japan and overseas" (RDC2011: 19). Also recognizing the importance of appropriate skill sets and the need for organizational hierarchy to coordinate implementation of the overall regional construction plan, the report calls for a "master planner" to lead this boldly ambitious project.

Back to the top

The Reconstruction Design Council report is an important milestone that appears to successfully coalesce the disparate ideas and concerns expressed in the four months since the disaster into a coherent and well-organized set of recommendations. It gives context by which to evaluate and judge the independent efforts developed so far by communities such as Onagawa, and while not perfect it does, as a first draft, give ample evidence that comprehensive, objectively critical and profound design thinking is possible with the resources available at the national level. The quality of debate in those "heated discussions," at least with respect to matters concerning community reconstruction, was no doubt high and passionate, as reflected in the report's earnest conclusions and imperatives.

The challenge, as always, will be establishing a streamlined implementation process by which these recommendations can take flight, and avoiding the dangerous drag that comes with politics, bureaucracy and self-interest.

The report has brought the Reconstruction Design Council back from the periphery of relevance to an exalted position at the top of the pyramid, in large part due to the qualifications and personality of the Council members and their Study Group. The government at both national and prefectural level now has a clearer lens through which to focus its view of the future. As post-disaster fatigue sets in, energies are diverted from long-term goals to short-term necessities, and it takes a good plan and strong leadership to stay the course, and to invest in processes that will result in greater safety and a higher quality of life for the nations' citizens and heirs. It will take a long time for Japan to recover its collective wits after a thousand-year event that knocked the Earth off its axis. If Japan's postwar history is any indication we are likely to see, with the right commander, a sound map, and a stoic and determined crew, a spirited race to a far better future for coastal communities of Tōhoku and the people of Japan.

Notes

1   The Tōhoku region saw a 5 percent decline in public works projects in the April–June period, which according to the *Nikkei* report "will inevitably have a large impact on local construction businesses because public investment accounts for more than half the money funneled into construction" in the region.

2   A seismologist at the University of Colorado, Roger Bilham points out the movement of stress fractures along the eastern Japanese seaboard converging ultimately at the intersection between the Eurasian, Pacific and Philippine tectonic plates, an area under Tokyo reaching out to Mount Fuji.

3   There are varying reports of wave heights from 3 m to over 38 m, generally result from poor understanding of the hydrodynamics of a tidal wave. While it appears the tsunami came on shore as an 11–15 m high wave front in places, higher elevations were reached

by the channeling of the surge by buildings and topography. Planning should therefore consider surge energy concentration and dissipation, not just land elevation.

4   The pace of debris removal is also being blamed (*Nikkei* 2011) for the delay in commencement of public works reconstruction projects.

5   The story published by the *Japan Times*, "Disaster plans need overhaul after tsunami," on June 27, as well as numerous others suggests that prior to March 11, government planners had succumbed to a willful amnesia regarding major tsunami events in Japan's recorded history, as though a realization of the impossibility of defending against such forces negated the need to contemplate their mitigation.

6   These and other touching and tragic stories can be found in this excellent reportage, which unfortunately, currently is only in Japanese.

7   These 12 were of a total of 25 sites in Onagawa, all above 6 m. In Minamisanriku, Miyagi prefecture, 31 of 80 designated sites were washed away.

8   This would suggest, as evidenced by the few structures left standing, that buildings can in fact be constructed to withstand tsunami, thus providing evacuation sites on flat land or in concentrated urban areas where rapid escape to higher ground might be infeasible.

9   This representative group was formed in anticipation of central government recommendations to promote community inclusiveness in reconstruction efforts, an objective also found in Iwate prefecture reconstruction policy which intends to "promote the development of towns based on the hopes and dreams the victims had for their hometowns" (*Basic Policy* 2011).

10 Saigo Mariko, the only professional urban designer in the combined Council and Study group, graduated from Meiji University Faculty of Architecture in 1975. She is also a part-time lecturer at the Tokyo Graduate School of Town Planning at the University of Tokyo. The only town planner is Council Member Professor Onishi Takashi, PhD, at the University of Tokyo, Graduate School of Engineering. His expertise is primarily transportation planning. This leaves architect Ando Tadao as the only other member who has the expertise and skills to visualize and execute urban design, although his built work has never been larger in size than a museum or hotel resort.

11 As already indicated, of the 35 members of the Council and Study Group only three have training in the specific expertise necessary to design and build. This seems oddly disproportionate to the anticipated expenditure of reconstruction funds to the design and construction of new towns, relative to all other recovery activities. This notwithstanding, those three members have clearly left their imprimatur on the substantial community reconstruction language of the report.

References

Architectural World (2011) "Japan Earthquake and Tsunami Situation Summary – 1: Mechanics of Earthquakes," April, online, available at: http://architectural-world. blogspot.com/2011/04/japan-earthquake-and-tsunami-situation.html.

AIJ (Architectural Institute of Japan, Tōhoku Chapter) (2011) *Reconnaissance Report (12) on Tsunami*, April 3, online, available at: www.eqclearinghouse.org/2011-03-11-sendai/2011/04/25/tohoku-chapter-aij-%E2%80%93-april-12-reconnaissance-report.

Basic Policy (2011) "Basic Policy for the Great East Japan Earthquake and Tsunami Reconstruction Efforts," Iwate Prefecture, April 11, online, available at: www.pref. iwate.jp/view.rbz?cd=32121.

Bilham, Roger (2011) *Japan's Killer Quake*, Nova DVD.

Cabinet Office (2011) *Conditions of Lifeline and Infrastructure in the Affected Areas*, Government of Japan, May 13, online, available at: www.cao.go.jp/shien/en/0-infra/infra-e.html.

Cabinet Secretariat (2011) *The Reconstruction Design Council in response to the Great East Japan Earthquake*, Cabinet Public Relations Office, July, online, available at: www.cas.go.jp/jp/fukkou/english/index.html.

Chang, Kenneth (2011) "Quake Moves Japan Closer to U.S. and Alters Earth's Spin," *The New York Times*, March 13, online, available at: www.nytimes.com/2011/03/14/world/asia/14seismic.html?_r=1.

Hirano, Hideki and Yoshihara, Shōko (2011) "Protecting Our Land from a Post-Quake Fire Sale", The Tokyo Foundation, June 15, online, available at: http://tokyofoundation.org/en/articles/2011/post-quake-firesale.

Hongo, Jun (2011) "Nation's Unpreparedness Ahead of Disaster is Blasted," *Japan Times*, April 12, online, available at: www.japantimes.co.jp/text/nn20110412f1.html.

Kyodo (2011a) "Disaster Plans Need Overhaul After Tsunami," *Japan Times*, June 27, online, available at: www.japantimes.co.jp/text/nn20110627a6.html.

Kyodo (2011b) "Regions Review Disaster Prevention: Localities Take Own Steps to Ready for Nuke Crises, Tsunami," *Japan Times*, April 20, online, available at: www.japantimes.co.jp/text/nn20110420f1.html.

Kyodo (2011c) "Tsunami hit more than 100 evacuation sites," *Japan Times*, April 14, online, available at: www.japantimes.co.jp/text/nn20110414a4.html.

Martin, Alex (2011) "Farmers Struggle Amid Tsunami Aftermath," *Japan Times*, April 8, online, available at: www.japantimes.co.jp/text/nn20110408f2.html.

Ministry of Foreign Affairs (2011) *Reconstruction Design Council Recommends Means of Rebuilding Northeastern Japan Areas Hit by Disasters*, July 12, online, available at: www.mofa.go.jp/announce/jfpu/2011/7/0712.html.

Nakamoto, Michiyo (2011) "Kan Under Pressure After Minister Quits," *Financial Times*, July 5, online, available at: www.ft.com/cms/s/0/d8bd2c54-a6ec-11e0-a808-00144feabdc0.html#axzz1dOmnLyuy.

Nikkei (2011) "New Push For Building Safety In Tsunami Danger Zones," July 13, online, available at: http://e.nikkei.com/e/fr/tnks/Nni20110713D13JFF03.htm.

Ogawa, Kiyoko (2011) "Members of Firefighters Closed Floodgates on a 'Sense of Mission'," *Sankei News*, June 26.

Onagawa Town Reconstruction Planning Committee (2011a) *Committee Activity Report, Onagawa, Miyagi Prefecture*, May 9.

Onagawa Town Reconstruction Planning Committee (2011b) *Committee Activity Report, Onagawa, Miyagi Prefecture*, June 10.

RDC (Reconstruction Design Council) (2011), *Towards Reconstruction: "Hope beyond the Disaster,"* Report to the Prime Minister's Office in Response to the Great East Japan Earthquake, June 25, online, available at: http://reliefweb.int/node/435471.

Singer, Jane (2011) "Disaster Expert Seeks Better Tsunami Defense," *Japan Times*, April 23, online, available at: www.japantimes.co.jp/text/fl20110423a1.html.

Walker, Brian (2011) "Researchers: Hawaii may get hit with trash from Japan's tsunami," *CNN.com*, April 7, online, available at: www.cnn.com/2011/WORLD/asiapcf/04/07/japan.debris.map/index.html.

World Bank (2011) *Global Economic Prospects, Volume 3*, June, online, available at: http://siteresources.worldbank.org/INTGEP/Resources/335315-1307471336123/7983902-1307479336019/Full-Report.pdf.

16

CAN POST-3/11 JAPAN OVERCOME TWENTY YEARS OF DRIFT?

Tōgo Kazuhiko

Introduction

3/11 was a wakeup call for many Japanese who already thought that something was wrong in Japan. Since that day newspapers, top journals, books, television and the Internet have all provided a cascade of news and opinions about the triple disaster of earthquake, tsunami and nuclear meltdown and what should be done to overcome this catastrophe and achieve reconstruction. I participated in this national discourse by writing in the mass media and also started sending personal letters to those who were in a position to make decisions about reconstruction, including Iokibe Makoto, Chairman of the Reconstruction Design Council; Tasso Takuya, Governor of Iwate prefecture; and Kondō Seiichi, Commissioner for Cultural Affairs.[1] On April 22 I also participated in a tripartite discussion with Masuda Hiroya, former Governor of Iwate prefecture and Kawakatsu Heita, Governor of Shizuoka prefecture, that was published as a book entitled, *Tōhoku Kyōdōtai kara no Saisei (Resurrection from the Tōhoku Community)* (Kawakatsu *et al.* 2011). This paper first introduces the vision I expressed there, then explains three disappointments and three hopes that I felt since April and concludes by assessing where Japan stands at the end of July 2011.

Creating a dreamland of twenty-first century civilization in Japan (my vision expressed on April 22, 2011)

Twenty years have passed since the Shōwa era ended and the Heisei era commenced in 1989. That change coincided with the end of the Cold War. After World War II, Japan shifted its course from "rich country and strong military" to "rich and peaceful country." Japan achieved remarkable success by the end of the Cold War to become the second largest economy in the world, a remarkable story of rising from the ashes of defeat in 1945. But after achieving the post-World War II goal of "rich and peaceful country," Japan lost its national objective and began to drift in the subsequent twenty years. In the wake of the earthquake/tsunami on March 11, I immediately thought that precisely because of the enormous scale of this calamity and the absolute need to concentrate people's energy to overcome it, Japan might be able to turn this tragedy into a "mandate from heaven" for reconstruction. If the Japanese people could mobilize their inherent energy and discipline to tackle reconstruction of Tōhoku (northeast) region, I thought it possible to end two decades of drift and turn this region into a dreamland of twenty-first century civilization. While the Fukushima nuclear meltdown resulted in a calamity of an entirely different nature from the tsunami/earthquake, I also consider this as another trial from heaven. If Japan is able to become the leading country for renewable energy, then it ultimately could realize the opportunities created by disaster.

Five dimensions

But how can we realize these opportunities? At least five dimensions have to be taken into account:

1. First, the feeling of the people who actually suffered naturally must be the starting point. For them, more than anything else, restoring ordinary life with a house and livelihood, even on a temporary basis, is critically essential. Eventually the reconstruction of Tōhoku must be something of which they themselves are proud and happy.
2. To come up with concrete planning for reconstruction and its implementation, local and regional leadership is essential from villages, towns and municipalities up to the prefectural level. Local leaders are the ones who best understand the feelings and needs of the survivors and can play a critical role in expressing their voices to the outside world.
3. The central government naturally has to play a decisive supporting role because it has access to the greatest available resources both financially and intellectually. Concrete measures for reconstruction of new Tōhoku have to be adequately guided and supported by the central government in tune with local sentiments.
4. Funding reconstruction is a critical issue. Immediately after 3/11, we saw an enormous explosion of goodwill and generosity from all corners of Japan. The Japan Red Cross was flooded with *gienkin* (assistance money). This initial enthusiasm must develop into a long-term determination that shakes off the languor that has enveloped Japan over the last twenty years, and enter into a new post-3/11 era of resolute action. There are many options to raise money for recovery and reconstruction such as higher consumption taxes (currently 5 percent), a new special income tax or special bonds for Tōhoku reconstruction. But whatever option is chosen, ultimately reconstruction will depend on hard

work and inspiration. The Japanese have an expression, *gashin shotan* (working harder, enduring hardship as ever), that seems apt for the challenges that lay ahead.[2]

5. The Japanese cannot achieve this reconstruction on their own. Immediately after the disaster, Japan received many offers of international assistance. The Japan-US alliance was reinvigorated by Operation Tomodachi (friendship), while China, Korea and Russia, neighbors with whom Japan has some difficult issues, also offered generous assistance. Japan, as in the past, should learn from the world and solicit wisdom, ideas, technology and advice from all countries that have knowledge and experience useful for the Tōhoku reconstruction. The Dutch, for example, have a long experience and knowledge of construction of dikes in harmony with the surrounding environment. Even a developing country like Bhutan has embarked on an inspiring modernization where its traditional architecture and culture is preserved, creating harmony with nature.

Reconstruction agenda

A twenty-first century reconstruction dreamland in Tōhoku can be achieved based on the following five guidelines:

1. All industries in the region must be rehabilitated, including agriculture, forestry, fisheries, industrial and technological production, and service sectors. The new society naturally should meet all conditions required for economic and societal development. A new concept of zoning for these activities should distinguish the reconstruction from just restoring communities as they were pre-3/11.
2. Reconstruction should be based on the principle of respect for and harmony with nature. Relocating communities to safer, high ground must be achieved so as not to destroy nature.
3. Reconstruction must respect and revivify traditional culture. That restoration should serve as a foundation for a holistic and future-oriented harmony between nature and human activities.
4. Reconstruction of houses, villages, towns and cities should strive to emulate European policies that consider the external structure of buildings as a public good that should conform to aesthetic criteria in harmony with nature.
5. Last but not least, there is the issue of nuclear energy. It is not feasible to consider the immediate abolition of nuclear energy, but 3/11 must be the starting point for Japan to develop clean renewable sources of energy and gradually shift towards a post-nuclear era. Radiation contamination is affecting the lives of people in the vicinity of Fukushima, forcing many to evacuate their homes and live in grim shelters. This radiation crisis resonates in a disturbing way among the only people to have endured atomic bombings so it seems fitting that Japan assumes global leadership in realizing a post-nuclear renewable energy era.

Three disappointments

Too slow, too little

Three months have passed since I shared my vision for reconstruction on April 22 with Governor Kawakatsu and former Governor Masuda. Where do we stand now? Three fundamental disappointments cannot but be noticed. The most serious issue is that daily life of those who suffered from the disaster has been slow to recover. Initially 450,000 people who lost their housing or whose houses became contaminated found refuge in emergency shelters. By June, 91,500 evacuees were still living in these emergency shelters: 23,500 in Miyagi prefecture, 10,000 in Iwate prefecture (officially 21,000, but 11,000 out of them actually returned to their damaged houses), and 59,000 in Fukushima prefecture, including 36,000 outside the prefecture and 23,000 inside the prefecture (*Yomiuri Shimbun* June 10, 2011). Aside from where to live, there is also the problem of restoring livelihoods; 60 percent of the mayors and heads of the most seriously damaged villages responded that people in their towns and villages have no income (*Asahi Shimbun* June 11, 2011).

In such circumstances it is natural that people who lost everything lose hope and become frustrated. Koshizawa Akira, Professor of Hokkaido University wrote,

> If asked whether "*fukkyū* (restoration)" or "*fukkō* (reconstruction)" should take precedence, *fukkyū* should come first … Taking into account the mindset of Tōhoku people, it is hard to believe that they desire a long term extravagant vision of reconstruction to become a model of Japan or of the world. The majority of the people who suffered would prefer to live in houses where minimal necessary equipment is furnished and become engaged in local fishery and other industries as they used to do … I fear that if one tries to create an ideal land to be built in ten years' time, the bulk of senior people who have to sustain life in that ideal village would leave, never to return
>
> (Koshizawa 2011: 26–27)

Professor Koshizawa's view differs from my vision to transform Tōhoku into the dreamland of twenty-first century civilization. However, it is understandable that if initial relief and recovery is delayed too long, the patience of people would reach its limit, and pressures will build to attend to immediate needs rather than follow a grand vision.

Indeed it is a race against time. John Dower, professor emeritus of Massachusetts Institute of Technology, also expressed his concerns about not missing the window of opportunity. He wrote,

> Likewise in personal life, there is a moment in the history of a nation or of a society to suddenly realize what is important after a sudden accident or disaster. There emerges a space to rethink everything with new methodology and creative measures. Historic moments such as the great Tokyo earthquake or the

defeat at WWII created such space. This is happening again. But if you do not hurry, that space closes down quickly

(*Asahi Shimbun* April 29, 2011)

Fukushima's special situation neglected

One of the most striking points that enlightened me in my talk with Governor Kawakatsu in April was his very clear distinction between the two prefectures of Iwate and Miyagi, which suffered mostly tsunami damage and Fukushima, where the damage came from the tsunami and nuclear radiation. Kawakatsu emphasized that the land of many farmers was contaminated and they were forced to leave without a timeline for returning. They have suffered enormous material and psychological damage and in his view, they deserve special attention. Relocation is a key priority, but Japan does not have abundant land. Fortunately there is the vast hill and meadow area called *Nasuno,* geographically located at the entrance of the Tōhoku region that is reasonably close to Fukushima. This is one of the regions once proposed as a possible future capital of Japan.

But what is the reality? The tsunami disaster was beyond the risk expectations and emergency preparations of Tokyo Electric Power Company (TEPCO) and the Ministry of Economy, Trade and Industry (METI) that oversees the nuclear industry. Those who were close to Kan argue that TEPCO was totally incompetent and irresponsible.[3] But whatever the case, inadequate preparation and coordination amplified by a lack of transparency made a bad situation worse. On April 22 the government of Japan formally designated the area 20 km from the nuclear plant as a "No-Entry zone," and the area 20 to 30 km from the plant as an "Emergency Evacuation Preparation Zone" and another specific area to the Northwest (where winds carried the radiation) as a "Planned Evacuation Zone." Some 78,000 within the 20 km zone were evacuated (*Yomiuri Shimbun* June 17, 2011) while evacuation from beyond that radius started from May 15 (*Asahi Shimbun* May 16, 2011). By the end of June, 59,000 of the evacuees remained in limbo, packed into emergency shelters, facing the stressful situation of not knowing when their ordeal will end, if ever.

The "Emergency Evacuation Preparation Zones" may be reduced in August (the future, as at this writing), but nothing indicates that "No-Entry zones" and "Planned Evacuation Zones" might be reduced (*Asahi Shimbun* July 16, 2011). When the *Kōteihyō* (roadmap to cold shutdown) to bring the Fukushima plant under control was announced by TEPCO on April 17, the Minister of Economy and Industry (METI) Kaieda Banri commented that returning home could be possible after the second step of the Roadmap was achieved in three to six months' time after the first step was completed (*Asahi Shimbun*, April 18, 2011). On July 17, after achieving this first step, Hosono Gōshi, the minister in charge of the nuclear crisis, stated on NHK TV that the schedule for returning remained unchanged. The question is whether everyone whose life has been so fundamentally disrupted should wait patiently for another three to six months to elapse. Could not the government give, right from the early days of the crisis, an indication that the situation is so serious that the alternative to "coming home in the foreseeable future" would be something drastic like resettling in Nasuno? No such decisive direction has been given.

Leadership deficit

It is not easy to give a comprehensive evaluation of what actually took place in the whole decision making process at the center of Prime Minister Kan's government after 3/11. To give a comprehensive analysis one should have primary source information on what took place. But even so, through media reporting and some information that I heard from a source with direct access to that decision making, the following observations can be made:[4] first, there was a fundamental lack of organizational discipline and effective command capacity; top leaders often shouted around with cellphone in hand, people assembled did not know what to do, and views from experts did not reach decision makers; second, therefore, some important decisions were made by the prime minister with very few advisors involved, and because of initial lack of consultation, these decisions subsequently had to be revised, causing confusion and discrediting the prime minister; third, because of this organizational weakness criticism of the prime minister became widespread, but there was no one to help him improve policy implementation, either in his inner circle or among his critics.

Whether or not this is an accurate report of Kan's crisis management performance, the political struggle against Kan peaked on June 2. The leading opposition party the Liberal Democratic Party (LDP), decided that it was time to oust Kan and on June 2 presented to the House of Representatives a motion of no-confidence. The Ozawa Ichiro faction of the Democratic Party of Japan (DPJ) decided to support this motion and there was widespread speculation that it might pass. However, on the very morning of the voting, former Prime Minister Hatoyama Yukio and Kan met and apparently Hatoyama agreed to oppose the motion on the condition of Kan stepping down. The conditions for his departure were apparently the adoption of a basic law for reconstruction and a second supplementary budget for reconstruction. Having survived the no-confidence motion, Kan immediately began to waver on the timing of his exit (*Asahi Shimbun* June 4, 2011). The Basic Law for Reconstruction was adopted on June 20, and Kan stated on June 27 that, "the adoption of the second supplementary budget, adoption of a Special Public Bond Law, and a Special Measures Law on Renewable Energy should become one criterion for retirement" (*Asahi Shimbun* June 28, 2011). At a time when real policy discussion was needed for Tōhoku reconstruction and Japan's future energy policy, power politics centering around Kan's ouster absorbed too much energy to the detriment of effective policy making.

Three hopes

Post-nuclear energy policy

As for the actual measures taken to bring the Fukushima nuclear plant under control and restore normal life for those who suffered from that disaster, the current situation is disappointing. In contrast, there are some hopeful developments in moving away from nuclear power and making the transition to renewable energy. Prime Minister Kan articulated a vision for renewable energy. At the same time, however, the "nuclear village" of pro-nuclear advocates in the bureaucracy, utilities, LDP, business community, media and academia is resisting the shift towards renewable energy. The power struggle at the center seems to be closely tied to this policy rivalry as advocates of nuclear and renewable energy fight over the future course of Japan's energy strategy.

Let us review this battle chronologically:

1. On May 6, Kan requested that Chubu Electric Company suspend operations at the Hamaoka nuclear plant immediately and a few days later it complied. Hamaoka is located in Shizuoka prefecture and some experts believe that it is located on an active fault line and is therefore vulnerable to a large earthquake and possible tsunami. Kawakatsu Heita, Governor of Shizuoka, immediately stated that, "he respected that wise decision." On May 25, Son Masayoshi, Chairman of Softbank Ltd., met with the governors of Kanagawa, Shizuoka and others and proposed the idea of starting a mega-solar project that should eventually supply solar energy capable of meeting both household and industrial needs. On May 26 at the G8 summit, Kan spoke about a program of installing solar panels in 10 million houses (*Asahi Shimbun* June 27, 2011).

2. The LDP obtained leaked information from TEPCO, later discredited, that Kan was against the injection of sea-water immediately after 3/11 in order to blame him for the meltdown. METI Minister Kaieda Banri, an advocate of nuclear energy, stated that he did not know about Kan's renewable initiative announced at the G8. In this context, the June no-confidence motion can be seen as part of the fight over nuclear vs. renewable energy policy. Kan later told his advisors that, "The counter-attack by the TEPCO-METI alliance after the suspension of Hamaoka was truly terrifying" (*Asahi Shimbun* June 27, 2011).

3. After June 2, Kan focused on enacting the Special Measures Law on Renewable Energy. This law, which introduces a comprehensive Feed-In Tariff (FIT) to stimulate expansion of renewable energy was adopted by cabinet decision, coincidentally, on the morning of March 11. On June 15, Diet members and other supporters held a special meeting to have this law enacted (*Asahi Shimbun* June 16, 2011). On June 19, there was a special meeting of main members of Kan's cabinet and the DPJ at the prime minister's residence, where Kan stated that enactment of this law would be another condition for his retirement, although consensus could not be reached on that day (*Asahi Shimbun* June 21,

2011). On June 28, however, he publically made it one of the conditions of his stepping down.

4. Meanwhile restarting idled nuclear reactors gained momentum on June 18 when Kaieda announced that reactor safety had been confirmed (*Sankei Shimbun* June 18, 2011) and on June 29 he visited Saga prefecture to assure local politicians that it was safe to restart the Genkai nuclear reactors. The nuclear village hoped that restarting these reactors would build momentum in favor of nuclear energy.

5. Kan, having secured his position on renewable energy, then took an offensive in July against the resumption of operations of idled reactors in the near future. On July 6, Kan announced that a "stress test" in line with European standards was now going to be required before the final decision to resume activities of idled nuclear reactors. Genkai plant's operation was, at least temporarily, put on hold. On the following day there was speculation that Kaieda would resign because of his dissatisfaction with Kan's zigzagging (and being overruled on the stress tests) (*Kyōdō Tsūshin* July 7, 2011). On July 11, the government issued a *Tōitsu kenkai* (unified view) stipulating a two-step stress test. Then on July 13, Kan gave a press conference and stated, "we are going to reduce nuclear dependency in a planned and gradual manner so that in the future we can realize a society without nuclear power" (*Asahi Shimbun* July 14, 2011).

6. *Asahi Shimbun* carried an editorial on July 13 calling for phasing out nuclear energy, as if to herald Kan's policy of gradual denuclearization articulated later that day. On July 14, however, other newspapers carried editorials weighing in on the issue. There was no disagreement about expanding renewable energy in general, but the necessity of preserving nuclear energy was emphasized to varying degrees, with the *Mainichi* staking out a position closer to *Asahi*, while *Sankei* and *Yomiuri* emphasized the importance of nuclear energy with Nikkei somewhere in the middle. Kan's "self-righteous approach," and failure to seek consensus, was criticized widely.[5] The lack of prior consultation angered many DPJ members and in the parliamentary debate on July 15, Kan declared that his July 13 press statement was his "personal view" (*Asahi Shimbun* July 16, 2011). The situation is admittedly confused, but a new approach toward renewable energy resulted from Kan's maneuvers with the passage of renewable energy legislation in August 2011.

Vision for reconstruction

On June 20, the Basic Law for Reconstruction was finally adopted. It established the *Fukkōin* (Reconstruction Ministry), *Fukkō tokku* (Special Reconstruction Zone), and *Fukkōsai* (Reconstruction Bond). Reconstruction Headquarters chaired by the prime minister is in charge of reconstruction until the Reconstruction Ministry is established, reportedly by April 2012 (*Asahi Shimbun* June 21, 2011). On June 25, the Reconstruction Design Council finalized its report and presented it to Kan. The Council was established on April 11 just one month after 3/11 by cabinet decision and entrusted to 16 members, chaired by Professor Iokibe Makoto, Dean of the Defense University, to formulate governmental policy guidelines on reconstruction in regions affected by the Tōhoku Earthquake.[6] Iokibe's report has five major characteristics:

1. Several philosophical points are emphasized at the beginning: 3/11 highlighted the problems that post-war Japan was unable to resolve, and the report questions the nature of Japanese civilization. It recommends that reconstruction be implemented with an eye toward "reducing" the impact of future disasters rather than futilely "preventing" them. The report also emphasizes the need to pursue reconstruction of tightly knit communities that connect people in the twenty-first century.
2. The report presents five different patterns of reconstruction based on local situations with convincing simplicity and illustrations. It discusses sensitive and difficult issues of land utilization and extraordinary measures for relocation and recovery.
3. Each industry, ranging from manufacturing, agriculture, fisheries and tourism is analyzed respectively identifying various needs for reconstruction.
4. Nuclear disaster is given an independent chapter and the need to address the Fukushima crisis is highlighted.
5. "Open Reconstruction" is the heading of the concluding chapter and the necessity of mobilizing the best of Japanese as well as foreign wisdom is articulated.

Thus the report contains some key concepts that I underlined in my vision stated above.

1. "Rebuilding the regions must ... take into account other factors, including ease of living, landscapes, environment, public transportation, energy conservation and anti-crime measures. Above all, with regard to landscape, it would be preferable to rebuild the regions that have a sense of unity, based on thorough discussion and consensus among local residents" (p. 13 of its English translation on the prime minister's homepage).
2. "It is necessary to advance the repair and restoration of the cultural properties of the 'community's treasures' and 'the community's spirit'. Furthermore, assistance will be sought for the restoration, preservation, and succession of traditional events such as festivals and dialects. In this way it is important to maintain the community identity by valuing the history and culture of the communities and passing on the cultural heritage" (p. 24).
3. "It is important to carry out community development that takes beautiful views into account and turns them into tourism resources in the reconstruction process. Furthermore, there is a need to incorporate a tourism perspective into local industries such as agriculture, forestry, and fisheries, and to devise creative

new methods such as forming new tourism routes with an awareness of approaches from the sea" (p. 31).

4.   "It is necessary to introduce cutting-edge independent and decentralized energy systems in accordance with regional characteristics. Those systems comprehensively combine firstly efficient utilization of energy-saving systems, and next the use of diverse energy sources including renewable energy" (p. 33).

5.   "In reconstruction, it is important to absorb the validity of other countries in various ways. One of the means of achieving that is through promoting foreign direct investment ... Japan should thus promote the acceptance of foreign nationals who can contribute to the revitalization of Japan" (p. 43).

The information collected and the direction shown does seem to be right. Can we really implement them? That is the question.

Strength of people and local communities

It is now almost a truism to say that in the wake of disaster what impressed the world most were the perseverance, restraint, discipline, compassion and mutual help among those who suffered most. TEPCO-METI and ultimately the government itself merit criticism for not preparing adequately for a potential nuclear disaster, but the TEPCO employees and contracted workers, firemen, Japan Self-Defense Forces (JSDF) troops who have been coping with a complex and dangerous disaster deserve kudos for their efforts. Leaders of villages and municipalities played a remarkable role in maintaining order in their communities. The June 9 *Economist* article "Japan's recovery: Who needs leaders?" well described that situation and mentioned two exemplary leaders:

> Jin Sato, mayor of Minamisanriku, [who] survived the tsunami by clinging to a fence on the top of a building as water washed over his head for three minutes, [and] since then has worked all hours, sleeping in a cot in his office

and

> Katsutoshi Sakurai, mayor of Minamisōma, who in the heat of the crisis went on NHK, the national broadcaster, to berate the country's authorities for failing to come to the aid of his town, which faced rising radiation levels from the nearby Fukushima Daiichi nuclear-power plant.
>
> (*The Economist* 2011)

Three governors of Miyagi, Iwate and Fukushima became members of the Reconstruction Design Council and worked as a bridge between the central government and local municipalities. The hope of Japan, and the recovery, rests on the resilience of local communities and listening to their voices.

Conclusion

Overall the situation in Japan remains confused. The Kan government seems to have established, albeit slowly and with a lot of zigzagging, basic guidelines for reconstruction embodied in the Report of the Reconstruction Council; a roadmap to bring the Fukushima meltdown under control; and articulating a new policy direction toward gradual reduction of nuclear energy to move towards a nuclear free society. The Reconstruction Headquarters estimates that the minimum cost for restoration will be ¥12 trillion over five years and favors making the devastated regions the base for renewable energy development (*Asahi Shimbun* July 16, 2011).

But these developments are slow and rest only on a fragile political foundation. Significantly, the powerful nuclear village opposes the new direction toward renewable energy. Kan's support ratings plummeted up until his resignation with many criticizing him for his inability to create consensus even within his own party and cabinet and for his provocative moves against organizations involved in the nuclear crisis, ones he considered incompetent and irresponsible. Critics, and even some supporters, also charged that a lame duck premier should not have been taking initiative on such vital issues as the future course of Japanese energy policy.

Alas, four months after 3/11, Japan's future remains uncertain. There are a few glimmers of hope, including the prospect of becoming a twenty-first century renewable energy superpower, but Japan still seems adrift and risks squandering the opportunities created by the Tōhoku Earthquake.

Notes

1   My public writing on the disaster in Japan includes *Kyoto Shimbun*, March 31; *Mainichi Shimbun*, May 4; *Asahi Shimbun*, May 23; *Kyoto Shimbun*, May 30; *Gekkan Nihon*, May 2011, pp. 50–55 (Tōgo 2011a); and *Shinchō 45*, May 2011, pp. 162–165 (Tōgo 2011b).

2   This slogan expression was typically popular after the humiliation of the Triple Intervention by Russia, Germany and France to force the retrocession of the Liaotung peninsula, which Japan gained as the result of its victory in the Sino-Japanese war (in 1894–1895). It was ten years before Japan regained control of this territory following victory in the Russo-Japanese war in 1905.

3   Terada Manabu, former assistant to Prime Minister Kan, stated in a recent interview that, "In the initial days for a week after 3/11, Kan forced TEPCO against its will to 'vent' the reactors, instructed TEPCO people not to evacuate the plant as they planned on doing, and instructed that pumping of seawater to cool the reactors not be stopped." Online, available at: www.jiji.com/jc/v?p=politician-interview_terada_manabu-01 (accessed July 16, 2011).

4   Anonymous source who personally observed the situation in the prime minister's inner circle who shared his knowledge with me on June 4 and July 16.

5   http://y-sonoda.asablo.jp/blog/2011/07/14/5953337 (accessed July 16, 2011).

6   The full Japanese version is posted at the Prime Minister's Office home page as follows: www.cas.go.jp/jp/fukkou/pdf/fukkouhenoteigen.pdf. Its English translation is posted as follows: www.cas.go.jp/jp/fukkou/english/pdf/report20110625.pdf (both accessed July 17, 2011).

References

Kawakatsu Heita, Masuda Hiroya and Togo Kazuhiko (2011) *Tōhoku Kyōdōtai kara no Saisei* (*Resurrection of the Tōhoku Community*), Tokyo: Fujiwara Shoten.

Koshizawa Akira (2011) "Fukkō wa Jikan to no Shōbu de aru" (Reconstruction is a fight against time), *Chūō kōron*, June.

The Economist (2011) "Japan's recovery: Who needs leaders? The aftermath of the March 11th disasters shows that Japan's strengths lie outside Tokyo, in its regions," June 9.

Tōgo Kazuhiko (2011a) "Tōhoku fukkō no tame ni Sekai no chie o Katsuyō seyo" (Mobilize the wisdom of the world for the reconstruction of Tōhoku), *Gekkan Nihon*, May.

Tōgo Kazuhiko (2011b) "Higashi Nihon Daishinsai to Nichibei dōmei" (The Great East Japan Earthquake and the Japan-US alliance), *Shinchō 45*, May.

INDEX